Student Quick Tips

Use this Student Quick Tips guide for a quick and easy start with McGraw-Hill Connect. You'll get valuable tips on registering, doing assignments, and accessing resources, as well as information about the support center hours.

Getting Started

TIP: To get started in Connect, you will need the following:

- Your instructor's Connect Web Address

  Sample of Connect Web Address:

  http://www.mcgrawhillconnect.com/class/instructorname_section_name

- Connect Access Code

TIP: If you do not have an access code or have not yet secured your tuition funds, you can click "Free Trial" during registration. This trial will provide temporary Connect access (typically three weeks) and will remind you to purchase online access before the end of your trial.

Registration and Sign In

1. Go to the Connect Web Address provided by your instructor
2. Click on **Register Now**
3. Enter your email address

TIP: If you already have a McGraw-Hill account, you will be asked for your password and will not be required to create a new account.

4. Enter a registration code or choose **Buy Online** to purchase access online

(Continued: Registration and Sign In)

5. Follow the on-screen directions

TIP: Please choose your Security Question and Answer carefully. We will ask you for this information if you forget your password.

6. When registration is complete, click on **Go to Connect Now**

7. You are now ready to use **Connect**

Trouble Logging In?

- Ensure you are using the same email address you used during registration

- If you have forgotten your password, click on the "Forgot Password?" link at your Instructor's Connect Course Web Address

- When logged into Connect, you can update your account information (e.g. email address, password, and security question/answer) by clicking on the *"My Account"* link located at the top-right corner

Home (Assignments)

TIP: If you are unable to begin an assignment, verify the following:

- The assignment is available (start and due dates)

- That you have not exceeded the maximum number of attempts

- That you have not achieved a score of 100%

- If your assignment contains questions that require manual grading, you will not be able to begin your next attempt until your instructor has graded those questions

(Continued: Home Assignments)

TIP: Based on the assignment policy settings established by your Instructor, you may encounter the following limitations when working on your assignment(s):

- Ability to Print Assignment

- Timed assignments – once you begin a *"timed assignment,"* the timer will not stop by design

TIP: *"Save & Exit"* vs. *"Submit"* button

- If you are unable to complete your assignment in one sitting, utilize the *"Save & Exit"* button to save your work and complete it at a later time

- Once you have completed your assignment, utilize the *"Submit"* button in order for your assignment to be graded

Library

TIP: The *Library* section of your Connect account provides shortcuts to various resources.

- If you purchased ConnectPlus, you will see an *eBook* link, which can also be accessed from the section information widget of the *Home* tab

- *Recorded Lectures* can be accessed if your instructor is using *Tegrity Campus* to capture lectures. You may also access recorded lectures when taking an assignment by clicking on the projector icon in the navigation bar

- Many McGraw-Hill textbooks offer additional resources such as narrated slides and additional problems, which are accessible through the *Student Resources* link

Reports

TIP: Once you submit your assignment, you can view your available results in the *Reports* tab.

- If you see a dash (-) as your score, your instructor has either delayed or restricted your ability to see the assignment feedback

- Your instructor has the ability to limit the amount of information (e.g. questions, answers, scores) you can view for each submitted assignment

Need More Help?

CONTACT US ONLINE

Visit us at:

www.mcgrawhillconnect.com/support

Browse our support materials including tutorial videos and our searchable Connect knowledge base. If you cannot find an answer to your question, click on "Contact Us" button to send us an email.

GIVE US A CALL

Call us at:

1-800-331-5094

Our live support is available:

Mon-Thurs: 8 am – 11 pm CT
Friday: 8 am – 6 pm CT
Sunday: 6 pm – 11 pm CT

Speak Well

Liz O'Brien
Phoenix College

Special Edition for
MERCER COUNTY COMMUNITY COLLEGE

2 3 4 5 6 7 8 9 0 GPC GPC 16 15 14

ISBN-13: 978-1-259-24221-2
ISBN-10: 1-259-24221-8

Learning Solutions Consultant: Jennifer Schmellick
Associate Project Manager: Vanessa Estrada

Speak up and speak out. You can and you must.

Dedication

To my parents.

You continue to earn an A+ in all things family.

About the Author

Liz O'Brien serves as residential faculty in Communication and Director of the Honors Program at Phoenix College, one of the Maricopa Community Colleges. She earned a B.A. in communication from the University of Arizona and an M.A in communication from the University of Maryland. With nearly twenty-five years of experience in the college classroom, she continues to enjoy the interaction with her diverse, urban student population. She received her campus' Distinguished Teaching Award in 2000, was named Educator of the Year by the Arizona Communication Association in 2009–2010, and has been honored with several national awards for teaching excellence. Additionally, she is a professional watercolor artist, avid traveler, scuba diver, yoga enthusiast, and wedding officiant. Liz lives in a historic home in Phoenix with her husband Steve Emrick, cats Masala and Haggis, a garden full of plants, and a pond full of fish.

Brief Contents

Resources
A. Sample Student Speeches
B. Guide to Documentation Styles
C. Speaker Evaluation Forms

Create your own *Speak Well* at www.mcgrawhillcreate.com.

These three appendices are available exclusively through McGraw-Hill's Create customization site.

Contents

2 Listen to the Speeches of Others 29

3 Create Confident Presentations 47

4 Commit to Ethical Speaking 68

5 Analyze Your Audience and the Speaking Situation 95

6   Determine Your Speech Purpose, Topic, and Thesis 121

7 Incorporate Research 140

8 Support Your Ideas 171

PART **3**

Developing Your Message 195

9 Organize Your Ideas 197

10

Outline Your Speech 216

11

Create Introductions, Conclusions, and Transitions 239

PART **4** Presenting Your Speech 265

14 Communicate with Your Language, Body, and Voice 318

PART **5** Types of Public Speaking 341

17 Develop Your Arguments 377

18 Speak on Special Occasions and in Groups 396

Three appendices, written by Liz O'Brien for Speak Well, are available exclusively through McGraw-Hill's Create customization site:

Appendix A   Sample Student Speeches
Appendix B   Guide to Documentation Styles
Appendix C   Evaluation Forms:
              Speaker Evaluation Form
              Speaker Self-Evaluation Form

Begin creating now at **www.mcgrawhillcreate.com.**

Boxed Features

create
converse
connect

SPEAK
Responsibly

A Note from the Author

Students have important things to say. Above all, when they share their ideas publicly, they want their voices to be genuinely heard, not just politely tolerated. They see the value in building positive relationships with audiences so that their ideas can take hold and affect others. They want to add their voices to society's dialogue. This in turn demands they accept and practice personal responsibility for

1. the development and delivery of their messages,
2. the needs of their listeners, and
3. their growth as credible speakers who engage others in important conversation.

Students want to be good public speakers—they're just not always sure how to make that happen. I wrote *Speak Well* to help students get there. My goal was to create an approachable, readable, and practical text that today's on-the-go students can use as a reference for all their public presentations—in class and in all aspects of their daily lives.

After decades of experience teaching the introductory public speaking course, listening to thousands of speeches in and out of the classroom, and working with all levels of students to help them craft and deliver their messages, I have found that the most effective public speakers

- speak on topics they're personally invested in and communicate their ideas about that topic with a passion that is infectious;

- create and communicate organized messages that make listening and following the ideas easy;

- deliver their speeches in their authentic voices using their own words and style, using comfortable, everyday communication behaviors, not verbiage, or movements that feel forced, unnatural, or overly performative; and

- view public speaking as creating a dialogue with their listeners about their message, not as a performance sport.

In essence, effective speakers know how to speak responsibly and they practice listener-centered communication—they *create* well-constructed speeches, and *converse* and *connect* with their audience.

Speak Well was developed with those qualities and speaking goals in mind. In all aspects of the text, from the narrative to the examples to the exercises, students are encouraged to engage in public speaking as responsible conversation with their audience members. In doing so, they truly begin to understand that their primary goal is to get their listeners to access, understand, and interact with their ideas—rather than merely perform for them—and they learn how to incorporate numerous concrete strategies into their speechmaking processes to achieve that goal.

The results of this approach have been very telling. Students from different backgrounds and with different levels of speaking experience find that from the outset, it greatly diminishes speaker anxiety, one of the biggest challenges in every public speaking course.

> I can now go into any situation and speak in a way that my ideas will have an impact on the listeners. It's really made me believe in myself again.
> — *Brenda Toscano, Phoenix College student*

Students who begin to practice and embrace the strategies they learn about in *Speak Well* speak more confidently, naturally, and engagingly from the start, and their speeches are unquestionably more successful.

The experience of a recent public speaking student, Brenda Toscano, can perhaps describe the effect of this approach best. Brenda took the introductory public speaking course twice. Public speaking was presented as a performance in the first course, and by Brenda's own admission, she didn't put in much effort because she "thought it [public speaking] was just about getting over shyness," and she wasn't shy, so she didn't think she needed to practice or work actively to engage her listeners. When she took the course a second time, a listener-centered approach was used, and the difference in her experience and in the quality of her speeches was dramatic:

After reviewing all the recordings of the speeches I gave this semester, I was very pleased and proud of the growth I have made as a speaker. I learned that public speaking is all about the listeners and whether or not they have understood the message that you attempted to convey. I can now go into any situation and speak in a way that my ideas will have an impact on the listeners. It's really made me believe in myself again. With this power comes great responsibility, and I plan to use this knowledge to promote my ideas and hopefully, one day my words will inspire social change.

Preface

Create Converse Connect—*Speak Well*

Liz O'Brien teaches students that to speak well is to speak responsibly, confidently, and authentically—to *create* well-researched and soundly constructed speeches, and to *converse* and *connect* with their audience. Through *Speak Well*'s listener-centered approach to public speaking, in which the speaker engages in a vibrant, important conversation with listeners rather than giving a static performance, students learn that their primary purpose as speakers is to communicate ideas. The result is reduced student anxiety about speech delivery, increased self-assurance, and more authentic, successful speeches. *Speak Well* also offers invaluable practical strategies throughout the speechmaking process, demonstrating that effective public speaking is about learning to make responsible choices across different speaking situations.

So, how is this accomplished in *Speak Well*? A combination of unique chapter presentations, step-by-step discussions of core skills and techniques, and useful supporting features helps students focus on responsible speech development and delivery that successfully engages their listeners.

An Accessible and Flexible Approach to Effective Public Speaking

Speak Well's **listener-centered approach** acknowledges that effective public speaking skills are essential for living, working, and thinking in today's interconnected world. *Speak Well* enables students to prepare and deliver speeches in an authentic, conversational style that will engage their listeners. **Chapter 1, "Public Speaking Is an Act of Communication,"** establishes the foundation, introducing students to a focus on public speaking as a communication event and dialogue between a speaker and a group of listeners. The chapter offers an overview of the ways students will learn to take responsibility for creating listener-centered communication, as well as a brief look at the rich history of public speaking.

An emphasis on communication, not performance, supported by meaningful examples that provide honest, conversational-based speech models, demonstrates that public speaking is an excellent medium for creating worthwhile public dialogue.

Speak Well's **tabbed sections and modular handbook structure** complement the flow of a traditional public speaking course, allowing instructors to easily identify concepts as they lecture, lead discussions, and build assignments, and students to rely on the text as

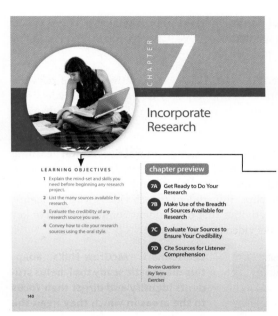

a reference guide. Parts 1 through 5 are comprised of the eighteen main chapters. Three appendices—a set of sample student speeches with commentary, a guide to documentation styles, and speech evaluation forms—are also available exclusively through McGraw-Hill's Create customization site at www.mcgrawhillcreate.com.

Learning objectives that reflect that assessment challenges are a reality on most college and university campuses. The beginning of each chapter highlights clear chapter learning outcomes of student skills that can be used or incorporated into assignment, course, department, or campus assessment efforts.

Speak Well **focuses on building student speaker confidence** and shows readers how to use their adrenaline effectively. **Chapter 3, "Create Confident Presentations,"** is built upon research showing that communication-oriented speakers (as opposed to those who are performance-oriented) experience lower anxiety levels. A focus on "speaker's energy," the term preferred by communication-oriented speakers, assures students that adrenaline is something they can harness and manage to serve their speeches rather than hinder them.

Ethics and civility are introduced early in the text in **Chapter 4, "Commit to Ethical Speaking,"** and presented as a required platform for speaking effectiveness.

Speak Well **places a strong emphasis on practice as one of the main keys to effective public speaking.** The importance of practice cannot be emphasized enough as a responsible speaker's priority and thus has its own dedicated chapter.

A commitment to inclusiveness is evident throughout the text. O'Brien's accessible and engaging new voice and innovative approach to teaching public speaking are uniquely suited to today's busy multicultural and age-diverse classroom.

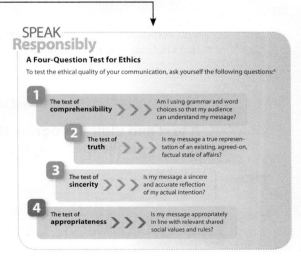

A unique chapter emphasizes the use of narrative. Many contemporary public speakers capitalize on listeners' tendencies to engage with narrative. Chapter 8 spotlights narrative as a way to support ideas and keep audiences with you.

Reflections from real students integrated into the main text narrative provide relevant, real-life examples of techniques and approaches in action. These also show readers that they're not alone in their challenges and that they too can gain skill and confidence in public speaking.

Connect Public Speaking, McGraw-Hill's groundbreaking, interactive digital learning platform, allows students and instructors to access the fully integrated, media-rich ebook. As students read the book online, linked icons guide them to embedded media-rich, interactive features, including speech video clips, full student speech videos with pedagogy, pre-tests and chapter quizzes, matching activities that test student comprehension of key terms, outlining activities, and TED Talks video activities.

LearnSmart, McGraw-Hill's adaptive diagnostic study tool, helps students identify and direct their focus to the areas in which they need the most help. Accessible within Connect Public Speaking, LearnSmart adapts to individual students based on their responses, enables them to absorb and internalize key ideas faster and more effectively, and prepares them better than ever for quizzes and exams. By tracking student responses in LearnSmart, instructors can also use class time to hone in on subjects that students find most challenging.

Noteworthy Text and Digital Features

A text and digital program that addresses the needs and realities of today's public speaking instructors and students

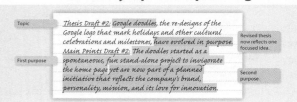

Annotated student speech examples walk readers through different parts of the public speaking process step-by-step, demonstrating how one student applied chapter concepts and showing specific public speaking skills in action.

Student speeches on Connect Public Speaking provide models of major speech genres. Sixteen full student speeches, as well as more than thirty techniques video clips, illustrate specific skills and concepts from the book. Icons in the margins of the main text direct readers to the appropriate online videos.

Sample student speech transcripts, with commentary, available exclusively at www.mcgrawhillcreate.com through McGraw-Hill's Create customization site, present extended speech examples with annotations that highlight the application of particular public speaking skills. (These speeches are also available online in video form in Connect Public Speaking.) The accompanying marginal commentary points out effective student choices as well as where different choices might have been made to improve the speech.

> Available exclusively through McGraw-Hill's Create customization site.

Public speaking concepts and examples are presented graphically for visual learners. In keeping with today's highly visual world and today's students, concepts, examples, and processes described in the text narrative are paired with relevant visuals—four-color infographics, highlighted and annotated examples, tables, flowcharts, images, and other graphic displays.

Unhelpful (abstract) feedback

Helpful (concrete) feedback

Your eye contact was poor.

Your eye contact favored the left side of the room. I felt left out.

You had good visuals.

The graph you used to show the correlation between diet and classroom performance was not only well designed but it really helped me to buy into your argument.

I liked your speech.

Your thesis was well chosen and clearly communicated. Your topic was made relevant to me, and your enthusiastic delivery helped me stay connected to your ideas.

I got lost.

Because I never heard a preview of your main points in the introduction, I had trouble following your flow of ideas in the body. More overt transitions also would have helped me stay with you.

figure **2.2**   Abstract vs. Concrete Feedback for Evaluating Another's Speech

Extensive help with the public speaking skills and processes students find most challenging

Hands-on, step-by-step help with every stage of the research process, with an emphasis on source evaluation. *Speak Well* recognizes that for today's students, one of the biggest challenges in doing research is in establishing the credibility of the sources they find. **Chapter 7, "Incorporate Research,"** offers students an overview of the different types of sources they can incorporate into speeches as support, as well as the many ways they can access those sources. Particular attention is given to the evaluation of sources; the chapter

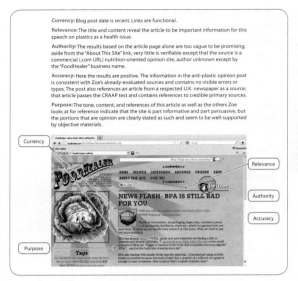

Currency: Blog post date is recent. Links are functional.

Relevance: The title and content reveal the article to be important information for this speech on plastics as a health issue.

Authority: The results based on the article page alone are too vague to be promising; aside from the "About This Site" link, very little is verifiable except that the source is a commercial (.com URL) nutrition-oriented opinion site, author unknown except by the "FoodHealer" business name.

Accuracy: Here the results are positive. The information in the anti-plastic opinion post is consistent with Zoe's already-evaluated sources and contains no visible errors or typos. The post also references an article from a respected U.K. newspaper as a source; that article passes the CRAAP test and contains references to credible primary sources.

Purpose: The tone, content, and references of this article as well as the others Zoe looks at for reference indicate that the site is part informative and part persuasive, but the portions that are opinion are clearly stated as such and seem to be well-supported by objective materials.

Currency

Relevance

Authority

Accuracy

Purpose

figure **7.3A** **FoodHealer Blog, Article Post on Plastics as Packaging**

SPEAK
Responsibly

Managing Difficult Behaviors within the Group

Kaitlin dominates. Brady makes sexist comments. Jaime refuses to participate. Many groups have to deal with individual behaviors that create barriers for effective group interaction. Here are some ways to manage these difficult behaviors[17]:

Dominating behaviors	What you can do
Interrupting	• Speak up assertively that you're not done talking.
	• If another person was interrupted, insist that you want to hear his or her complete thought.
Making authoritarian or know-it-all statements	• Politely request backup information, evidence, or justification.

Objectionable behaviors	What you can do
Making jokes at the expense of others	• Do not laugh.
	• Say that those jokes bother you.
Behaving unethically	• Don't remain silent; it can be seen as con-

walks students through the criteria they can use to analyze any given research source—currency, relevance, authority, accuracy, and purpose—and then presents a sample evaluation of a commercial blog.

Current, extensive coverage on using visuals in presentations. Chapter 12, "Select and Incorporate Visual Support," reflects the latest research on the best slideshow (PowerPoint, Prezi, etc.) practices and highlights the increasingly popular use of storyboarding one's ideas to keep audience members visually engaged in the message. The chapter also presents numerous examples of different types of visuals and how to incorporate them, visual examples of effective design principles, a checklist that walks students through using technology in ways that make sense for their presentation needs, as well as a student sample, "Choosing Images in Action: A Student's Process."

"Speak Responsibly" boxes. Interspersed throughout the text, these spotlight the tasks speakers must undertake to make the most of their listeners' time and energy. The boxes inform and remind students to respect the message, the audience, and themselves. Topics include responding to a perceived ethical breach, navigating Wikipedia, and using polled data.

"Create Converse Connect" boxes. These boxes appear in every chapter and provide more detail on a specific topic or strategy, including tips on engaging through the five senses, how to explain a citation, and the uses (and limits) of statistical and subjective support.

create
converse
connect

Engagement through the Five Senses

People interact with the world around them throu... touch, taste, and smell. Keep these in mind as you ... ence engagement.

Auditory appeals:
Can the audience listen to anything (other than your voice)? Make a noise, have them repeat something, share a song clip, or play an instrument.

Visual appeals:
Can the audience look at anything to stay involved i... your message? Show colors, action, textures, animation, beauty, or novelty.

Olfac...
engag...
some f...
and-sn...
you're ...

G...
to...
y...
y...

Extensive opportunities for practice, review, and assessment through *Speak Well*'s print and online pedagogy

Interactive assignments in Connect Public Speaking. Connect enables students to access pedagogy in a new interactive context and offers a wide range of assignable and assessable online activities. These include chapter quizzes, speech videos with questions for analysis, scrambled outline exercises, key-term diagnostics, and TED Talks video activities.

Critical thinking questions in select "Speak Responsibly" and "Create Converse Connect" boxes. At least one box in every chapter ends with critical thinking questions that prompt students to reflect on the highlighted tasks, topics, and strategies in the context of their own habits and public speaking practices and choices.

End-of-chapter review questions and exercises. To promote retention of the chapter's main points, review questions prompt students about each major chapter section, addressing the learning objectives presented at the beginning of the chapter. Likewise, chapter exercises, designed for both individual and group use, help students practice and apply chapter concepts and skills.

Tools that enable student speech practice and facilitate student speech evaluations

McGraw-Hill SpeechPrep app. On-the-go students can practice their speeches on their Apple- or Android-based smartphones or tablets using the McGraw-Hill SpeechPrep app. This mobile tool is designed to help students create and organize note cards, as well as practice, record, time, and review speeches. To learn more or download the app, search "Speech Prep" in iTunes, the App Store, or the Android Market, or go to www.mhhe.com/speechprep.

User-friendly speech tools in Connect Public Speaking, McGraw-Hill's groundbreaking, interactive digital learning platform

Speech Capture. Connect's Speech Capture gives instructors the ability to evaluate speeches live, using a fully customizable rubric. Instructors can also upload speech videos on behalf of students, as well as create and manage peer-review assignments. In addition, students can upload their own videos for self-review and/or peer review.

Outline Tool, with enhanced user interface. The Outline Tool guides students systematically through the process of organizing and outlining their speeches. Instructors can customize parts of the outliner, and also turn it off if they don't want their students to use it.

Topic Helper, as well as access to EasyBib and Survey Monkey online tools. The Topic Helper helps students select a topic for speech assignments. EasyBib is a web-based tool that simplifies and automates the formatting of citations and bibliographies. Survey Monkey, also a web-based tool, helps students create and manage audience-analysis questionnaires.

McGraw Hill **create**, because customization for your course needs matters

Design ideal course materials with McGraw-Hill's Create, www.mcgrawhillcreate.com. Rearrange or omit chapters, combine material from other sources, upload your syllabus or any other content you have written to make the perfect resource for your students. Search thousands of leading McGraw-Hill textbooks to find the best content for your students, then arrange it to fit your teaching style. You can even personalize your book's appearance by selecting the cover and adding your name, school, and course information. When you order a Create book, you receive a complimentary review copy. Get a printed copy in three to five business days or an electronic copy (eComp) via e-mail in about an hour. Register today at www.mcgrawhillcreate.com, and craft your course resources to match the way you teach.

Three appendices, written by Liz O'Brien for *Speak Well,* are available exclusively through McGraw-Hill's Create customization site:

Appendix A   Sample Student Speeches

Appendix B   Guide to Documentation Styles

Appendix C   Evaluation Forms:
Speaker Evaluation Form
Speaker Self-Evaluation Form

The **Best** of **Both** Worlds

ADDITIONAL RESOURCES FOR INSTRUCTORS

Easier online course management through full Connect-Blackboard integration and single sign-on capability with other Learning Management Systems. Connect Public Speaking has full integration with the Blackboard CMS, features single sign-on capability with a host of other Learning Management Systems, and also makes the management and grading of assignments easier for instructors.

Online Learning Center. *Speak Well*'s Online Learning Center includes an array of comprehensive resources to aid instructors. See www.mhhe.com/speakwell.

Instructor's Manual. Written and updated by the author, the Instructor's Manual provides a range of tools for each chapter to help structure the course and use the *Speak Well* text effectively for particular course needs—discussion questions, assignment ideas, lecture ideas, and other resources.

Test Bank. The Test Bank offers multiple-choice questions, true/false questions, fill-in-the-blank questions and essay questions for each chapter.

PowerPoints for each chapter. Complementary PowerPoints have been provided for instructors who choose to teach using slides or formulate their lesson plans based on them.

Campus, a one-stop teaching and learning experience

McGraw-Hill Campus is the first of its kind institutional service providing faculty with **true single sign-on access to all of McGraw-Hill's course content, digital tools, and other high-quality learning resources from any learning management system (LMS).** This innovative offering allows for secure and deep integration and seamless access to any of our course solutions such as McGraw-Hill Connect®, McGraw-Hill Create™, McGraw-Hill LearnSmart™, or Tegrity®. McGraw-Hill Campus includes access to our entire content library, including ebooks, assessment tools, presentation slides, and multimedia content, among other resources, providing faculty open and unlimited access to prepare for class, create tests/quizzes, develop lecture material, integrate interactive content, and much more.

CourseSmart   Visit coursesmart.com to purchase registration codes for this exciting new product

CourseSmart offers thousands of the most commonly adopted textbooks across hundreds of courses from a wide variety of higher education publishers. It is the only place for faculty to review and compare the full text of a textbook online, providing immediate access without the environmental impact of requesting a printed exam copy. At CourseSmart, students can save up to 50 percent on the cost of a printed book, reduce their impact on the environment, and gain access to powerful web tools for learning, including full text search, notes and highlighting, and e-mail tools for sharing notes among classmates. Learn more at www.coursesmart.com.

Contributors

I am grateful to the numerous public speaking instructors who lent their expertise by examining, reviewing, and evaluating all components of the *Speak Well* program during its development—including the text manuscript, the interior design and cover, and the online tools, activities, and offerings in Connect Public Speaking:

BOARD OF ADVISORS

Rebecca Carlton, *Indiana University Southeast*
Michelle Coleman, *Clark State Community College*
Emily K. Holler, *Kennesaw University*

Kristine Warrenburg, *Flagler College*
Kay Dukes Weeks, *Abraham Baldwin Agricultural College*

REVIEWERS AND SYMPOSIUM PARTICIPANTS

Shae Adkins, *Lone Star College–North Harris*
Melanie Anson, *Citrus College*
Ronald Arnett, *Duquesne University*
Sheila Austin, *Johnson & Wales University*
Vera Barkus, *Kennedy-King College*
Chris Bell, *University of Colorado*
Raymond Bell, *Calhoun Community College*
Mardia Bishop, *University of Illinois, Urbana-Champaign*
Ferald J. Bryan, *Northern Illinois University*
Sakile Camara, *California State University–Northridge*
Jon Camp, *Abilene Christian University*
Rebecca Carlton, *Indiana University Southeast*
Shani Clark, *Darton College*
Melissa Click, *University of Missouri–Columbia*
Michelle Coleman, *Clark State Community College*
Leslie Collins, *Modesto Junior College*
Melanie Conrad, *Berry College*
Diana Cooley, *Lone Star College–North Harris*
Glenda Davis, *Central New Mexico Community College*
Cynthia De Riemer, *J. Sargeant Reynolds Community College*
Audrey Deterding, *Indiana University Southeast*
Lisa Dimitriadis, *Central Carolina Technical College*
Belle Edson, *Arizona State University*
Jennifer Ehrhardt-O'Leary, *Pensacola State College*
John Galyean, *Abraham Baldwin Agricultural College*
Carla Gesell-Streeter, *Cincinnati State Technical and Community College*
Joanie Gibbons-Anderson, *Riverside City College*
Patricia Hill, *University of Akron*
Emily K. Holler, *Kennesaw University*
Jessica Kane, *Adirondack Community College*
Tressa Kelly, *University of West Florida*
Mary Catherine Kiliany, *Robert Morris University*
Jay Leightner, *Creighton University–Omaha*
Marc Martin, *San Francisco State University*
Ted Matula, *University of San Francisco*
Patricia McDonald, *John Tyler Community College–Midlothian*

Tracy McLaughlin, *Northwest Mississippi Community College*
Martin Mehl, *California Polytechnic State University*
Rick Merritt, *Northeast State Community College*
Laurie Metcalf, *Blinn College*
Joe Mirando, *Southeastern Louisiana University*
Mike Monsour, *Metropolitan State College of Denver*
David Moss, *Mt. San Jacinto College*
Emily Lamb Normand, *Olivet Nazarene University*
April Nunn, *Calhoun Community College*
Jennifer O'Donnell, *Mitchell College*
Rick Olsen, *University of North Carolina Wilmington*
Beth Patrick-Trippel, *Olivet Nazarene University*
Andrea Pearman, *Tidewater Community College*
Brandi Quesenberry, *Virginia Tech*
Rita Rahoi-Gilchrest, *Winona State University*
Jason Ramsey, *Indiana University Southeast*
Laura Rapozo-Davis, *Butte College*
James E. Reppert, *Southern Arkansas University*
Kristen Ruppert-Leach, *Southwestern Illinois College*
Lisa Samra, *Triton College*
Janet Shiver, *University of New Mexico*
Alisa Shubb, *University of California–Davis*
Paul Spampanato, *Brevard Community College*
Kerrigan Sullivan, *John Tyler Community College–Midlothian*
Donna Thomsen, *Johnson & Wales University*
Jeffrey Tischause, *Triton College*
Becca Turner, *Abraham Baldwin Agricultural College*
Alice Veksler, *University of Connecticut–Storrs*
Heidi Winters Vogel, *Eastern Mennonite University*
Kristine Warrenburg, *Flagler College*
Brenda A. Washington, *Houston Community College–Central*
Kay Dukes Weeks, *Abraham Baldwin Agricultural College*
Micherri Wiggs, *Riverside City College*
David Zanolla, *Western Illinois University*

Acknowledgments

Oliver Wendell Holmes was right. *Many ideas grow better when transplanted into another mind than the one where they sprang up,* he said, and such is indeed my experience with my writing project, this textbook in your hands. What started as a nugget of an idea more than a decade ago, triggered by two pages in a book, has evolved—thanks to an array of other minds—into something I'm honored to attach my name to.

First, I'm indebted to my professional colleagues. Andy Wolvin, thank you for awakening my listening all those years ago and for writing those influential two pages in your text. Belle Edson, I treasure your patience and wisdom, and am grateful to you for helping me strengthen this story. Jennifer Linde, teacher extraordinaire, I hope to be your perpetual student. Richard Doetkott, I'm so sorry we lost you too soon, but I'll do my best to carry on the philosophy we shared. BCD folks, may your lively conversations continue to guide me. Dianne Miller, thank you for the breathing space. Ann Roselle and Kelly Lambert, the world of research is a better place with you in it.

To all my students at Phoenix College, you've undoubtedly shaped my ideas the most. You embrace this listener-centered approach to public speaking with little to no resistance and run with it. You want your voices to be heard—they're passionate, creative, and diverse—and they continue to inspire and challenge me. Colossal appreciation to all of you, too many to name, who provided examples for the chapter concepts, end-of-chapter student samples, and videos. To think that I earn a living by getting to interact with you and your ideas—how lucky can I be? And keep sending that feedback; you know where to find me.

What a prize to work with the McGraw-Hill team, so many of whom lend the bounty of their talents in promoting and shaping my ideas. Thanks first and foremost to sales representative Sherree D'Amico, for being the spark that ignited it all. I'm also endlessly appreciative for the advocacy, candor, and guidance of director of communication Susan Gouijnstook. Susan, your cute wardrobe and reading recommendations only make me adore you more. I'm equally indebted to the creative marketing efforts of Leslie Oberhuber and Clare Cashen, and to the market development expertise of Suzie Flores. Rhona Robbin, it's a great comfort to know you're always there for consultation on all things editorial. Deep appreciation, too, to Vicki Malinee for her leadership in the early stages of development, to Jinny Joyner, Elizabeth Murphy, and Tara Hack for late-stage editorial help, and to editorial coordinator Jamie Daron and marketing coordinator Emily Moore for their impeccable support on project tasks big and small. A huge shout-out goes to the talented production team members who enabled the print and digital components of this project to come together, including production editor Carey Eisner, design manager Preston Thomas, art editor Ayelet Arbel, photo researcher Joanne Mennemeier, digital product analyst Janet Byrne Smith, and media project managers Danielle Clement and

Katie Klochan. Mikola De Roo deserves a parade in her honor—complete with tumbling cheerleaders, funky music, fireworks, and a phalanx of bespectacled Chihuahuas—for her expert development. You are *very* good at what you do, Mika, and I'm authentically grateful that Susan "let you off the leash."

Finally, raucous applause goes to all my friends and mishpucha, too many to list, for creating entertaining diversions and such a supportive network. Extra big hugs go to my parents, Barbara and Alan O'Brien—long live Cawfee Tawk! And to my endlessly patient and accommodating spouse, Steve Emrick, you deserve all the plants you want.

Public Speaking as Listener-Centered Communication

Every journey needs a beginning. Whether your approach to this course is enthusiastic or tentative, you need a place to start thinking. These first four chapters present some ideas about public speaking that help you create a foundation for your course experience and any speaking you may do in the future. The first step is to perceive public speaking as an act of communication—and more specifically, a listener-centered act of communication. You'll also learn about the importance of public listening, how communicating (as opposed to performing) in public settings leads to increased confidence, and about your responsibility to make your communication ethical, civil, and credible.

• • •

Public Speaking Is an Act of Communication

LEARNING OBJECTIVES

1 Explain how listener-centered public speaking is effective.

2 Articulate the link between effective public speaking and fulfilling speaker responsibilities.

3 Identify the components of public communication.

4 Describe the benefits of being an effective public speaker.

5 Summarize the nature and history of the public speaking course.

chapter preview

1A Explore Listener-Centered Public Speaking

1B Identify Speaker Responsibilities

1C Understand the Public Communication Process

1D Capitalize on the Benefits of Public Speaking

1E Discover the Traditions of Public Speaking

Review Questions
Key Terms
Exercises

Dorothy Sarnoff, an American operatic soprano, musical theatre actress, and self-help guru, once said, "Make sure you have finished speaking before your audience has finished listening." Sarnoff recognized the need to be keenly aware of those gathered to hear her. She understood the power of being listener-centered. The first chapter's aim is to help you begin to see the advantages of a listener-centered approach to public speaking as well. The first two sections describe how successful public speaking is a listener-centered communication event (rather than a speaker-centered practice that many believe it is) and relay the historical and scholarly framework that provides a foundation for listener-centered speaking. You'll then learn that to become a listener-centered public speaker, you must fulfill a set of speaking responsibilities. Finally, you'll get an overview of the communication process and how it works, of the many additional benefits that public speakers enjoy, and of public speaking's rich history and traditions.

1A Explore Listener-Centered Public Speaking

How many speeches have you listened to? Tens, hundreds, thousands? If you thought about those speeches, you would probably agree that some were better than others. But what made them so? Most likely, those you enjoyed most made a point, were easy to follow, and engaged you visually, emotionally, or with humor. The speaker was prepared, personable, and confident. He or she talked to you rather than read to you. You walked away with something to think about or were inspired to do something. Are you remembering such a speech right now?

I certainly am. Like you, I'm a public listener who responds positively to certain speaker actions. Unlike you, though, I'm a seasoned public speaking instructor, and it's my job to help you *be* the speaker that others will want to listen to. Your course instructor is another such person. We've got strategies and tips of all kinds to share with you. We continue to rely on these tools for one reason: they make the public speaking course experience richer and more enjoyable for students and because they result in more successful, memorable, and even inspiring speeches. Numerous novice public-speaking students have made use of these strategies, and as a result, they're speaking more effectively than they ever thought they could. You can be that kind of speaker, too—in and outside of the classroom.

Public speaking is part of the human experience. It's an important form of communication that, as you'll read later in this chapter, goes back at least to ancient Greek times. While many of the classical public communication theories and skills still ring true today, times have obviously changed. We have moved from a speaker-centered way of thinking about public speaking to an inclusive understanding about the roles of public messages and the people who present *and* listen to them.

This book embraces a contemporary framework known as listener-centered public speaking. Briefly, **listener-centered public speakers** make their ideas (whether simple or complex) easy for listeners to access, understand, and interact with—to listen to. Why? Because when real listening—genuine accessibility of, understanding of, and interaction with ideas—happens, real communication occurs, and a speech becomes a genuine ex-

SPEAK
Responsibly

Understanding Your Speech's –*ability*

"Listenability" may sound like an invented term, but it isn't. It's found in academic papers in the field of communication going back to the early 1950s. When you tack the suffix *-ability* onto any given action verb, you transform it into a noun, one that refers to the quality that makes that action possible. As you may recall, in 2008 Bud Light launched a successful "drinkability" campaign touting that the beverage is "neither too heavy nor too light" but is *easy to drink*.

   "Listenability" functions the same way. When we refer to "listenability" in this text, we're focusing on creating and delivering a speech that is *easy to listen to*. All aspects of the speech process—from topic selection to organizational structure to supporting examples to visual aids—impact your listener's ability to access, understand, and interact with your ideas. You have the "-ability" to make this happen.

change of ideas. In essence, listener-centered speakers make conscious decisions throughout the speech process that maximize their speech's **listenability,** or its quality of being easy to listen to.[1] Listener-centered public speaking embraces and values everyone involved in the transfer of public messages—speakers *and* listeners. As one student explains:

> *I learned to experience public speaking as a genuine communication event. It's not about a person who stands up and "spits out" ideas to audience members who are waiting to judge or are just sitting there to be nice. It is so important to talk with our listeners, relate our ideas directly to them, and embrace them throughout the speech. And when we do this, we'll see that they are there, truly listening and sending messages of their own right back at us.*

Why listener-centered messages matter

When your public messages are listener-centered, you will:

- Engage your listeners in a conversation they find meaningful.
- Reduce speech anxiety by focusing on communicating, not performing.
- Enhance your credibility through your use of contemporary public speaking skills.
- Exercise your creativity and critical-thinking skills as you develop a message for your particular audience.
- Make the most of the time with your listeners.
- Gain practical skills you can use in all areas of your life—academically, professionally, and personally.
- Make an impact by adding your voice to public discourse.

1. Make listener-friendly choices

As a listener-centered public speaker, you consciously think about other people as listeners and consider the consequences your own speaking behaviors have on their listening. You present to a group of people who use their ears and eyes to access your ideas and their minds to interact with you in real time as you speak. All the choices you make as a public speaker either help or hinder listeners in those efforts. When you commit to being listenable, you say, *I've decided that when you are in my audience, I'm going to do my best to take advantage of what you do well as a public listener and do what I can to meet your public listening limitations at least halfway.*

Good listening requires energy and engagement on the part of an audience, but asking your audience to work too hard, to "listen uphill," is not smart speaking. It makes for ineffective speaking because it increases the chances that you'll lose your audience's attention and interest. In short, they may stop listening. You need to make presentation choices—without compromising the integrity or complexity of your ideas—that help you meet your communication goals, not that fight against them. If effective listening is the audience's responsibility (and it *is,* as you'll read in Chapter 2), creating and achieving a listenable speech is yours.

Table 1.1 helps you understand the nature of **public listeners,** the people actively working to access, understand, and interact with your public message. Learn how to take advantage of what your public listeners do well while keeping in mind their shortcomings. Throughout this text, the listener-centered "What should I do?" strategies mentioned in Table 1.1, plus many others, will be discussed in detail.

Qualities of a Listener-Centered Public Speaker

Throughout this text, you'll learn numerous strategies for effective listener-centered public speaking. In sum, public speakers with a high degree of listenability know how to:

- **Create.** With a focus on your listeners, you choose and develop relevant and meaningful topics and organize them in patterns that are easy to follow.
- **Converse.** You deliver your speeches by infusing your own style and using comfortable, everyday communication behaviors, not language, movements, or vocal qualities that feel forced or unnatural.
- **Connect.** You view public speaking as creating a dialogue with your listeners about your message, not as a performance sport.

table **1.1** **Taking Advantage of What Public Listeners Do Well and Don't Do Well**

Traits of public listeners	Why is this so?	What should I do?
They are naturally predisposed to listen to you.	The human brain is wired for listening. When you present ideas in public, you face a lively, sensing group of people ready to take in what you say and do.	• Keep working to build your skills and confidence so that you look forward to more public speaking interactions. • Choose meaningful topics. • Research your topics fully and ethically. • Develop a clear thesis and supporting points.
They create new meaning after listening to your ideas, thereby helping you see things in a new way.	As a speaker, you work with listeners in the public communication transaction to achieve mutual understanding and to create a meaning none of you had before.	• Seek feedback from listeners about your message. • Consider this feedback nondefensively.
They may lack listening training or skills.	Strong listening skills tend to be the exception rather than the rule.	• Use conversational patterns of language. • Clearly communicate the structure of your speech.
They may have a bias or prejudice when listening to you.	It's difficult for some to listen when they think they know everything about your topic, may hold strong prior opinions about your topic, or may perceive too much of a difference between your and their values, ideas, background, or appearance.	• Analyze your audience. • Acknowledge the controversial nature of your topic. • Avoid using a superior tone that can create defensive listening. • Present yourself as someone who's open and friendly. • Use language inclusively.
They may be apprehensive about their listening in some situations.	If listeners perceive your topic as complex, obscure, or difficult, or they know they may be tested on the information presented in your talk, they may tune out before giving you a chance.	• Define terms. • Use conversational patterns of language. (Don't read a dense essay.) • Develop a clear thesis. • Tell stories.

(continued)

table **1.1** *(continued)*

Traits of public listeners	Why is this so?	What should I do?
They may not have an inherent interest in your topic.	People's age, culture, socioeconomic status, education, and previous experience combine to create their differing views of the world. You cannot expect all listeners to share your enthusiasm about your topic.	• Be generous and authentic with your passion and enthusiasm toward your topic. Listeners are more likely to get excited in return. • Work hard to establish relevance between the topic and the audience.
They may have trouble retaining your ideas.	Studies show that the average listener remembers 50 percent of what you say in your talk. By the next day, an additional 50 percent evaporates, leaving the average listener with about 25 percent of your message. As time passes, further erosion occurs.[2]	• Emphasize your thesis and main supporting points in the introduction, during transitions in the speech body, and again in the conclusion. • Use visual support that enhances your ideas.

2. Public speaking is a unique form of communication

While there are overlaps with other forms of communication, namely writing and informal conversation, listener-centered public speaking is its own form of communication.

Similarities and differences between writing and public speaking

It's common to hear someone say, "I need to write my speech" or "That was a well-written speech." These comments reflect the belief that a good speech is based on a well-written text. In some specialized speaking contexts, this is true. Presidents, for example, have speechwriters who hone their every word. Good writing, however, doesn't necessarily enhance the everyday presentations most of us give in school, at work, and in our communities. To put it another way: An essay that's effective on the page, when performed aloud, rarely makes for a listenable speech.

People who write for readers need to communicate differently than do people who speak to listeners. Two students, Angie and Rick, are both enrolled in courses focusing on communication: Angie is taking English composition, and Rick is enrolled in public speaking. Angie and Rick both spend the school term studying how to communicate their ideas to their respective audiences—Angie to readers and Rick to listeners—but they learn to do so in different ways.

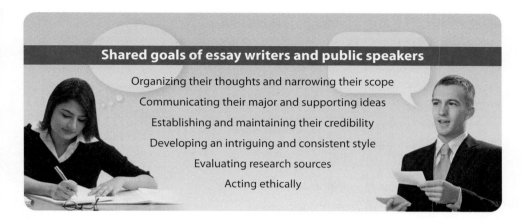

Shared goals of essay writers and public speakers

Organizing their thoughts and narrowing their scope

Communicating their major and supporting ideas

Establishing and maintaining their credibility

Developing an intriguing and consistent style

Evaluating research sources

Acting ethically

As a writer, Angie aims for a **literate,** or **written, style;** she uses patterns of formal English that are appropriate when expressing ideas through the written word. Rick, on the other hand, is more successful in reaching his audience if he focuses on an **oral,** or **conversational, style.** His listeners respond positively when he speaks naturally, using patterns people rely on when talking with one another. Rick does not need to consciously work at adhering to this style; he has been using it his whole life. It will come with limited self-consciousness during his presentations—if he lets it.

While readers and listeners are both receivers, they are different kinds of receivers. Whether the writing style is popular, scholarly, or somewhere in between, a reader has a great deal of control in processing another person's writing. He or she can read it again and again if need be to understand the writer's point. Listeners are a different type of

Qualities of a literate, or written, style

- Adherence to grammar conventions—
  correct sentence structure, subject-verb agreement, etc.

- Correct spelling and punctuation

- Elevated, formal vocabulary

- Clarity—through succinct sentences,
  sentence variety, properly placed modifiers, etc.

Qualities of an oral, or conversational, style

- Short sentences
- Simple sentence structure
- The use of first- and second-person pronouns (*I* and *you*)
- The speaker's individual style
- Adaptations to the listeners' language style (if known)
- The use of contractions (*isn't, we'll, you've*)
- The use of repetition for emphasis and effect
- Occasional slang, jargon, and colloquialisms

receiver. If they must, they can process written-styled language, but it is much easier to access, understand, and interact with oral-styled discourse. Listenable speakers recognize listeners' preference for conversational language—and use it in their presentations.

Similarities and differences between informal conversation and public speaking

Public speaking shares some characteristics with the informal conversations at which you are already relatively competent. Both the conversationalist and the public speaker

- address ideas appropriate to the listener(s) and the circumstances.
- know about and believe in their ideas.
- organize their ideas in a logical pattern so as to make sense to the listener(s).
- support their ideas with examples, stories, facts, and reasoning.
- monitor the audience for feedback.
- speak loudly enough to be heard in the specific speaking space.
- use their voices, facial expressions, and bodily gestures to convey emotion.

It's crucial to recognize that despite the above similarities, the conversational style emphasized in public speaking is not the same as informal conversation. As with the differences between written and oral styles, if you are to be effective, you need to recognize the important differences between the two speaking situations and, in turn, make different choices as a public speaker than you do as an informal conversationalist. See Table 1.2.

Because of the many significant differences between conversation and public speaking, you do not want to transfer all daily conversational qualities into your public communication transactions. Unlike most conversations, which occur spontaneously and for which there is little to no preparation, the public presentation is a *listener-specific, prepared*

table **1.2** Differences between Everyday Conversations and Public Speeches

As an informal conversationalist, you . . .	As a public speaker, you . . .
typically come up with topics spontaneously.	typically have time to plan your topic.
cover meaningful topics often, but not always.	choose a meaningful and relevant topic.
rarely practice ahead of time.	have time to practice to create a familiarity with what you will say.
are often interrupted with questions and side comments.	usually remain uninterrupted until completing your thoughts.
usually speak without the pressure of a firm time limit.	show respect for the audience by presenting within a time allotment.
may or may not toss in information picked up through research or hearsay.	must competently and ethically consider relevant research and cite the source(s) if you use it in a speech.
may converse just to strengthen relationships, to pass the time, or to be polite.	must make a point in your speech.
may use linguistic distractions—verbal "junk" (*um, uh, er,* and *like*), slang, epithets—without significant consequence.	eliminate, or at least minimize, linguistic distractions, which can impede listening and damage your credibility.

conversation. But to the extent that you can consider the public speech a type of conversation, what quality of conversation works best?

Treat your public presentation as an **important conversation.** Think of the style of conversation you use when interacting with someone you respect. How would you speak if you were being interviewed? Talking to a professor you admire? to your employer? to a valued customer? In these contexts, the style of speaking most likely differs from the familiar and informal style you use with family or friends. In important conversation, you attempt to convey meaningful messages and are generally more aware of how you are being perceived by the other person. You are more careful with word choices, more attentive to grammatical conventions, and more focused on better posture and eye contact. In important conversation, you also hold yourself straighter, look the other person in the eye, and are aware of the placement and movements of your body. In other words, in important conversation, *you are trying to be your best.*

This high level of attentiveness and care is the communicative quality you want for the majority of the speeches in your classrooms, at work, and in your community. Different public speaking situations call for assorted topics, varying levels of formality, and a range of strategies. Sometimes the content is more serious than at other times. Likewise, some audiences are tougher to convince than others. An advantage of the important-conversation style, however, is that it works for nearly all public speaking contexts. Your elevated conversational quality reflects the importance of your ideas, your self-respect, and the respect you have for your listeners.

3. Explore the foundations for listener-centered speaking

A public speech—by definition—is a kind of dialogue. Let's examine what some important thinkers have to say about the role of dialogue in human interaction. These ideas, valued by many communication instructors, provide a basis for embracing listener-centered speaking as a logically sound framework.

Twentieth-century Russian philosopher Mikhail Bakhtin, in his thinkings about the classical Greek concept of **dialectics**—using reasoned arguments to find a truth about a topic—notes that all human interaction is based on dialogue.[3] This may sound obvious, but it is important. Bakhtin's concept of **dialogism** explains that each of us becomes who we are—takes shape—based on the push and pull of discussion, exploration, and debate with others. In other words, the interaction of another's individual voice with our own voice, by virtue of the interplay and dialogue, creates new ways of thinking within both participants. For example, you weren't born with your current knowledge and opinions about topics such as immigration, sex before marriage, and the value of a higher education. You needed a buildup of multiple interactions with others to arrive at your current perspectives.

Bakhtin goes on to observe that these perspectives aren't static or permanent. Just as they've taken shape and evolved in the past, they will continue to take new shape—again through dialogue with others—as time progresses. Through social interaction with others, we change—sometimes a little, sometimes significantly. Likewise, we alter those with whom we communicate. This cycle continues throughout our lives; we are forever changing.

Communication scholars Leslie Baxter and Barbara Montgomery expand on Bakhtin's ideas with their concept of **relational dialectics,** which says that communication—interacting with others—is used to construct relationships and understanding within those relationships.[4] When interacting with another person, they note, we each start in our own place of knowing or believing, and these places are by nature different from those of the other person to some degree. Through the push and pull of speaking and listening to one another, which can get contentious along the way, we come to a new place, one of understanding. You may not like or agree with what you learn, but you understand it, thereby altering yourself to some degree. In the process, you also alter the relationship, because "changed" people are now involved in it. In short, communication with others helps us gain a new perspective.

When we expand to the public sphere[5] we see that public speakers and listeners need one another. It is the very nature of our dialogue—the opposing forces at play—that leads to gradual but eventual change in our individual lives and in our society. For example, nearly all of us living today in Western societies strongly believe that women should have the right to vote. In fact, that policy is so commonplace, most of us don't even think about it. But women's suffrage was among the serious national dialogues open for debate well into the twentieth century. It's intriguing to envision what the tone of some of today's hot-button dialogues, including climate change, same-sex marriage, and the role of government in health care, may be like one hundred years from now. How will individuals and societies view these ideas next century?

Modern public speaking, by its very nature, positions speakers and listeners in dialogue. You present ideas to a group, and they listen and respond. You then reconsider and perhaps alter your message, if ever so slightly, presenting those ideas again. The cycle continues through additional dialogue, creating change, however gradual, among individuals and societies. Change happens because the act of speaking in public includes more people in the exchange. The speaker, while in dialogue with an audience, is actually in dialogue with each individual listener comprising the audience. The potential effect of a speaker's message, then, is multiplied by a number equal to those listening. To return to our women's suffrage example, advocates of suffrage like Susan B. Anthony, Elizabeth Cady Stanton, Lucy Stone, and Julia Ward Howe used public speech, as well as marches and dramatic acts such as locking themselves to doors, as a way to engage in a dialogue/conversation with lawmakers and a voting public about this important civil right for American women. The power of their messages eventually prevailed over those of their opponents and led to a new development—the passing of the Nineteenth Amendment in 1920 and ultimately to our current, practically unremarkable views toward a woman's right to the ballot box.

It's important for speakers to effectively engage in dialogue with their listeners. Yet sometimes, a speaker's actions—stiff reading straight from a manuscript, poor eye contact, disorganized ideas, offensive or distracting language choices—prevent good listening, and therefore dialogue, from taking place. When speakers instead make their ideas easy for listeners to access, understand, and interact with—if, in effect, they are listener-centered, achieving a high degree of listenability while speaking—listeners can engage and respond to the messages being conveyed. This push and

Suffragist Julia Ward Howe, c. 1908
In Howe's speech at a suffrage hearing before the Massachusetts legislature, she disputed the opposition's point that allowing women a voice at the ballot box would "double the ignorance vote," arguing, "If with others the hod carrier, the railroad hand, the factory operative, had power to elect a decent and creditable legislature, why should not the school teachers and shop girls and servant maids of Boston, with all these ladies to help them, be able to do as well?"[6]

SPEAK Responsibly

Adding Your Societal Voice

Though our democracy includes the right for all to engage in the public dialogue, some voices, for a variety of reasons, are more dominant than others. For social change (like suffrage, for example) to occur, however, all voices—dominant and otherwise—must engage in dialogue with each other. Everyone has a unique perspective to offer. We each have the responsibility to speak up and speak out.

- Is there any social change you would like to see occur?
- If you have a naturally soft or politically nondominant voice, do you remain relatively quiet or do you make yourself heard? How does it feel when you do speak up? What are the challenges in getting others to listen to you? How do you want to overcome these?
- If you have a charismatic, forceful, or otherwise powerful voice, are you aware of it? Do you use it to your advantage? Why or why not? Do you ever temper your voice so as to give room for other voices? If so, how do you do this?

pull of ideas keeps individuals and societies dynamic, providing the very essence of what it means to be alive in a particular time and place. A commitment to dialogue through listener-centered communication ultimately offers speakers greater opportunity to reach others and potentially effect change.

1B Identify Speaker Responsibilities

The well-known phrase "**power of the podium**" refers to the inherent respect that public communicators enjoy as soon as they approach the speaking space. If only it were as easy to keep that respect. To fully connect with your audience, you must fulfill a series of responsibilities during speech preparation and delivery. This network of responsibilities, described in detail below, includes accountability to the message, to your listeners, and to yourself. Throughout this text, you'll learn how to master these responsibilities and ultimately become an effective listener-centered public speaker.

1. Responsibilities to the message

Your ideas are central to your public presentation; they are the very reason you're speaking. In order to be true to those ideas and successfully relate them to other people, your responsibilities to the message include the following:

Select meaningful topics

First, you need to know whether your overall goal is to inform, to persuade, or to mark a special occasion. Then, you must choose a relevant topic that is mutually beneficial to you and your listeners. (See Chapter 6.)

Narrow the scope of your discussion

It's important to narrow the scope of your topic and craft a meaningful thesis statement— the specific message about your topic you want to communicate. (See Chapter 6.)

Evaluate and cite relevant research

Responsible research increases your own understanding of your topic, helps strengthen your main points, and increases the confidence that you—and in turn, others—have in your ideas. (See Chapter 7.)

Support your ideas in a multitude of ways

By elaborating on your ideas, you reduce your listeners' need to make inferences and thus make the speech easier to understand. However, not all ideas call for the same kinds of support. Some topics benefit from the use of narrative, or story. Others are better suited to objective support—facts, definitions, and statistics. Still others can best be served by illustrative support—examples, descriptions, and explanations. Most speeches, however, will be enhanced by a combination of support methods. (See Chapter 8.)

2. Responsibilities to listeners

Responsible speakers work during speech preparation and delivery to show that the communication event is indeed for the benefit of the audience. You'll do this through the following actions:

Analyze and engage your listeners

You are more likely to communicate your message successfully when you know who's listening. Tailoring your message to the specific group gathered tells the audience you did your homework. (See Chapter 5.)

Create a clear structure

A well-organized message helps listeners stay with you as you convey your ideas and avoids their getting lost or left behind. (See Chapters 9, 10, and 11.)

Use visual support when appropriate

While not all messages require visual accompaniment, effective speakers know how to capitalize on it when needed. (See Chapter 12.)

Practice and manage your time

Procrastination and poor time management are among the top reasons that speeches don't go as hoped or planned. Managing your own time wisely rewards both you and those who make a time commitment to listen to you. (See Chapter 13.)

Use appropriate delivery skills

Responsible speakers understand the communicative power of their language, voice, and body. Talking in conversational patterns and moving in ways that make others comfortable help them stay with you to fully access, understand, and interact with your message. (See Chapter 14.)

3. Responsibilities to yourself

Take your time before an audience seriously, and approach speaking tasks as an opportunity to expand your knowledge base and your scope as a critical thinker, a productive professional, and a thoughtful citizen. The following are your responsibilities to yourself:

Increase your confidence while being honest about your own speaking growth

Most speakers contend with nerves prior to a presentation. However, you can harness that energy to present with ever-growing self-assurance and authenticity. An honest and realistic post-speech self-evaluation helps you reflect on your speech delivery and refine your skills. (See Chapter 3.)

Be ethical, civil, and credible

Your integrity and reputation are tested each time you speak. It's critical to abide by ethical standards throughout speech preparation and delivery in order to engage in civil dia-

Responsibilities...

to the message	to listeners	to yourself
• Select meaningful topics. • Narrow your scope. • Craft a clear thesis statement. • Evaluate and cite research. • Use multiple, strong forms of support.	• Analyze and engage your listeners. • Create a clear structure. • Use visual support as needed. • Practice. • Manage your time. • Use appropriate delivery skills.	• Increase your confidence. • Grow through self-evaluation. • Be ethical, civil, and credible. • Listen to others.

logue with your listening audience. Focus on creating your own ideas while avoiding the dangers of plagiarism. (See Chapter 4.)

Listen effectively to others

This course offers the bonus of enhancing your own skills as an active, ethical, and civil public listener. (See Chapter 2.)

1C Understand the Public Communication Process

Another responsibility you have as a speaker is to "learn the lingo" and see how participants in the public speaking event interact. Several components are at play during the public speech (Figure 1.1, p. 18). Knowing them helps you better visualize your role as speaker and provides you with important terminology you'll use as you progress through the public speaking course.

1. Sender

When speaking in public, you are the **sender,** the person motivated to share your ideas. These ideas may be informative, persuasive, or geared to a special occasion such as an anniversary party or a funeral. In the role of **encoder,** you create meaning by taking the ideas in your mind and translating them into various codes perceptible to others, such as words, gestures, facial expressions, pictures, and tone of voice.

2. Receivers

The audience members are the **receivers** in a public speaking event. Also known as **decoders,** they are the listeners who assign and create meaning from the speaker's words and behaviors. Some decoding is basic: only receivers who speak English can assign and create meaning for English words, and only then for the English words within their vocabulary.

Most decoding is more complex and subjective. When receivers see you choosing and using engaging visual support, they make assumptions about your preparation and competence. On the other hand, when they hear you make a claim without providing sufficient evidence, they may view your entire message with suspicion.

3. Frame of reference

All communicators in the public speaking transaction, both sender and receivers, bring with them a **frame of reference,** an individual worldview based on characteristics such as age, education, gender, politics, economic status, culture, occupation, and health. As a speaker,

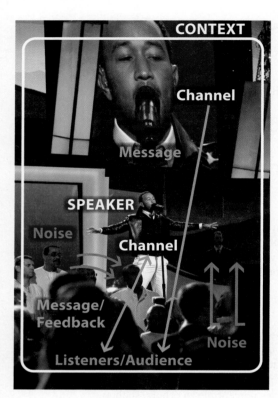

figure **1.1** **The Transactional Communication Process** John Legend speaks at the 2008 Democratic Convention.

you have a frame of reference that influences the creation of your message; each of us says and does things based on our worldview.

Individual audience members also have a frame of reference that influences their reception and interpretation of your message. A peace activist and a military leader, for example, may interpret the same speech on U.S. foreign policy differently. A cash-strapped student listening to a presentation on investment strategies would not perceive things in the same way as a wealthy worker nearing retirement.

An audience as a whole is also considered to have a frame of reference. Your role as listener-centered speaker is to do your best to understand, prepare for, and respond to the audience's frame of reference through a process called *audience analysis* (which you'll read about in Chapter 5).

4. Message

The **message** is the set of ideas you (as the speaker) transmit to the audience. You send messages in the form of content—what you want your listeners to learn, believe, do, or feel. You also send messages about yourself—your knowledge of the topic, your confidence, your preparation, and your personal feelings about the audience, the topic, and the situation.

Listeners send messages as well, known as **feedback.** Audience members communicate their degree of participation, their interest in you, or their understanding of the content. Some feedback is immediate and simultaneous. Direct eye contact, nods, and smiles all let you know how your message is being received as it is being delivered. Because of this feedback, a public speech is an example of **transactional communication.** Essentially, messages of all kinds are being sent both ways; if these messages could be made visible, you would see hundreds of messages flying back and forth through the air. As your audience members transmit their own feedback and messages, you interpret them and respond in turn. For some beginning speakers, high levels of adrenaline may make it hard to see and process audience feedback. If this happens to you, understand that it's quite normal. After a few presentations, the "fog" will lift, and you'll be able to perceive and consider the messages your audience is sending back to you.

Other kinds of feedback are delayed, such as questions and comments at the end of a presentation. Reviews and evaluations from an instructor, a supervisor, or audience members may arrive hours or days after the speech.

Listen to any feedback you receive with an open mind. You may not agree with it, but accept it as another person's perception. Feedback helps you see how your message with your listeners, those for whom you shaped your talk, and provides direction for future presentations.

5. Channel

Your goal in any communication event is to transfer the ideas in your mind into the minds of your listeners. The means by which messages and feedback are transmitted between you and your audience is called a **channel.** Visual channels include gestures, posture, eye contact, dress, photographs, and pie charts. Auditory channels include spoken words, tone of voice, and sound clips. Some speakers use a form of media, like television or a web broadcast, to get their message to their audience.

6. Noise

It is nearly impossible for your message to arrive purely as intended at a listener's ear. **Noise** is anything that interferes with the audience's ability to fully understand your message. Both you and the listeners are responsible for lessening or eliminating noise. As you can see from Table 1.3 (p. 20), there are many different types of noise—not just the obvious—and there are practical ways to avoid or deal with noise.

7. Context

Each public speaking transaction takes place in a specific environment or situation. This **context** affects how you create your messages and how listeners create meaning from those messages. For instance, you would present one way to peers at a campus meeting and another when arguing for neighborhood rights at City Hall. New employees at a workplace orientation listen differently than family members at a fiftieth wedding anniversary celebration.

1D Capitalize on the Benefits of Public Speaking

Your immediate goal may be to excel in this class, but of all the classes you take in college, this course in public speaking may arguably help you develop skills that provide the most far-reaching benefits. From your life as a student to your life in the working world and in your community, proficiency in public presentation enhances your interaction with others by allowing you to share important ideas, shape opinion and policy, and participate meaningfully in special occasions. There are personal benefits as well. If you're not yet doing so, there are many good reasons to join in public dialogues.

table **1.3** **Types of Noise**

Type of noise	Examples	Ways to reduce or eliminate noise
Psychological/internal noise	Daydreaming, worries, distractions	**For speakers:** Stress the relevance of your ideas. Use listener-engagement techniques (described throughout the text). **For listeners:** Make a conscious choice to pay attention. Your daydreams and worries can wait.
Environmental/external noise	Ringing electronic devices, crying babies, loud air-conditioning systems, people shuffling in late	**For speakers:** Ask people to turn off electronic devices. Close doors to noisy hallways. **For listeners:** Find a spot where it's easy to hear the speaker. Do your part to keep the noise down so as not to create distractions.
Social noise	Biases, unyielding attitudes, prejudices	**For speakers:** Openly address the controversial nature of your content. **For listeners:** Acknowledge your bias. You never have to agree with the speaker, but it's ethical to listen fully before making judgments.
Organizational noise	Poor structure; listeners can't follow the speaker's train of thought	**For speakers:** Have a clear structure, know it well, and openly communicate it to listeners. **For listeners:** Take notes. Listen for main ideas. Listen actively.
Physiological noise	Listeners are hungry, tired, or sick	**For speakers:** If possible, schedule complex presentations early in the day. Provide food and drink. **For listeners:** Eat before you arrive. Try to manage physical discomfort or distraction.

1. Academic benefits

The skills learned in this course extend far beyond excelling in your public speaking class. Preparing for and listening to others' speeches is a chance to expand your knowledge base on a breadth of topics, to learn new technologies, and to polish research skills. The act of exchanging public messages is also an opportunity to look inside and see who you are—your commitments, your values, your ideals. Here are some specific academic skills you'll learn or build on in this course:

Speaking skills

Rare is the college student who is not required to orally present a paper or project in at least one course. Recent surveys of undergraduates showed that 70 percent of community college students give formal presentations,[7] and 86 percent of first-year university students and 94 percent of seniors do the same.[8] Knowing how to present your ideas to classmates is essential in any academic or workforce area of study. One graduate of a public speaking course, an engineering major, shared her experience:

> *I made a presentation in my calculus class today, and I think it's fair to say I was among the best. Most others read off their papers in a monotone voice and never even looked at the audience. I'll admit I walked away from some of those presentations with no new understanding of calculus. In contrast, I spoke conversationally from only a few notes and really engaged my classmates. My visuals were big, bright, and helpful, and people even asked questions at the end. They were listening. And I got an A on the assignment.*

Critical-thinking skills

Critical thinking, the ability to skillfully use and analyze your thought process in order to make effective judgments, is a requirement for college success. Throughout this course, you'll have multiple opportunities to exercise your analytic and evaluation skills because they're needed at every step of the speechmaking process. You make strategic, conscious choices about what to say and do based on your assessment of the speech purpose, the audience, and the speaking occasion.

You also exercise your critical-thinking abilities through your role as a public listener. As you listen, you work to identify your classmates' central themes, evaluate the effectiveness of their organization, and question the support they use to sustain their arguments. You should find your critical listening improving with each listening opportunity.

Writing skills

As discussed earlier, although public speaking and composition writing are two very different forms of communication, there are some areas of overlap. Public speaking students repeatedly report that they can now write tighter essays, craft clearer central messages, and better structure and support those messages.

Expanded campus involvement

Most colleges and universities offer extensive opportunities for formal and informal involvement with others in the campus community. The skills you learn and practice as a speaker can increase and enhance your social, philanthropic, or political interaction with others. These relationships may even come in handy in a future job search.

2. Career benefits

You'll enhance your current and future professional life when you learn how to speak in public. Expertise is one of the most critical economic resources in this interconnected world. Whether you work for yourself, for a government agency, or for a multinational corporation, chances are you'll need or want to communicate your ideas to others at some point, if not many times, in your working career.

Better communication during your job interview

Successful job applicants articulate their experience and vision in an organized manner. They tailor their responses to the specific needs and culture of the interviewing organization. Eye contact, formal use of language, clear pronunciation, and a confident speaking voice—essential interviewing skills—are all skills used by public speakers.

Better communication on the job

Speaking up at meetings, training other employees, selling ideas to clients, and presenting at conferences are only some of the public communication situations for today's working people. Employers value the skills possessed by effective public speakers. In fact, having the "ability to communicate with persons inside and outside the organization" was the top key skill for new college hires in a recent survey.[9] Many other desired job requirements, such as listening skills, analytic and research skills, problem-solving skills, planning and organizing skills, as well as multicultural awareness, reasoning, creativity, adaptability, and self-confidence are also taught in the public speaking course.[10] Employers are happy to train you in job specifics, but are not always willing or able to spend valuable organizational resources to teach you such general practical workplace skills. Your public speaking training and experience can give you and your employer increased confidence in your ability to connect with clients, customers, and others within the organization.

Workplace presentations Survey your friends, family, and acquaintances working in education, law, business, public service, the military, entertainment, various trades, government, law enforcement, science, health care, and numerous other occupations. Most of them likely engage in some degree of public presentation. Some address large audiences; others, smaller groups at work. But for most, presenting to customers, supervisors, clients, and colleagues is part of the job. Mike Rumpeltin, an architect at RSP Architects in Tempe, Arizona, is typical:

I present my ideas, thoughts, and designs constantly to a wide array of people with varying backgrounds. This means that even within a single presentation, I may have to represent an idea or concept in multiple ways but still keep a certain level of excitement and engagement with the audience. I am certain that my techniques, along with the energy and passion I communicate about my work, are what lead to my repeat clientele.

Speaking skills and self-employment Public speaking skills are also essential for people who are self-employed or working in seemingly solitary professions. Mark Duran, a self-employed commercial photographer specializing in "planes, trains, and automobiles," attributes his success, in part, to his public speaking skills:

I have to make presentations to companies to convince them to hire me. Though my knees literally knocked the first few times I did it, I am now quite comfortable with speaking. First of all, I'm prepared. There's nothing that substitutes for that. I then go into the presentation seeing it as my room to work. I know I have more expertise in photography than anyone else sitting there. I'm confident. And I believe it gives me an edge. It's usually a slam dunk that I get hired for the job.

Speaking skills and workplace training Duran also uses his speaking skills to train others. He makes presentations on photography tips to students and talks to marketing departments on topics such as "What to Expect When You Hire a Photographer." Duran's engaging personality and confidence as a public speaker get him repeated requests to make presentations.

3. Community and personal benefits

Finally, public speaking skills are advantageous in your community and personal life. Speakers experience increased levels of engagement in their communities and increased confidence in social situations. One speaker, reflecting on her public speaking training, said,

I learned a lot about public speaking in this class, but I also learned a lot about life. I learned that people don't want to see a presentation of you; they want to see you, the real you, just as you are. I've learned, as absolutely corny and grade school as it sounds, that it's okay to be myself. I now feel confident that I have the tools and experience necessary to succeed and communicate in an honest and effective way with whomever I want.

Engagement in your community

People participate in their communities in a variety of ways. Parents join school committees, car enthusiasts gravitate toward the local lowrider club, and a variety of caring individuals get involved with the Boys and Girls Clubs of America. Public speakers have added influence in the start-up, maintenance, impact, and success of community organizations.

Benefits of public speaking

Confidence in social situations

People often say that "finding their voice" through their public speaking experience leads to stronger feelings of personal empowerment. They value their ability to teach, influence, and reach others through words and actions. Many also testify to increased levels of self-esteem and to feeling less intimidated in social situations.

1E Discover the Traditions of Public Speaking

When you begin studying public speaking, you are participating in an endeavor with a rich history. Most human societies have created the need or the opportunity for one person to stand before others with the intent of teaching, convincing, or even entertaining. Though the earliest beginnings of public speaking may go back even further, the roots of contemporary public speaking lie in the great cultural shift from aristocracy to democracy that took place in ancient Greek society 2,500 years ago.[11] Whereas "tyrants may have ruled other nations by torture and the lash, the Greeks made their decisions by persuasion and debate."[12] Soon, skill in persuasion—more than social class—became a key factor in a person's success and public influence.[13]

Greek teachers and philosophers such as Protagoras, Plato, and Aristotle studied and taught specific methods of persuasion to their fellow citizens. Romans such as Cicero and Quintilian followed a few centuries later. Sought out enthusiastically by those who could afford their services, these men enjoyed high status. For example, a course in the rhetorical arts from one famed Greek teacher, Isocrates, cost 1,000 drachmas at a time when a day laborer made roughly 1 drachma per day.[14]

The teachings of these early scholars are still studied and remain relevant today. A good number of the concepts and skills found throughout this book, including the arrangement of ideas, speaker credibility, and listener-centered language, stem from classical origins. In fact, except for philosophy and grammar, no other area of study has such deep roots.

As times change, however, so does a subject of study. Thinkers in the late eighteenth century began questioning some of the classical ideals.[15] These later philosophers believed that they could discover truth through life experience, rather than purely through persuasion, and that they could communicate this new truth only by re-creating or narrating their experience for listeners. The narrative, a valued component of modern presentations, thus became important. The speaker "was expected to develop his or her own understanding by reflecting on experience, and then explain those ideas to the audience by appealing to the faculties of mind, which included both understanding and imagination."[16]

By the nineteenth century, orators were expected to be "larger than life." Because this was a time before modern media, public speaking was as much a common spectacle and an entertainment as it was a means of conveying and exchanging ideas. The most charismatic speakers drew large crowds and enjoyed celebrity status. To learn the presentation skills of the day, students joined debating societies that allowed them to sharpen their talents. Books taught people how to participate in "deliberative assemblies." Schools trained children through the use of anthologies of published speeches.

The study, practice, and discussion of public communication, as an academic discipline and as an everyday practice, continues today and remains as relevant to our modern-day world as it was to the Greeks 2,500 years ago. Today, people in many countries study public speaking in schools, colleges, and universities. Others hire private coaches or get together with like-minded people through organizations like Meetup.com or Toastmasters. While the speaking methods you learn today are based on foundational core concepts and skills used, tested, and refined over millennia, they have been adapted for today's culture and today's listeners. Public speaking success in the twenty-first century requires unique methods and tools and, certainly, a different speaking personality than was valued in past eras. We have moved beyond the age of speaker-centered oratory to the age of listener-centered presentation. This book, your instructor, and perhaps even your classmates will all play a role in teaching you the most current, effective techniques for presenting your contemporary ideas in modern public settings.

Listener-Centered Speaking in Action
A Student's Process and Shift in Approach

Brenda Toscano enrolled for a public speaking course that she had taken once before, several semesters previously. This time, the course relied on a listener-centered approach, which was new to her. To Brenda's surprise, that new perspective made her treat the course, her speeches, and her role as a speaker in an entirely different way. The first time she took the course, however, public speaking was presented as a performance, with the focus on Brenda as a speaker. By her own admission, she didn't put much effort into the course—because she didn't think she needed to.

Brenda, on Public Speaking—Then:

Before this [second] class I used to think that public speaking was just about getting over the shyness and the fear of talking to large crowds. But since I've never been shy, the course seemed like a complete waste of time. However, the course was required for me, so I had to start somewhere, and I started with the goal of being funny. I figured "funny" was a way to bond with the audience and gain their acceptance. I now realize this is very performance-based. It was not about communication. It was about me.

The listener-centered approach required Brenda to work and reflect on her choices as a speaker. At the core of her shift in perspective was the notion that a speech is a public conversation with listeners—not just a speaker performing and talking at a captive, passive audience of people, being charming, and expecting praise and applause.

Brenda, on Public Speaking—Now:

I've learned that I didn't need to be funny. I learned instead to keep my listeners in mind and speak in a way that will be meaningful to them. Most of all, I learned that public speaking is all about listeners and whether or not they have understood the message that I attempted to convey. By my final speech I think I had it mastered. I spoke about the conditions that illegal farm workers face, which is something that most people in class had never given any thought to, and I tried to make it meaningful by telling them how it is that we ourselves are affected—without that, I think they wouldn't have cared and would have missed my message completely. By strategically involving them in my message, I appealed to their sense of compassion and some of my classmates even mentioned a sense of guilt. This was exactly what I wanted to do, because by awakening these feelings in them I hope

connect

See Brenda's listener-centered persuasive speech in the online speech video "Migrant Farm Workers."

they will do as I have suggested and spread the word to others so that together we can make a change for those without any rights.

For the first time ever, I feel like I can really be understood. When I speak now, I feel I have the power to make people listen, as well as the tools to present my ideas in ways that listeners understand the messages in my words.

review questions

1. What is listener-centered public speaking? Why is it beneficial to study public speaking through this framework?
2. Why is dialogue an appropriate foundation for listener-centered public speaking?
3. How is it that fulfilling a network of responsibilities makes you a better public speaker?
4. What are the components of a public communication transaction?
5. How does becoming a public speaker benefit you as a student, in your career, and in your community?
6. How does modern public speaking compare and contrast with public speaking of the past?

key terms

listener-centered public speaker 4
listenability 5
public listener 6
literate, or written, style 9
oral, or conversational, style 9
important conversation 11

dialectics 12
dialogism 12
relational dialectics 12
power of the podium 14
sender 17
encoder 17
receiver 17
decoder 17
frame of reference 17

message 18
feedback 18
transactional communication 18
channel 19
noise 19
context 19

exercises

1. Have you been invited to see public speaking from a listener-centered lens before? If so, describe your experience and your reactions to the concept. If not, does it sound intriguing? Why or why not? Write up your thoughts in a brief reflection paper.

connect

For online exercises, quizzes, and hands-on activities, see the Chapter 1 assignments in Connect Public Speaking.

2. What are the current societal conversations going on at your school, in your community, your region, or the nation? As a class, write all the topics on the board. Are there people in class who are on opposite ends of these social conversations? Is there a potential for true dialogue in your class?

3. Pair up with another person in class. Share your thoughts on the "important conversation" style promoted in the chapter. Are you capable of this? What might you sound like when engaged in it?

4. Interview a person working in your chosen field of study or in one that interests you. Ask this person to tell you about the role public presentations play in his or her work life. How often does this person give and/or listen to presentations? What kinds of messages are typically shared during these presentations? Who is in the typical audience? Report your findings to your teacher and classmates.

Listen to the Speeches of Others

LEARNING OBJECTIVES

1 Describe the characteristics of active public listening.

2 Explain how to combat problems at each stage of the listening process.

3 Summarize the four listening levels within the public speaking context.

4 Articulate the skills and behaviors of an excellent public listener.

chapter preview

2A Know What Good Listening Is

2B Understand the Listening Process

2C Position Your Listening

2D Be an Excellent Public Listener

Review Questions
Key Terms
Exercises

S
N
L

Your public speaking course delivers a bonus—the life-enriching skill of public listening. Many students are surprised to learn that listening plays a central role in a course that emphasizes public speaking. It may be hard to predict how, when, and where you'll give public presentations in the future, but it's guaranteed you'll listen to them throughout your life—in your classes, at work, in your community, and in society. Listening is an underrated skill. Because we've been doing it all our lives, many of us believe that we already do it well. In reality, listening takes work, but it is work that is absolutely worth the effort. This chapter focuses on your responsibilities as a listening member of the audience by describing what listening is and how it works. You'll also learn various ways to position your listening, how to overcome barriers to effective listening, and how to practice excellent public listening.

2A Know What Good Listening Is

The act of listening is often taken for granted. While you most likely remember receiving formal and informal instruction in reading, writing, and speaking, listening is something we're just expected to know how to do. Yet few have been taught how to listen effectively, and most people could do a better job of listening than they do. That's changing, though. Fortunately, many schools, businesses, and health-related fields are seeing the value in listening training. There is even a professional organization, the International Listening Association, whose members share research, exchange ideas, and promote the practice and teaching of effective listening.

The rewards of good listening include:[1]

- Gathering ideas and information—for academic or work-related projects or for personal use
- Finding opportunities that you may not have known existed
- Sharpening your analytic skills
- Asking intelligent questions
- Increasing your chances for job success by learning more about how your organization operates and how you can best function within it
- Improving your social connections
- Improving your public speaking skills
- Maintaining the health of our democracy by listening to opposing points of view

1. The role of the listener in the public speaking transaction

As a public listener, you are one-half of an essential partnership between speaker and audience. You might be tempted to think that the speaker is more important than the listeners, but as you read in Chapter 1, listeners and speakers are equal players. They have no purpose without each other. Though speakers and listeners need one another, each faces different obligations for creating a successful communication interaction. This book is filled with the responsibilities required of the public speaker, but as a public listener you assume obligations as well, including:

- Understanding that listening is an active skill requiring intention and energy
- Being willing to listen
- Showing the speaker that you are listening
- Interacting with the message and providing feedback
- Not creating distractions
- Ignoring distractions and focusing on the speaker
- Being a civil and ethical listener

You'll find more details about these listener responsibilities as you continue reading the chapter.

Speakers and listeners also need each other to make the other stronger and more accountable in public contexts. In essence, the greater the number of capable public listeners there are, the greater the demand for capable speakers. One student looked at the speaker-listener relationship this way: "Having the desire to hear good speeches inspires me to give them."

2. Hearing versus listening

Do you remember the last time you suddenly realized that someone was saying something to you? You were hearing the person's voice, but for whatever reason—perhaps you were distracted by something else—you weren't processing the words and assigning meaning to them. You were hearing but not listening.

Hearing is the foundation of listening. It is an involuntary, biological process that occurs when your ears pick up a sound within range; if your ears are working, you cannot help but hear. **Listening,** on the other hand, requires you to take what you hear, choose to attend to it, assign it meaning, and somehow respond to it. Listening is a voluntary, mental process that, when done well, takes energy. You engage in the complex and fascinating listening process hundreds, if not thousands, of times a day.

We also "hear" and "listen," in some sense, with our eyes. While our ears pick up words and vocal intonation, our eyes catch the nonverbal messages in the speaker's facial expression, body movement, and gestures, enriching the overall message we receive. The brain processes these visual stimuli in the same manner as aural stimuli. Deaf people, for example, rely on intonation for meaning just like hearing people do, but the intonation comes through visual information such as the pace of signing, accompanying facial gestures, and whether the sender signs in a big space or a small space.[2]

3. Active versus passive listening

We don't listen to everything in the same way. **Passive listening** takes relatively little energy, as you know when you pay halfhearted attention to incoming stimuli (someone's voice outside a room, the car radio) either by choice or by habit. Passive listening can be appropriate at the end of a long day when you just need to relax in front of the TV or when your favorite uncle tells you—for the umpteenth time!—how he won that weight-lifting tournament back in 1982. But passive listening is not appropriate when you're assuming the role of public listener.

Active listening, listening with the intention of understanding what another person is saying, is what you strive for during a public presentation. It begins with a willingness and desire to listen and requires you to expend high levels of energy. Active listening includes behaviors such as making eye contact, taking notes, and identifying main ideas.

The goal of active listening is to fully *comprehend* what the other person is saying; you don't necessarily need to agree or obey. People often say "I hear you" when they actually

How to Take Useful Notes

Note taking is not just jotting down random words. It is a conscious and deliberate process that helps you stay active as a listener and develop a thorough understanding of the speaker's message.

Tips for Effective Note Taking

- Bring the most efficient tools for note taking, be it old-school pen and paper, or new technology like a tablet computer. If you're using a computer for taking notes in class, always check with your instructor first—and save your notes often.
- Limit distractions. Turn off your cell phone, move away from that chatty person next to you, and sit as close to the speaker as is comfortable or possible.
- Create a system of shorthand. Your notes have to make sense only to you.
- Write down any unfamiliar words or concepts you don't understand; you can look them up later and then work their meaning into the overall context of the speech.
- Record the speaker's primary organization, including the central idea (thesis), main points, and essential subpoints, but don't attempt to write everything down. If these major ideas are hard to detect, keep at it. Sometimes a speaker's structure becomes apparent as the speech progresses.
- Attempt to put these major ideas that you detect into a visual outline so you can literally "see" the relationships of the ideas to one another.
- Use the margins to write down any questions you'll want to ask post-speech.
- Clean up, fill in, and summarize your notes as soon as possible after the speech, while everything is still fresh.

mean "I agree with you." We use "I should have listened" to mean "I should have done what I was told." But these phrases are just figures of speech. As an active public listener, you aim to fully understand what the speaker is attempting to say. Only then do you decide whether to agree or comply.

Like piano playing or stilt walking, active listening is a skill that requires practice. The more active listening you do, the better at it you become. Not only do you become a stronger listener, able to follow more complex ideas and speech structures, but you are also able to listen for longer stretches of time. You'll have many opportunities to practice your active public listening throughout your academic and working career.

2B Understand the Listening Process

1. The steps in the listening process

In Chapter 1, you learned that listenable speakers help audience members access, understand, and interact with their messages. In this chapter, we break down the listening process in more detail and explore it from the listener's perspective. The process of listening is the same; as highlighted in the color-coded verbs below, speakers and listeners use different words to describe the steps from their respective viewpoints.

> As a speaker, I will make choices to help you access, understand, and interact with my message.

> As a listener, I will work to hear, attend, interpret, and respond to your message.

As a listener, you must successfully achieve each step in the listening process before moving on to the next. Figure 2.1 (p. 34) shows the process in action.

2. How the listening process can break down and what you can do about it

The process of listening should be simple, but breakdowns and distractions lurk at each step. The average listener, however unintentionally, often creates obstacles to successful public communication. Here are some ways to help you improve your active public listening. Determine which ones work best for you by applying them, for example, during speech presentations, class lectures, or meetings at work or in your community.

Hearing problems and solutions

Some listening difficulties occur with hearing. If you are not picking up aural or visual stimuli clearly, it's difficult, if not impossible, to process the message further. Table 2.1 (p. 34) lists some common hearing problems and solutions.

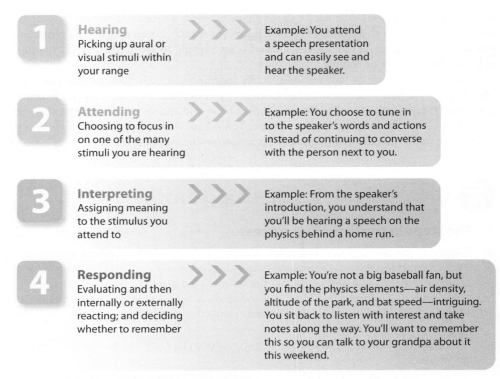

1 Hearing
Picking up aural or visual stimuli within your range

Example: You attend a speech presentation and can easily see and hear the speaker.

2 Attending
Choosing to focus in on one of the many stimuli you are hearing

Example: You choose to tune in to the speaker's words and actions instead of continuing to converse with the person next to you.

3 Interpreting
Assigning meaning to the stimulus you attend to

Example: From the speaker's introduction, you understand that you'll be hearing a speech on the physics behind a home run.

4 Responding
Evaluating and then internally or externally reacting; and deciding whether to remember

Example: You're not a big baseball fan, but you find the physics elements—air density, altitude of the park, and bat speed—intriguing. You sit back to listen with interest and take notes along the way. You'll want to remember this so you can talk to your grandpa about it this weekend.

figure **2.1**   **The Listening Process, Step by Step**

table **2.1**   **Hearing Problems and Solutions**

Hearing problems	Hearing solutions
Impairment, damage, illness, or age-related hearing loss.	• Sit as close to the speaker as possible. • Wear a hearing or vision-correcting device, if required.
Distracting sounds from outside or other people sitting next to you.	• Close doors or windows. • Move to another seat or ask others to keep their voices down.
Inadequate amplification of the speaker's voice.	• Cup your hand over your ear in a nonverbal request for more volume. Make sure the speaker sees it. • *Speak up please* or *Can't hear you* are acceptable things to say, and the speaker is usually grateful for your comment.

Attending problems and solutions

You may hear what the speaker is saying, but if your attention is otherwise diverted, you cannot assign meaning or respond to it. Attending is about choice. No one forces you to be distracted; you control whether you let something or someone draw your attention away from the speaker and his or her message. Table 2.2 lists some common attending problems and ways to better attend to the speaker.

table **2.2** **Attending Problems and Solutions**

Attending problems	Attending solutions
Focusing your attention on your text messages or other electronic devices.	• Put your electronic devices away prior to the start of the speech. While you can switch tasks, your brain cannot multitask, especially when you're trying to learn.[3]
Daydreaming, worrying, spacing out.	• Be a **meta-listener:** Be consciously aware of yourself engaging in the listening process. • If you catch yourself drifting off, come out of it by listening closely for key words or phrases that might help you get back on track.
Assuming an incompatible listening stance such as slouching, looking away, or tightly crossing your arms.	• Adopt an alert and open posture, and give eye contact to the speaker.
Perceiving that the speaker's ideas are not relevant to your life.	• Recognize that every idea has a place. Not every idea will change your life, but a new thought may help you better understand others or make a small improvement in the world around you.
Being fearful of not being a good listener.	• Listening is a skill to be exercised. Know that you become a better listener with every speech you listen to.
Imagining the topic is too difficult to follow.	• Determine that you will get all you can out of any presentation.
Not having enough mental or physical energy to give to the speaker.	• Take some mind-clearing breaths. Focus on the present. Acknowledge the other issues on your mind, but leave them for later. • Take care of any relevant physical needs before the presentation begins—eat, visit the restroom, and so on. • If it's permissible in the speaking space, bring water or some other beverage to keep you alert.

Tune In or Tune Out?

Stuttering, or stammering, is a communication disorder that interrupts the flow of speech. People who stutter (roughly 1 percent of people worldwide) participate in all aspects of daily life, including public speaking.[4] Jude is one such person. He's a smart guy with lots to share. Though he has endured his share of teasing because of his stuttering, he wanted to communicate his ideas to others. He signed up for a public speaking course to learn how.

Jude stuttered on every speech. Did the audience notice? Yes. But did his stuttering affect his ability to communicate? Because Jude's unique topics, thorough research, excellent organization, and engaging personality were what mattered, his stuttering, for the majority of his listeners, was relegated to a mere observation. He quickly emerged as a speaker others looked forward to hearing.

When listening, do your best to tune out a speaker's communication differences—stuttering, heavily accented English, lisping, unique phrasing or intonation—and focus on the message instead. Recognize that speakers with delivery challenges are trying their best. Be patient and respectful. Most likely, there's a worthwhile message waiting for you.

Interpreting problems and solutions

The goal of interpreting is to understand the message as the speaker intended. We don't always find common ground, however, despite our best intentions. Some common interpreting problems and ways to improve your chances of getting the message are shown in Table 2.3.

Responding problems and solutions

Most of your responding—evaluating and deciding whether to remember—occurs while listening to the message, though you may make further responses after the presentation, when you have more time to think. But problems can arise when your responses create barriers to or shut down your listening. Table 2.4 offers common responding problems and suggestions for improvement.

2C Position Your Listening

Scholars have identified several major types of listening.[5] While each of these listening levels is familiar to you, identifying and understanding them as discrete activities allows you to better position your listening—consciously—depending on the context. As you

table **2.3** Interpreting Problems and Solutions

Interpreting problems	Interpreting solutions
Not having enough background knowledge to follow what the speaker is saying.	• If you know the topic in advance, prepare by doing some general research before the presentation. • Use the context of the ideas you do understand to try to determine and follow the speaker's points. • Take notes on ideas and themes to research or questions to ask later.
Not knowing the definition of an essential word, phrase, or concept.	• Record words or ideas to look up later, but use the context to try to derive the approximate meaning for now. • Write down questions to ask at the end of the presentation. • If appropriate, politely interrupt the speaker to request clarification.
Getting lost due to the poor organization of the speaker's ideas.	• Write down the ideas you can detect, and attempt to figure out later what the main idea was. Sometimes a speaker's organization becomes evident midway through or near the end of a presentation. • Listen for transition words and phrases that connect ideas, such as *therefore* and *because*. • Listen for internal previews and summaries that help indicate how the presentation is organized.

table **2.4** Responding Problems and Solutions

Responding problems	Responding solutions
Sensing interference from your personal bias or prejudice about the speaker.	• Acknowledge your bias or prejudice and then separate your feelings about the person from your responsibility to understand the speaker's message. There's plenty of time for evaluation after the speech.
Sensing interference because you disagree with the speaker about the content.	• Take note of the speaker's biases, use of evidence, omissions, and construction of arguments to prepare yourself for post-speech discussion, but keep listening for now.
Thinking of something unrelated in response to something the speaker said.	• Take notes about what you want to say, think over, or remember. Get back to the speaker's message so that you are not left behind.

read about these levels here, note that you can employ more than one type during any presentation. (See Table 2.5 for a handy recap of the various levels.)

1. Pseudo-listening

Also known as fake listening, **pseudo-listening** is an imitation of the real thing. It's a passive activity that takes very little energy. Whether this is due to laziness, an inability to ignore distractions, or just bad habit, pseudo-listeners give every indication that they are present in mind and body, yet they are not. They are elsewhere, reflecting on the events of last weekend or checking out someone's new hairstyle.

Pseudo-listeners are so wrapped up in their thoughts that they waste their own valuable time and fail to get anything out of the presentation. They may think they're being polite and helping the speaker by pretending (*At least the speaker thinks someone is listening.*), but in reality they're wasting the speaker's time as well as their own. Speakers want people to listen, and most are doing their best to meet their listeners at least halfway. Pseudo-listeners are definitely not giving their half.

If you're sometimes a pseudo-listener, try to figure out why. Perhaps it's just become a bad habit. If you're quick to label something as "boring," take responsibility for your own interest level by finding some personal relevance in the speaker's topic. (Sections throughout this chapter offer tips and suggestions for improved active listening.)

2. Appreciative listening

Appreciative listening takes place when people listen for personal pleasure. Of all the listening levels, it is the most highly individual. While the shrieks of playing children or the sounds of improvisational jazz may bring you great listening pleasure, they may grate on another person's nerves.

Appreciative listening is mostly passive. In public settings, appreciative listening may occur during an entertaining after-dinner presentation, a lighthearted anecdote, or an opening joke. You know you don't need the content for later and can sit back and enjoy the present moment.

Other instances of appreciative listening engage your mind more. It may give you pleasure to listen intently to any presentation about your favorite topic or to realize that you are able to follow a complicated argument. You may enjoy listening to another speaker argue the same ideas that you confidently plan to refute when it's your turn at the podium.

Still, there are few public speaking contexts where it is appropriate to listen purely for appreciation. Most of your public listening takes place at the more active listening levels described below, where your mind is energetically engaged and interacting with the message. However, because people can easily switch between the different types of listening, appreciative listening can play a role in parts of even the most serious or controversial topics.

table **2.5** **Listening Levels**

Type	Definition	Active or passive: Energy required by the listener	Relation to public speaking
Critical	Listening to analyze or evaluate.	Highly active.	Used in most speeches in school, at work, or in the community.
Comprehensive	Listening to learn or understand. (Also a prerequisite for critical listening.)	Highly active.	Used in most speeches in school, at work, or in the community.
Appreciative	Listening for personal pleasure.	Mostly passive.	Sometimes used in parts of a speech or in speeches meant to entertain.
Pseudo	Fake listening.	Highly passive.	Should be avoided.

3. Comprehensive listening

Comprehensive listening occurs when you listen to learn or to understand. It is highly active and requires a significant amount of concentration and energy. You should be using comprehensive listening during your classes, at work, or whenever it is necessary to accurately receive, understand, and retain information. Comprehensive listening is successful when the message you understand is the same as the message intended.

Two requirements must be met to listen comprehensively:

- First, the listener must ignore distractions and focus on the speaker and his or her message.
- Second, the listener must make a commitment to interact with the message. This may mean distinguishing between main and supporting ideas, detecting pieces of evidence, following narratives, and making sense of visual data.

Good comprehensive listening takes effort. Read, travel, expand your vocabulary, interact, put yourself in new situations, and experience life. Aim for a broad and deep knowledge of the greater world around you. If you do find yourself struggling to understand a given speaker, don't give up and tune out. Follow what you can. Everything you learn today makes you a better comprehensive listener tomorrow.

4. Critical listening

Critical thinking, as you'll recall from Chapter 1, is the ability to skillfully use and analyze your thought process in order to make effective judgments. **Critical listening,** a closely related concept, takes place when you listen to analyze and to evaluate the speaker's ideas. It's an exceptionally active form of listening, requiring a high degree of mental engagement and energy. In order to listen critically, you must first listen comprehensively—or listen to understand. Once you have understood what the speaker is saying, you then make judgments, draw conclusions, form opinions, or take action.

Critical listening requires you to actively engage your thinking and reasoning skills. It means not only listening intently to what the speaker is saying but also listening "between the lines," to figure out what is being said by omission. Critical listening is also needed to protect yourself from the hidden agendas and camouflaged intentions of less ethical speakers. The First Amendment allows all voices to be heard; it's up to you to decide which ones are worth listening to. Many marketers, celebrities, and media organizations have enormous resources for persuasive communication, and many attempt to change your thinking and behavior. Critical listening is what you need to employ to figure out what they are really saying. Analyze their methods and tools; recognize the use of personal, logical, and emotional appeals; question their substance and validity; and actively decide how to respond.

Critical listening, in turn, makes speakers more accountable. Your teacher needs to listen critically to your speeches, giving you constructive criticism to help you become a better speaker. Employees and management need to listen critically to each other, helping the organization meet its objectives in an ethical way. Citizens need to listen critically to each other and to our government, ensuring the health of our democracy and the strength of our nation.

SPEAK Responsibly

Become a Better Critical Listener

To grow as a critical listener you must:

- Maintain an open mind and recognize how your own biases and prejudices affect your listening.
- Try not to rush to judgment; be willing to suspend a question until you can analyze it from multiple angles.
- Ask questions that might fill in missing information, better explain the speaker's sources, or better clarify the speaker's intentions.
- Establish your own personal criteria that others must meet in order to persuade you.
- Place yourself in increasingly complex thinking and listening situations.
- Continually educate yourself. The more you know, the better you're able to listen to a greater breadth and depth of topics.

2D Be an Excellent Public Listener

You know by now that listeners are as important as speakers in the public speaking event. Additionally, because preparing and delivering a speech takes a significant amount of work, you appreciate it when others listen to you while you speak. When you're in the role of the public listener in class, at work, or in your community, you can do several things to increase the value of the communication event and to recognize the dignity of the speaker.

1. Civil listening

Civil listening is the counterpart to civil speaking, which you'll read about in Chapter 4. In public speaking, **civility** goes beyond, but certainly includes, the use of courtesy and good manners. It more broadly refers to abiding by a code of decency and showing respect, honesty, fairness, and tolerance to others. **Civil listeners** work to suspend judgment while also giving notable feedback to the speaker.

Come to the speech with an open mind

Few of us are free of biases or prejudices, and such predispositions can get in the way of our understanding each other. So can our culture. See the "Create Converse Connect" box on page 42 for some examples. Civil listeners strive to actively listen to others with an open mind. For some audience members, this is a natural tendency. One student, because of his own public speaking training, looked forward to hearing others speak:

> *As a listener, I find myself paying more attention and respecting the speaker, because now I know what they're going through. I come away from speeches now not only with new content, but with public speaking tips I can use.*

For others, having an open mind is more challenging. Put aside judgments about the speaker's topic, dress, or speech patterns, and listen instead for the speaker's content. Recognize that you are under no obligation to agree with the message but that you are obliged to remain actively engaged during the presentation. If you're required to be at the speaking event for work, school, or other reasons, yet would prefer to be elsewhere, don't take your frustrations out on the speaker. By giving your best attention, you may be pleasantly surprised to learn something interesting and relevant.

Show courtesy and good manners by providing nonverbal feedback

Speakers don't expect you to agree with everything they say (though they may like you to), but they do want to know that their ideas are getting through. They are reassured when they can see their ideas connecting and are energized to continue speaking when they can see listener feedback.

While you may listen well when you're slouched back in your chair with your eyes closed, imagine how your posture looks to a speaker. It's demoralizing for a speaker to see audience members checking phones, doing math homework, putting their heads down on

Cultural Influences on My Listening

Our culture affects how we understand each other. Read what these three students had to say about how their cultural habits and expectations clashed with American cultural trends:

AYUMI (JAPAN):
: Americans can be blunt. In Japan, we cannot say things that hurt people. We can think them, but we cannot say them! It's a little hard to get used to hearing things like that.

GENE (HOPI TRIBE, U.S.):
: It bothered me when people fidgeted or played with their hair or their phone while listening. We are still when we listen.

CHII (ZIMBABWE):
: The freedom that Americans have to criticize or make fun of their president or their government still shocks me. We just can't do that. Our speakers are also much more formal. Here, the informality of some topics and the language used, like slang and contractions, are still a struggle for me. On top of that, many Americans mumble. Listening can be a real challenge sometimes.

- What advice would you give to these students, if any, about adapting to their perceptions of mainstream American culture?
- Do speakers representing the dominant culture have a responsibility to accommodate for those members of the audience who were acculturated elsewhere? If so, how can they do that? If not, why?

their desks, or chatting with friends. It's discomforting, if not intimidating, for a speaker to look out on a wall of blank faces. As a listener, you have a civil responsibility to provide visible feedback that tells the speaker you are actively listening. Here's a list of ideas and suggestions to help you create a friendly and constructive environment for your speaker:

- Be on time so you don't create distractions for the speaker or other audience members by coming in late. Better yet, be early so you can get a good seat.
- Make eye contact with the speaker. Nap, text, or do your catalog shopping on your own time.
- Smile and show that you're interested in being in the audience.
- Sit up straight and lean forward in your chair.

SPEAK
Responsibly

I'll Be Posting That One on YouTube

Today's mobile and compact technology allows us to record the world around us—including others' speeches—with the click of a button. Just because you *can* capture public messages, it doesn't mean you're entitled to. Respect others' intellectual property and rights to privacy. Always ask the speaker or the speaking host if you want to record, much less post, someone else's public speeches.

- Create no distractions once seated—put away your electronic devices, bring a cough drop, take your crying baby outside, sit near the door if you must leave early, avoid talking to other audience members, and get your pen out ahead of time so you don't have to rustle around in your backpack looking for one.
- Nod your head to show that you're following what the speaker is saying.
- Provide comments or ask questions at the end of the presentation. Such feedback makes most speakers feel honored. It shows that you were listening.

2. Ethical listening

In Chapter 4, you'll read in depth about ethical speaking. Its counterpart, ethical listening, is our focus here. Exact definitions vary, but in general, **ethics** are the standards society uses to determine right action from wrong, or good action from bad. **Ethical listeners** listen actively to increase their own worldview and to hold speakers accountable to society's moral principles.

Seek out opposing viewpoints

It's natural to seek out only those sources of information that agree with our own point of view and to avoid those that contradict or refute it. (Psychologists call this the *confirmation bias*.) We join groups and organizations whose viewpoints are comforting to us, cheering on the reinforcement of messages we already know and believe. We often consider those who believe otherwise to be ill informed, misled, and out of step. Ethical listeners acknowledge the complexities of human intention and communication. They realize that every story usually has two or more sides, and they take the time to seek out multiple perspectives. Democracy thrives on the exchange of ideas, no matter how radical they may appear. Genuinely listening to opposing views can raise valid questions about your own. Critically reconsidering your own perspectives can give you the opportunity to change, refine, reshape, or strengthen what you believe or think you believe, leading to personal growth.

Hold speakers accountable to ethical standards

Ethical listeners recognize the potential influence speakers have and therefore hold them to ethical standards.

Ethical listeners question
- whether the speaker appears informed and prepared.
- whether the speaker promotes positive cultural values.
- whether the speaker is up front about his or her intentions.
- whether the speaker's language is clear or tries to needlessly complicate the issue.

Ethical listeners evaluate
- the reliability of the speaker's research sources.
- how inclusive the speaker is in topic selection, examples, and language.
- the potential for the speaker's message to have negative consequences on others.

If you find yourself questioning or doubting the speaker's adherence to ethical standards, challenge it aloud (respectfully) during the question-and-answer period, or discuss it with the speaker in private at a later time. See the "Speak Responsibly" box below for one challenging example.

Remaining silent in the face of perceived ethical breaches is to condone the speaker's actions. However, there is no need to attack, boo, or call the speaker names. Instead, begin by checking your perception and asking the speaker whether what you heard was what was intended. If the speaker is unable to provide an acceptable clarification or defense, politely but forcefully voice your concerns. When you do so, other listeners will probably start speaking up, too. Ethical speakers will in turn respond appropriately, making the communication a richer experience for all.

SPEAK
Responsibly

Responding to a Perceived Ethical Breach

One audience felt compelled to confront a speaker who presented a speech about the Nazi concentration camps during World War II. Many listeners felt that the speaker had included too many gratuitously violent examples and, worse, appeared to enjoy himself while doing so. Because he expressed no remorse or sympathy for the camp victims during the post-speech discussion, he lost the attention and respect of his listeners for the remainder of the school term.

- Were the audience members in this case justified in confronting the speaker?
- Would you have added to the discussion? If so, what would you have said?

3. Know how to give constructive feedback to another speaker

You may be asked to evaluate fellow class-mates or an out-of-class presentation. These are great opportunities to exercise your critical-listening skills and to provide a speaker with some additional angles of critique.

Before you begin your analysis, it is helpful to have a set of criteria with which to make the most of your role as a critic.

Watch with both your eyes and ears

Good listening begins with both of these senses activated.

Set specific evaluating criteria

It can be overwhelming to provide feedback on the whole speech. Limiting what you are looking for ahead of time may make the evaluation fairer for the speaker and easier on you. Your instructor can provide you with specific criteria and/or a detailed form you can use while evaluating another's speech. These criteria are also easily modified for any task.

Be specific in your feedback

Concrete examples are more helpful than abstract language. Figure 2.2 shows some comparisons.

Be ethical in your evaluation

Provide constructive criticism rather than just pointing out "mistakes." Also, apply the same standards to all speakers. It is unfair to call one speaker on something you let slide with another speaker.

Understand that providing meaningful evaluations is an art and a skill

Keep at it. You improve the more you do it.

Unhelpful (abstract) feedback

Your eye contact was poor.

You had good visuals.

I liked your speech.

I got lost.

Helpful (concrete) feedback

Your eye contact favored the left side of the room. I felt left out.

The graph you used to show the correlation between diet and classroom performance was not only well designed but it really helped me to buy into your argument.

Your thesis was well chosen and clearly communicated. Your topic was made relevant to me, and your enthusiastic delivery helped me stay connected to your ideas.

Because I never heard a preview of your main points in the introduction, I had trouble following your flow of ideas in the body. More overt transitions also would have helped me stay with you.

figure **2.2   Abstract vs. Concrete Feedback for Evaluating Another's Speech**

review questions

1. What are the responsibilities of a listener in public speaking situations?
2. What are the differences between hearing and listening? Active listening and passive listening?
3. What are the primary steps in the listening process? What are some potential listening problems and solutions for each step?
4. What are the major types of listening and the major differences between them? How much energy does each type require of listeners?
5. What are civil listening and ethical listening, and what behaviors embody these concepts?

key terms

hearing 31
listening 31
passive listening 31
active listening 32
meta-listener 35

pseudo-listening 38
appreciative listening 38
comprehensive
   listening 39
critical listening 40

civility 41
civil listeners 41
ethics 43
ethical listeners 43

connect

For online exercises, quizzes, and hands-on activities, including a TED Talks activity, see the Chapter 2 assignments in Connect Public Speaking.

exercises

1. On a typical day, keep a log of your listening. How much of your day was spent listening? What kind of listening (see Section 2C) did you engage in the most? Does this surprise you? Would you like to spend more or less time listening at any of the levels?

2. Everyone has at least some personal barriers to good listening. What are yours? What steps could you realistically take now to remove these barriers and become a better listener? Which others can you work toward in the future?

3. If a hidden camera took a picture of you listening in class, what would you look like? As a speaker, what does your ideal listener look like?

4. Choose a topic about which you feel passionate. Go on the web and find a video in which someone argues the opposite of that belief. Were you able to listen to the whole video with an open mind? Why or why not?

CHAPTER 3

Create Confident Presentations

LEARNING OBJECTIVES

1 Understand and describe what's happening to your body when you "feel nervous" prior to a public speech.

2 Contrast the communication and performance orientations toward public speaking.

3 Identify psychological and physiological strategies for reducing excess speaker's energy.

4 Explain how learning to become a public speaker is a manageable and continual process.

5 Adopt strategies for conducting a purposeful and realistic post-speech self-evaluation.

47

I f your stomach performs triple backflips at the mere thought of speaking before others, you're not alone. Contending with nerves is a concern for nearly all speakers, even those with experience. Effective public speakers learn to harness the body's energy and use it to their advantage by first understanding what's happening to them and then adjusting their preparations accordingly. This chapter explores some of the reasons you may get nervous before speaking in public, and it offers solutions—perceptual, psychological, and physical—for using that energy for positive outcomes. Finally, you'll get some insights into managing the public speaking learning process, and gain strategies for meaningful, honest, and confidence-boosting self-assessment.

3A Understand Why You Feel Nervous

Caitlin, a college sophomore, admitted how fearful the prospect of public speaking made her feel after her first speech: "I was terrified about talking for two minutes in front of the class. I was shaking, couldn't see straight, and had a horrible stomachache. Somehow I got through it." Caitlin's experience is common, even typical. After all, speaking before a group is consistently listed among the top human phobias—along with confined spaces, heights, spiders, and thunderstorms. Still, phobias are usually based on perceptions rather than on reality. For example, you're much more likely to be hurt in a car accident than to get struck by lightning. Yet most of us hop into our cars every day without a second thought and, paradoxically, some of us are petrified of lightning, despite the unlikeliness of being harmed by it.

If you're experiencing feelings of discomfort prior to a public speech, take comfort that your sensations are normal—and there are numerous solutions that work. At the end of the term, after making use of some of these practical remedies, Caitlin reflected on what a difference it made: "I can't believe I just spoke for ten minutes on my last speech in front of a full classroom with all eyes looking at me. Public speaking is not scary if you prepare for it. If I can do this, anyone can."

Some common reasons for pre-speech anxiety

In rare cases, people experience severe, deeply rooted public communication anxiety beyond the situational anxiety experienced by the typical public speaker. If none of the perceptual shifts and other strategies in this chapter ultimately work for you, you may need additional assistance. Your instructor can direct you to available and relevant outside resources.

For many of us, however, the perceptions or individual interpretations about public presentation that function like a negative filter don't have to have that effect. The fact is, people have been speaking in public for centuries, and all have lived to tell the tale. To speak well in public, you need to be temporarily vulnerable and face potential hurdles to the acceptance of your ideas. And as you saw in Chapter 1, the benefits greatly outweigh the risks. You stand to gain far more than you may realize.

One more thing troubles a lot of people: sheer physical nervousness. When you offer to speak, or are asked or required to do so, your body reacts by releasing **adrenaline,** a hormone that helps the body adjust to sudden stress. Adrenaline increases the strength and rate of your heartbeat, heightens brain activity, and encourages the famous fight-or-flight reaction by sending energy to your muscles. It's this increased adrenaline that makes your body feel as it does.

Everyone's body manifests adrenaline differently. For people like Caitlin, the stomach feels chaotic, and the heart seems to relocate to the throat. For others, hands or knees may get jittery, the voice may tremble, skin may flush, or palms may sweat.

Your challenge lies in interpreting your physical sensations. You might be quick to label these feelings "fear," "apprehension," or "anxiety." Once you attach a negative label, however, you'll probably want to avoid whatever it is that brings the feeling on: *When my body feels like this, it means I'm afraid. I don't like to experience fear. I should avoid public speaking.* But as the sections that follow will demonstrate, there are other, more positive interpretations of these physical sensations.

3B Make Use of Adrenaline

Experienced speakers channel their perceptions and physical sensations into beneficial energy and look forward to putting them to use. You can, too. As one anonymous quote says, "Never accept the negative until you've thoroughly explored the positive." The next two sections of this chapter show how you can harness adrenaline for its benefits.

1. Move away from the performance orientation

Michael T. Motley, a professor of communication at the University of California–Davis, has found in his research that a **performance orientation** toward public speaking creates unnecessary and uncomfortable physical stress. Motley says that when we view public speaking as a performance, a judgmental perspective—the notion that being ourselves isn't sufficient or desirable when we speak publicly—soon follows:

> *We view the speaker's role as that of satisfying an audience of "critics" set on evaluating our behaviors—gestures, language, eye contact, etc. Speakers with the performance orientation cannot exactly describe with much precision just what kinds of behavior the audience-critics expect, but they assume that "proper" public speaking behaviors should be rather formal and artificial—somehow "better" than their everyday natural speech.*[1]

In other words, if we believe that we're mainly being judged on the quality of our gestures, eye contact, language, and other delivery skills—rather than on our ability to connect to others with our coherent message—we decide that nothing less than a speech *performance,* free of all delivery errors, is the most important outcome to achieve. The burden of trying to produce a flawless technical performance—like that of a professional dancer or musician—increases nervousness. Once we feel all these symptoms, we interpret them irrationally and disproportionately, often as fear of failure. What is it that we fear in a performance? Being evaluated? Being criticized? Needing to be a "perfect 10"? These interpretations lead to further physical stress and thus, a self-perpetuating negative cycle is born. The end result is a speaker with high psychological and physical anxiety.

Other research supports Motley's view that most public speaking anxiety stems from the perceptions a speaker holds well before the speech even begins. The anxiety associated with a performance-oriented perception, these researchers say, can be damaging because it may steer us away from otherwise desired courses or careers just because we know or expect that they entail public presentation.[2] When speaking is unavoidable, performance-oriented speakers are more likely to prepare so as to needlessly shorten their speaking time. Such speaking situations lead to increased stress for the speaker and, most likely, a shallower speech for the audience to listen to.

Another problem with viewing public speaking as a performance is that it turns the focus of our presentation inward. We start asking ourselves self-centered questions about whether we have the

The worries of a performance-oriented speaker

Will the audience like my speaking style?

Will I be better or worse than the other speakers?

Do I have what it takes to be considered a good speaker?

needed skills and the ability to perform them, and we may start to see the speaking occasion as a competition. Once you focus inward, your audience becomes secondary. Yet the audience is exactly where your focus should be.

2. Adopt the communication orientation

Motley's research, supported by other scholars,[3] shows that nervousness about speaking publicly diminishes once people move away from a performance orientation and its emphasis on pleasing an audience of critics. A **communication orientation** toward public speaking, with its familiar goal of conveying ideas to listeners (similar to what you do during your everyday interactions with other people), can be gratifying, fun, and effective, and just as importantly, it is far less stressful for you. The body still releases adrenaline, but as a communication-oriented speaker, you use the additional energy to improve your focus and appear more animated and interesting. A communication orientation allows you to think more rationally. You feel excited and ready to share your prepared ideas. You know that the listeners are there to interact with those ideas and will accept delivery "mistakes" should they happen, just as listeners do in any other communication interaction. The end result is a speaker alive and alert in mind and body. Lance, a first-year college student, is an example of how this shift in approach can alter the experience for both speaker and listeners:

> In my first speech, I was over the top. It was obvious to others that I was playing a part, and doing so not particularly well. However, as the class went on I was able to adopt the communication orientation. By my last speech you can see that my audience and I are both focused on what I am saying— rather than what I'm doing—and our connection with one another is genuine.

The communication orientation allows you to direct your energies toward your listeners and the occasion; you are no longer facing pressure to perform a set of skills labeled "perfect public speaking."

The focus of a communication-oriented speaker

I have a worthwhile message.

I want my audience to pay attention to my message, to understand it, and to interact with it.

This experience is about what I have to say.

3. Keep your listeners in communication mode

The orientation you adopt as a speaker also influences your listeners' reactions. Performance-oriented speakers, trying to live up to those unknown audience expectations, usually end up delivering their presentations in an affected and unnatural style. When confronted with this style, audience members are more likely to become performance-oriented listeners—more evaluative, wanting to be pleased, more focused on delivery, and less accepting of mistakes or awkward moments. The resulting irony is that the very audience characteristics and reactions a performance-oriented speaker dreads facing—a hypercritical, judgmental mind-set focused almost exclusively on technical delivery—are exactly those brought out in the audience through a performance-styled speech. Yet another negative cycle is born.

Research even suggests that a performance-oriented style eliminates some of the responsibility an audience feels to provide feedback.[4] Audiences feel less obligated or inspired to be responsive when they sense that the speaker is presenting mainly for external rewards, such as gaining public speaking experience or getting a good grade, rather than for genuine communication purposes. If the speaker is not interested in communicating, why should the audience expend the energy and interest to listen?

A natural and direct delivery style consistent with a communication orientation, on the other hand, encourages audience members to remain in listener mode. Listeners stay focused and are interested in understanding and interacting with the ideas presented. Research suggests they even retain more of your message.[5] See Table 3.1 for a side-by-side contrast of the performance and communication orientations.

table 3.1 Performing vs. Communicating

The performance orientation	The communication orientation
The speaker perceives the need for perfection and views the speaking event as a competition.	The speaker relies on his or her communication experience and applies it to the public speaking context.
The speaker's focus turns inward to the performing self, inviting uncertainties and anxieties.	The speaker's focus is outward, toward the audience and the exchange of ideas.
The speaker strives for "perfect" delivery skills, resulting in artificiality.	The speaker uses natural delivery skills, like those used in important conversation.
The needs of the audience become secondary.	The needs of the audience remain primary.
Listeners are invited to unleash their inner-critic.	Listeners are likely to remain in communication mode and respond with constructive feedback and discussion.

Word Power

Language theory tells us that thoughts and experiences can be influenced by the words we use. As you've read, performance-oriented speakers tend to label the sensations of adrenaline flow with terms that drum up negative emotions. When faced with a public speaking situation, avoid using these terms in your internal mental dialogue in favor of terms with effective, positive associations.

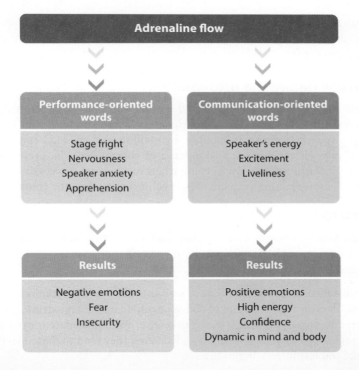

Who, after all, wants to suffer apprehension or endure anxiety? Instead, use the term **speaker's energy**—a term loaded with positive connotations. You *should* be energetic and on your toes during important communication interactions; a public speaker with no speaker's energy (adrenaline) would likely be dull and uninteresting. Speaker's energy makes your eyes bright, brings liveliness to your voice, helps you think on your feet, and gives you confident posture. It's speaker's energy that flows out of you and influences your audience.

3C Reduce Excess Speaker's Energy

You've learned to welcome the effects of speaker's energy. But what if you still have excess energy that may be hard to control during your presentation? Below are some tried-and-true tips for dealing with too much of a good thing before and during your speech. Practice these techniques and experiment with them, and you'll soon find the ones that work for you, and will probably come up with additional strategies of your own. One student did so to great effect:

> *I even went as far as naming my fear for public speaking. When I saw it as a separate entity, it made me want to be better than it. That objective awareness and interaction with my fear caused it to slowly melt away.*

Remember that you don't want to eliminate your adrenaline; you want to have some level of speaker's energy to get you through your speech. But certainly, you want to "be better than it." And you can be.

1. Tips to use before the presentation

Besides developing a great listener-centered speech, you must get your body and mind ready to successfully channel your speaker's energy. When you treat your body right via a physical, pre-speech "training program"—by making sure you're sleeping, eating, and drinking properly—it can heighten your sense of control over the presentation. Likewise, psychological tips are effective because when you forecast success, it becomes a self-fulfilling prophecy, increasing your chances of achieving it when the actual event arrives.

Physiological tips

- **Make sure you are energized, well rested, and ready, physically and mentally.** Pulling an all-nighter practicing for a morning presentation may leave you sluggish and disoriented.

- **Avoid substances that overstimulate as well as those that slow your reflexes and reactions.** Pass on that extra cup of coffee or caffeinated energy drink, which may be counterproductive to thinking clearly. Likewise, avoid pharmaceutical depressants (unless prescribed by your physician) and alcohol; they tend to flatten your affect and make you less interesting to listen to.

- **Stay hydrated and energized.** To "soak up" the extra energy and help avoid potential lightheadedness, drink juice or water, and eat something nutritious an hour or two before the speech. Your food choice should fill you up just enough to give you the energy you want—oatmeal, for example, or a bagel or sandwich.

- **Keep the blood flowing to your head, not your stomach.** Avoid a heavy meal before your presentation. A quick snack of an apple or a granola bar is easy to carry with you and can give a last-minute boost of healthful energy.

- **Rely on calming rituals.** Breathe deeply for a minute or so prior to speaking; count to a slow six for each breath in and out. Borrow a calming and centering technique from the practice of shiatsu, a traditional form of Japanese massage therapy: gently massage the pressure point in the web between your thumb and first finger for three to five minutes.

- **Do everything to ensure you look your best and feel physically comfortable and confident.** Choose clothing that breathes well, lets you move easily, and won't show perspiration. Light-colored cotton is better than dark-colored silk or polyester. A jacket can help boost your confidence. Visit the restroom and perform a last-minute appearance check. The confidence you get from looking your best can carry over to the presentation.

- **Work through any excess nerves beforehand.** Take a brisk walk, and literally shake the excess energy out of your hands and feet.

- **Your mouth and voice are your instruments, so be mindful and take care of them.** If you suffer from a dry mouth, chew a mint or a candy to get the juices flowing. Be sure to finish it or throw it away before beginning to speak.

- **Sit up straight while waiting to be called.** Good posture improves your breathing and gives you confidence.

Psychological tips

- **Stay idea-centered rather than self-centered.** Remind yourself that your job is to communicate your ideas to your audience.

- **Genuinely adopt a communication attitude.** Use the style of important conversation you rely on when talking to someone you respect—someone like your boss, your professor, or a loan officer at the bank.

- **Be prepared.** Start practicing aloud early to identify and work through challenges. The sooner and more you practice, the more time you have to own the material. The more you own the material, the higher your confidence will be and the better the speech will go. (See Chapter 13 for more on effective practice.)

- **Use positive self-talk.** Rather than saying, *I'm going to forget everything and look like I don't know my topic*, think, *If I get a little distracted from what I meant to discuss, the audience won't notice. They don't know what I've prepared.*

- **Use positive visualization.** Find a quiet space, and close your eyes. Envision yourself in the speaking room, being called on, and walking up confidently with your prepared notes and visuals. See an engaged, interested audience looking back at you. Picture yourself beginning to speak, confidently and competently.

2. Tips to use during the presentation

The techniques you can employ to maintain and manage excess energy aren't limited to the prep time prior to giving the speech. The presentation itself offers numerous ways and opportunities to harness your energy, again both physically and mentally, and to let that energy fuel your speech instead of letting your nerves distract you and your listeners and derail your message.

Physiological tips

- **Just start.** Walking up to the front of the room can be the hardest part, and most speakers progressively relax as the speech continues. Also, take comfort that many of your physiological reactions to excess speaker's energy, such as sweaty palms or pounding heartbeat, will go unnoticed by your listeners.

- **Adapt your presentation to de-emphasize physical signs of nerves.** If you experience visible signs such as blotching skin or shaking hands, wear a high-collared shirt and avoid demonstrations requiring fine-motor control (like threading a needle).

- **Bring water with you and drink it if your mouth gets dry.** It's perfectly acceptable to pause while speaking to take a quick sip.

- **When mistakes or fumbles happen, take a deep breath to re-orient yourself, and then pick up where you stopped.** Don't beat yourself up or let "mistakes" distract you or paralyze you. This tip applies whether the stumbling point is mental or physical. Should your mind suddenly go blank, pause, coolly and calmly review your notes, and get back on track. If you can't remember where you left off, humbly ask listeners to remind you. They're usually happy to do so. Likewise, if you mispronounce a word, and realize it right away, simply correct it. If you realize you've forgotten to share an idea, quickly do so if it's still appropriate or just move on. If trembling hands cause you to drop your notes or the laser pointer, just pause, pick up the item, and return to what you were discussing. Making loud apologies or pointing out how nervous you are only draws attention away from your message.

Psychological tips

- **Have faith in your listeners and try to stay optimistic about possible interactions with them.** Some speakers fear audience hostility, heckling, or aggressive questioning. Such feedback is rare (and if it happens, it's typically with high-profile speakers). Most audiences want to see you accomplish your goals.

- **Remind yourself that heightened energy comes with the public speaking territory.** Extra feelings of energy are a natural part of the speaking experience. As you continue speaking, you learn to manage, through experience and personal techniques, those sensations you perhaps once felt intensely. Recent research backs this up; the more you speak, the more relaxed you become.[6] Embrace, then, the fact that you'll have several opportunities to give speeches in your public speaking class. The next section looks briefly at the unique experience of taking advantage of those opportunities.

3D Manage Your Learning Process

Learning anything new can leave people feeling either eager and excited or anxious and apprehensive; few look at the prospect of standing before a group and competently communicating ideas with a "take it or leave it" attitude. Whether you are starting this course with much, some, or no past speaking experience, at the end of the course, you should be a changed person, with new tools in hand for negotiating future speaking situations.

It's natural for everyone to experience this course in their own unique way to work toward highly individualized goals. If you have spoken in the past, you may want to use your class time to fine-tune your current speaking strengths and experiment with higher-level skills. Bear in mind that there's always something new to learn in any subject we study. The listener-centered approach, especially, is most often a welcome addition to people with previous speaking experience. Kristopher, a software engineer, told the following story about how he realized that despite a fair amount of public speaking experience, he had been relying heavily on a less effective, performance-oriented orientation:

> *I had given presentations on multi-million-dollar projects to several groups of people before with no problems; everyone understood me. Or so I assumed. But I can see now that I wasn't really communicating with people in a way that made it easy for them to connect to me and my ideas. I was really just talking at them. This class has taught me that there is more to public speaking than reading off some slides that I might as well have just emailed to everyone.*

By contrast, if you are experiencing public speaking for the first time, consider yourself in good company. Hundreds of thousands of people each year learn to speak in classes and workshops taught around the country and the world. Every well-known public speaker, including presidents, CEOs, and circuit speakers earning $50,000 per speech, started from point zero at one time and moved forward from there.

1. Frustrations and accomplishments are part of any learning process

Public speaking differs from many of your other college courses in that it requires you to exercise your voice and body in the learning process. While most of us did this freely as children, as adolescents many of us probably became more comfortable being part of the background. Yet this course asks you to conspicuously place your body before your peers and open your mouth with the intention of having something brilliant emerge. Our society's preoccupation with outward appearance makes it easy to worry about how others will perceive us. Evie, a second-year college student, fell into this trap:

> During my early speeches, I was constantly worried. I was trying to hide flaws and was very self-conscious. Internal commentary such as What are they thinking about me? and How do I look? is counterproductive when you are trying to deliver an engaging speech. But when I really thought about it, I know what I look like and can stop worrying about that. I'm focusing on my audience instead.

Evie reminds us that our job as public speakers is not to impress; instead, it's to effectively communicate our ideas to a group of people. Each opportunity we get to practice doing that is beneficial.

Like riding a bike, public speaking is a skill you have to do in order to learn. Expect to face some setbacks along the way. You may not articulate an important element of your argument as well as you had planned; your visual support may not make the impact you thought it would; you may say "um" more than you would like. But frustrations are part of any worthwhile endeavor. Your instructor is doing all he or she can to create a comfortable environment for trial and error. Your job is to try your best, to learn from each speaking experience, and to press forward. You *will* live to complete the course and emerge a stronger person.

Achievements are also part of the learning equation. Every speech offers the chance to connect to listeners through your ideas, to show off speaking strengths, to discover or practice something new, and to improve upon or overcome speaking challenges. For instance, you may choose an especially engaging topic or may use a new piece of technology smoothly and expertly. You may discover that you're very comfortable in the spotlight. You have real opportunities to make a genuine impact on your classmates and instructor. Many others have done it before you. Audience members have learned new things, reconsidered their viewpoints, and been inspired to change their behavior based on class presentations. When you communicate relevant ideas in a passionate manner, listeners can't help but get caught up in the action.

2. Your classmates are valuable resources

Students are consistently surprised at how much they enjoy their public speaking course. One explanation lies in the relationships that form among classmates. People realize that they're "in this together," so the support system for the individual speaker is strong. Your classmates are a rich resource for guidance and feedback. Look to them as you brainstorm and contemplate topics. Because they're familiar with the assignment criteria, they are uniquely qualified to provide assistance as you organize and develop your ideas. You should also find them a highly supportive and welcoming audience on the days you speak.

You'll also benefit from the speaking choices your classmates make while they prepare and present. Pay critical attention as other people try out the same skills you are learning. Both their successful and their not-so-successful speaking choices are highly instructive for everyone in the class. One student was surprised at how much she learned from her classmates:

> *At first I thought I'd be learning about public speaking only from my teacher and the book and maybe a video or two. But I probably ended up learning more from watching and listening to my classmates. One of them, Eric, was an amazing role model. He walked up there, and on his first speech he stole my attention. He was obviously prepared. He looked relaxed, was dressed nicely, spoke naturally, and engaged the audience. And he only got better after that!*

3E Evaluate Yourself Honestly

Your speaking confidence will also grow the more mindful you are of yourself as a public communicator. Once you commit to self-improvement and are open to constructive criticism, you should see each speaking opportunity as a rich mine of data, usable for future presentations. An honest self-evaluation gives you insight into your strengths and weaknesses, helping you choose the best ways to reach your audience, keep their attention, and ultimately succeed in achieving your speech's purpose.

1. An honest self-inventory: Try an adapted SWOT analysis

Anyone undertaking a productive endeavor benefits from identifying his or her current knowledge, attitude, and level of skills, but it's not always obvious to know how to assess them. An adapted form of **SWOT analysis** is a useful place to start. Standing for "Strengths, Weaknesses, Opportunities, and Threats," a SWOT analysis is a tool that businesses and organizations use to distinguish themselves from their competitors and successfully compete in their markets.[7] Because you are not trying to compete against other speakers, a full SWOT analysis is not appropriate. But you can use a version of it to help identify your current strengths and opportunities in public speaking. After reading the following descriptions of the SWOT steps, use the self-inventory form in Table 3.2 (p. 60) to draft one for yourself.

- **What are your *strengths* as a public communicator?** Many people are quick to point out what they feel are their "speaking faults," saying, "Where would you like me to begin?" In all likelihood, much more goes right for you than not in your presentations, far more than you may realize. Use your communication orientation, and reflect on the things you do that help your listeners access, understand, and interact with your ideas. Perhaps you organize your thoughts well, use humor appropriately, or know how to be brief. Perhaps you're good at building credibility with solid documentation or at telling a compelling story. Knowing your speaking strengths gives you confidence to keep moving forward. Ask for an honest assessment from a trusted friend, supervisor, mentor, or teacher, too; all are usually happy to discuss your strengths with you.

- **What are your *weaknesses* or challenges as a public communicator?** Perhaps your weaknesses have to do with poor structuring of your speech or with using insufficient support or flimsy argumentation. Perhaps your clothing choices detract from your credibility, or you're looking at your notes more than you'd like. Your own and your instructor's evaluations should help you identify your weaknesses. In addition, listen and watch for the communication challenges other speakers are facing. There's a good chance they're struggling with some of the same things you are, and you can learn from their solutions.

- **What are your speaking *opportunities*?** Speaking opportunities of all kinds provide you with chances for potential growth and advantage. This course obviously offers multiple occasions to try new skills. But what opportunities exist outside this course to improve your speaking skills? Do you have an oral-presentation assignment in another course? Can you practice some of your new skills at work, on campus, or in your community? Perhaps this is the time to research a topic you have wanted to know more about or to finally learn how to use a particular piece of technology or software. Public speaking can open a variety of doors, even some you never knew existed.

- **Are there any potential *threats*?** Sometimes, obstacles block the way to speaking growth. For example, do you need to better understand current research methods and appropriate technology? Are you short on preparation time? What if someone else has chosen a similar topic? Do you lack internal motivation to think, organize, and prepare ideas? Acknowledge these potential threats, and ask yourself whether

table **3.2** **Self-Inventory Form for SWOT**

Use the prompt in the right-hand column to create your own SWOT inventory on a separate piece of paper or electronic device.

Strengths	What goes right for me in my presentations?	My current strengths:
Weaknesses	What speaking skills are not as developed as I would like?	My current weaknesses:
Opportunities	Are there any circumstances that could help my growth as a public speaker?	My opportunities:
Threats	Are there any obstacles blocking my way to growth, and can I turn them into opportunities?	My threats:

SPEAK Responsibly

Make Self-Evaluation a Consistent Practice

Good employees don't wait for their annual performance review to assess whether they're on target with goals, nor do good students wait until receiving a final grade to assess whether they've understood the course material. Likewise, speakers should evaluate themselves periodically and not just rely on others for feedback.

Manage your self-inventory throughout your speaking career—it pays off. The greater your breadth and depth of speaking experience, the more you'll watch weaknesses become strengths, opportunities present themselves, and threats diminish.

you can open up any opportunities by minimizing or eliminating them. Tackling your research skills now, for instance, provides you with a skill set you can continue using throughout your academic career and beyond.

2. A concrete personal goal for each presentation

Students often announce that they want to be better speakers. What does that really mean in practice? Being a "better speaker" is an abstract and relative goal. Better than what? Better than you were last time? Better than your classmate sitting next to you? Better than Steve Jobs, the former CEO of Apple? How will you know when you are a "better speaker"?

A **personal speaking goal**—one specific, measurable skill on which to focus for a particular presentation—is a helpful tool. Though you strive for a listenable speech every time you speak, you should also have a personal goal that focuses on one key part of speechmaking. Here's a two-step process for identifying one:

Make your speaking goal personal, specific, and measurable

Your speaking goal should be concrete and clearly defined (rather than general and abstract) so that you can better determine if and when you have reached it. Table 3.3 (p. 62) offers some examples of the differences between a general, abstract goal and a specific, measurable goal.

Acknowledge your goal in some explicit way

Some speakers write their goal down, keeping it visible during preparation and practice. Others share their goal with a teacher, classmate, supervisor, mentor, or colleague. You don't have to make your goal public, but once you say it aloud to others, you're more likely to take it seriously and feel accountable for it.

table **3.3** **General vs. Specific Personal Goals**

General personal goal	Specific personal goal
I want to make a stronger audience connection.	I will increase my use of personal pronouns, especially *you, we,* and *us.*
I want to use better language.	I will refrain from obscenities and slang, such as *it sucks,* by expanding my vocabulary.
I want to be more prepared.	I'll plan and practice my closing statement ahead of time.
I want to be more credible.	I'll adopt a confident posture and clearly cite my research sources. Also, no apologies!

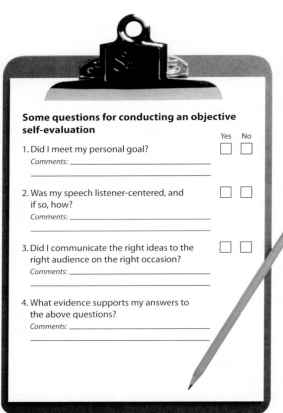

Some questions for conducting an objective self-evaluation

Yes No

1. Did I meet my personal goal?
   Comments: _____
   _____

2. Was my speech listener-centered, and if so, how?
   Comments: _____
   _____

3. Did I communicate the right ideas to the right audience on the right occasion?
   Comments: _____
   _____

4. What evidence supports my answers to the above questions?
   Comments: _____
   _____

3. Conducting your self-evaluation

Many public speaking instructors require students to do post-speech self-evaluations. These exercises may be formal or informal, spoken or written, simple or in-depth. Whatever form they take, self-evaluations provide a structure and direction for self-improvement. More importantly, they help you create a habit of self-reflection and ongoing goal-setting you can rely on once you finish the course and continue speaking. There is an art to public speaking, and like any artist, you must learn to critique your work so that you can continue to grow and evolve. Vince, a first-year college student, noted the effectiveness of evaluating his recorded presentation:

Our instructor said, "You are your own best teacher," and I believe that. When something happens to you firsthand, you're going to learn and remember it a lot better than hearing about it. When a teacher tells you about your speech, you can pick up only so much. But a picture is worth a thousand words. A video, then, must be worth at least ten thousand, because that is what you get when you watch it. You are showing yourself everything you have done. And then you can focus on things and improve.

Evaluate yourself soon—but not too soon—after the presentation

Give yourself some time after your presentation before engaging in a detailed evaluation. First, enjoy the natural high created by the release of endorphins. These biochemical compounds, produced in the pituitary glands at the base of your brain, make you feel light and energized, creating a sense of well-being. Students often report a pleasant floating sensation after a speech. Enjoy your well-earned endorphin buzz.

Get to your self-evaluation in the next day or so, while the presentation is still fresh in your mind. (But don't wait too long or you might get distracted or lose interest in the important evaluation process.) When you do start your evaluation, be as specific and objective as possible about your work.

Use multiple sources for self-evaluation

There's no singular "best" source for self-evaluation. Ideally, you have access to several sources to evaluate a given presentation. The more sources you can use to see and hear yourself, the richer your overall picture is. Here are some of the methods you can use:

Use video. Video captures your exact content and delivery, providing a look at your presentation from your listeners' point of view. It offers many benefits. First, it's often difficult (especially if you are a newer speaker) to remember what you did or said while presenting. Video provides a reminder, allowing you to see and hear your communication strengths and weaknesses, and to set personal goals for the next time you present. Many students like to evaluate their video several times, each time focusing on a different aspect.

Video also produces a valuable tangible record; at the end of the school term, students often enjoy watching their entire speaking progress from start to finish. Many speakers also like being able to share what they do as students—such as their in-class public speeches—with important people in their lives.

Watching yourself on video can be awkward at first because video captures a nonmirror image, a reflection you are probably not used to seeing. If you were to draw a line down the middle of your face, you would likely find the two halves asymmetrical. For example, one eye might be slightly higher than the other or the left side of your nose a bit more rounded than the right side. This is the way others see you. If you are like most speakers, however, you soon get used to your likeness on video.

Use audio. If video is not available, an audio recording of your speech is the next best thing. An

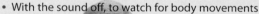

Multiple ways to view speech videos
- With sound and image for the full effect
- With sound only, eyes turned away from the screen, in order to concentrate fully on the words
- With the sound off, to watch for body movements

audio recording at least captures your verbal and vocal content, letting you hear the flow of your ideas, the words you used, and your vocal qualities such as intonation and pace.

Read or listen to your instructor's evaluations carefully. All instructors give feedback to their students. Some instructors give written feedback, while others provide it orally after the speech. Sometimes you get a combination. Whichever form the feedback takes, it is a rich source of material for your own self-improvement. Take this feedback seriously and aim to incorporate any suggestions and comments during your next speech project. Clarify any comments as needed with your instructor.

Ask a trusted source for feedback. Some instructors form evaluation groups, in which students take turns sharing their perceptions of each other's speeches. These can be valuable sources of feedback, because the others in the group are aware of the evaluation criteria you're working toward.

For presentations outside the classroom, look to a coworker, mentor, or supervisor. Find someone you can trust to give you honest and detailed feedback on both your strengths and weaknesses. You may have to prompt your source for specifics. If he or she provides abstract feedback such as "Your speech was good," ask for concrete examples supporting the ways it was "good." (Use Table 3.3 on page 62 for guidance on how to be specific.) You may also want feedback on your specific speaking goals. If you were working on the clarity of your thesis, for example, ask your source to paraphrase the thesis back to you to see whether it was indeed clear.

Complete a self-evaluation exercise or assignment. Many instructors have students engage in some type of formalized self-evaluation. These exercises may be oral or assigned in the form of a worksheet, some short questions, or an essay. Their purpose is to concentrate your focus on certain presentation criteria and to train your analytic skills for use beyond the course.

4. Increasing the sophistication of your self-evaluations over time

Remember that preliminary SWOT analyses will help you determine your current skills and comfort with public speaking. Throughout your academic and professional career, as you gain more public speaking experience, you will want to continually re-assess your abilities and goals. Correspondingly, as your skills expand and improve, you will soon learn to evaluate your presentation skills on an increasingly sophisticated level. At first, you may be concerned only with having a clear thesis, maintaining good conversational tone, having strong eye contact, and meeting the minimum time limit. As these skills become second nature, you can begin to focus on advanced qualities such as using a more complicated (but still clearly communicated) thesis, incorporating more intricately designed visuals, avoiding errors in persuasive reasoning, and managing a difficult question-and-answer session. As your understanding of public speaking grows, so you grow as a public speaker and self-evaluator.

Speaking Confidence in Action
A Student's Progress and Evaluative Process

Kat Kelman, before the public speaking course

- Kat had done a small amount of speaking as part of her summer job as a volleyball coach, but lacked confidence in her abilities.
- She thought successful public presentation was about receiving applause and praise from the audience.
- She enrolled in the course to fulfill graduation requirements, but also knew she'd need effective speaking skills for her larger career plans in product design.

   Kat's speaking confidence = 3 (on a scale of 1–10)

Kat, after the first speech

Based on her instructor's feedback and what she saw and heard on the recording of her speech, Kat started an informal SWOT analysis on the inside cover of the folder she used for speech class.

My strengths
- *Decent eye contact.*
- *Enthusiasm—passionate about my topic.*
- *Pretty strong organization of ideas.*

My weaknesses
- *Excessive verbal junk. Um, um, um!*
- *Conclusion not well planned. Weak.*
- *I do <u>NOT</u> practice enough. Very nervous.*
- *Credibility was pretty thin.*

My opportunities
- *Really focus on the communication orientation—still focused too much on my performing self.*
- *Maybe join campus speaker's club?*

My threats
- *Working while going to school.*
- *I know only the bare bones of PowerPoint.*
- *Prep time—not enough of it. I'm also a skilled procrastinator.*

   Kat's speaking confidence = 4

Kat, near the end of the school term, after having given several more speeches:

My strengths

Much improved

- ~~Decent~~ eye contact.

- Enthusiasm—passionate about my topic.

Very
- ~~Pretty~~ strong organization of ideas.

- PowerPoint. It was so easy to learn.

- Successful building and maintaining of credibility.

- Using several audience engagement techniques.

- I fully believe in this listener-centered approach.

- I manage my speaker's energy pretty well.

My weaknesses

Way less   *Just a few here and there—no biggie.*
- ~~Excessive verbal junk. Um, um, um!~~

                 much richer though I still need a more audience-specific take-aways.
- Conclusion ~~not well planned. Weak.~~

                        Better, but still need more practice.
- I do <u>NOT</u> practice enough. ~~Very nervous.~~

- ~~Credibility was pretty thin.~~

- Argumentation principles still not my strong suit.

My opportunities

- ~~Really focus on the communication orientation—still focused too much on my performing self.~~

                Their meeting schedule conflicts with work. Maybe next term.
- ~~Maybe join campus speaker's club?~~

- Find out which design courses require oral presentations and sign up for at least one of those.

My threats

- Working while going to school.

- ~~I know only the bare bones of PowerPoint.~~

                     But I'm better at prioritizing my time.
- Prep time—not enough of it. ~~I'm also a skilled procrastinator.~~

Kat's speaking confidence = 8

review questions

1. What is happening to your body when you "feel nervous" prior to a public speech?
2. What is the difference between the communication orientation toward public speaking and the performance orientation? Why is the communication orientation preferred?
3. What are some psychological and physiological strategies for reducing and managing excess speaker's energy? Which ones might work best for you?
4. How can you best learn to manage the continual process of becoming a public speaker?
5. What are some strategies for conducting a purposeful and realistic post-speech self-evaluation?

key terms

adrenaline 49
performance
   orientation 49

communication
   orientation 51
speaker's energy 53

SWOT analysis 59
personal speaking
   goal 61

exercises

1. Pair up with a partner in class. Take turns discussing your degree of anxiety about public speaking. Explore the reasons why each of you feels the way you do. Ask yourself whether your feelings are based on perception or reality.
2. Once your first speech is completed, pair up with your partner again. Talk out the experience with each other. Were there any commonalities between what you were thinking and feeling? any differences? What can you learn from each other?
3. Look at the lists of tips in Section 3C (p. 54) for lessening excess speaker's energy. Would any of these tips be helpful to you? If so, which ones? Can you come up with any of your own?
4. Reflect on a skill or an activity—whether rock climbing or webpage designing—you recently learned or undertook. Describe the challenges you faced and the steps, both physical and psychological, you went through during the learning process. Do you think that experience can help you in this class? If so, in what ways?

connect

For online exercises, quizzes, and hands-on activities, see the Chapter 3 assignments in Connect Public Speaking.

4

Commit to Ethical Speaking

LEARNING OBJECTIVES

1 Define ethics and their relationship to successful public speaking.

2 Identify the ways that speakers adhere to ethical guidelines.

3 Explain why plagiarism is a serious breach of ethics.

4 Describe the relationship between civil speaking and ethical speaking.

5 Explain the role speaker credibility plays in successful public speaking.

chapter preview

4A Know What Ethics Are

4B Make the Choice to Be Ethical

4C Avoid the Costs of Plagiarism

4D Use Civility as a Companion to Ethical Speaking

4E Use Additional Ways to Earn Speaker Credibility

Review Questions
Key Terms
Exercises

Your goal in public speaking is to gain a desired response from your listeners. But you don't have the freedom to use any means necessary. Every culture has standards and rules—some clearly defined, some less so—delineating right and wrong ways to interact with each other. Because listeners expect a speaker to abide by these ethical standards, your integrity and reputation are tested each time you speak. Your trustworthiness, your ability to convince, and even your grades suffer greatly when listeners perceive you as unethical. This chapter examines the role of ethics in the public speaking interaction and offers guidelines and suggestions for ethical speaking, highlighting the responsibility to avoid plagiarism. The chapter also looks at the role civility plays in ethical speaking. The discussion then broadens to include additional ways to gain speaker credibility.

4A Know What Ethics Are

1. What are ethics?

Exact definitions vary, but in general, **ethics** are the standards society uses to determine right action from wrong, or good action from bad. While values and morals are inherent in this definition, the emphasis on conduct is important. Communicating ideas in public, after all, is comprised of a set of actions, so it's crucial that public speakers pay attention to ethics as something foundational to their efforts. The German philosopher Immanuel Kant (1724–1804) asked this profound question: "If it would be wrong for everyone to do what you are doing, would you still do it?"[1] While Kant's position is philosophically pure, and most "real world" situations contain complexities of all sorts, it's still a worthwhile place to start. If, for example, telling untruths were a common public speaking practice, then anything any individual speaker said would be questionable. If every public speaker felt free to attack the personal reputation of others without solid evidence of wrongdoing, then few people would listen when personal criticism was warranted. If people could say and do anything they pleased at the podium without retribution, we would not be well served as a society.

Thus, every public speaker—including you and me—must consciously consider the role of ethics in our presentations. Nearly every stage of the speaking process, from topic selection to research and from visual support to language choice, requires that we make ethical decisions. But *who* gets to say what is right and wrong or good and bad?

2. Who decides what is right or wrong?

People construct ethical standards by establishing guidelines for themselves and for groups to which they belong, letting them live together and interact in relative safety, trust, and harmony. Ethics may apply to a larger culture (such as the United States or China), to a broad field (biomedical ethics or business ethics), or to an occupation (law enforcement officer or broadcast journalist). The field of public speaking, too, has its own ethical guidelines, which we'll explore in this chapter.

Consequences of unethical speaking

 On the outcome Strains or destroys your present and future relationship with the audience

Reduces your chance of meeting communication goals

EXAMPLE: A manager who was found out to knowingly use self-serving (and bad) data at last month's meeting will be hard pressed to get colleagues to cooperate this month.

 On the speaker **In the classroom**
- A failing grade on an assignment or a class
- Expulsion from class or a degree or certificate program
- Expulsion from school

In the workplace
- A weakened position, which puts the success of your organization at risk
- Possible violation of company policies and city, state, and federal regulations; and/or the guidelines of accrediting agencies or professional organizations, and resulting related penalties
- A lower performance review for the job
- Loss of the job

EXAMPLE: Recall radio personality Don Imus, who was fired for making racial slurs about a college women's basketball team.

 In your community
- A diminished community reputation
- Loss of responsibilities or position within the community organization

 On the audience Complete or partial untruths passed on from speaker to unsuspecting listeners, who may themselves spread the untruths

Listeners who are inspired to act in unethical ways themselves

EXAMPLE: Hitler's influence on the German people during World War II.

Why does it matter if someone violates these ethical guidelines, either intentionally or unintentionally? Who is harmed, for example, if you "borrow" an idea from an article and pass it off as your own? Ultimately, each individual action *does* matter; the way each of us makes and acts on decisions affects our own spiritual health as well as the fabric of our society. Because of your power to inform and persuade others while speaking, you have a serious responsibility to abide by ethical guidelines.

3. What are the consequences of unethical speaking?

Choosing to act ethically can at times be a challenge, especially given some of our cultural messages and habits, as well as the perception that some people appear to be rewarded for unethical behavior. These gains, however, are often short-term, and offenders pay high prices when caught.

Like all unethical acts, unethical speaking has consequences. Whether this public communication behavior takes place in the national spotlight or in your classroom, it has effects on the speech outcome, on the speaker, and on the listeners.

Because ethical speaking operates within the larger culture, it can be difficult for an individual speaker to successfully navigate an ethical path. Ethical speaking is a choice, and some choices are difficult to make. While some people violate ethical speaking codes knowingly and willingly, most people do so unintentionally through a lack of awareness or training. That's where this chapter can help you.

4B Make the Choice to Be Ethical

One fundamental ethical question each speaker must consider is the relationship between public speaking and the right to freedom of expression. The **First Amendment** to the U.S. Constitution provides protection for free, uncensored speech. This means that speakers are legally protected if they choose to use bigoted, intolerant, or offensive language. Most American adults believe this protection is necessary to maintain an open, free, and democratic society. That said, not all types of speech are covered under the First Amendment. In fact, some speech is illegal.

In an effort to maintain an environment conducive to learning, many colleges and universities have adopted codes against **hate speech,** words that harass or promote discrimination or violence against social or ethnic groups of people or against a member of such a group. For instance, saying something demeaning or intimidating to or about someone because they are Hindu, are Native American, or use a wheelchair could constitute hate speech. What are the policies of your campus in regard to hate speech?

Take seriously your rights under the First Amendment; but at the same time consider your communication goals and your relationship with your audience. What is legal and protected is not always ethical. You must therefore make conscious, thoughtful choices and live by the results.

Types of illegal speech

- **Slander,** false statements that defame another's character and potentially harm that person's standing in the community or at work.
- Speech that incites people to lawless behavior or imminent violence.
- **Fighting words,** intimidating speech directed at a specific individual in a face-to-face confrontation, especially if it inflicts injury or incites an immediate breach of the peace.[2]
- Speech that invades another's privacy.
- Defamatory falsehoods about public officials, punishable *only* if the offended official can prove the falsehoods were published when they were knowingly false or with "reckless disregard of whether it was false or not."[3]

Though most speakers do make ethical speech choices, some speakers commit errors because they don't think things through or do not realize that their words and actions are problematic. One student expressed the wish that he had another chance to remedy a seemingly inconsequential but ultimately questionable ethical public speaking choice:

> *I wanted to show photos of the demonstration march I participated in, but I didn't have any personal ones. Figuring one photo of a march was as good as the next, I used one I found online. That was a bad decision. My credibility suffered when I was asked why there were leaves on the trees in the background of the photo when my march supposedly occurred in February. I should have been honest and contextualized the photograph differently.*

Make conscious choices that afford dignity to others and build or maintain your own integrity. Each of our individual actions *does* matter. Find inspiration in these words of Edward Everett, a powerful nineteenth-century American orator and scholar:

> I am only one.
> But still I am one.
> I cannot do everything,
> But still I can do something;
> And because I cannot do everything,
> I will not refuse to do the something
>   that I can do.

The following sections outline several general and specific guidelines for ethical public presentation.

1. In your speech preparation

Increase your understanding of ethics

For millennia, people have thought, written, and talked about ethics. Individuals, groups, and societies continue to consider, shape, and debate the ethics under which they operate. Numerous workshops, classes, essays, books, organizations, institutes, websites, blogs, and web feeds are dedicated to ethics. (To find them, go online and type in keywords: ethics resources.) There are even professional ethicists, people whose life work is to help others navigate the sometimes difficult ethical terrain of society.

Always be ethical

Ethics must be a consistent, fundamental part of your actions as a public speaker. It's not just something to attend to when convenient. The podium is a powerful symbol of truth and authority, and you have a responsibility to use its power ethically throughout the speechmaking process.

Speak up and speak out

Don't hesitate to address topics you believe to be morally right. You may speak up for people who cannot speak for themselves (e.g., victims of human rights abuses). You may take unpopular positions (e.g., being in favor of genetically modified foods). You may speak out against policies you consider harmful. Whatever the case, support your positions responsibly with appropriate rational and emotional appeals to justify your stance.

Choose topics that promote positive cultural values

Human values differ across cultures, but honesty and causing others no harm are near universals. Speeches informing listeners "How to skip out on a restaurant tab" and "How to get drunk and still avoid a DUI" may technically meet the criteria for a "how-to" speech, but they are obviously unethical. Speeches encouraging listeners to falsely "enhance" résumé data or to join a hate group, while within the legal protection of the First Amendment, embody negative values. Speaking skills are not inherently good or bad, but speeches can promote either good or bad purposes. Choose your speech topics carefully, and make sure your speaking skills promote positive cultural values, including compassion, respect, fair play, cooperation, perseverance, and tolerance.

Be informed and prepared

Once you have committed to a presentation, you're ethically obliged to manage your time to allow for necessary thought, research, organization, preparation, and practice. Spend the energy necessary to fulfill audience expectations of listening to truthful, accurate, and well-supported content. Don't plan to get away with just the bare minimum of preparation.

Acknowledge shades of gray

Few topics can be argued in black-and-white terms. Acknowledge the complexity of human thought and actions and avoid speaking about the world as if your answers were the only clear and obvious solutions. This doesn't mean that you can't argue that certain things are true, take a certain position, or share feelings and opinions. To say and do such things is the very reason people speak in public. But when speaking, you have an ethical obligation to acknowledge that others look at the world differently than you do, based on their own culture, values, beliefs, and experiences. None of us has a lock on the truth.

2. While speaking

Use truthful, accurate supporting materials, and give credit to sources

For presentations requiring research, work hard at finding a wide variety of information, critically analyzing the sources of that information, and giving credit to those sources while speaking. Chapter 7 and the following section in this chapter on plagiarism further discuss the use of research sources.

Examples of doublespeak[4]

- *Nonperforming assets* for bad loans

- *Biosolids* for sewage sludge

- *Privatization* for the transfer of former public sector services to management by private firms

Use concrete language

Language that is vague, ambiguous, or abstract can give the impression that you're trying to hide something or are not being fully truthful. One type of vague language, known as **double-speak,** serves to intentionally hide, distort, manipulate, or even reverse true ideas. People using doublespeak are only pretending to say something, and tend to be more concerned with making the truth seem more pleasant than it is.

Realize that concrete language encourages, not hampers, a listener's ability to make rational decisions about the ideas addressed in a presentation.

create
converse
connect

No Hidden Agendas Here

Be up front about your intentions.

Don't lure an audience with one topic ("A Breakthrough Discovery in Arthritis Research") and then switch to another topic ("A Fantastic New Arthritis Cream!") the listeners may not have voluntarily shown up for. Don't lead an audience to believe you're being informative when your hidden agenda is to manipulate the information and lead the audience to only one subjective conclusion.

Most audiences are quick to realize when they've been duped, and they're not quick to forget or forgive it. Clearly communicating what you would like your listeners to know, do, or believe affects your reputation and your speaking goals.

- As an audience member, have you ever experienced speakers and speeches with hidden agendas? If so, what were they?
- What was your reaction?

Be inclusive

Take all potential listeners into account. A thorough analysis of the audience, which you'll read about in Chapter 5, assists you in your goal of being inclusive in actions and words. It's ethical to choose a topic of interest to as many people as possible—not only to you or a few others—and to use language that *includes* rather than excludes.

Avoid personal attacks

Focus on issues and separate people from the problems you choose to address. It's an abuse of the podium to wage verbal combat against others who may not have the opportunity or means to defend themselves. Belittling another's character in order to prove him or her wrong is to use poor reasoning. It can also threaten any goodwill the audience has toward you as the speaker. Personal attacks are unethical because they focus an audience's emotional energy on character judgments about a person rather than focusing listeners' rational thoughts on ideas. For example, if you support the proposed local tax increase for public libraries, argue for it on its merits; there's no need to attack the city council member who opposes it as "an idiot who obviously doesn't support reading."

The motivation to engage in a personal attack is not always malicious; sometimes, it's easier to default to this route than it is to convey complex or abstract points, or to argue against points that stand in opposition to your ideas. Nonetheless, work to substantiate your statements and claims in their own right; don't reject them because of another person's stance on them.

Avoid the overuse of emotional appeals

Appealing to listeners' emotions is a powerful way of gaining their attention and encouraging them to interact with your ideas. Recognize, however, that while people feel, they can also think. Respect the power of the heart *and* mind, and increase your persuasiveness by combining emotional proof with logical proof.

The "Speak Responsibly" box (p. 76) gives you a chance to test your own messages for their ethical quality.

4C Avoid the Costs of Plagiarism

1. Plagiarism is a serious matter

Plagiarism, from the Latin word for "kidnap," is a familiar topic from your years studying writing and composition. It's an attempt to pass off another person's idea or image, or a close imitation of it, as your own.

Types of plagiarism—*all* of which are unethical—can be classified in two major groups: sources not cited and sources cited, but still plagiarized.[5] Plagiarism can occur in written or spoken work.

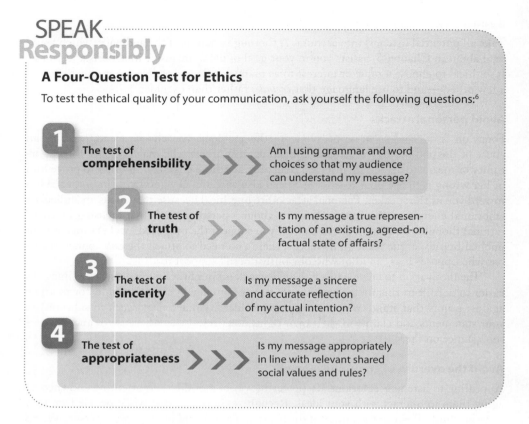

SPEAK
Responsibly

A Four-Question Test for Ethics

To test the ethical quality of your communication, ask yourself the following questions:[6]

1 The test of **comprehensibility** > > > Am I using grammar and word choices so that my audience can understand my message?

2 The test of **truth** > > > Is my message a true representation of an existing, agreed-on, factual state of affairs?

3 The test of **sincerity** > > > Is my message a sincere and accurate reflection of my actual intention?

4 The test of **appropriateness** > > > Is my message appropriately in line with relevant shared social values and rules?

Plagiarism is a form of stealing and cheating, and those caught plagiarizing suffer consequences to their grades, reputations, and careers. Claiming that your plagiarism was unintentional carries little weight now that you're in college—it's your responsibility to know what plagiarism is, why it's wrong, and how to avoid it. You should also know that while the enormous wealth of online material makes pirating another person's work easier than ever, resources allowing teachers to detect plagiarism, such as SafeAssign and Turnitin.com, have become more numerous and easier to use as well. Your college or university undoubtedly has clearly written policies on cheating and plagiarism; your course syllabus probably does as well. Know them. Every school term, students are caught and prosecuted for cheating and plagiarism. If your campus is typical, plagiarists face consequences ranging from a zero on the assignment to expulsion from school.

Plagiarism is also a serious matter for speakers outside the academic context. Consequences at work or in the community may range from a diminished reputation to a scaling down of duties to removal from an official position. Moreover, sometimes a documented record of the plagiarism is long-lasting or permanent: many speeches in business, community, or special-occasion environments are formally recorded, and the popularity of portable recording devices, especially mobile phones and tablet computers, makes it more likely that an audience member may choose to record and perhaps post your speech, with or without your permission. These public messages become part of your digital footprint, readily available for scrutiny by any interested parties. Because plagiarized content can negatively impact your professional and personal standing, it's best to avoid including any in your speech in the first place.

2. The kinds of material that need to be cited

Public speakers, like writers, need to give credit to others who created or gathered material such as:

- Facts, especially those that are debatable or unusual
- Statistics
- Quotes or testimony
- Novel ideas, examples, or strategies
- Class notes
- Opinions, analyses, and interpretations
- Paraphrased material (of yet another's work)
- Images like photographs, videos, graphs, and charts

In contrast to writers, however, speakers give credit orally. Chapter 7 provides guidance on how to create and deliver these oral citations (depending on the kind of source they're found in—a book, database, website, journal, and so forth).

Examples of sources not cited

- **The ghost writer:** presenting another person's work in its entirety as if it's your own.
- **The potluck:** taking pieces from several sources, patching them together as a new whole, and passing it off as your own.
- **The poor disguise:** changing key words or phrases but essentially retaining the original content of the source.

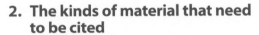

Examples of sources cited, but still plagiarized

- **The forgotten footnote:** providing an abbreviated citation but failing to retain or have on hand the full information about the research source.
- **The misinformer:** providing an inaccurate citation, making the true source difficult or impossible to trace.
- **The perfect crime:** properly citing and quoting in several instances, yet failing to cite other material from those same sources thereby passing them off as your own.

It's also helpful to know the kinds of material that don't need to be cited. These include common knowledge and accepted facts, information that is generally known to everyone or is easily referenced in multiple sources. Examples of common knowledge facts that don't require citation include that human gestation is nine months, that Lil Wayne's birth name is Dwayne Michael Carter Jr., and that most paper is a by-product of trees. Because gray areas about what constitutes common knowledge exist, check with a librarian or your instructor if you have questions as to whether given material needs to be cited.

3. Avoiding plagiarism while speaking

Plagiarism—intentional or otherwise—violates an audience's trust and damages the relationship between you and your listeners. This ethical failure ultimately inhibits your ability to achieve your communication goals. On the positive side, sifting through and choosing relevant ideas, and synthesizing existing material while creating something new, are not only ethical choices, but they also are a sign of intellectual strength, which will increase your standing with listeners and heighten the chances of achieving your communication goals. Here are realistic ways to avoid plagiarism:

Begin preparation early and manage your time

The temptation to lift material is greater when you're up against a looming deadline. Choose your topic and start your research as soon as possible after you've volunteered or been asked or assigned to speak.

Create a system for taking notes

Before beginning your research, create a system for tracking the bibliographic data of your sources. It's difficult otherwise, especially if you're using digital sources, to remember later which idea came from which source, much less where those sources can be found. Perhaps you'll use a notecard system, putting the citation details of each source (title, author, publisher, year, page, URL, etc.) on a card and noting which idea in the speech it connects to. Another option is to keep a running list on a piece of paper. Online citation-management systems like EndNote, NoodleBib, or Zotero include the added bonus of exporting your sources as a bibliography formatted in any of the major citation styles. No matter what system you use, be sure to chart which citation connects with which speech idea.

Create something new by combining research with your own knowledge and beliefs

Some speakers may feel that the enormous amount of information already available makes it difficult, if not impossible, to say anything new. But you can. For instance, Jen, having recently heard a presentation on the medieval medical practice of bloodletting with leeches, was preparing a speech for a psychology of medicine course. Recalling that earlier presentation, she researched current medical uses of leeches and ended up talking about the value in learning from the past rather than just favoring the promise of new medical technologies. Jen's creative thought, however, took time. An incubation period, during which the "new" and "old" ideas had time to mingle in her brain, was necessary—and was one more reason she was glad she had started her speech preparation early.

Use multiple resources

Some objective data require only one reliable source. For example, if you want to tell your listeners the nesting habits of the Northern Parula, a small blue and yellow wood warbler, the Boreal Songbird Initiative, a nonprofit organization dedicated to conserving boreal forest birds, can quickly give you the accurate description of "4 or 5 brown-spotted white eggs in a woven basket-shaped nest of grass, bark, and vegetable fibers . . . neatly hidden in moss or lichen."[7] You don't need a second source. For subjective ideas, however, you're more likely to develop a fresh viewpoint if you look at more than one research source. For example, health care workers and scientists disagree about how likely it is that a given flu virus can create a global pandemic. Using only one source on such a topic limits your scope. Multiple sources allow you to research multiple angles, increasing your chances of creating something unique to share with your listeners.

Abide by fair use

Copyright laws protect original creative work, including music, art, graphics, and pictures. **Fair use** regulations help people figure out how to maneuver in the complex and debatable world of copyright law. In general, you will not need to secure permission for works you use for a classroom presentation because your use is for an educational purpose and your speech is not generating money. However, citing the source *is* required no

table **4.1**   **Identifying Fair Use Material**

Questions	Determining Fair Use
What is the character of the use?	If you are speaking for nonprofit or educational purposes, the work you are using is probably considered subject to fair use. If you are speaking for pay or commercial purposes, you will need to obtain copyright permission for works used.
What is the nature of the work to be used?	Published works of fact are more likely subject to fair use. Works that are imaginative tend to require permission.
How much of the work will you use?	While the law does not set exact quantity limits, consider the amount you are using in proportion to the entire original work. Using only a small amount of a work tips the scales toward fair use. Using large portions or the full work tips the scale toward requiring permission.
If this kind of use were widespread, what effect would it have on the market for the original or on permissions?	If your analysis of the first three questions is leaning toward fair use *and* the original work is password protected or out of print, if there is no ready market for permission, or if the copyright owner is unidentifiable, your use is probably fair. No permission is needed. But if your analysis is leaning toward needing permission *and* you determine that your use would take sales away from the creator, or if you are avoiding paying royalties in an established permissions market, your use is probably not fair and you must seek permission and, if required, pay a permission fee to the copyright holder, which may be the author, the publisher, or both.

matter what your purpose is. Your school library most likely provides guidance in fair use to your educational community; know how to access it—and use it. For example, the University of Texas system interprets the United States Copyright Office's four factors for determining fair use[8] and says that individuals have the responsibility to examine each of the four factors and weigh the result of the combined answers. (See Table 4.1 on page 79 for the questions to ask.) If the ultimate decision tips toward fair use, you are most likely protected. If it doesn't, you must secure copyright permission (or not use the material).

4D Use Civility as a Companion to Ethical Speaking

Throughout the discussion of ethics, you've probably noticed many connections between being ethical and maintaining a positive relationship with your audience. You want to be an ethical speaker not only because it's the right thing to do but also because it's a civil thing to do. In public speaking, **civility** goes beyond, but certainly includes, the use of courtesy and good manners. It more broadly refers to abiding by a code of decency and showing respect, honesty, fairness, and tolerance to others.[9]

When you display civility—familiar territory for many of you—it tells your audience that you consciously consider your words and actions. Some of the words and actions describing civility are similar to the ones you read about earlier in the section on ethics, including:

- Being aware of and acknowledging others
- Being inclusive
- Separating people from problems
- Respecting others' opinions
- Respecting other people's time
- Speaking kindly of others
- Not shifting responsibility and blame

A civil speaker is aware that words and actions have consequences, which, in turn, either enhance or damage the relationship with the audience. As a listener-centered speaker, you want to create a good relationship with your audience. When you do so, you tell your audience that they are valued members of the communication interaction. Using codes of civility while speaking in public is more likely to produce the following outcomes:

- **Civility makes the practicing of ethical speaking choices easier.** When you care about the consequences of your words and actions, you're more likely to work harder at being ethical, including avoiding plagiarism.

- **Your audience is more likely to keep listening.** Some speaker-listener relationships last only as long as the presentation, as you have further interaction with listeners in the workplace, community, or classroom. No matter how great the degree of the connection, when your listeners sense that you care about the relationship you establish with them, they are more likely to stay engaged and listen to you. You are thus more likely to achieve your communication goals.

- **Society as a whole benefits.** When you model civility, you set an example for others and enrich your own life by doing your part to create a more positive experience for your fellow citizens. You show that there are preferred alternatives to the types of discourse we encounter all too frequently on television and online, in which speakers position themselves as combatants, speak loudly and aggressively, make unsubstantiated claims, and engage in personal attacks. While such forms of communication may make for good TV, most of us prefer to reap the rewards of daily living in a civil society.

Is civility always required in our public communication? No. History, including the Vietnam War protests and the more recent Occupy and Tea Party movements, shows a need in our democracy for uprisings and uncivil discourse. But in the majority of your interactions in your classrooms, at work, and in your communities, civility leads to more effective communication.

At the same time, civility doesn't mean you choose only "nice" topics that make people comfortable; you can present the most complex or controversial topics in a civil fashion. Numerous workshops, books, websites, and organizations provide guidance on how to do this. Here are just two examples:

- Guy Burgess and Heidi Burgess, codirectors of the Conflict Information Consortium at the University of Colorado, teach people how to use "constructive confrontation," a type of interaction utilizing civil behaviors, during public discourse.[10] They say, "While continuing confrontation is inevitable, the enormous destructiveness which commonly accompanies these confrontations is not." Each of us, according to the Burgesses, "can work individually and collectively [through civility] to increase the constructiveness of public debate."
- Designed at Arizona State University, Civil Dialogue,[11] according to cofounder Jennifer Linde, "offers people an opportunity to speak openly about difficult topics in a productive manner. It encourages them to listen with respect and speak with civility."[12] Volunteer participants explore controversial issues such as the war on terror, immigration, and taxation from positions ranging from *strongly agree* to *strongly disagree,* following guidelines for civility that include "disagreeing without demonizing, . . . expressing beliefs and values in a passionate yet responsible and truthful manner, and . . . listening to others with patience and empathy."[13] The broader audience is then invited to respond, extending the civil dialogue.

P. M. Forni, author of *Choosing Civility: The 25 Rules of Considerate Conduct,* sums up the need for civility: "Through civility we develop thoughtfulness, [and] foster effective self-expression and communication. . . . Civility allows us to connect successfully with others."[14]

4E Use Additional Ways to Earn Speaker Credibility

Your attention to ethics and civility plays a vital role in the way listeners perceive you as a public speaker, affecting the degree of success you'll have at meeting your communication goals. But additional factors determine whether listeners will perceive you as a likeable, trustworthy, and competent person who cares about the relevant ideas you are discussing.

1. Speaker credibility

connect

For a sample student video on establishing credibility in an actual speech, see the online student speech techniques video clip "Establishing Credibility."

It's impossible for you to separate yourself from your presentation. *You* are the person at the front of the room with something to say. All eyes and ears are on you, anticipating a worthwhile, meaningful message. Each of us has our own image, personality, degree of charisma, intelligence, experience, credentials, and demeanor to bring to the public speaking event.

Speaker credibility, defined as the way your character directly influences the listeners' willingness to receive and accept you and your ideas, is essential to speaking success. Also known as **ethos** (a term coined by the Greek philosopher Aristotle), credibility is something you want to establish as thoroughly as possible.

Credibility is a *perceived* quality, not an inherent one. The audience, not you, determines the degree of your credibility. You can know everything possible about your topic and be the best person to talk about it, but if you don't communicate your credibility to the audience effectively— verbally and nonverbally—then that credibility doesn't exist to your listeners. Credibility does not happen without effort.

Listeners who perceive you as credible are much more likely to attend to and interact with your message, whether that message is informative, persuasive, or entertaining.

2. Establishing credibility for all speakers in all contexts

The very fact that you're speaking in front of a group lends you initial credibility, but this takes you only so far. You need to establish yourself in other ways. Show your audience through your words and actions that you have thought about your ideas, are fully prepared to discuss them in a personable and ethical way, and genuinely want to communicate them in a civil fashion.

Be prepared

If the motto in the real estate industry is "location, location, location," the motto for public presentation is "preparation, preparation, preparation." Prepare your content, your speaking notes, and your visuals. Practice thoroughly so that you know your structure inside and out. An organic-chemistry major described the critical role of preparation perfectly:

> *There is no substitute for having done your homework. Audiences have a sixth sense when it comes to a speaker trying to fake something. You know when you aren't fully*

prepared, and the audience can just feel it. Knowing your stuff always helps you come through in a more positive light, affecting your credibility in a good way.

Show that you are competent

Audiences want to be assured that you are knowledgeable, have thought in-depth about your ideas, and have done your homework. Demonstrate your competence by discussing your credentials, your research, and your connections. Use your visual support or any technology with ease. Pronounce words, people's names, and names of places correctly. Show that you are up-to-date through your choice of topics, ideas, examples, and appearance.

Show that you own the material by speaking conversationally

Speaking conversationally shows that you know what you are talking about, have absorbed the materials, and care enough about listeners to speak with them in language patterns that are easy to listen to. Don't perform a written essay aloud. Instead, own your material in your heart and your head. Listeners quickly sense when you do and when you don't.

Use an objective tone when citing credentials

Some speakers initially feel uncomfortable when establishing their credibility because they think it requires bragging or drawing undue attention to themselves. But, as one student said, "Speaking is not about acting like you're better than everyone. It's about being your best and, when necessary, stating some facts." As you mention your research, experience, and credentials, use an objective, matter-of-fact vocal tone and a confident facial expression and stance. Superior-than-thou messages—verbal or nonverbal—are rarely well received, and most audiences find modesty appealing. As you practice balancing the need to establish credibility with the need for modesty, you may have to ask a trusted source for feedback on how well you achieve both aims.

Use first-person pronouns

First-person pronouns—I, me, mine, we, us, ours—are a natural part of conversational speaking. Connect yourself to the topic and main idea, share your feelings, talk about your perceptions, and share your experiences. Audiences like to know that you are one of them and are reassured when they hear that you have an interest and a stake in your message.

Read the following two paragraphs aloud. The one without first-person pronouns communicates, but it does so in a way that distances the ideas from both speaker and audience. The paragraph with first-person pronouns, on the other hand, creates relevance and makes the ideas expressed seem more central to the people involved in the public discussion.

Without First-Person Pronouns

Sexual activity without commitment is nothing new. After all, it takes place among each young generation. What changes are the words describing it, the rules governing it—if it can be said that there are any—and the reactions to it. "Hooking up" is among the terms used by today's generation. Hooking up can mean different things to different people, but in general it covers anything from kissing to having sex with another person outside the bounds of commitment.

With First-Person Pronouns

I'm probably not telling you anything you don't know when I say that sexual activity without commitment is nothing new. It's been going on for generations, and it's still happening today. What changes are the words we use to describe it, the rules governing it—if we can say that there are any—and our reactions to it. "Hooking up" is among the terms our generation uses. Hooking up can mean different things to you and to me, but in general it covers anything from kissing to having sex with another person outside the bounds of commitment.

> First-person pronouns connect the speaker to the listeners and to the ideas being discussed.

Be dynamic

Audiences want to see a real person speaking. You want to put forth your best face, but there is no need for that face to be overly serious and unemotional. Let your personality come through as you show that you are friendly and approachable. Communicate your emotions as well as your content. Should the topic call for it, smile and laugh, sound angry, or look exasperated. Be careful to avoid drama and histrionics, but don't hold back on emotions that surface naturally during your presentation.

Some people have a natural **charisma,** great personal charm or a magnetic personality that draws others toward them. These speakers rarely have to work at being dynamic; they just are. Not everyone is charismatic, however, and because charisma is a trait and not a skill, it's difficult to learn how to display it. Nonetheless, you can overcome a lack of charisma. As one speaker said,

> *Though I have many good qualities, I am being honest when I say I don't have huge amounts of charisma. So I build my relationship with my audience in other ways—I'm prepared, I use lots of pronouns, and I choose topics I know we'll all care about. That way my audience can sense my passion and connect with me there.*

Show that you want to communicate

Walk to the front of the room with confidence and enthusiasm. No matter what your message is, enthusiasm goes a long way toward attracting and retaining the audience's attention. In public speaking, enthusiasm doesn't mean the rah-rah of cheerleaders but rather your passionate interest in your ideas. It's easy to speak enthusiastically about a fantastic vacation or favorite sport, but you can also speak with passionate seriousness about domestic violence or environmental destruction. Your passion in turn tells listeners that they should view those ideas the same way.

If you present with a ho-hum attitude, speak tiredly or sarcastically, or appear to be speaking only because you have to, the audience quickly gets the message that it's okay to stop listening because nothing valuable is being said. Listeners may even resent having their time wasted. Find that passion, hold on to it, and share it generously with your audience.

Dress appropriately

A first impression has tremendous power. Fair or not, people make snap judgments about others, often within three to six seconds.[15] First impressions are hard to overcome and can positively or negatively influence future interactions. A nice appearance can never compensate for a lack of ideas. Still, presenting an appropriate appearance is important. Remember: Your audience sees you before they hear you.

Professional and/or appropriate dress increases a speaker's credibility by commanding respect, attention, and cooperation.[16] It tells your audience you respect them enough to look your best; they respect you for this in return and are more likely to give you their attention. A well-considered appearance also reflects preparation and good time management; it says that you had time to give to your appearance and were not struggling with your presentation up to the very last minute.

Just as good appearance can attract respectful attention, inappropriate clothing, a hat that hides your face, or flashy jewelry can prove distracting and create a negative image.

There are no absolute rules when it comes to your appearance on speaking day because each audience and occasion is different. It may be smart, for instance, to dress like your audience in situations when you need to stress your role as an "ordinary" person, as one of them. Though exceptions are sometimes necessary, here are two general rules:

- **In academic or community speaking contexts.** Appear at least one degree nicer in your attire than your audience. If you are speaking in front of a neighborhood group in a casual setting, look at least as formal as you would if you were going into the office on casual Friday.

- **In work or ceremonial contexts.** Appear according to the standards of the profession or ceremony. Business and professional people are expected to appear businesslike whether they are serving in speaking or listening roles. Ceremonial events, such as weddings or memorial services, often call for more formal attire than everyday wear.

Look at your audience

Although this is not true of all cultures, mainstream U.S. audiences expect eye contact. Your willingness to look at your listeners conveys confidence, truthfulness, and a desire for personal connection. These characteristics are important to your credibility. See Chapter 14 for more nonverbal ways to increase your credibility.

3. Establishing credibility for individual speakers in individual contexts

Every speaker has different strengths on which to capitalize and weaknesses to overcome. An analysis of your audience and the occasion, which you'll read more about in Chapter 5, is important as you consider specific ways of establishing your credibility. Your past gang affiliation, for instance, may lend you credibility as you convince young audiences to stay

SPEAK
Responsibly

Who's to Blame?

Sometimes, things don't go so smoothly during your speech. Enhance your credibility by avoiding the blame game and taking the ethical high road instead.

Tips for Avoiding Bumps in the Road During a Speech
Double-check the accuracy of your content. Don't blame others for giving you bad information.

- Be overt about the arrangement and relationship of your ideas. Don't think poorly of your audience for not following your message.
- Have a backup plan for technology; be sure you can access your digital files through another channel such as a Yahoo! or hotmail account. Don't curse the computer for not reading the flash drive that holds your slideshow.

  • What are additional examples of speakers (perhaps even yourself) who have acted appropriately—or not—when something didn't go as planned during their speech?

away from gangs, but it's doubtful you would want to mention it during a sales pitch to clients at work.

Consider using the following factors to your advantage.

Education, training, and occupation

Mentioning these factors can be a shortcut to enhancing your credibility with most audiences. Listeners tend to admire the years of study and community service required to become a firefighter and the educated palate of a fine-dining chef. Referencing your education or training also lends you the credibility conferred by your degree and its granting institution and conveys the qualities you needed to earn it—self-discipline, creativity, persistence. Many jobs require specialized degrees or training, and the mere mention of your occupation implies these other levels of preparation.

Age

Depending on the topic and idea being discussed, age can bestow credibility. A 72-year-old most likely has more credibility on the topic of grandparenting than does a 17-year-old. The teen, however, would probably be perceived as more credible than the older person during a speech on the latest video-game technology.

Life experiences

You have innumerable life experiences from which to draw that can enhance your standing before an audience. The experiences you choose to share should be relevant to the idea you are discussing. While presenting on the ancient rock city of Petra, mention your travel experiences in Jordan. While speaking about the designer Alexander McQueen, tell about the fashion show you helped stage.

Expertise

Your accumulated knowledge, training, and experience on a given topic lead to a level of expertise, thereby increasing your credibility. Though you are most likely not the world's leading expert on nineteenth-century violins, perhaps you have played the violin for more than a decade, own an older instrument, and have done a lot of relevant research. For your presentation on antique violins to the local high school orchestra, you *are* the relative expert. Be sure to talk up your expertise if it's appropriate for you and your topic.

Personal connections

Speakers strengthen their own credibility by associating with people who are already perceived as credible. Name-dropping for its own sake is unbecoming, but you can appear more credible when you connect yourself socially or professionally to other people your listeners see as important and reliable. Cite personal connections only when they are truthful and relevant, of course. Mention how you were coached for a summer by the highly ranked table-tennis player. Point out your Capitol Hill internship with your state's senator.

Memberships

Relevant affiliation with a group can also strengthen your credibility. Your work with the campus chapter of Amnesty International is appropriate to mention in your presentation on the CIA's program of extraordinary rendition. Talk up your eleven years as a card-carrying member of the National Rifle Association during your presentation on the World Black Powder Rifle Championship.

Culture

While it's naïve to think that any one person can represent an entire culture—and distasteful to present yourself as a stereotype—drawing on your role as an individual from a particular culture or co-culture can lend you credibility. Because most listeners associate tango with Argentina, referring to your relevant experience with or membership in Argentine culture could heighten your credibility, especially if you had instruction in the dance as well. Refer to your family's history as rodeo riders for added credibility while discussing the history of the cowboy hat.

Speaking of culture, bear in mind that credibility is won in different ways in different cultures. While one culture may value a high-intensity, rational, and relatively egocentric delivery style, that same style can cause other audiences to perceive you as heavy-handed. Some cultures perceive as credible those who demonstrate humility, the ability to listen well, the willingness to share credit for good ideas, and the ability to compromise. Always get additional training from an expert or the speaking host if you are speaking to a cultural group with which you are unfamiliar.

4. Managing your credibility to your advantage

Credibility should be uppermost in your mind at all points during the speechmaking process. Tables 4.2 and 4.3 present some do's and don'ts.

table **4.2** **Presentation Do's: Managing Your Credibility**

Before the presentation	What you can do	• Have all materials (like notes and visual support) ready to go. • Walk confidently when you're introduced or called on to speak.
	What another person can do	• If requested, provide this person with your topic, credentials, and relevant biographical data so he or she can properly introduce you. • Give this person your full attention while they're introducing you and thank them warmly once you start speaking.
	What printed materials can do	• If requested, provide accurate information in a timely manner. • Ask to see a proof before the materials are printed or posted.
During the presentation	Things you do and say	• Be fully prepared. • Show that you want to communicate. • Follow the many other recommendations throughout this chapter.
After the presentation	Things you do and say	• Graciously accept the applause. • Remain at the front of the room and/or return to your seat with confidence. • Thank your audience for their attention.

table **4.3** **Presentation Don'ts: Actions That Are Counterproductive to Your Credibility**

Action	Example	Why it's a problem	What to do
Primping while waiting to speak	Fixing your hair, picking lint off your clothes	These self-absorbing behaviors are the opposite of the listener-centered speech you are expected to give.	Be fully prepared before coming to the speaking space.
Apologizing	For your nervousness, a forgotten item, or a stuffy nose	It needlessly draws attention to the "problem."	Don't apologize.
Making excuses	For a source you meant to find but didn't, for your lack of PowerPoint skills	Audience members realize that they are now going to be on the receiving end of a second-best effort and may get resentful.	Put forth your best effort. Audiences don't know what you have planned.
Putting yourself down after the conclusion	Slumping over the lectern, emitting a huge sigh, commenting on how many times you said *um*	You can bring the audience down with you (yet they may have enjoyed your speech).	Perhaps everything did not go as planned, but reserve your self-evaluation for later.

Ethics and a Plagiarism Lesson in Action
A Student's Process

During high school, Ben Racasa received only rudimentary instruction on plagiarism. He knew he was supposed to cite if he used another's work, but, by his own admission, he had "gotten away" without doing so on a few occasions and, frankly, had become academically lazy. His poor use of time management, too, found him tackling assignments at the last minute, thereby increasing the temptation to cut and paste.

But Ben realized college was different. A friend's plagiarizing had recently earned her a zero on a written essay, and Ben knew it was time to get serious before he faced similar consequences. He was grateful that his public speaking course focused on ethics and invited him to see the problems of plagiarism in ways he had never before considered. The guidelines for avoiding plagiarism were clear, and he learned that his campus library's website was an excellent resource for helping him navigate any citation questions he would have.

Next speech assignment: Biography on a notable (but not famous) person

My topic: Ashrita Furman, *Guinness World Records holder of the most Guinness World Records*

Three required sources:

1. *Wilkinson, Alex. "Higher, Faster, Madder," The New Yorker, December 19 & 26, 2011, pp. 60-70.*
2. *Furman, Ashrita. Official website, http://www.ashrita.com.*
3. *"A Record Record Holder," News Videos, ABC News, January 16, 2011, http://abcnews.go.com.*

Ben's side comments: I actually chose this topic the day after the assignment was given. Nice . . . no procrastinating.

Ben's side comments: I found these credible sources a few days later.

With a week to go before his speech, Ben created this list to track the specific ideas from his sources that he'd be using in his speech. This list would help him distinguish the borrowed ideas from his own and would indicate where in the speech he'd need to provide a citation.

IDEA FOR SPEECH	SOURCE
Furman's interesting Eastern spirituality has taught him that nothing is impossible.	• *Furman's website*
Furman has set more world records than anyone, including the record for the most records.	• *Wilkinson article, p. 62*

review questions

1. What are ethics? What is their relationship to effective public speaking?
2. What are some steps public speakers can take to abide by ethical guidelines before the presentation? during the presentation?
3. Why is plagiarism problematic? What are some ways to avoid plagiarizing?
4. How are civil speaking and ethical speaking connected?
5. How does being a credible speaker increase your chances for successful speaking?

key terms

ethics 69
First Amendment 71
hate speech 71
slander 72
fighting words 72

doublespeak 74
plagiarism 75
copyright laws 79
fair use 79
civility 80

speaker credibility 82
ethos 82
charisma 84

exercises

1. Look over the guidelines for ethical speaking in Section 4B. Are these realistic for you to follow? Why or why not? If you were to rewrite the guidelines, what would you leave in, add, or delete?

2. Visit the Doublespeak website hosted by the nonprofit Center for Media and Democracy (http://www.sourcewatch.org/index.php?title=Doublespeak). Choose five to ten items from the list of words and phrases, and ask friends if they understand their meanings. Report back to your public speaking class, and use your findings as a springboard for a class discussion on the advantages and disadvantages of doublespeak.

3. One of the suggestions for avoiding plagiarism is to use multiple sources (p. 78). Choose a current topic that is being widely covered by legitimate news organizations, and read how at least three different outlets are covering it. Prepare to summarize the topic to a classmate, blending what you have learned from each source while adding your own ideas, thereby creating something new.

4. Find a speech by a speaker you respect. This person can be someone you know from the media or in real life. Chart any civility behaviors you notice displayed in the

connect

For online exercises, quizzes, and hands-on activities, see the Chapter 4 assignments in Connect Public Speaking.

speech. In other words, what does the speaker do to enhance the relationship with his or her audience?

5. As a class, discuss the role of appearance in relation to speaker credibility. Does a speaker's appearance matter? Be sure to analyze speakers under several different circumstances.

Preparing for Responsible Public Communication

There are several "behind-the-scenes" tasks you must complete before you step in front of your audience. These four chapters provide direction on creating the right message that's given at the right time for the right group of listeners. You'll learn first why it's essential to consider your audience and the speaking situation before making any communication choices. Once you know who's listening, you'll then learn how to choose an appropriate topic, narrow your topic into a coherent thesis, and use research to support that central message.

• • •

CHAPTER 5

Analyze Your Audience and the Speaking Situation

LEARNING OBJECTIVES

1 Explain the role of audience analysis in a public speech.

2 Describe the benefits of a successful audience analysis.

3 Identify the steps of a thorough audience analysis.

4 Explain the purpose of a context analysis.

5 List several ways to keep listeners engaged in your message.

Talking to a group of wildlife activists about the joys of largemouth bass fishing on the Mississippi River is probably not the smartest choice. Talking to them about the role of the bass in preserving the river ecosystem probably is. Bottom line: successful public speakers adapt their messages to their audiences. Before you can aim your communication at your specific listeners, however, you must know who they are. As you learn details about your audience and then target the message specifically for them, you make your presentation more "listenable." In other words, a listener-centered speaker is one who knows who's listening. This chapter explains the role of audience analysis and provides strategies for analyzing the audience and the context of each speech. Additionally, you'll learn some techniques for putting your audience analysis into action.

5A Understand the Role of Audience Analysis

Public speaking is not about putting an arbitrarily selected speaker in front of a randomly selected group of people. On the contrary, effective public speaking occurs when a particular speaker creates a comprehensive plan to gain a desired response from a specific audience.

1. Audience analysis is a deliberate step

Audience analysis, the process of gaining an understanding of your audience members and then acting on that information, is a key element for success. It makes your presentation more listener-centered because it helps you choose relevant ideas and communicate them for maximum attention, comprehension, and interaction. In essence, audience analysis *personalizes* the public communication transaction for the intended listeners.

2. Your audience may be different from you

We all have a tendency toward **ethnocentrism,** which occurs when one person views his or her culture, co-culture, or viewpoints as the standard and judges others accordingly. Ethnocentrism creates misunderstandings because it involves viewing other people through one's own cultural lens rather than understanding them through the lens of their own cultural context.

It's ethnocentric (as well as unrealistic) to assume all members of your audience value the principles of capitalism, have patriotic tendencies, or operate on the basis of Western legal codes and moral values. They may not, especially if they were raised in a different part of the world. As a public speaker, you must take extra precautions to engage in a thorough audience analysis and avoid broad messages or specific comments that are founded on ethnocentric views. You can't assume that your audience is like you.

3. Audiences differ from one another

Every audience is comprised of individual listeners who differ from one another—and from you. Likewise, every audience differs from the next. They may differ in **demographics,**

Examples of ethnocentrism

or characteristics such as age, socioeconomic status, education level, and gender. They may differ in their purpose for gathering or in their attitudes toward you or the occasion. However they differ, you need to know. If you're an expert on hawks, for example, you need to be one type of speaker when talking before an excitable second-grade class, another when presenting in front of colleagues at a conference, and yet another when leading a tour group around a wildlife sanctuary.

Be sure to analyze the audience even if you present to the same group on a consistent basis. What you find even from the same set of listeners may change over time, vary from one topic to another, or shift depending on other contextual factors and influences. Managers who speak to their employees twice a month, for instance, must be aware of the current politics of the organization, current relationships between employees and management, and relevant issues of employee concern. Because these contexts are ever-shifting, audience analysis must be done before every presentation.

4. Audiences have expectations

Your listeners have most likely attended (and perhaps even given) many speeches. These multiple experiences mean that people have expectations when they show up to listen to you speak—expectations about the format and the tone of the message—and they use these expectations to evaluate the success of your speech. Of course, there's plenty of room for your personality and creativity in any speech, but in general, adhering to these conventions help you meet those expectations and avoid creating distractions.

Format

Your listeners know from experience that "good" speeches make a point, and that most follow an introduction/body/conclusion format. For example, audience members at an informative speech expect you to answer a "now what?" somewhere near the end of the speech. If you stop speaking at the end of the speech body and fail to provide a sense of summary, listeners may feel that something is missing, and their perception about the speech event and you may be irrevocably tarnished. Audiences at a wedding reception, on the other hand, expect brief toasts that are respectful but don't necessarily follow a formal structure.

The message and its tone

Different speeches have different tones. For example, listeners in a work, educational, or organizational environment expect speakers to address important topics of mutual concern. The speaker who unintentionally speaks in a cheerful tone when talking about contaminants in the water supply makes her audience feel uncomfortable and distracts them from her serious message. Memorial service reflections are expected to shine a positive light on the deceased, even if his or her life was far from perfect.

5B Adapt Your Presentation Based on Audience Analysis

Because one audience differs from another, listener-centered public speaking requires the ability to adapt. Your assessment creates a picture of the people in your audience, along with their needs and attitudes, and it gives you direction and confidence as you prepare your ideas. Your ability to properly adapt your message also affects your credibility. Listeners expect you to have properly analyzed your audience, chosen a relevant topic, and done the necessary planning to communicate your topic in an audience-specific way. There's a bit of irony at play here: effective audience analysis takes work, but audience members rarely comment on it. However, they'll quickly notice an analysis that's poor or lacking.

Here are the ways an audience analysis helps improve your presentation:

1. Audience analysis helps you choose and shape your topic for maximum interest and relevance

Knowing the needs and desires of your audience enables you to select a meaningful topic, organize it appropriately, and support it for maximum audience benefit. General and specialized audiences need different treatments of a topic. (Recall the earlier hawk example.)

Older and younger audiences have different attention spans. Gatherings of men may be interested in different topics than audiences composed of women.

2. Audience analysis helps you speak at the listeners' knowledge level—not above or below it

Understanding your audience's education level or previous experience with your topic helps you to decide, among other things, the complexity of your thesis (the central idea you're communicating), the sophistication of your visual information, and the depth of your presentation. Bear in mind, for example, that the ability to think abstractly begins around age 12, and children are not capable of adult reasoning until age 15.[1]

Knowledge levels among adult audiences vary in many more ways. In contrast to a general audience, groups with specialized shared interests may enjoy and require higher-level ideas and concepts. Freudian analysts, for example, appreciate complex psychoanalytic theory, but a general audience would need the fundamentals of Freudian psychology explained first before they could understand it and be engaged by it. The knowledge level of your audience also affects the types of proof, references, and examples you use. General audiences would probably require a review of the basics and simpler examples during your presentation on climate change, whereas with a group of meteorologists you could go straight to intricate scientific discussions.

Audience analysis checklist

Choose and shape your topic

- What should I talk about?
- How do I make the topic relevant?
- How can I keep my listeners interested?
- How long should I talk?

Audience analysis checklist

Speak to the listeners' knowledge level

- How much does my audience already know?
- Do I need to provide any background information?
- What kind of examples should I give?
- How deeply should I discuss the topic?

3. Audience analysis determines the language best suited to communicate your message

The results of your audience analysis will dictate which words you need to define and the sophistication and formality of your language. To interact with your ideas, your listeners must understand the words you use. A marine biologist, for instance, can and should use scientific terms like *photic zone* and *commensals* when talking to a general audience but should also explain them. On the other hand, these terms require no definition for an audience of marine biology graduate students.

Your audience also determines the tone or feel of your language. Most speakers use a formal tone and lofty style of language when presenting to people gathered for a special occasion such as a historical commemoration; a professional tone and the language of the

Audience analysis checklist

Determine language choices

- Does this group expect certain terms to be used?
- Do I need to define some terms and concepts?
- Should my language be formal or informal?
- How much of my "language personality" should I share?

Audience analysis checklist

Avoid alienating or offending listeners

- How can I be inclusive with my language?
- Are my examples too violent, too sexual, or unsuitable in any way?
- Are my ideas patronizing?
- Are any words or topics taboo with this group?

field when presenting to colleagues and coworkers; and a lighter tone and informal language—perhaps even some slang—when presenting to a familiar audience at a campus club gathering.

4. Audience analysis decreases the chance of alienating or offending listeners

Speakers want to invite their audience members into their presentations, not exclude or alienate them through offensive language or behavior. Certain topics, examples, and language choices are more appropriate for some audiences than for others. Some people gather to hear political commentary, whereas others find politics boring. Some audiences like to hear people speak openly and forthrightly about religious values or sexual practices, whereas others think these topics are better discussed privately. Racist and sexist remarks are offensive to most audiences and should always be avoided. (Read more about language choice in Chapter 14.)

While the risk of offense and alienation can arise in many contexts, you need not choose only safe or bland topics. The most provocative and controversial ideas can—and should—be discussed publicly; the health of our democracy requires it. If necessary, acknowledge the controversial nature of your ideas and do your best to discuss them in an honest, ethical, and civil way. You gain a lot of ground right at the start if you verbally recognize a hot-button topic as potentially touchy; it shows a measure of respect for your audience's diversity and that you have thought about the broad range of viewpoints your listeners may have. One speaker, Anurahda Mittal, the director of a policy think tank, knew that some of her ideas on economic human rights, especially those that favor the global poor, had the potential to stir up heated opposition among some members of her mainstream audience at a large community lecture. In her introduction, Mittal recognized the controversial nature of her ideas yet asked listeners to at least hear her out as she attempted to reframe the public debate and provide answers that would ultimately be in everyone's best interest. Most listeners seemed willing to do so—and it made for quite a rousing question-and-answer session.

If you think your speech idea has the potential to offend your listeners, talk it over with a friend, colleague, or teacher. You may choose to switch topics, revise certain sections, or go ahead with your original plan. Regardless of what you decide, remember that individual values and experiences can cause some listeners to take offense despite even the most thorough audience analysis and best-laid plans. In other words, it's impossible to please and adapt to every listener 100% of the time. But as long as you've taken as many steps as you can, before and during your speech, toward understanding your listeners' needs and attitudes, most people will recognize your efforts and be willing to keep an open mind and suspend their personal judgments at least for the duration of your presentation.

5C Know When and How to Analyze Your Audience

To effectively analyze your audience, you must do the analysis at the right time; where you are in the speechmaking process affects the choices you will make. You also need to know the kind of information to collect, how to collect it, and then what to do with it.

1. When to conduct your audience analysis

The majority of your analysis should take place at the outset—it will be your first or second step, depending on whether or not your topic is predetermined. Still, audience analysis can continue to take place at later stages of the process; you can fine-tune your analysis right before or even during the presentation.

Do your audience analysis first if you have yet to select a topic

Many speakers choose a topic only after they know their expected audience. Classroom speaking frequently works this way. Your instructor gives you an assignment with several parameters, and you then select a topic that fits both the assignment and your listeners. Take your task seriously; your classroom speaking is not just an exercise. Know this group of people, and use the opportunity to choose topics relevant to their lives. There are countless examples of students being informed, persuaded, and inspired by "just a classroom speech."

An increasingly popular speaking assignment is to have students make presentations elsewhere on campus, such as the Aggie Club or Film Society. Some instructors have students speak to community groups such as the American Lung Association or Big Brothers Big Sisters International as part of service learning projects. Opportunities such as these require an in-depth understanding of your listeners before you can pick an appropriate topic. They are excellent training for future real-world speaking situations.

If your topic is predetermined, use audience analysis to further shape it

Many people are asked to speak because of their expertise on a particular topic. Job-related and community speaking typically work this way. Kristen Rosati, an attorney specializing in genetic privacy and the use of electronic health information for research, is one such speaker. Rosati tours the country and speaks to all types of audiences, shaping each presentation to the specific needs of her gathered listeners:

- To other attorneys, she provides detailed analyses of the laws that affect genetic privacy and the use of that information for research.
- To university researchers, she provides guidance on how to apply relevant laws in a way that does not create barriers to research.
- To hospital compliance officers, she discusses how hospitals can provide their electronic health information to researchers in a way that complies with federal and state privacy laws.

Rosati's ability to modify this complicated issue and meet the needs of her specific audiences has earned her prestige in her field.

Other speakers are not as successful as Rosati in their audience analyses. A prominent nutritionist once spoke to a large general community audience on the importance of health and diet. At first, the speaker was doing well; she was organized, showed a lot of relevant visual support, and was charismatic. About forty-five minutes into the hour-long presentation, however, things took a wrong turn when she began providing guidelines on how to forward her message when out working with clients. *Out working with clients?* This presenter was suddenly speaking as if all 500 listeners from the general community were fellow professional nutritionists. The speaker's failure to properly analyze her audience weakened her whole presentation. Listeners felt confused and unimportant. How was any of the professional strategizing being relayed relevant to them? Had they just sat there for an hour listening to a speech prepared for a different audience?

Last-minute analysis

You must be prepared for changes that could affect your speech plan. New people come into organizations, new policies are enacted, roles shift, and outside influences affect internal politics and thinking. As your speaking date approaches, double-check your audience analysis. Call your speaking host, stay current with the news, and check the organization's website to see whether you need to revise your speech plan. Arrive early on your speaking day. Ask the speaking host what the audience has been doing before the presentation and what they will be doing afterward. Listen, observe, and be hyperaware. For instance, one student speaker replaced a planned example with a new one he picked up through informal interaction with audience members before class started. The fresh example "starring" one of the listeners created a welcomed intimate vibe in the room. And many a speaker has wisely abbreviated a presentation when realizing that all-day meetings have left the audience looking a bit worn out. Bring a flexible mind-set and a pencil on speech day. You just never know.

Analysis during the presentation

By the time your presentation begins, you should be confident about your knowledge of your audience. Nonetheless, there may still be opportunities to keep learning more.

Tips for Analyzing While Speaking	**"How Do I Say It?/What Do I Do?"**
Ask a question and for a show of hands to quickly assess audience demographics, behaviors, or attitudes. ⟶	*How many of you have seen the Body Worlds exhibit?*

Watch for listeners' body language. It can help you make some quick decisions:

Are they enjoying themselves (smiles, nods, engaged posture)? ⟶	Keep doing what you're doing.
Are they looking perplexed (wrinkled foreheads)? ⟶	Clarify the point of confusion—it's okay to ask if something is or isn't clear—and then provide a definition or an example or explain the idea in a different way.
Are they looking bored (wandering eyes, slouched posture)? ⟶	Can you shorten this section and move on?

2. The types of information to collect

There are two general categories of audience information—demographics and attitudes. Demographics, as stated earlier in the chapter, look at the statistical traits of the audience. **Attitudinal information** looks at audience attitudes, values, and beliefs.

Some Typical Demographics Categories	**Some Attitudinal Information Categories**
Abilities/disabilities	Societal or local attitudes toward issues like immigration, urban sprawl, or personal freedoms
Age	
Education level	Group values and beliefs
Ethnicity or cultural background	
Gender	Feelings about your topic
Geographic location	Level of agreement with your speech's thesis
Occupation	
Political or religious affiliation	Feelings and attitudes toward you as the speaker
Sexual orientation or identity	Attitude toward attendance (Is the audience present voluntarily or out of obligation?)
Socioeconomic status	

3. Where to collect audience information

You can gather information about your specific audience in several ways: through existing research, by asking the speaking host, by using an expert, by conducting surveys and questionnaires, and by using personal contacts.

SPEAK Responsibly

Using Polled Data

If you are using polled data, be sure to evaluate the credibility, as well as the interests and possible biases of the organization conducting the poll. Polls sponsored by ideological organizations or companies with something to sell are usually skewed in order to produce results favorable to their agendas. Nonpartisan, independent polling organizations such as Gallup, Roper, PollingReport.com, and Zogby design their surveys to ensure random sampling and low statistical margins of error.

Use existing research

Information is often available to speakers needing to conduct research on a potential audience. First, many organizations collect data on themselves and provide it in brochures, reports, and websites. If you were asked, for example, to speak to the Gulf Citrus Growers Association, its website would tell you that it represents growers in five southwest Florida counties, produces one-fifth of Florida's citrus, has a $1 billion impact on the regional economy, and produces the first grapefruit of the growing season.[2] Information like this helps you tailor your talk to your particular audience, accurately meet your listeners' needs, and increase your credibility by showing listeners that you "did your homework."

Polled data are another source of information about audiences. Polls collect current opinions in a wealth of categories—politics, current events, pop culture, and more. Polls also gather information about habits ranging from shopping practices to travel preferences to leisure behavior. Polls may not give you the exact opinions and habits of your particular listeners, but they do provide a random sampling of society at large, and in many instances you can assume that your specific audience is a random sampling of society. Moreover, some available polling data are specific to geographic location or other demographic criteria and can therefore be narrowed to apply more specifically to your listeners.

Ask the speaking host

Your speaking host, the person representing the group who has invited you to speak, can provide unique insights about the demographics and attitudes of your upcoming audience. This person can also, if necessary, update you on the politics of the group and pinpoint people in the room who need to hear your message. Some speaking hosts automatically provide audience information when inviting you to speak. If yours does not, be sure to ask questions clarifying listeners' demographics and attitudes until your needs are satisfied.

Use an expert to help you understand an unfamiliar audience

Consulting an expert whose knowledge pertains to your speaking situation can help you navigate cultural or organizational intricacies; those nuances and how you handle them can make or break your presentation. You may be asked to speak to a group from a country, culture, or co-culture different from your own. If you do, be aware that customs, humor, gestures, and references do not always translate well. For example, your reference to a "yardstick" may mean little to audience members from countries that use the metric system. Not all cultures consider it appropriate to address people by first names; addressing someone informally could insult that person and the audience. Each culture has its own taboo topics you'll want to avoid.

Type of Expert	Examples of audience analysis expertise
Academic consultant. Scholarly field experts can offer a unique perspective on cultures, nations, and demographic groups specific to their academic disciplines.	• A graduate of the Hawaiian studies program at the University of Hawaii–Hilo would be of great assistance for your presentation to a local Hawaiian audience. • A professor of Islamic studies could provide essential guidance for your speech before a Muslim organization.
Professional in a specific, relevant field. A representative of a profession or trade can provide valuable insights into the lives of those working in a particular occupation.	• Consult a tourism specialist for your speech about time-shares. • A master pipe fitter could be helpful for a speech to apprentice students interested in the trades.
Books, websites, and blogs. Many experts across numerous fields of study write books and host websites or blogs.	• A book on Cambodian culture can help as you prepare your presentation for a group about to visit Phnom Penh. • A blog written by an organic-chicken farmer can help you with your talk about sustainable food trends.

Conduct surveys and questionnaires

Some speakers like to conduct a survey or create a questionnaire to gain additional information about their specific audiences. Give yourself at least a few days to develop and administer a questionnaire and interpret the data. (Free web-based software like Survey-Monkey or PollDaddy can facilitate your task.) Also, be sensitive to people's busy schedules. Make sure your survey or questionnaire is easy to understand, takes no more than a few minutes to complete, and gives you the information you were seeking without the need for additional questions. Figure 5.1 (p. 106) gives tips for creating a survey.

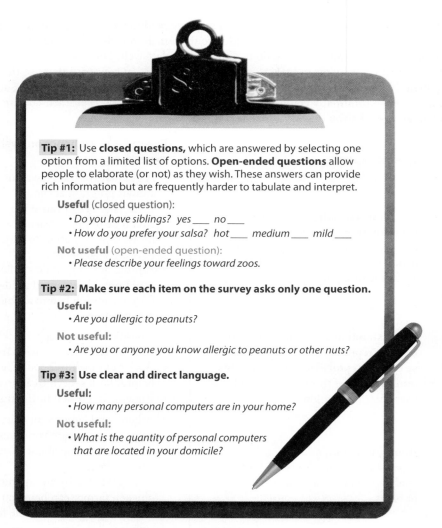

Tip #1: Use **closed questions,** which are answered by selecting one option from a limited list of options. **Open-ended questions** allow people to elaborate (or not) as they wish. These answers can provide rich information but are frequently harder to tabulate and interpret.

Useful (closed question):
- *Do you have siblings? yes ____ no ____*
- *How do you prefer your salsa? hot ____ medium ____ mild ____*

Not useful (open-ended question):
- *Please describe your feelings toward zoos.*

Tip #2: **Make sure each item on the survey asks only one question.**

Useful:
- *Are you allergic to peanuts?*

Not useful:
- *Are you or anyone you know allergic to peanuts or other nuts?*

Tip #3: **Use clear and direct language.**

Useful:
- *How many personal computers are in your home?*

Not useful:
- *What is the quantity of personal computers that are located in your domicile?*

figure 5.1 **Three Tips for Creating a Useful Survey**

Use your personal contacts

On occasion, speakers present their ideas before groups to which they belong. These are familiar audiences composed of classmates, coworkers, fellow organization or club members, family, and friends. Your membership in this group should provide you with a solid understanding of your listeners' characteristics and attitudes. When you know a speaking date is approaching, pay extra attention to those around you to gauge their attitudes and to learn about their current topics of conversation. The information you pick up could help you shape your speech.

4. Applying the information to your presentation

Once you've gathered audience demographic and attitudinal information, you have the additional challenge of making sense of it and applying it to your presentation. One way to start is to examine the data and decide whether your audience is homogeneous or mixed.

Homogeneous audiences

Homogeneous audiences are groups that share at least one important demographic or attitudinal characteristic. Examples of homogeneous audiences include:

- Soldiers in an army platoon
- A college class of pharmacy majors
- A group of soon-to-be retirees
- Members of a women's soccer team
- The Asian American Hotel Owners Association

These listeners gather to hear topics relevant to their shared interests. When you are presenting to a homogeneous group, play up audience commonalities. Show the audience that you are aware of their issues, and stress the relevance of your ideas. Focusing on the listeners' commonalities reinforces their bonds with one another and increases the chance the audience will act as one, thereby easing your job of reaching them.

SPEAK Responsibly

Stay on Topic

Despite any significant commonalities, homogeneous audiences are still made up of individual listeners. It's not safe to assume that you can venture off onto other topics and still have an agreeable audience. People in a gun-rights organization share a common ideology about guns, but they do not necessarily share views about certain politicians, environmental issues, or cultural issues such as immigration. Monitor your language, too. Though a men's football team as a group displays traditional masculinity in many ways, it's never appropriate or ethical to make off-color remarks, particularly those that are sexist or homophobic.

General audiences

A mixed audience—often referred to as a **general audience**—can be a challenge. Your job of finding a topic of interest and creating relevance becomes more demanding when presenting ideas before a group that is widely mixed in terms of demographics and attitudes.

When choosing a topic for a general audience, consider its range of appeal. Few—though surely some—people are interested in obscure topics like "The Winter Appetite of Northeastern Slugs." Search instead for topics with universal appeal. All people eat, need clean water, and are interested in health issues. Most people value family and friends, are concerned about safety, technology, and self-improvement, and like to be entertained.

A general audience also requires you to use content and language appropriate for listeners at all knowledge levels. Take extra care to define specialized words and jargon, explain allusions, and provide background to concepts so that you don't lose less knowledgeable audience members. Mastering that technique takes practice, and even experienced speakers can struggle with it. For example, when journalist Ray Suarez presented his speech "The Old Subdivision: American Life and American Culture in the First Suburban Century" to a large community audience, he twice alluded to a show called *The Goldbergs*. Listeners older than 50 who had grown up in the United States immediately got the reference to the popular radio and television situation comedy featuring the home life and assimilation struggles of a Jewish family in New York City. But listeners outside these demographics were lost. A quick explanation of *The Goldbergs* reference would have allowed all listeners to participate in that particular section of the speech.

Values, attitudes, and beliefs of general audiences most likely run the gamut. Be sensitive to these variations, and beware of the trap of ethnocentrism. Pay attention to relevant polls to see how the majority of listeners are thinking, feeling, and behaving. You have a right to communicate your message, but at the same time, acknowledge varying points of view to encompass as many listeners as possible.

Adapt to listeners with disabilities

If you know that listeners with visual or hearing disabilities will be in your audience, there are some specific things you can do to facilitate the public communication. First, don't assume that all listeners with disabilities want or require accommodation. Generally, people needing accommodation request it ahead of time. If you need extra assistance in providing accommodation for your listeners, seek out experts in adaptive technology, often found in campus student-services offices. The following tips assist all listeners in your audience, those with and without disabilities.[3]

For Listeners Who Are Blind or Have Other Visual Impairments

- Reserve a few front-row seats.
- Accompany visual support with an oral narrative. Describe in detail what is shown, be it contrasting pie charts or a photograph depicting an aerial view.
- Provide large-print copies of any handouts. Black ink on white paper makes for the best contrast.

- Avoid darkening the room or turning lights too low.
- Vary your vocal expression, and alternate the pace of your delivery.

For Listeners Who Are Deaf or Hard of Hearing

- If an interpreter is present, situate yourself and the interpreter so that deaf and hard-of-hearing audience members can easily see both of you. The interpreter can provide guidance about how best to do this.
- Speak at a normal rate, maintaining eye contact with the audience, not the interpreter.
- Reduce any background noise: shut doors and ask people to remain seated until the presentation is over so as not to block the view of the interpreter.
- Repeat or paraphrase questions or statements from other audience members before you answer or address them.
- When referring to a visual or a handout, provide extra time for deaf and hard-of-hearing audience members to look at it, and then return their attention to you and the interpreter.

5D Know How to Analyze the Speaking Situation

Part of your pre-speech analysis goes beyond the people in attendance and looks at the speaking environment or situation, which, as you read in Chapter 1, is also known as the context.

1. Context analysis is important

The speaking situation leads audiences to expect certain types of messages and behaviors. They consider a speech more listenable when it meets these expectations. Conversely, when those expectations are not met, listeners tune out quickly. For example, a newspaper columnist evidently misread the context when he was invited to speak as part of a well-established lecture series geared toward a scholarly audience. The presentation's title looked promising; the audience had high expectations that this speech would be yet another in a long line of interesting, intellectually rigorous, and well-developed talks on the year's chosen theme. The speaker provided a superficial overview and a few amusing anecdotes throughout the hour, but he never developed any major idea in depth. The presentation might have satisfied listeners expecting a lighter, more entertaining speech, but it did not fulfill the expectations of the lecture-series audience. The evening was a disappointment to them, and the speaker was viewed as an intellectual lightweight.

Here are some assumptions about certain speech-giving contexts:

- Presenters at a work meeting are expected to discuss topics furthering the mission of the organization and to meet the standards of the organization for clothing and appearance.

- Classroom speakers are expected to discuss relevant topics and to use language learned in the course.
- Graduation speakers are expected to look optimistically toward the future.
- Slang is unsuitable for a formal presentation to clients at work, but casual language may be acceptable in an informal speech in front of a high school group.
- Leaning comfortably against a desk may work for a speaker long familiar with his group of listeners, whereas an interview candidate making a presentation before a group should sit or stand with good posture.

2. Context is physical, temporal, and psychological

Each presentation has its own unique context, made up of three narrower contexts: the physical, the temporal, and the psychological. You want to give the right message in the right place at the right time to the right audience.

Physical space considerations

The characteristics of the speaking space make up the **physical context.** The physical space, including location, size, and purpose of the room, determines many of the logistics and practicalities of the presentation. It also influences the feel of the event. For example, you may be bound to the microphone when speaking in a large room. The language and clothing appropriate for the presentation in your history classroom may not be acceptable when talking to coworkers in the conference room. A bright auditorium lends a different atmosphere than a dimly-lit banquet hall.

Temporal considerations

The point at which a speech is given—relative to the time of day, to the time in history, or to other presentations on the same topic—is the **temporal context.** A speech presented midmorning after most people have had a coffee break is heard differently than a speech given at the end of a long afternoon when most people feel like they need a break. Some speeches make sense only in relation to another message; for example, the final speaker on a panel can refer to concepts addressed earlier in the day without having to fully discuss them again.

Audience analysis checklist

Analyzing the physical context

- How big is the room and what's the expected head count?
- How close will my audience be sitting to me and to each other?
- How are the seats arranged?
- How is the room's lighting?
- What technology is available?
- Am I expected to use a microphone?

Audience analysis checklist

Analyzing the temporal context

- How does my presentation relate to what has been said before?
- How does it relate to what may be said afterward?
- At what time of day am I speaking?
- What has my audience been doing prior to my speech?
- What are they doing afterward?

Psychological considerations

The **psychological context** encompasses the moods and frames of mind of audience members and how they react to your message. For example, many special-occasion speeches are expected to be lighthearted; audiences are quick to laugh and enjoy themselves. In business environments, where time is money, speakers are expected to get to the point quickly.

The social roles of the speaker and people in attendance also create a psychological context. For example, a CEO sharing a recent company success story in front of a friendly and familiar audience faces a different psychological context than does a manager attempting to persuade a hostile employee group to adopt a new contract. The "Create Converse Connect" box (p. 112) highlights how context played a role in one of the most famous speeches in United States history.

Audience analysis checklist

Analyzing the psychological context

Organizational and cultural considerations

- Do my listeners share an organizational or societal culture of which I should be aware?
- What is the internal political climate in this organization?
- Is money or someone's reputation on the line today?
- Is there a certain protocol, or expected customs or rules, I need to follow?

Speaking-occasion considerations

- What is my audience's attitude toward this speaking occasion and toward me?
- Is this a formal or an informal occasion?
- Are my listeners attending voluntarily or out of obligation?
- Are there certain people in the audience of whom I should take special note?

5E Engage Your Audience by Connecting Them to Your Ideas

Now that your upcoming presentation is tailored for your audience and the speaking context, you can use several strategies during your presentation to keep your listeners actively engaged and better connected to your ideas. Most of these strategies fall into two larger categories that are explored in greater detail in the two sections below: your language choices and audience interaction opportunities.

Involving your listeners can enhance your presentation. One frequent public listener said,

> *Of all the speeches I hear, the best ones are not necessarily the most eloquent. To me, the best are those involving the listeners to the highest extent possible. When I am in the audience, I expect speakers to make me feel that they are giving the speech to me and not to themselves or some generic audience.*

Inviting your listeners to get involved is easy once you adopt the right frame of mind. You'll soon find the connections happening quite naturally. Max, a first-year college student who at first found himself planning his audience connections, provides inspiration:

Reading the Context on a Day in 1963

The story of Martin Luther King Jr.'s famous "I Have A Dream" speech[4] provides a classic example about a speaker reading the context and taking advantage of the moment. King actually had a different speech prepared for the March on Washington for Jobs and Freedom that famous day of August 28, 1963. He had prepared the text earlier in New York City and put the final touches on it upon his arrival in Washington the night before the march.

Nearly a quarter of a million people were gathered on the Mall in front of the Lincoln Memorial. Despite predictions of violence and mass rioting, the crowd was peaceful, and the mood was bright. King was among a slate of speakers, all enthusiastically supported by the crowd.

King started his intended speech but never finished it. Instead, he took advantage of the crowd and its energy (and quite possibly gospel singer Mahalia Jackson's cry of "Tell them about the dream, Martin!") and switched midstream to words he had delivered in a smaller context a few months before in Detroit. Those words included the famous "I Have a Dream" section, which became part of one of the most moving speeches of the civil rights movement, if not the twentieth century.

- What are the physical, temporal, and psychological contexts King was reading and acting upon?
- What does King's story say about the benefits of public speaking experience?

I had to force those sections of relevance in my first few speeches. I've been taught to be more subtle when writing papers, but I can see how I need to be more obvious while speaking. By the last few presentations, it was becoming second nature. I just keep seeing more and more opportunities to connect.

Seizing these opportunities for connection is a way to capitalize on the audience analysis information you've gathered in advance. Here are just some of the many strategies you can use to highlight connections between your listeners and your ideas as you speak:

connect
For sample student videos that use audience engagement strategies, see the online student speech techniques video clip "Engaging the Audience."

- Tell your listeners directly how your ideas can benefit them, help them learn, or cause them to think in new ways.
- Refer to the issues that matter in people's daily lives—family, love, money, and health.
- Appeal to listeners' goals or beliefs.

- Comment on areas of shared experience and mutual acquaintances.
- Base other connections on geography, occupation, nationality, education, age, or common interests.

Whether you decide to engage your audience through your language choices, through audience interaction, or both, keep in mind the importance of doing so ethically and civilly. Luring audiences in with audience engagement techniques but under false pretenses is not ethical. Neither is forcing engagement through any position of power you might hold. Begging an audience to participate or making them feel guilty for not doing so only alienates them. Audience engagement must be voluntary to be effective.

1. Connect with your language

The language choices you make as a speaker influence your audience's decision to keep listening to you and interacting with your ideas. Chapter 14 explores several categories of language that—depending on the speaker, the ideas, and the context—can create a bridge between speaker and audience. Here we'll look at techniques that allow your listeners to feel that they are an intrinsic part of an "in the moment" communication event.

Use specific terms your listeners can relate to

A listener-centered public speech is designed for a specific audience. Your speech is not a generic message that could just as easily be given down the hall, in a different room, on another day. When you have specific names, locations, and mutual references that can build your rapport with listeners, and subtly remind them that you know who they are and are talking to *them*, the effect on the mood of the room and the receptivity of your listeners is palpable:

- Names—*If you recall, Nina told us yesterday . . .*
- Locations—*You can find examples of those wall graphics in the basement of the Hannelly Center next door . . .*
- Mutual references—*We all know our company struggled in the first quarter, and . . .*

Use personal pronouns, especially *you*

Recall the discussion in Chapter 4 about using personal pronouns to increase your personal credibility. You can also use these pronouns, especially *you, yours, we, us,* and *ours,* as a way of creating a bond with your audience. These pronouns are a way of saying, "What we are talking about is important to all of us, here and now."

Listener-centered pronouns are easy to incorporate throughout your presentation once you're in a listener-oriented frame of mind. One student put it succinctly:

> *I paid attention to how I used pronouns during everyday conversation, and it was simple to transfer that skill to my speeches. These pronouns really draw an audience in. When I hear someone speaking directly to me, I want to listen. We as humans automatically perk up at the use of the word you.*

connect

For a sample student video that uses personal pronouns, see the online student speech techniques video clip "Using Pronouns to Connect Listeners and Speaker to the Topic."

These pronouns may not be appropriate for every presentation, however. Your audience analysis can help you determine how much to use them. If the topic is considered negative or might make people feel bad, too many *you* references could make listeners defensive. For example, when discussing alcoholism with a group of people who suffer from it, audience-connecting personal pronouns are appropriate. But you'd want to use qualified language when discussing this topic with a mixed audience. Using phrases like *If you are among the adult population who has a problem with alcohol . . .* helps establish everyone's individuality.

2. Connect through audience interaction

Maintain the energy and support of your in-the-moment, dynamic speech by inviting the audience to participate. Most audience members are happy to contribute in any way asked, whether through a direct question, rhetorical participation, or actual participation. If you choose to engage your listeners through interaction, check with your instructor first. Some assignments may not lend themselves to audience participation as well as others.

Question the audience

Questions are a common device for opening a presentation as well as a terrific way to refresh and maintain audience interest throughout your talk. Don't ask a question merely for its own sake; be sure that it connects to the ideas you're discussing. Questions should be short, easy to understand, and easy to answer with only a few words by at least one person in the room. Closed questions, those answered with a yes or a no, also work well. Avoid questions that could spark a long-winded answer and take your planned discussion in a direction for which you are not prepared. Soliciting answers for particular facts, experiences, attitudes, and habits, however, can be very effective:

- Facts—*Does anyone know the percentage of U.S. adults who have a college degree?*
- Experiences—*Can I see a show of hands from those of you who have been to the Caribbean?*
- Attitudes—*How many of you enjoy country music? How about if it has a punk flair?*
- Habits—*What was the last electronic gadget you purchased?*

Allow time for a response. It's insincere to ask a question and then move on to your next thought without waiting for an answer. Also, consider the size of the audience and the speaking venue when asking direct questions. If the room is large, you may need to repeat an audience member's answer for everyone to hear. When a listener responds, acknowledge the answer and, if appropriate, comment on it.

Invite rhetorical participation

Rhetorical participation asks your audience to contemplate an issue, consider a scenario, reflect on a value, or mull over a proposal without making a verbal response. It's a common device for opening a presentation and can also effectively refresh and maintain listener engagement throughout your talk. You don't want to invite rhetorical participation for its own sake; instead, look for opportunities to connect to the ideas you're already discussing. Here are some examples:

- *Think back to that first day of elementary school.*
- *How do you illustrate your commitment to your community?*
- *You all were here when our company president was fired last month. How did that affect your relationship with this workplace?*
- *If you were faced with the same choices I just described, what would your response be?*

If you invite rhetorical participation in your presentation, be comfortable with a small amount of silence following your appeal. Otherwise, you risk the perception that your invitation to ponder was artificial. Consider the depth of your request when deciding how much silent response time to allow. Some questions need only a few seconds; complicated invitations require more time.

create
converse
connect

Engagement through the Five Senses

People interact with the world around them through their five senses—sight, sound, touch, taste, and smell. Keep these in mind as you create opportunities for relevant audience engagement.

Auditory appeals:
Can the audience listen to anything (other than your voice)? Make a noise, have them repeat something, share a song clip, or play an instrument.

Visual appeals:
Can the audience look at anything to stay involved in your message? Show colors, action, textures, animation, beauty, or novelty.

Olfactory appeals: Can an odor or scent engage them in any way? A classic perfume, some freshly baked croissants, or a scratch-and-sniff sticker may be relevant to what you're talking about.

Gustatory appeals: Is it appropriate to let the audience taste anything? Your famous cake recipe, an exotic fruit, or a new sour candy just might work.

Tactile appeals: Is there anything the audience can touch? How about the back of their chairs, their ribs, a piece of soft fabric, or a unique object?

Invite actual participation

Audience members respond positively when "one of their own" becomes involved in the presentation. Consider audience participation if you want to demonstrate something, provide a fresh and relevant example, or reinforce a point. Table 5.1 outlines some ways to maintain listener engagement through audience participation.

table 5.1 Audience Participation Techniques

Technique	Example	Tips
Make an open invitation for general participation.	Yasmin: "I got my audience involved by asking them to apply the critical-thinking theory I had just discussed to some new images. Not only did it make me feel more at ease, but I think it helped their understanding and brought them much closer to the presentation."	• Be genuine and enthusiastic when making the invitation. • Have a sample response in case you need to jump-start the interaction.
Call on a specific audience member.	*Andre, we all know you've been through this before, and you told me you came out of it with real positive feelings. Could you quickly fill everyone else in?*	• Be sure that the person you are calling on is willing and able to come through with a response.
Conduct a verbal poll—to introduce a topic, quickly gauge listener knowledge or beliefs, or as a pre-test/post-test for your material.	In your speech on the health benefits of soy milk: *Who's tried soy milk? Now, keep your hand up if you drink it regularly.*	• Keep questions brief and to the point. • If relevant, make a quick comment to acknowledge listeners' responses. This helps further the sense of dialogue.
Invite your listeners to write something down.	Dave's speech-opening material: *Write down the first five words you think of when I say freedom.*	• Be silent while they write. • Be sure to go back to this list at some point in the speech. Dave did so midway to support a point he was trying to make about abstract language.
Ask for a volunteer.	To prove how light your new titanium bicycle is, ask someone to pick it up and report exactly how easy it is to lift 2.6 pounds.	• See pages 287–288 for more on using real people as visual support.
Ask the audience to do something.	Ask audience members to pat their heads while rubbing their stomachs as you discuss coordination.	• Make sure the task can be done quickly and safely.

Successful Audience Analysis in Action
A Student's Process

The upcoming assignment halfway through the term asked students to prepare a five-minute informative speech on a topic in which they had a degree of expertise. Adam Chang had worked as a tattoo artist for nearly five years before deciding to return to school, and immediately knew what he'd talk about—tattooing.

How am I going to appeal to this audience?

I've noticed tattoos on several classmates, but I'm assuming that, like the general American population, not everyone has one or wants one.

Considering a classroom audience: Adam's informative speech

Adam first did some research on national behaviors and attitudes toward tattooing:

- *15% of the adult population has a tattoo (Food and Drug Administration), up from 7% in 1936 (Life magazine).*
- *36% of people aged 18–25 and 40% of people aged 26–40 have a tattoo (2006 Pew Research Center poll).*
- *75% of 18–25 year-olds think the increase in people being tattooed has had a positive or no discernible impact (Pew Research Center, 2010).*
- *There are an estimated 15,000 tattoo parlors in the U.S., making roughly $2.3 billion annually (Inc., 2007).*

These statistics confirmed that Adam had chosen an appropriate topic for this group of classmates, most of whom were in the 18–25 age range. He then brainstormed a list of ways to make the relevance of his topic even more apparent and engaging:

> - *Tattooing is very popular in our culture (as per my stats), and most people are at least curious about the practice. Also, in a pre-speech poll, 45% of my classmates claimed to have at least one tattoo.*
> - *I also noticed from working in the industry that colorful tattoos were gaining in popularity, especially among women, and since the class is about 60% women, color may be an attractive angle.*
> - *I think I'll talk about how new expressions in tattooing are possible because of advancements in pigment and dye technologies.*

Adapting the speech to a classroom audience

Adam crafted his speech, tailoring it specifically for his classmates.

Ways to keep my listeners engaged	
	- *Play up the curiosity angle in my introduction. I'll appeal to those who are thinking about a new tattoo, and to those who don't have or want one but could nonetheless appreciate the aesthetics.*
	- *Prepare a slideshow of my most colorful tattoo work.*
	- *Incorporate tattooing jargon, like carving (the process of tattooing), the irons (the machine you do it with), and meat (someone who really likes a particular artist's work), to enhance my credibility, but will define all terms so that no one gets lost.*

Spontaneous audience analysis and interaction during the speech

On the day of the speech, Adam's classmate Cristina came in showing off her new tattoo—a colorful one. Adam seized the opportunity and worked her tattoo in as a fresh example for his presentation. Cristina beamed, as did the audience. They all enjoyed being part of an in-the-moment communication event that was meant just for them.

review questions

1. What is an audience analysis? Why must it be a deliberate step in your speechmaking process?
2. How does a thorough audience analysis help you achieve your speaking goals?
3. What are some strategies for conducting a successful audience analysis?
4. What is the role of a context analysis? What are the three specific contexts to analyze?
5. What are some ways to connect your ideas to your audience?

key terms

audience analysis 96
ethnocentrism 96
demographics 96
attitudinal
  information 103
polled data 104

closed question 106
open-ended question 106
homogeneous
  audience 107
general audience 108
physical context 110

temporal context 110
psychological context 111
rhetorical
  participation 114

exercises

1. With a partner, take turns sharing a recent experience where ethnocentrism created a misunderstanding or misinterpretation of an event or another person. Discuss how you (or the speaker, if it was someone other than you) realized that ethnocentrism was present.
2. Choose a topic in which you have a keen personal interest. A general audience may or may not share your passion about the topic. Brainstorm a list of at least five different ways you could make your ideas relevant to general listeners during a presentation on the topic.
3. Explore alienating, taboo, and offensive topics and speech behaviors and discuss as a class. Research how attitudes toward such topics and behaviors have changed in the United States over the past ten years; twenty years; forty years. Why do you think things have changed? What topics and behaviors are currently acceptable when discussed by certain speakers in certain contexts yet are unacceptable when discussed by other speakers in other contexts? What costs are paid by speakers who alienate and offend? Real-life examples will enrich your discussion.
4. In groups of three to five, assign each person to research a different polling organization to see how it is reporting public opinion on topics such as:
   - The president's approval rating
   - Attitudes toward abortion, gun control, or the death penalty

connect

For online exercises, quizzes, and hands-on activities, see the Chapter 5 assignments in Connect Public Speaking.

- The state of the economy
- Issues affecting older people such as Social Security or prescription drugs
- Attitudes toward same-sex marriage

Did the polling organizations report different findings? If so, discuss or research why. What implications do these different findings have for a public speaker?

5. Review one of your recorded speeches. Find at least five places where you did not make an audience connection but could have. Explain what those connections might have entailed.

6

Determine Your Speech Purpose, Topic, and Thesis

LEARNING OBJECTIVES

1 List the circumstances in which people find themselves speaking in public.

2 Articulate the difference between informative, persuasive, and special-occasion speaking.

3 Explain the link between a well-chosen topic and a successful listener-centered speech.

4 Describe the role of the thesis statement.

chapter preview

6A **Know Why You're Speaking**

6B **Communicate in Public for a Reason**

6C **Select Your Topic**

6D **Move from Topic to Thesis Statement**

Review Questions
Key Terms
Exercises

121

Your choice of topic can make or break your speech. Your passion for and knowledge of well-chosen subject matter make a speech more listener-centered because ultimately they determine how you communicate about the topic and, in turn, how your listeners attend to, respond to, and interact with your ideas. This chapter introduces the three major speech purposes—to inform, to persuade, and to mark a special occasion. It then examines the importance of choosing a relevant topic that is mutually beneficial to you and your audience. Finally, it introduces the thesis statement—the central idea of your presentation.

6A   Know Why You're Speaking

Why are you speaking? Answering that question helps you narrow your focus and begin your speech preparation in the right frame of mind. Your choice of **topic,** the subject matter you discuss, often depends on whether you're being asked to speak, being required to speak, or offering to speak.

1. Being asked to speak

You may be asked to speak by a boss, a group leader, or a host of an outside organization. The person making the request typically tells you the general purpose of the gathering and provides specific or general parameters for your topic. In the workplace, in some cases, your boss may make a specific request, and in others, his or her request may be general:

- **Specific workplace request:** Prepare a presentation on how your team met last year's sales goals.

- **General workplace request:** Choose a topic for the bimonthly training session.

Either way, if you agree to the request, you must abide by the constraints and choose a topic that helps the other person—in this case, your boss—meet his or her goals.

2. Being required to speak

On occasion, you may be required to speak, whether at work, at school, or in your community. Some classroom assignment topics will be specified; others will allow you more leeway. Employees in all fields are often required to speak, as are community members.

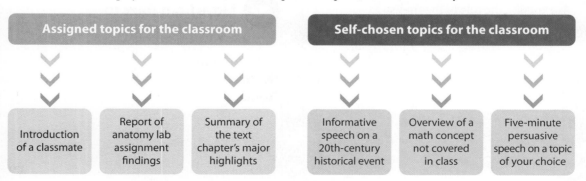

Assigned topics for the classroom			Self-chosen topics for the classroom		
Introduction of a classmate	Report of anatomy lab assignment findings	Summary of the text chapter's major highlights	Informative speech on a 20th-century historical event	Overview of a math concept not covered in class	Five-minute persuasive speech on a topic of your choice

On-the-job required speeches

- Project managers introduce new products.
- Public-safety officers inform the public about security policies.
- Salespeople make client presentations.

SPEAK
Responsibly

Sometimes We're Assigned a Topic

Being assigned a topic often doesn't initially sound appealing, but it helps to keep a positive attitude. Prescribed assignments are designed for a reason—to help you meet academic goals or a work or community organization's aims. In most instances you'll find the topic intriguing once you dig into it. If not, just remember that adult life has compulsory aspects and these presentation experiences can provide as much growth as the things we choose freely. The best way to engage with a required topic that doesn't compel you is to reflect on what you can learn from the experience.

- Will it allow you to work outside your comfort zone?
- Can it introduce you to intriguing people or useful ideas?

Required presentations in the community

- School boards present annual budgets to parents.
- Neighborhood volunteers describe a fund-raiser to local businesses.
- Club officers train members for a creek clean-up day.

3. Offering to speak

Finally, many people *choose* to speak, as evidenced by the prevalence of different public speaking forums—community and campus lectures, as well as idea conferences like the Aspen Festival of Ideas or TED (Technology, Entertainment, and Design) Conferences. Those who offer to speak often relish the opportunity to choose topics that reflect their passions and then present those ideas in a public venue.

6B Communicate in Public for a Reason

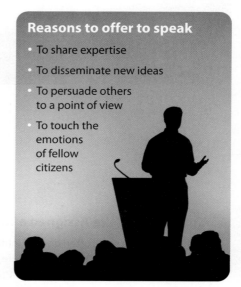

Reasons to offer to speak

- To share expertise
- To disseminate new ideas
- To persuade others to a point of view
- To touch the emotions of fellow citizens

Your topic selection and subsequent speech preparation are easier when you know the reason for your presentation. There are three major purposes for public communication—to inform, to persuade, and to mark a special occasion. Chapters 15 through 18 look at each of these general purposes in greater detail. Here is a quick overview.

1. Speaking to inform

Speeches to inform help your audience understand new or useful ideas from the world around them. Informative topics examine objects, events, processes, concepts, and issues that broaden listeners' intellectual horizons.

2. Speaking to persuade

Speeches to persuade aim to create, change, or reinforce the thinking or actions of others. Persuasive topics run the gamut from the accepted to the controversial and are based on questions of fact, value, or policy.

3. Speaking to mark a special occasion

Speeches to mark special occasions celebrate important people or places, honor memorable events, or share humorous ideas. People at ceremonies or rituals often speak to evoke feelings, strengthen bonds, or create memories.

Sometimes it's difficult to determine a single purpose for a speech. A persuasive speech often has informative sections. Likewise, to get and keep your audience's attention on an informative topic, you may first need to persuade them that it's relevant and important. Even a special-occasion speech, such as a tribute, may persuade listeners to think of someone in a new way.

connect

For sample student speeches—speeches of introduction, as well as informative, persuasive, and special-occasion speeches—see the Library tab in Connect Public Speaking.

Sample informative speeches

- The process of admission into the police academy
- Current meat cloning research
- How to read a sonogram
- Nutritional benefits of duck eggs

Sample persuasive speeches

- All Google searches must be free of government influence.
- Genetically engineered potatoes should be funded with tax dollars.
- Breastfeeding is better for infants than is formula.
- NASCAR's Jimmie Johnson is America's most influential athlete.

Sample special-occasion speeches

- Paying tribute to your coach upon her retirement
- Accepting a scholarship award
- Inspiring kids with physical disabilities
- Commemorating Veterans Day

Still, imagining a primary outcome for your speech helps you make listener-centered choices about how to get there.

6C Select Your Topic

1. Where to find your topic

We live in a unique time. Technology allows us to do and know more than any previous generation. We can fly to the other side of the planet within 24 hours. We can also find the world literally and instantly at our fingertips by turning to technology or opening a book or magazine. Despite this incredible access to ideas, some speakers still complain that they have nothing to talk about. The truth is, topics surround you.

Look inside yourself: You already know a lot

Just as writers are encouraged to write about what they know, speakers should speak about what they know. You know things. You have not made it this far in life without picking up a thing or two. You have had experiences, travels, interactions, education, and training. You think about things. You have talents. This is not to say you know all there is to know about any topic, but you at least know something—and additional research is easier to do than ever before. For now, however, your first task is reflecting on ideas for topic selection. *You* are an excellent resource for speech topics. Don't underestimate yourself.

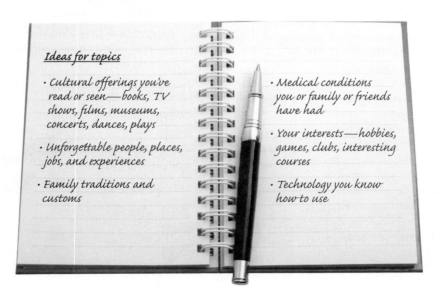

Ideas for topics

- Cultural offerings you've read or seen—books, TV shows, films, museums, concerts, dances, plays
- Unforgettable people, places, jobs, and experiences
- Family traditions and customs
- Medical conditions you or family or friends have had
- Your interests—hobbies, games, clubs, interesting courses
- Technology you know how to use

Consider topics you want to know more about

Many people find an upcoming speech the perfect opportunity to delve into a topic that has long interested them. Perhaps you've been meaning to learn more about type 2 diabetes, the history of nuclear energy, or the differences between the Sunni and Shiite branches of Islam. Students often appreciate an assignment that "forces" them to finally look into topics of interest. Many speakers also report a newfound interest in and enthusiasm about their topic once their research is under way. This awakening has led some students to start blogs, take classes they had not previously considered, get involved in their communities, and even change majors.

Talk to others

Other people in your life are likely resources for topics. Through your interactions with them, you are exposed to things they know, do, and have experienced. One student found stimulating topics by going back to talk with her high school biology teacher, a valued instructor who had played a significant role in her intellectual development. Other students have gone to grandparents, mentors, coaches, community leaders, neighbors, and friends. Not only are other people helpful in choosing a topic, but speakers find their enthusiasm increases when a topic is "attached" to someone they love, admire, or respect. Learning more about that topic is a way to strengthen your bonds with that person. Use the same list of topic sources found on page 126 (in the "Look inside yourself" section) to get your conversation started.

Professional contacts are also helpful with topic selection. It's astounding what reference librarians know and have access to. Talk to a photographer, a firefighter, a poet, an electrician, a physical therapist, a journalist, a helicopter mechanic, a judge, or an international aid worker. These people have access to worlds beyond your boundaries and are usually happy to share what they know.

Browse

Those who take the time to browse find thousands of topics waiting to be discovered. Sometimes, an idea will come from reflecting on something familiar. Fascinating speeches have been given on the golf ball, deer antlers, and platform shoes. Other times, venturing into unknown territory can bring an unexpected idea to light. Even if you're not a car buff, pick up a car magazine. You might be amazed at what's happened in the world of cars while you weren't paying attention—engines are more efficient and powerful, new designs are on the horizon, and alternative fuels are being incorporated. Here are some ideas for browsing:

- Check out something you usually skip or have never looked at—a TV channel, a newspaper section, a magazine, someone's Twitter feed.
- Scan breaking stories through online portals (e.g., Yahoo! News, BBC News Android).
- Type a word into a search engine and see what comes up.

- Look at photos for reminders of your past—experiences, places, people.
- List everything you touch in a given day, and reflect on these objects' histories and purposes.

Use online resources

The web offers many sites for topic browsing and selection. Below are a handful of helpful starting places, some geared toward factual information, others better for new perspectives or humorous examples. Each example includes keyword search terms to locate the corresponding website.

- **The U.S. National Library of Medicine and the National Institutes of Health**—health-related topics. (Keywords: nih health topics)

- **Government Information by Topic for Citizens**—topics relating to government information and services. (Keywords: government information topics)

- **Library of Congress American Memory project**—U.S. historical events, people, places, and ideas. (Keywords: American memory browse)

- **ScienceDaily**—topics in science, health, and computers. (Keywords: science daily news)

- **Newseum**—the front pages of newspapers across the world, from Melbourne's *The Age* to Beirut's *The Daily Star*. (Keywords: newseum today's front pages)

- **News of the Weird**—media stories of strange and wacky events (e.g., a judge's ruling on mooning one's neighbors). (Keywords: news of the weird archives)

Brainstorm

Brainstorming is a technique for generating ideas. A *quantity* of ideas is your goal; you evaluate their *quality* only after you've generated as many as you can.

Once you've generated as many ideas as possible, go back and begin the evaluation process. Keep your specific audience and occasion in mind as you do.

Use a mind map

One particularly effective brainstorming method is called a web or **mind map** (see Figure 6.1, p. 130). Mind maps are visual representations of how ideas connect to each other. It's easy to do one yourself. Begin by choosing a word, writing it in the middle of a piece of paper, and circling it. Draw lines radiating from the circle, and for each line, make an association with your central word. Take one of these new ideas and draw lines out from it. Begin brainstorming through association again. Experiment with using different colors for different categories of ideas on the same mind map. Keep repeating this process until you've filled the paper, and you should have a significant number of ideas. If you prefer to mind-map in digital format, use free software programs like FreeMind, bubbl.us, or MindMeister.

Brainstorming session tips

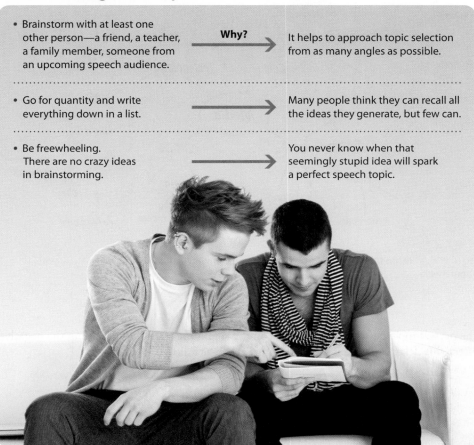

- Brainstorm with at least one other person—a friend, a teacher, a family member, someone from an upcoming speech audience.

Why? → It helps to approach topic selection from as many angles as possible.

- Go for quantity and write everything down in a list.

→ Many people think they can recall all the ideas they generate, but few can.

- Be freewheeling. There are no crazy ideas in brainstorming.

→ You never know when that seemingly stupid idea will spark a perfect speech topic.

2. Choose your topic early

Speakers fail to choose a topic early enough for two major reasons. First, many people—especially college students—are skilled in the arts of procrastination and avoidance behavior. Innumerable rooms have been cleaned, video games played, and ringtones downloaded—all in the name of postponing the inevitable. Second, some speakers have trouble choosing from the multitude of available topics. So many things interest these people that they feel paralyzed when faced with choosing just one. They wait and wait, hoping for yet a better topic to surface, for their professor to tell them what to do, or, perhaps, to find

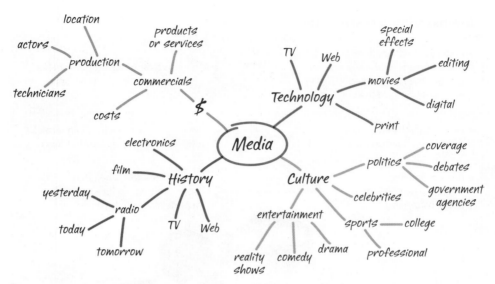

figure **6.1** **Mind Map** Use a mind map when brainstorming your topic. This idea generates ideas about media.

the perfect topic between the cushions on the sofa. One student summed up the negative effect this delay can have on the resulting speech as follows:

> *I am an admitted procrastinator, and as long as I didn't have a topic, I didn't have to begin work on my speech. Finally, it got to the point where I just had to choose some-thing, and because I didn't care about that topic, neither did my audience.*

The upshot: Whatever your tendencies, the sooner you choose your topic, the bet-ter. Students report that a fixed topic frees up energy; they're no longer psychologically stuck for what to do. By removing the focus from yourself and your inability to choose a topic, you can begin to focus on your audience instead. Early topic choice means a greater understanding of your material, and more time for research, organization, and practice. These strengthen your passion for communicating your ideas, and that passion, in turn, appeals to your listeners. Here's what the same procrastinating student quoted above had to say about the benefits of committing early to a topic:

> *The best thing for me—and therefore for my listeners—happened when the instructor required us to publicly announce our topic for the informative speech well before the due date. I found that when I had time to actually dive into my topic, I became so much more interested in it. I actually got hooked on the information and couldn't wait for my speech day. Imagine!*

Early topic selection also allows time for creativity. Speaking is partly a creative process, and as any creative person can tell you, time is creativity's best friend. All speakers need time to think, to let other thoughts filter in and out, and to nurture ideas by letting them incubate, bounce around, and latch onto other ideas. These are creative processes.

3. Choose a topic of general audience interest

While you want to select a topic in which you have an interest to ensure motivation and enthusiasm, you must also choose one that's appropriate and of interest to other people. What do audiences in general like to hear?

Audiences like topics about themselves

Pique your audience's interest by giving them topics relevant to themselves. All people eat and rely on a clean, functioning environment. Most people are concerned about their local communities; their own health and appearance; safety; and sufficient resources, such as money and time. They engage in relationships with family, coworkers, significant others, and fellow citizens. Most seek information to make themselves smarter and more efficient at work. Topics relating to these personal interests tend to have wide appeal.

Audiences like current topics

Listeners are interested in what shapes their world today. Issues regarding global or domestic current events bring all kinds of speakers and listeners together. Campaign seasons are wildly popular for public communication. New inventions, technologies, and theories that help people navigate the ever more complex world are of great interest to most audiences. Scientific theories and discoveries give us a sense of the physical world. Pop culture topics can generate lots of attention. The public seems to have an insatiable appetite for learning about people in the news, from Lady Gaga to Michelle Obama.

Audiences like historic or future-related topics

Topics grounded in the past can help listeners connect with people in other cultures, times, and places. A good historical topic may explore changes in economics, politics, war, fashion, or customs. Most listeners are also curious about what life will be like tomorrow. Topics allowing your audience a peek into the homes, cars, computers, doctor's offices, trends, and travels of the future have wide appeal. Futurists, people who study trends to predict the world of tomorrow, usually draw large crowds of curious listeners.

Audiences like topics that satisfy their curiosity

Most people are naturally curious about topics that answer questions about the nature or roots of things: What are the origins of certain words, customs, belief systems, or ideologies? How do successful relationships actually work? Why is a "time-out" an effective disciplinary tactic? Why is Venus the first visible "star" at night? How and why do consumer habits differ regionally? Why are there more U.S. women getting college degrees than men?

4. Choose a meaningful topic

Because audience members give time and listening energy during a public presentation, they deserve a meaningful experience in return. The definition of *meaningful* depends on the audience and the occasion, but overall, your speech should make an impact on the listeners. It may teach audience members something new and useful, or it may inspire them to action. It may encourage them to consider a new viewpoint, or it may touch their feelings. It may allow them to take the world or themselves more or less seriously.

Show respect for your audience's intelligence and listening time by avoiding stale topics. Most audience members have heard and read a lot about steroids, marijuana, the death penalty, abortion, and anorexia. You don't want them to tune you out before you have even begun. You, too, are probably tired of these topics—often known as "high school topics"—and may have trouble generating your own interest and enthusiasm. If you must choose or are assigned an overdone topic, give it a new and relevant take.

Stale	New Take
Rising steroid use in high school athletes	The role of doctors accused of giving performance enhancers to pro athletes
Marijuana: gateway drug?	Relationship between state medical marijuana laws and federal drug laws
The rights or wrongs of abortion	Political pressure to satisfy party views on abortion

SPEAK
Responsibly

So, What Do *You* Think?

Say you come across this question: "What kind of thinker are you?" The options are:

a. I'm intellectually curious and willing to work at satisfying my curiosity.
b. I mainly look to be entertained or to have information served up to me in easy-to-access-and-digest packages.
c. I'm somewhere in the middle of the first two.

Whatever your answer, it's an intriguing question for public speakers because in order to have something to say, we need to have ideas to share.

- So, what kind of thinker are you? What types of information do you take in to satisfy that style of thinking?
- Are you satisfied with your current "thinking" status, or would you like to change?
- What connections to public speaking are there from your answers?

6D Move from Topic to Thesis Statement

Once you've selected your topic, you need to decide *how* to talk about it to your particular audience. In other words, you need a **thesis**—one main idea to which everything else in your presentation connects.

Sometimes known as the central idea, purpose statement, or core idea, the thesis is usually offered somewhere in the introduction of the speech and lets the audience know exactly what point you are trying to make and how you intend to make it.

1. A true thesis versus a false thesis

Jacqui, a college sophomore, describes a common point of confusion about the concept of the thesis statement:

> *I always thought a speaker talked "about" a topic and that a thesis was the sentence that told what that topic would be, such as "My speech will be about Thailand." I now understand that the thesis is so much more. The thesis statement actually tells the audience how the topic will be discussed in a narrower way.*

Jacqui is right—every speech should have a thesis, but you have probably heard one that did not. Don't confuse the thesis statement with the topic; ineffective speeches may have a topic (subject matter) but no thesis statement. No matter how enthusiastic a speaker is or how interesting the details of the speech are, when you explore a topic from several random angles yet leave listeners with no single coherent new perception of their world, you have employed a **false thesis:**

> **False Thesis:** *My speech will be about date rape.*
>
> *I'll first discuss victims of date rape, then look at how date rape occurs, and, finally, talk about some prevention measures you can take.*

In the example above, it sounds like there's a central plan (or thesis), but there's not. The "thesis" is false. How can you tell? Because the "main points" could just as easily be other random ideas.

> **False Thesis, Version 2:** *My speech will be about date rape.*
>
> *I'll first discuss the history of date rape as a college problem, then look at some common date-rape drugs, and, finally, talk about penalties paid by those convicted of date rape.*

If there were a **true thesis**, there would be one central idea and the main points would be inevitable and not easily substitutable. Here's how you might revise the "date rape" topic to contain a true thesis:

Sentence 1 introduces topic

Sentence 2 shows how topic will be discussed. But these are random directions disguised as main points, so the "thesis" is false.

Topic

Thesis is "false" because main points can be easily swapped out for others.

Topic narrowed
to one idea.

Topic

True Thesis: *College campuses across the United States are using a variety of unique strategies to combat the problem of date rape.*

A speaker cannot address everything about a topic in one speech. Date rape among nonstudent populations, drugs used in date rapes, and what happens to those convicted of date rape are important topics, but are not the focus of *this* presentation. A good speech is one that does not attempt too much. Instead, it makes one point and makes it well. This focus is what enables audience members to leave this speech perceiving their world in one new way—college campuses are addressing the issue of date rape through multiple strategies. The speaker can provide many kinds of interesting details in the body of the speech, but those details are discussed and organized within the chosen main points, which are the strategies campuses are using.

Table 6.1 provides more examples of a true thesis that could support the given topic. You'll see how the main supporting points stem naturally from the thesis. Main supporting points are discussed in detail in Chapter 9.

2. Other thesis considerations

Phrase the thesis as a declarative statement

A thesis statement is exactly that—a statement. It's a complete sentence that contains a noun and a verb that form an idea. The thesis is not a question or a phrase.

connect

For a sample student video on stating the thesis in an actual speech, see the online student speech techniques video clip "Stating the Thesis."

table **6.1** True Thesis Statements

Topic	True thesis	Focused main supporting points, not easily substituted
Richard Wright	*Richard Wright's childhood experiences are evident in his later literary themes.*	Those **childhood experiences** include racial segregation and the violence he witnessed.
Adolescent depression	*There are several effective treatments for depression among teenage girls.*	The **treatments** include serotonin reuptake inhibitors and psychotherapy.
Mythology	*While details of their stories differ, all mythic heroes follow the same stages in their quest.*	The **stages** include selection from the general populace, the fulfillment of the quest, and the return as a hero.
Palestine	*There are numerous factions battling for political control of Palestine.*	The most powerful **factions** include Hamas, Fatah, and the PFLP (Popular Front for the Liberation of Palestine).

Incorrect (question):	What constitutes an orangutan's diet?
Incorrect (phrase):	The orangutan's diet.
Correct (declarative statement):	The components of an orangutan's diet reflect its status as an opportunistic forager.

What words and phrasing would you use to communicate this central idea to your audience?

Less is more

A successful thesis does not try to do too much—it does not, for example, aim to solve all the United States' domestic problems or relay everything about taxidermy. Less is more when it comes to communicating ideas to an audience. It's fine, for example, to teach your audience just about the material composition of a baseball. You don't need to also pay homage to Babe Ruth, inform people about the history of the All-Star game, or convince listeners that the legendary curse on the Chicago Cubs will come to an end someday. One idea, fully developed, is preferable to a hodgepodge of undeveloped ideas of equal "importance." Save those other ideas for another speech. Your presentation is an opportunity to make a point, not to show how much you know by engaging in a data dump.

A good thesis helps you focus on your audience, not yourself

The confidence gained by knowing what you are talking about and where you are going with it allows you to expend your energies on your audience instead of on yourself. Terese, a college junior, tells it from her point of view:

> *The benefits of having a great thesis are that it frees me to allow my personal style to emerge, and it enables me to connect with my audience so much more effectively. The speech is no longer about me wading desperately through a haze of details. I can now confidently stand on a firm platform of a single idea and look at and really communicate with my audience.*

Listeners appreciate a meaningful thesis

Audience members come to your presentation hoping to make good use of their time. They can get frustrated and resentful when they have to sit through meandering and unrelated thoughts. On the other hand, a great thesis, well developed in the body of the speech, makes them glad they have come and grateful for the time and energy you put into broadening their horizons.

create
converse
connect

Phrasing Your Thesis in Your Own Words

You know that the thesis needs to be phrased as a full declarative statement, but what will your thesis sound like in your actual speech? Returning to the example about the orangutan's diet, we see that on paper, the thesis may read:

The components of an orangutan's diet reflect its status as an opportunistic forager.

- But what would that thesis sound like if YOU said it?
- As long as the central idea is conveyed, feel free to use word choice and phrasing that are more authentic to who you are.
- Do any of the declarative statements in Figure 6.2 sound more comfortable?

figure **6.2** **Declarative Statements**

Topic Selection and Thesis Creation in Action
A Student's Process

Ian Kotko's next assignment in his public speaking class was a five-minute informative speech about an object.

Choosing his topic

Topic selection was Ian's first task. So many objects interested him; he had trouble narrowing it down to just one. He decided to make a quick list of listener-centered criteria his topic would have to meet:

Ian then spent the next few days being especially aware of the things around him—in his room, on campus, at the retail shop where he worked—and while many objects caught his attention, none were getting him excited and meeting his criteria.

About a week before his presentation, Ian's speech topic "appeared" to him during the course of doing research for another class. It was St. Patrick's Day, and Google was displaying yet another of their doodles—the artistic versions of the Google logo that appear frequently to celebrate holidays and to commemorate anniversaries and birthdays of famous scientists and artists. Ian always smiled when a doodle appeared, and would often click on the doodle to learn more about what or whom the doodle was honoring, but he didn't know much about the doodle's history or its behind-the-scenes operations. He guessed his classmates were in a similar position.

Moving from topic to thesis statement

Now that he had a topic, Ian knew that he needed a thesis so that his research, and later, his actual presentation would have a coherent point and focus. His first attempt, however, turned out to be an overly general false thesis.

Ian was able to identify his first-draft thesis as "false" by asking himself whether the two main points could be easily exchanged for others; the answer was "yes," and he realized that no matter how many cool and interesting anecdotes he was amassing through his research on Google doodle history, if he wasn't making a clear point about his topic, his speech would fall flat. He started doing preliminary research and, in doing so, realized that what really intrigued him is how Google was using a seemingly small, fun, and simple design element to reflect its values as a company.

> *Thesis Draft #1:* My speech is about the Google doodles, the adapted re-designed versions of the Google logo that sometimes show up on the home page on holidays and special occasions.
> *Main Points Draft #1:* I'll first discuss the origin and history of Google doodles and then present some examples of the most popular ones since the company's founding.

Topic

Thesis is "false" because the main points can be easily substituted for others. Essentially, this is an "about" speech.

Topic

First purpose

> *Thesis Draft #2:* Google doodles, the re-designs of the Google logo that mark holidays and other cultural celebrations and milestones, have evolved in purpose.
> *Main Points Draft #2:* The doodles started as a spontaneous, fun stand-alone project to invigorate the home page yet are now part of a planned initiative that reflects the company's brand, personality, mission, and its love for innovation.

Revised thesis now reflects one focused idea.

Second purpose

Once Ian found his focus, his research process had direction, and his speech went well. His list of audience-centered criteria had been especially helpful, and by starting early, he had given himself plenty of time to let topic selection happen in a way that felt almost organic. Ian's personal interest in the topic was genuine, and it fueled his desire to learn more about it and then craft a message that would appeal to an interested and enthusiastic audience.

review questions

1. What are the circumstances in which you'd find yourself speaking in front of others?
2. What are three major reasons for public communication? What are the differences between these three types of speeches?
3. How does a well-chosen topic help lead to a listener-centered speech?
4. What is the purpose of a thesis statement?

key terms

topic 122
speeches to inform 125
speeches to persuade 125

speeches to mark special
   occasions 125
brainstorming 128
mind map 128

thesis 133
false thesis 133
true thesis 133

exercises

connect

For online exercises, quizzes, and hands-on activities, including TED Talks and video activities, see the Chapter 6 assignments in Connect Public Speaking.

1. With a partner in class, take turns sharing your individual creative processes. Where, when, and how do your best ideas come to you? Can you easily describe your creative process to someone else (and to yourself)?

2. In a small group, brainstorm at least ten topics under each of the following categories. After brainstorming, pick the top two in each category that your group would like to hear a presentation on.

   • Domestic and international current events
   • Societal trends
   • People in the news
   • Medicine and technology
   • Local or state issues of concern or interest
   • Business and industry

3. As a class, generate a list of topics that you all consider stale and overdone. Break into small groups, and have each group choose one of the topics. Have each member of the group go home and research at least one new take on the topic. During the next class period, compile the individual findings, and then have all groups report.

4. With a partner in class, turn each of the following false theses into a true thesis.

   • This morning, we'll be focusing on the city of Washington, DC. You'll understand why it was chosen as our nation's capital, learn about its many famous monuments, and be inspired to go there on your next vacation.
   • I'll be speaking today about social-networking sites. We'll focus first on Facebook; we'll then look at some of the dangers for young kids using these sites; and finally, we'll look at how companies are using these sites to increase business.

7

Incorporate Research

LEARNING OBJECTIVES

1 Explain the mind-set and skills you need before beginning any research project.

2 List the many sources available for research.

3 Evaluate the credibility of any research source you use.

4 Convey how to cite your research sources using the oral style.

chapter preview

7A **Get Ready to Do Your Research**

7B **Make Use of the Breadth of Sources Available for Research**

7C **Evaluate Your Sources to Ensure Your Credibility**

7D **Cite Sources for Listener Comprehension**

Review Questions
Key Terms
Exercises

Although each of us has an impressive storehouse of knowledge and experience, it's impossible to know everything. Your informative, persuasive, and special-occasion presentations all benefit from looking beyond the borders of your own world. Information garnered from good research makes your presentation more listener-centered because it increases your understanding of your topic, and once you become better informed, you can better "own" and communicate the material clearly and confidently. Using credible research sources also increases the confidence your listeners have in your ideas because it reveals that you thoroughly investigated your topic, which enhances your credibility, and it adds specific support and evidence for the points you are making. This chapter provides tips for conducting research, examines various research sources, discusses recommended ways to evaluate and cite your researched material, and underscores the need for information literacy.

7A Get Ready to Do Your Research

Technology, especially the web, has made "looking things up" an almost automatic process. When you want to know what year *Wedding Crashers* was released or who will be teaching a certain course next term, you look it up. The easy availability of almost unlimited information has turned us all into everyday researchers; not so long ago, *google* wasn't a verb synonymous with online searching, but now that usage is familiar to nearly everyone.

Speech-related research, however, needs to go beyond everyday research skills. The good news is that you may possess several research skills—and perhaps some advanced ones—already. Whatever your level of experience, before beginning any research, there is a beneficial mind-set to adopt and some general tips to follow:

1. The research mind-set

It may sound obvious, but the best place to start is with your internal thinking and attitudes about research. To expend the effort in the most effective ways, and take full advantage of what good research can add to your speech, you first need to understand its value.

Believe in the power of good research

Some people look upon research as a necessary chore that has no inherent benefit. *My instructor said I have to use three sources for this speech.* Sound familiar? What these people are missing is how those three required sources, when chosen with purpose and care, are strengthening their public messages. In describing how he came to value research, one student, Jesse, noted what writers, speakers, and thinkers of all kinds know—that good research adds welcomed credibility and authority to their voices and ideas:

> *I am not going to lie and say I love research. However, speechmaking, in its own strange way, actually motivated me to go out and look at the greater world around me. I wanted to be perceived as a credible speaker, and I knew I needed some additional research to enhance what I already knew. I didn't want to run out of things to say and end up giving a relatively empty speech.*

Four goals of research

- Define a topic and identify multiple viewpoints.
- Understand the language used in the topic.
- Identify your speech's context.
- Search for, find, and evaluate relevant, credible sources.

The good news is that thanks to the web, the increasing availability of wireless and other fast, inexpensive web connections, and faster and more effective online search portals, locating these sources has never been easier. So the best place to start your research journey is by embracing these modern times when the vast world of human knowledge is so easy to access. But you've got work—interesting work—in front of you.

Understand the goals of research

Every speech-related research project has four goals.[1] One aim is to understand the "big picture," figuring out how the topic is defined and the different angles from which people approach it. Additionally, you need to understand the language, terms, and areas of discussion within the scope of the topic. Another goal is to conduct your research within the context of your project. As a student, you're attempting to meet your instructor's expectations, which are not always easy to define. As a workplace or community speaker, you need to keep the organization's mission in mind. Finally, you need to seek out, assess, and secure relevant, credible sources.

Know that the research phase can be frustrating

Research is rarely a straightforward process; in fact, it can be quite chaotic and stressful. You may not know exactly what you're looking for. The seemingly infinite amount of information can be overwhelming, and it's hard at the outset to separate the valuable sources from those that may be interesting but don't serve your speech purpose and points. You may hit a dead end. It's sometimes difficult to determine the quality and credibility of a given source. What you find may contradict what you thought you knew and cause you to rethink your speech purpose and points all over again. You may become fixated on satisfying that nagging desire to find "the perfect source," even if this source doesn't always exist.

These challenges are very real experiences, but they are a natural part of the research process for everyone. You *will* get through them, and the more you deal with the challenges, the better you become at using the guidelines covered in this chapter to find and evaluate effective sources. Once you accept that the research path is not always straight or smooth, you will stay focused on your ultimate goal of preparing something meaningful to say to others. Keep these tips in mind for reducing the potential stress of the research process:

- **A focused thesis makes for focused research.** The more narrowed your thesis (see Chapter 6), the more you'll be able to target the information you need. Remember, a speech needs to communicate one idea well; it needn't go beyond that and achieve herculean proportions.

- **Be open to whatever the research yields.** On occasion, your research can provide a new and better thesis and/or main supporting points than the one you had at the start of your journey for sources. You may come across an exciting and whole new way of looking at your topic that's much better suited for your intended audience.

- **Less can be more if the sources are the right ones.** A few comprehensive sources can be as helpful as multiple minor ones. An instructor or librarian can help you analyze the sources you find.

- **No research is a waste.** Research rarely goes unused. For instance, if your message is persuasive, knowing the opposing arguments can help you strengthen your own argument. Should you find yourself with "extra" research, know that new knowledge is never useless. That new information can come in handy during your question-and-answer session, and you also may save it for a future project.

2. The research tips

Follow these four basic guidelines, each described in greater detail below, to help you avoid the major pitfalls of the research process: start early enough to find your sources and make effective use of them; keep your particular listeners in mind as you research so that your sources result from a listener-centered mind-set; gather more material than you think you need; and create a documentation system to catalog what you find.

Start early

As just mentioned, a lot happens during the research phase, and you'll need time to deal with it. The earlier you start your research, the better you understand the topic and the more time you have to shape your topic, finalize a relevant thesis, and create your supporting points. Some speakers claim that they work best under the pressure of a deadline, but this is often an excuse for procrastination. Simply put, the more time you give yourself to research, the more you're able to create meaningful ideas, absorb your material, and increase your degree of ownership and confidence.

Keep your listeners in mind during research

Because you speak for the sake of your listeners, search for material relevant to what they need to know so that they can better interact with your ideas. Use your audience analysis (see Chapter 5), put yourself in your listeners' place, and ask yourself what *you* would need or want to know if you were an audience member. For example, before researching his assigned informative speech in his business class about what to expect in a pre-employment background check, Robert did a quick oral survey in class to assess classmates' knowledge of the screening process. Satisfied that their knowledge was as superficial as his own, Robert knew he needed to focus on the basics. He chose to begin his research by interviewing a professional in the pre-employment screening industry, assuming that this person knew from experience the typical questions asked by those being screened. The interview provided Robert a clear understanding of the basic information his audience would need. The professional was also helpful in directing him to some additional sources that would enhance his speech even further, saving Robert a lot of research time.

Gather more material than you think you need

While your research should be targeted to your thesis and main supporting points, remember that the greater your storehouse of background knowledge, the greater your chances for effective communication. Speakers report higher levels of confidence when they know a lot more than they end up sharing. Natalie, a second-year college student, shares her experience:

> As a first-generation college student, I am very interested in learning about the many ways—other than earning potential—a college degree is likely to make my adult life different from that of my nondegreed parents. I decided to use this topic for both my ten-page sociology paper and my ten-minute informative talk in speech class. Obviously, I was able to include many more ideas in the paper, but I realized that the amount of information I gathered for it actually ended up changing the whole experience of my presentation assignment. I liked going up there with all that knowledge. Though I had a clear plan for what I wanted to say, I knew I could change things at the last moment if I sensed the audience wanted it or needed it. And the question-and-answer session went really well. I had thought about these ideas so thoroughly that I was able to expand on my answers in unexpected ways.

Create a documentation system

Documenting researched ideas is one of your ethical responsibilities. If you haven't already read about plagiarism on pages 75–80, now is the time to do so. In addition to the ethics-oriented reasons to cite sources correctly, there's a practical reason as well: the flip side to our easy access to information is that if we plagiarize and don't document where the information came from, it's also easy to get caught. An increasing number of colleges and universities are using plagiarism-detection services such as Turnitin.com. You do not want to pay the price of slipping up—no matter how unintentional the plagiarizing. Consequences are often severe, ranging from a failed grade on the project to a failed grade in the course to academic probation to expulsion from school.

The best way to avoid plagiarism of all kinds is to make sure you have a complete record of all the sources you are considering using. When researching, create some sort of documentation system *at the beginning* of your project, and stick with it. You cannot rely on your memory to go back and find sources again later if your initial documentation was disorganized or incomplete.

Consistency in documentation is not only good discipline; it makes creating your bibliography or reference list much easier when you are required or asked to provide one. Additionally, if you ever develop your speech into another academic or professional project, your research notes will give you a great head start.

Whether you use a legal pad, notecards, an online bibliography management system like NoodleBib, RefWorks, or Zotero, or some other method, create a plan to link every

table **7.1** **Key Information Needed to Document Research Sources**

Type of source	Information you'll need to collect	Relevant tips
Web source	• Name of the website • Name of the site host or sponsoring organization (if applicable) • Title of the page • URL, or Internet address, for the particular page and the website's home page • Name of the author, editor, or compiler (if available) • Date published (if available) • Date you accessed the information	• Web links often go "dead," are moved, or link to altered contents over time. Print out the web source material so that you have something to refer to. • Make sure the URL is visible on your printout.
Book	• Title (and subtitle, if applicable) of the work • Name(s) of author(s) or editor(s) • Edition and volume (if applicable) • Page(s) on which the information is found • Date of publication • Publisher information (name, city, state)	• Do an online search of the author's name to check credibility and find related publications that may be useful. • See if the author has related publications that are more current.
Article	• Title of the article and periodical • Name(s) of the author(s) (if available) • Volume and issue (if applicable) • Date of publication • Page(s) on which the information is found	• Bookmark or make a copy of the original article in case you need to refer to it later for quotes or statistics.
Interview	• Name and title of the interviewee • Date and location of the interview	• Record complete contact information in case you need to get in touch with this person again.

speech idea to its source and use it fully and regularly. The citation style you use (MLA, APA, CSE) determines the formatting of the research source for a bibliography. It helps to know the style ahead of time; for academic research projects, the course area usually determines the citation style, but your instructor can confirm the preferred format. In general, however, you will want to keep track of certain key pieces of information for all research sources used, regardless of your particular speech context. Table 7.1 provides a handy reference for commonly used sources.

7B Make Use of the Breadth of Sources Available for Research

Research sources fall under two broad categories. **Primary research** collects data from first-hand sources—experiments, case studies, surveys, observation, and interviews. You may perform primary research yourself—create and conduct an experiment, a case study, survey, observation, or interview—or you may locate another person's primary research among the many sources discussed in this section. **Secondary research** summarizes and synthesizes existing research gathered, collected, or organized from other sources, and is found in print and electronic sources of all kinds.

The almost-instant ease of access from remote locations often makes using the web to locate research the first choice for students. While an impressive amount of quality research can be accessed online, not everything is available on the Internet, and a great deal of what is there is not reliable. Many other sources of research are still absolutely relevant, and your instructor may even require you to use some of them. Let's look at all your source choices, starting with digital information. The next section in the chapter (7C) provides guidelines on assessing the credibility of these sources.

1. Digital information

The Internet offers researchers an extensive array and amount of information. Separating what's useful and credible from what isn't becomes easier when you learn to recognize the basic categories and forms this web-based information can take: websites, search engines, specialized search engines, the invisible web, ask-an-expert sites, virtual libraries, databases, discussion groups, blogs, online reference resources, online journal articles, online newspapers and magazines, and online books.

Websites

Web-based information has become such a common part of our world; most people know what websites are because they use them for information gathering, big and small, every day. We use websites for everything from looking up a movie time to finding a campus building location to buying gifts for family and friends. For researching purposes, however, it's useful to define websites in specific terms: websites are locations on the Internet containing information, visuals, sound, and video on a given topic. Millions of individuals, companies, schools, and organizations—from AAMCO to the Miami Heat to the Zoological Society of Manitoba—own and manage their own websites. Many organizations provide search functions within their own websites, allowing you to quickly navigate their archive of online content. Many websites offer recommended links to other related sites as well, which are good sources of additional research paths. In the expansive online universe, more often than not, a website will be your virtual doorway to online research and sources, including to many of the other categories described below (e.g., ask-an-expert sites, blogs, and online reference resources, newspapers, magazines, and books).

Search engines

A **search engine** is a software program that allows users to access online information about a given topic through a **keyword search,** the act of entering a few topic-related terms to cue the search engine to narrow down the information you're looking for. Google, Yahoo!, and Bing are among the most popular search engines, though Google currently hosts about two-thirds of all web searches in the United States.[2]

Specialized search engines

Most people are familiar with general search engines like Google, but other specialized search options exist to help you find the research you need and want more quickly and efficiently. WebQuest provides a long list of specialized search engines and directories, including those for biographies, military information, federal legislation, and even TV episodes. Find the list by using keywords "specialized search engines webquest."

The invisible web

Not all information available on the web is fully searchable from general search engines like Google. The **invisible web,** or deep web, contains information that general search engines cannot access, including databases, virtual libraries, licensed information, and deliberately excluded pages. CompletePlanet and Infomine are two great places to access the invisible web. Most campus library websites also allow you to access the invisible web. Ask a reference librarian if you need assistance.

SPEAK
Responsibly

Keep Your Internet Research Skills Current

The rapid pace of technological progress makes it essential that you keep your Internet research skills up-to-date. Many college and university library websites provide helpful tutorials on all sorts of topics, including:

Recommended search strategies
Search engines
Subject directories
Meta-search engines
The invisible web
Evaluating web pages
Citing sources (The University of California–Berkeley Library is one such helpful site. Find it by typing *finding information on the Internet Berkeley* into your search engine.)

- What are you doing to stay up-to-date with online research skills?

Ask-an-expert sites

There are innumerable sites where you can post a question on a forum and receive an answer from—theoretically—someone who has expertise in the area, usually within 24 hours. Some sites charge a fee though several are free. Try AllExperts.com, DoctorsLounge.com, Answers.com, or Ask a Mad Scientist. As with all sources, however, you will need to confirm the site's credibility. Going to another site or sites to verify information that they send you is also smart practice.

Virtual libraries

Virtual libraries, or digital libraries, contain much of what you would find in print collections, but allow you to access it in digital format. Some virtual libraries are general (e.g., ibiblio and ipl2), some access international collections (e.g., Digital Library of India), some are discipline-oriented (e.g., arXiv, for scientific papers in math, physics, and astronomy), whereas others are topic specific (e.g., The Complete Works of Charles Darwin). Wikipedia has a relatively complete list of virtual libraries. Find it by searching for "list of virtual library projects" from the Wikipedia home page.

Examples of databases

Major databases for articles
- ProQuest
- LexisNexis Academic
- InfoTrac Newspapers

Academic databases
- JSTOR
- Google Scholar
- InfoTrac OneFile

Specialized Databases*
- WorldCat—catalog of libraries; allows searching of multiple libraries
- ABI/INFORM—business, economics, and management journals
- Scirus—enables searches of science-specific web pages
- CINAHL—Cumulative Index to Nursing and Allied Health Literature
- PubMed—U.S. National Library of Medicine database of biomedical literature citations
- PsycINFO—indexes and summaries of articles and content in psychology, psychiatry, and other similar disciplines

*Often accessible via college libraries

Databases

A **database** is a collection of data on a single topic or a variety of topics; it is organized so that the content can be easily accessed and managed. Databases exist for topics across the spectrum, including newspapers and periodicals, scholarly journals, flowers, genome projects, and U.S. patents. (See Figure 7.1 for an example of a search page from an academic database.) Some databases provide the full texts of articles, reports, and other content, while others provide **abstracts,** a summary of an article or publication.

Discussion groups

A **discussion group** allows Internet users to discuss topics of mutual interest. Discussion groups are good starting points for researching users' attitudes and opinions, and many of them also include topic experts. Because many postings are unverified and virtually anonymous, always go to other research material to enhance or confirm what you learn from a discussion group. Discussion groups exist for just about everything—Abyssinian-cat owners, military-history buffs, panic-disorder sufferers, and all sorts of people in between.

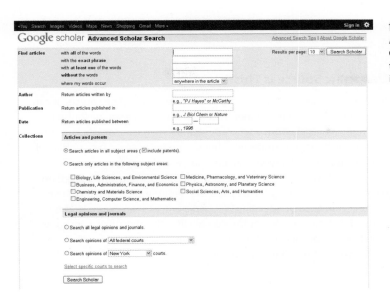

figure **7.1 Google Scholar Advanced Scholar Search Page**
Google Scholar is an academic database that you can use to find research and opinions in a variety of knowledge areas.

Blogs

Blogs contain dated entries of commentary, opinion, or news on a given subject, usually in reverse chronological order. Hosted by one person or a group of contributors, blogs typically combine text, images, videos, and links to other relevant websites. Covering topics ranging from politics to books to local issues, some blogs have become highly influential. Nonetheless, because most are based on personal opinion, you must conduct follow-up research from an unbiased or original source before relying on a blog's "facts." Credible bloggers provide links to their primary sources.

Online reference resources

The web has become a place to find sources once available only in print. Many credible encyclopedias, glossaries, and dictionaries are available digitally, including *Encyclopedia Britannica* and *Merriam-Webster's Online Dictionary*. Wikipedia is a highly popular online encyclopedia, but one that you'll want to use with caution. (See page 162 for more on online reference sources.)

Online journal articles

Journals contain research and opinion relevant to various professionals and specialists. The articles in most journals are **peer-reviewed,** meaning that they have been found acceptable by other experts in the field prior to publication. While a full electronic library of journals is not yet complete, more titles are archived online each year. Some are available free to the public, while others are accessible only through paid subscription. Google Scholar is one database for finding relevant articles, including those in journals that range

SPEAK
Responsibly

What Kind of Electronic Source *Is* This?

Many students report confusion when determining the nature of an online source.[3] It can require some investigation to figure out whether the electronic source you've found is a blog, web page, document, an article from a scholarly journal, magazine article, or some other format. Inspect the source to determine whether it is peer-reviewed fact, unbiased reporting, an open-source forum that anyone can edit, someone's opinion, or something else. Familiarize yourself with these various electronic sources and stay current on indicators that clue you in as to what they are (such as the "[edit]" indicator, which helps identify an open-source forum as such—see any Wikipedia entry for an example; the reverse chronological order of blog entries; or the domain identification, like .com, .gov, .mil, or .org, which you'll read more about later in this chapter). Your reference librarian or instructor can also help you scrutinize a particular source.

from the *International Journal of Tantric Studies* to *RePEc* (Research Papers in Economics). Your campus library is an excellent resource in helping you access online journals; in many instances, campus libraries pay the required subscription rates for the benefit of the campus community.

Online newspapers and magazines

Most newspapers, magazines, and other periodicals publish online as well as in print. It's worth noting that while many titles are simply online versions of print formats, as our technological world evolves, digital and print content from the same title is no longer always matched up. Benefits of the online versions include updated or expanded text-based information unavailable at the time the periodical went to print, and expansive digital-only content like discussion opportunities with authors; additional photographs and video; and interactive graphs, charts, and statistics. Newspapers from the *Los Angeles Times* to the *Marion Record* (of Marion, South Dakota, population under 1,000) and magazines from *The Nation* to *Bird Times* are available online.

Online books

Websites such as Online Books (hosted by the University of Pennsylvania) and Project Gutenberg are bringing full texts to the web, and you can download most of these for free to your computer or e-reader. Until recently, the percentage of books accessible online was pretty small, but with the advent of mobile ebook reading devices like the Kindle, the Nook, and the iPad, as well as smartphones, this digital format is the fastest-growing market in the book publishing industry and more books become available online each year. Commercial sellers like Amazon, Barnes & Noble, Kobo, and iBook all make ebooks available for purchase, usually at lower prices than print books, and books that are in the public domain—everything from the novels of Jane Austen to philosopher Friedrich Nietzsche's *Beyond Good and Evil* to American political revolutionary Thomas Paine's *Common Sense and Other Writings*—are available for free.

2. Librarians

The old stereotype of the stern librarian whose only job is to stack books and shush everyone is long gone. Today's librarians, especially at college and university libraries, are experts at access to information the majority of us probably don't even know exists—from databases to statistics resources to videos to digitized image collections. Some people are hesitant to approach a librarian, who always looks busy doing something else. On the contrary, the reference librarian's job is to help library users build proficient information literacy skills while finding and retrieving relevant, credible information. Phoenix College reference librarian Ann Roselle describes the profession this way:

> *Everyone knows that reference librarians answer questions. However, we can also help you create dynamic class presentations. We can assist you in finding and integrating all kinds of information and multimedia to support your ideas. We will also guide you in the use of proprietary and public information so that you are in compliance with copyright law and fair use.*[4]

Many students report talking with a librarian only as a last resort, after they have found too much or too little in their research efforts. Instead, consider contacting a reference librarian at the start of your research process. Share the details of your assignment with your librarian and let him or her save you a lot of time by pointing you in the right direction and helping make your research relevant, efficient, and ethical. In one recent study, a whopping 90 percent of college students said they were "overwhelmingly satisfied" with the services of their librarian and 80 percent agreed that these professionals add value to their search process.[5] Find your librarian at the reference desk or online through the home page of your library's website.

3. Books and other print resources

Though the Internet is easy to access and seemingly infinite, there is still much research that you can accomplish only through books and other print resources. A great many thinkers and creative people publish printed books on an endless number of subjects each year. Not all magazines, newspapers, and journals have a web presence. Reference sources, including encyclopedias, almanacs, atlases, and dictionaries, can be easier to use in hard-copy form; hard copies can also yield unexpected finds such as additional photos, informative figures, boxes, and graphs that aren't in the electronic record. Finally, many sources written before the information explosion of the web are not yet available online, and some may never be. If necessary, see a reference librarian for help in accessing these print resources.

4. Organizations

Most organizations compile, house, and distribute information to anyone wanting or needing it. Contact the American Lung Association when looking for the latest research on lung disease or lung health, Mothers Against Drunk Driving when looking for information about drunk driving or underage drinking, or Planned Parenthood when seeking information about sexual health.

5. Government data

The U.S. federal government, in addition to state, county, and city governments, is required to collect, manage, and make available to its citizens various types of data. For example, the Census Bureau provides information ranging from payroll data for public employees to state government tax collections to statistics on prisoners in federal correctional facilities. Counties and cities provide information ranging from local ordinances to their operating budgets to vendors with whom they do business. Data from some foreign governments are also available. Much of this information is available on the web. You can also request it in person or in writing through the office of the particular government.

The **Freedom of Information Act,** enacted in 1966, ensures access to federal documents outside the boundaries of nine specific exemptions, including national security and public privacy information. The Electronic Freedom of Information Act, passed in 1996, makes many federal records available online. Requests must be made in writing to access any of these print or electronic records. Know that it can take months to get your request approved, if it will be approved at all.

6. Interviews

The world is full of people who know different things than you do. Some are experts in their fields. Most people, especially when asked by a student, are happy to talk about what they know and believe, and you've got nothing to lose by asking for an interview. Audience members also tend to be impressed when they learn that you've taken the time to do some primary research by conducting an interview. Mentioning your interview with a knowledgeable, credentialed person increases both your own credibility and the reliability of your information.

Interviews—whether conducted face-to-face, by phone, or by e-mail—take time and preparation. (See page 154 for some cautions about the challenges with using other platforms for interviews.) Be sure that you can efficiently find out what you need to know by conducting the interview, and earn the good will of the interviewee by fully preparing yourself ahead of time. Books and websites on proper interviewing etiquette are widely available, but here are some basic guidelines.

Find the right interviewee

People know people who know other people, so it's easier than you may think to find the type of expert you're looking for. Ask those in your social circle—instructors, coworkers, neighbors, professionals, and classmates. Click on the Staff Directory link on an organization's website, or call them and ask the office secretary for recommendations.

Expand interviewee options through social networking

Social networking has also made locating people on the basis of common interests or areas of expertise easier and more efficient, even if you aren't linked directly through shared contacts. LinkedIn, a free networking site for professionals, allows people to search a database of members using a broad range of filters—by job title, location, skill set, company, and so on—and also offers the options of sending a message to potential new contacts. While it's more likely that you'll get a response from an interviewee if you have a mutual connection, in this age of near-instant communication, it's simpler than ever to identify and send an e-mail to someone who seems, in virtual form, to meet your interview criteria, even if that person is a stranger. Again, it never hurts to ask.

Be gracious

Although most people are happy to offer their help, keep in mind that no one is required to give you an interview. Should someone grant you the gift of his or her time, be thankful and courteous at all stages of the process.

Schedule ahead

Don't walk in to someone's office expecting to conduct an interview on the spot. Use the phone or e-mail to set things up in advance—to identify yourself, to find a time that works for both of you, and to tell the interviewee the specific purpose of the interview. For example, tell the tulip expert at the botanical garden that you are doing research for a presentation to your botany class on the recent pest infestation attacking tulip crops in Turkey. These specifics let the interviewee, if necessary, brush up on the topic to prepare for the interview. Also, if you're specific about what you need, even if the person can't help you, he or she can often steer you in the direction of someone who can.

Show up or call on time for the scheduled interview

People are busy. Be prompt, and don't overstay your scheduled interval. Respect your interviewee's time.

Open the interview with some pleasantries

Thank the interviewee for his or her time, and provide a reminder again of who you are and what information you're seeking. Fulfill your ethical obligations by being up front and honest about what you plan to do with the information you gather.

Plan questions ahead

Plan most of your questions ahead of time, but allow room for follow-up questions that may arise during the interview. Do the relevant research before the interview so that you don't waste the interviewee's time with questions whose answers are easily available elsewhere.

Be accurate

You don't want to compromise your credibility with errors. Double-check for correct grammar and spelling in your e-mails or any other printed materials the interviewee may see. Prior to phone and face-to-face interactions, learn how to pronounce any new or difficult words.

Plan a recording strategy

Documenting the interview can end up being a big challenge, and preparation will ensure you don't waste time during the interview itself. Will you take notes as the interviewee talks, or will you use a recording device? Or will you do both? If you decide to take notes, will you do it by hand or on an electronic device? Whatever your inclination, it's important to have a plan in place beforehand—pen and paper, a fully charged laptop or tablet, a recording device, a combination. If anything you're using requires an electric outlet, you'll need to make sure you're meeting in a space that has one. If your equipment requires a battery, make sure it's charged. And always ask for permission ahead of time if you plan to record the interview.

Dress professionally for face-to-face interviews

Look your best on the day of the interview. Don't undermine your credibility by dressing inappropriately or too casually.

Texting usually relies on abbreviated, shorthand language, making it ineffective for in-depth interviews.

Extend your thanks

Send a follow-up note thanking the interviewee for his or her time and information. Whether you send it by e-mail or as handwritten or typed is a judgment call; e-mail thank-yous have become acceptable etiquette and are now, in fact, the most common format, but keep in mind that some people are still traditional or not tech-savvy. Your best bet is to use the interview setup interactions to formulate an impression of how comfortable the interviewee is with e-mail and other computer-mediated communication.

If appropriate, you can use your thank-you note as an opportunity to share the results of your interview. Tell how impressed your listeners were with the collected information, report on any follow-up questions you answered in the question-and-answer segment, or share the grade you got on the assignment.

Be cautious and strategic about using digital platforms for interviews

If scheduling a phone or face-to-face interview isn't possible, conducting an interview by e-mail can be a viable default plan. Once your interview is confirmed, you can send your questions all at once, and the interviewee can send his or her responses by whatever deadline you have agreed on. However, keep in mind that this method can require more follow-up on your part than a phone or face-to-face interview. There's also the risk that your interviewee won't get back to you within the agreed-on time frame. Because it is asynchronous communication, an e-mail interview will also function less like a fluid conversation, and there may be limited opportunity for follow-up. On the plus side, e-mail's written format means that so long as your e-mail defaults to saving your correspondence, the medium itself documents your interview.

Other digital methods, like texting and instant messaging, should be avoided for actual interviews. If your interviewee uses these platforms, it's fine to rely on them for confirming the interview time and place, but, despite their convenience, they are ill-suited for conducting interviews. Texting, by definition, is used by most people as an abbreviated form of communication, and it's unlikely you will be able to explore any topic in depth or get a complex answer from an interviewee in this medium. In addition, most text messaging packages are set up such that a certain number of messages are saved only for a limited period of time and aren't easily exported into other formats.

Similarly, while instant messaging (IMing) is expedient, free, and easily accessible to anyone with web access, in most programs, the IM conversation is viewable only while you are signed in, and messages are automatically deleted as soon as you sign out. Some IM services enable you to save and export the messages, but you would need to follow the manual steps to do that for your specific IM platform. And again, even if you can export the conversation, the medium is going to affect the level of depth of the conversation; keep in mind that the IM format itself is geared toward multitasking—conversing while doing other tasks on the computer—and you want your interview to command the full attentions of both you and the interviewee.

7C Evaluate Your Sources to Ensure Your Credibility

Because your own credibility is directly tied to the quality of the material you present, you must ensure the credibility of your sources. A wide range of source material is available, and the quality and reliability run from the highly credible to the somewhat credible to the entirely incredible. It's your responsibility as the researcher to thoroughly examine each source you use. Your listeners are expecting you to do your homework in order to give them reliable information and well-supported opinions. Make sure your research sources are trustworthy and enhance rather than detract from your integrity and trustworthiness.

1. A need for information literacy

Information literacy is at the top of the list of skills required of today's citizens of an information society. An information-literate person is one who recognizes the need for information and can then "find, understand, evaluate, and use (that) information in various forms . . . for personal, social, or global purposes."[6] Six skills comprise the information-literacy process:[7]

1. *Task definition:* being able to define the problem and identify the information needed.

2. *Information-seeking strategies:* determining all possible sources and selecting the best sources.

3. *Location and access:* locating and finding information within sources.

4. *Use of information:* reading, hearing, or viewing the information and extracting that which is relevant.

5. *Synthesis:* organizing information from multiple sources and presenting it.

6. *Evaluation:* judging the effectiveness of the result and the efficiency of the information-seeking process you used.

These six skills are necessary whatever form your research source takes. Before looking at some of these forms, let's look at a tool you can use to assess the credibility of any research source you may use.

2. A tool for assessing the credibility of a research source

The Meriam Library at Chico State University presents several criteria for analyzing the credibility of *any* research source: currency, relevance, authority, accuracy, and purpose (forming the amusing acronym "CRAAP").[8] Be thorough—use all five criteria before you decide to trust the information in or from the research source, be it in print or digital form. Evaluating sources using the CRAAP test (see Table 7.2) and other guidelines covered in this chapter is like all the other aspects of the speechmaking process. It takes practice, and the more familiar and skilled you become with the steps, the easier it will become.

Let's look at an example that shows the CRAAP test in action on a commercial blog. Zoe, a second-year college student contemplating a health and wellness major, decided to research the rise in the use of plastics as storage in the food and beverage industries for an informative speech assignment. Zoe had some purely factual information from several credible print and web sources, but she wanted a source with personal expertise. Some additional online research led to a brief article on a commercial blog called FoodHealer. The annotated screenshots in Figure 7.2A and Figure 7.2B (pages 158–159) indicate how Zoe was able to assess the article, the blog author, and the FoodHealer site enough to feel comfortable with using it as a source.

Most of what Zoe found about the FoodHealer site was reassuring and favored its credibility, but the lack of any author information was enough of a red flag that Zoe pursued her evaluation further. First she checked the "About This Site."

Most people would have stopped there, rejecting the source because the author's anonymity would be suspect, despite all the other credible indicators. Zoe, however, took her analysis a few steps further. First, she sent a message to Celia the FoodHealer both via the site's Twitter account and to the provided e-mail address, explaining her assignment and research, and asking if she could get additional information to verify the site-provided credentials. She also did some creative online investigating. Because FoodHealer was a

table **7.2** **CRAAP Test for Assessing Research Source Credibility**

Currency	The timeliness of the information	• When was the information published or posted? • Has the information been revised or updated? • Is the information current or out-of-date for your topic? • Are the links functional?*
Relevance	The importance of the information for your needs	• Does the information relate to your topic or answer your question? • Who is the intended audience of this information? • Is the information at an appropriate level (i.e., not too elementary or advanced for your needs)? • Have you looked at a variety of sources before determining this is one you will use?
Authority	The source of the information	• Who is the author, publisher, source, or sponsor? • Are the author's credentials or organizational affiliations given? • What are the author's qualifications to write on the topic? • Does the author have a reputation? • Is there contact information, such as a publisher or e-mail address?
Accuracy	The reliability, truthfulness, and correctness of the informational content	• Where does the information come from? • Is the information supported by evidence? • Has the information been peer-reviewed? • Can you verify the information in another (credible) source or from personal knowledge? • Does the language or tone seem unbiased and free of emotion? • Are there spelling, grammar, or other typographical errors?
Purpose	The reason the information exists	• What is the purpose of the information? to inform? teach? sell? entertain? persuade? • Do the authors/sponsors make their intentions or purpose clear? • Is the information fact? opinion? propaganda? • Does the point of view appear objective and impartial? • Are there political, ideological, cultural, religious, institutional, or personal biases?

*For a web source only

Currency: Blog post date is recent. Links are functional.

Relevance: The title and content reveal the article to be important information for this speech on plastics as a health issue.

Authority: The results based on the article page alone are too vague to be promising; aside from the "About This Site" link, very little is verifiable except that the source is a commercial (.com URL) nutrition-oriented opinion site, author unknown except by the "FoodHealer" business name.

Accuracy: Here the results are positive. The information in the anti-plastic opinion post is consistent with Zoe's already-evaluated sources and contains no visible errors or typos. The post also references an article from a respected U.K. newspaper as a source; that article passes the CRAAP test and contains references to credible primary sources.

Purpose: The tone, content, and references of this article as well as the others Zoe looks at for reference indicate that the site is part informative and part persuasive, but the portions that are opinion are clearly stated as such and seem to be well-supported by objective materials.

figure **7.2A** **FoodHealer Blog, Article Post on Plastics as Packaging**

blog intending to help promote a nutritionist's private practice, chances were good that its author, if legitimate, would list her credentials elsewhere online.

Zoe was thorough and persistent, and in this case, it paid off with a source she could rely on with no doubts. After plugging "Celia" and "FoodHealer" into a basic Google search, Zoe turned up a LinkedIn professional profile page—basically, equivalent to a brief online résumé. The profile information was more complete: it listed the owner of

Authority (revisited): The "About This Site" page answered the previously unanswered questions about the author's credentials. The FoodHealer blogger was an accredited holistic health counselor and nutritional consultant with certifications and degrees from several well-respected institutions. The sole concern was that she gave only her first name on the site.

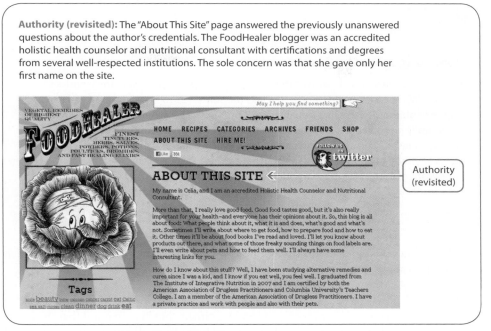

figure **7.2B** **FoodHealer "About This Site" Page**

FoodHealer as Celia Kutcher, a certified and accredited Brooklyn-based health counselor and nutritionist with more than a decade of professional experience in health and nutrition. Fortuitously, Zoe also heard back from Celia herself; not only did that exchange confirm Celia Kutcher as a knowledgeable expert in health and nutrition, it also resulted in an unexpected, follow-up interview that greatly enhanced Zoe's final speech.

Let's next focus our conversation on several research sources where information literacy skills are paramount.

3. Assessing digital information

A recent information-literacy national progress report found that "no matter where students are enrolled, no matter what information resources they may have at their disposal, and no matter how much time they have, the abundance of information technology and the proliferation of digital information resources make conducting research uniquely paradoxical: *Research seems to be far more difficult to conduct in the digital age than it did in previous times.*"[9]

Indeed, as citizens of information societies, we are interfacing with ever-evolving digital resources—and it can be an overwhelming and time-consuming experience. But the greater your degree of information literacy, especially in regard to digital sources, the more efficient your research will be, and ultimately, you'll be in a position of academic, career, and personal advantage.

SPEAK
Responsibly

.com, .org, .gov: The Revealing URL

A website's address, also known as the URL, can be helpful in assessing the website's purpose. While codes in the URL—especially the suffix—are a first indication of a site's degree of objectivity, they are not absolute. Commercial sites and blogs ending in .com are typically not objective. Governmental (.gov), professional (.org), and academic (.edu) sites typically are. The international organization that governs website addresses (ICANN) allows anybody to apply for new suffixes that can include nearly any word or phrase, complicating matters for those wanting to understand the author or source of a particular website. Always verify any information you find on the web with another credible source.

Here are a few digital sources you'll need for your speech-related projects to which you'll want to apply your information-literacy skills.

Websites

Information on many websites is complete and legitimate, but bear in mind that the Internet is a playground for commercial and ideological interests of all kinds; anyone can build a website. Personal knowledge about a site and everyday common sense, while helpful, can only take you so far. The CRAAP test is especially helpful in assessing the credibility of any website you may want to use as a research source. See the "Speak Responsibly" box above for another helpful indicator for evaluating a website.

Search engines

On average, 83 percent of college students begin an information search with a search engine such as Google, Yahoo!, or Bing.[10] Since commercial search engines are such popular tools, you should keep a few things in mind. First, research suggests that some Internet users confuse navigation—how they found a website—with the site's credibility.[11] The fact that a website shows up first on a reliable search engine may have more to do with complex, profit-driven algorithms[12] than with the credibility of the website. Many website owners seeking increased online attention, traffic, and consumer or user activity pay for-profit search engine companies (or hire a professional search engine optimizer) to ensure their website appears high up on any results list. The payment transaction can take various forms—paid placement, contextual advertising, pay-per-click—but the end result is the same: higher placement during a keyword search. These conspicuous placements can be helpful for the everyday research many people do when looking for travel bargains, but we require less biased, commercially focused information when researching for a speech. It's not always easy to figure out which results have been bought. Some results may indicate that they're "sponsored" (i.e., paid advertisements), whereas others may give no clue.

Again, as you read above, be sure to apply all five areas of the CRAAP test (Table 7.2) to any website you're considering for speech-related research.

Library websites are a good alternative to a commercial search engine. A multilevel evaluation process, in which librarians assess the database, the database managers rate the publications, and the publication editors evaluate the articles, ensures highly credible sources. Although a recent survey found college students reporting that commercial search engines trump library websites for speed, convenience, and ease of use, library websites came out on top in terms of trustworthiness and accuracy.[13] The size of your initial yield from a commercial search engine may be bigger, which seems to save time, but the CRAAP tests will often confirm that many of these sources aren't credible.

And don't forget your reference librarians. Isn't it preferable to let an information-literacy professional guide you early in your research process rather than rely on impersonal commercial search engine software? Put another way, unlike a commercial search engine, a librarian isn't directing you to sources with the aim of selling you something (whether it be a product, a service, or an idea).

Wikipedia

If you're like 88 percent of college students,[14] you rely on Wikipedia, a popular online encyclopedia, especially at the beginning of your research process. That's understandable. Students report using Wikipedia because it[15]

- identifies and defines the topic's terms;
- uses clear English;
- provides background and overview (the "big picture") for a topic;
- lists many legitimate citations for sources that can then be located by searching scholarly databases;
- frequently includes pictures, timelines, and charts that help with visual learning;
- has a highly usable interface (highlighted links, relatively short entries); and
- uses an open-source functionality (defined below) that allows for updates and changes that can increase the accuracy of the information.

If these first four points sound familiar, it's because they match most of the research project goals outlined on page 142. Given that, it's no wonder people like Wikipedia.

Wikipedia merits much of its attention, but using it for anything beyond the early brainstorming stages to generate ideas and narrow your topic can be risky. Most significantly, it is an **open-source website (or "wiki"),** meaning that anyone is invited to create or edit most entries. Because millions of Wikipedia pages in many languages are not peer-reviewed or fact-checked, their reliability and credibility as sources for research are not necessarily reliable. While experts administer and control some pages (identified by a lock symbol), people with agendas put a slant on others.

Treat any Wikipedia entry with a critical eye. The bottom line is that, ultimately, you cannot identify or evaluate the "author" of Wikipedia content. The most credible Wikipedia entries provide external links and references that lead you to other resources, sometimes even primary ones—sources and authors, in other words, whose credibility can be confirmed. Bear in mind, however, that content on Wikipedia pages is often copied from other places on the web, and vice versa. This complicates your task of verification through

SPEAK
Responsibly

The Evolving Experiment: Navigating Wikipedia

It's captivating to realize that as an information culture, we are in the middle of a huge and rapidly evolving experiment with open-source sites like Wikipedia. The conversation about Wikipedia's reliability is robust, with intriguing arguments on both sides. The company deserves credit for constantly working to increase the trustworthiness of its pages, and information-literate people pay attention to its many credibility indicators on the pages. While some believe that Wikipedia is already the premier source for many science and popular culture topics,[16] in the future, it may become the primary go-to resource for researchers of all kinds. But for now, and for as long as the reliability of its information and its authors remains in question, the rule of thumb is clear: don't use Wikipedia as your only or major source of information. Most instructors will not accept it as a reference in your bibliography, and citing it during your speech can weaken your credibility with listeners.

- Have you critically asked yourself how, why, and when you use Wikipedia?
- What conversations about Wikipedia are you having in your other courses?

cross-checking as the web makes it as easy to disseminate inaccurate data as correct data. Bad information may be replicated in several, even many, places. Always keep digging to locate the least-filtered sources.

Online journal articles—the open-access question

The open-access movement has created confusion for some researchers seeking and viewing journal articles. While some in the scholarly community believe that their peer-reviewed work should be purchased by those wanting to read it, others—those believing in **open access**—consent to make their intellectual work available for free online.[17] The open-access movement is growing, leading to more scholarly work available for free each year.

Don't confuse the quality of free scholarly journal articles you may find through a commercial search engine like Google with those available only from a library database; they're probably equal. Your reference librarian or instructor can help you with any questions you may have.

Social media

An increasing number of people are using social media like Facebook, Twitter, and LinkedIn. The jury is still out as to social media's role in the gathering and disseminating of research-worthy information, but it is a fascinating potential research source to watch, and signs are emerging that it may someday play a meaningful role. Social media is already being used to report on local events in real time, to track and communicate with subjects in medical research studies,[18] and to survey those within a social network about knowledge, behavior, and opinions. Journalists, academics, business professionals, and others continue to discuss and debate social media's role on a variety of levels. APA and MLA, the organizations responsible for two of the most common academic citation styles for different source materials, are currently creating guidelines for citing social media,[19] but if you refer in a speech to something you saw on a social media site, you should say so *(On February 5, 2011, from the middle of the Egyptian protests in Tahrir Square, activist Wael Ghonim said in a Twitter feed that . . .).*

4. Assessing books

Like digital information, books are not all equal in terms of credibility. Use the CRAAP test to analyze any book you may want to use. Additionally, the University Libraries at the University of North Carolina offer several questions you can ask to determine a book's credibility:[20]

Consider the following questions about the *author* and the *publisher*:

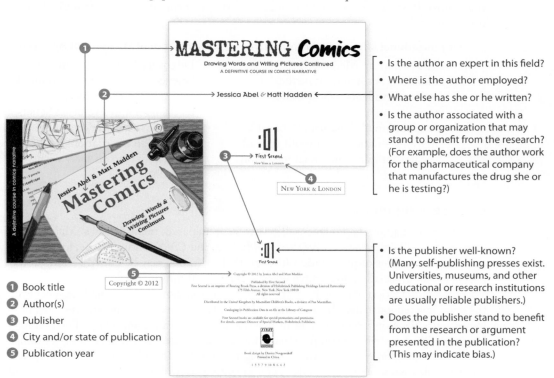

① Book title
② Author(s)
③ Publisher
④ City and/or state of publication
⑤ Publication year

- Is the author an expert in this field?
- Where is the author employed?
- What else has she or he written?
- Is the author associated with a group or organization that may stand to benefit from the research? (For example, does the author work for the pharmaceutical company that manufactures the drug she or he is testing?)

- Is the publisher well-known? (Many self-publishing presses exist. Universities, museums, and other educational or research institutions are usually reliable publishers.)

- Does the publisher stand to benefit from the research or argument presented in the publication? (This may indicate bias.)

figure 7.3 **The Cover, Title Page, and Copyright Page from *Mastering Comics*, a Textbook on Creating Comics** A book's preface, introduction, and "About the author" pages are particularly useful for assessing credibility, and the CRAAP test is as effective in evaluating book content as website material. The provided questions can offer additional help in evaluating a book's credibility.

5. Assessing organizations

Using information from a trusted and well-known organization adds to the credibility of your material. If you incorporate data from an organization that is not well-known, be sure to research its mission thoroughly so that you can explain it to your listeners. Also, keep in mind that many (though not all) organizations are based on a particular ideology and/or have a political agenda. Though their information is usually trustworthy, it may be slanted in ways that support their ideological mission.

The name of an organization is another thing to consider. Some names, such as the Occupational Safety and Health Administration, clearly state the organization's mission and purpose. Other organizations have names that are not as revealing. For example, just what does the Goldwater Institute do? Further investigation reveals it to be a conservative public-policy organization funded by a private foundation and individuals that promotes policies supported by the late Senator Barry Goldwater. This may or may not be useful for your speech purpose, but the lesson is that you need to have a clear sense of the organization's aims. Research any organization before using its printed or online material in your presentation.

Organizational Mission Clear from Name	Organizational Mission Not Apparent
• The American Medical Association—national consortium of medical doctors and students, whose aim is to promote public health • Association of America's Public TV Stations—national nonprofit that advocates for noncommercial television	• Discovery Institute's Center for Science and Culture—a nonprofit organization that advocates the teaching of anti-evolution beliefs • The Industrial Workers of the World—an international union whose aim is to do away with capitalism

6. Assessing media

Numerous media outlets produce well-researched, unbiased, relevant news. Major media organizations like the *Detroit Free Press, CBS News,* and *CNN* continue to be, for the most part, trusted sources of information (though their opinions may be biased). Many newspapers are an especially good source when seeking local information.

The politicization of some forms of the news media, however, has made suspect even the once-revered journalist. It's not uncommon today to see critics (and entertainers) posing as journalists on television and in newspapers, magazines, and blogs. For example, how would you describe the professions of Jon Stewart, Glenn Beck, or Arianna Huffington? Media conglomeration is another thing to consider. In today's media marketplace, fewer people own more media outlets, concentrating control over what we see, hear, and read.[21] The need to please advertisers is another concern.

The Society of Professional Journalists, a professional organization (since 1909) "dedicated to the perpetuation of a free press as the cornerstone of our nation and our liberty," says that true journalists have four ethical obligations, including freedom from

SPEAK
Responsibly

In or Out of Context?

To support a point, people may take quotes, statistics, and other material out of their original context. If you come upon out-of-context research and pass it along to your audience, your own credibility may suffer. When examining a piece of research, ask yourself whether it seems as if there's "more to the story." For example, it may not be fair to call for reduced funding for College X "because of its low graduation rates." More research would tell you that many people enroll at College X to fulfill goals *other* than graduation, such as taking a class for a professional credential or personal fulfillment. Ethical standards require that you understand the context of your researched material to the best of your ability before you present it to listeners.

any interest other than the public's right to know and accountability to readers, listeners, viewers, and each other.[22] Many such journalists work in print, over the airwaves, and online; their information is credible. Your reference librarian or instructor can help you evaluate any media source you may want to use.

7D Cite Sources for Listener Comprehension

It's necessary to follow specific formats when citing research sources in your written work (see Section B in Chapter 10 for details). The conversational style preferred by public speakers, however, allows flexibility in citing sources during a presentation. Whereas a reader may benefit from knowing the complete URL or the volume, issue, date, and page of a certain source, listeners quickly become bogged down by such details. This doesn't mean that you shouldn't cite your research sources in a presentation. You should—always. You just cite them less formally and with more flexibility. Check with your instructor for classroom speaking as he or she may have additional guidelines and/or requirements for verbally citing sources.

1. How to cite verbally

Simplify the citation

Although you must cite some details about the research source, your listeners do not need (nor do they want) every bit of information. Refer to the "Holistic Dental Association website" instead of mentioning the "Holistic Dental Association website found at http://www.holisticdental.org, which I accessed last week on February 27." In your speech on

Take Time to Explain Your Citation

Because listeners hear your reference only once in real time, they must understand it well enough to make sense of it as a credible source on which you are standing. For instance, the *Washington Post, Time* magazine, and WebMD are popular enough that they need no explanation. Other sources need some or a lot of explanation:

- Tell your audience that the Museu Picasso, located in Barcelona, Spain, is dedicated to helping people understand the formative years of the artist Pablo Picasso.
- Explain that the American Association of Swine Veterinarians, based in Perry, Iowa, is an organization dedicated to swine health and production, with strong ties to the pork industry.
- Describe *Mother Jones* as an independent, nonprofit magazine committed to achieving social justice through investigative reporting since 1974.

Never assume that audiences will understand who or what your source is. When in doubt, take the time to fully explain.

Navajo rugs, mention that you got much of your information from "a classic 1997 publication called *A Guide to Navajo Weavings* by Native American art expert Kent McManis." There is no need to cite the publication's title, its subtitle, the name of its other three authors, its publisher, its date of publication, *and* the page on which you found the information. Of course, even though you do not verbalize these details, you must *know* them and have them available. Should an audience member ask for your specific citations after your presentation—and don't assume no one will—you must be able to provide them.

On the other hand, beware also of oversimplifying the citation to the point where it's unidentifiable. It's not enough to say "according to the latest research" or "I read this article last week that said . . ." or "When I googled it, I discovered that . . . ." You must provide *some* specific source information to enhance and maintain your credibility. At the very least, give your audience the name of the website or the name, title, and credentials of the author from a printed source.

Limit the number of citations you mention

Even though you may have used eight sources for your speech, your listeners do not need to hear them all. Mention that you've looked at many sources, but cite only the two or three you relied on the most. Some speakers like to display digital images or show hard copies of their sources (such as a book) while mentioning them. Of course, if someone requires or requests a complete list of all your sources, you must make that available.

Pronounce citation details correctly

Don't undermine your credibility by mispronouncing a citation. Practice to ensure a smooth mention of book titles like *Paradox and Perspicacity* ("pers-pi-KASS-ity"). Practice so that you can refer correctly to the journal titled *Archives of Gastroenterohepatology* ("gas-tro-en-TER-o-hep-a-TALL-ogy") and to names like Krosoczka ("crow-ZAHS-ka").

2. Where in the speech to cite

Speakers have flexibility for choosing when and where to cite their sources. For academic speaking, check with your instructor to see which of the following three options he or she prefers.

Internal citations

The most popular option is similar to what you do when writing a paper—mention the research source as you use it during the presentation. Here's an example, in conversational form, from a speech on global efforts to combat malaria:[23]

> *Mosquito nets are actually one of the oldest and still most effective ways to prevent malaria infection. I read an article in the July 2007 issue of National Geographic called "Bedlam in the Blood," and the author, a journalist named Michael Finkel, notes that the nets—when used correctly—have been shown to cut malaria infection by one-half and child deaths due to malaria by a third.*

Conversational internal citation

Many speakers use this option because it helps distinguish between their own ideas and their borrowed ideas. Some ideas are so important to your message that you must highlight them with their own citations.

Front-loading of your sources

Another option is to front-load your sources, or mention them in the introduction of your speech.

> *I looked at several resources for this presentation. The two that provided the best information were Michael Finkel's "Bedlam in the Blood," from the July 2007 issue of National Geographic, and the website of Malaria No More, a nongovernmental organization based in New York City dedicated to ending malaria. The site has several reports and fact sheets that provided me lots of current information.*

Introductory paragraph relays all sources up front.

If you front-load, you may not choose to mention specific sources within the body of the presentation. However, it's still absolutely necessary for you to know which source connects with which idea. Should an audience member, your instructor, or your supervisor ask about the connection between any idea and its source, it is your ethical responsibility to provide an answer.

connect

For a sample student video that uses and cites research material, see the online student speech techniques video clip "Incorporating Researched Material to Support a Point."

Front-loading is more appropriate for an informative presentation than for other types of speeches. It assures your listeners that you are well prepared with credible sources. At the same time, front-loading can be more listener-friendly as it saves audience members the cumbersome task of processing numerous references, which can start to blend together after a while. Once you've mentioned your sources in the introduction, you can communicate your ideas, and your audience can sit back and interact with those ideas.

Front-loading is less effective for persuasive speeches. During persuasion, the quality and quantity of each of your sources are often tremendous assets in helping you achieve your communication goals. You want to ensure the connection of particular ideas with particular sources. Continue citing internally.

A combination of front-loading and internal citations

A final option is to combine the first two options—front-load some or all of your sources, but make important individual citations during the presentation.

Credible Source Citation in Action *A Student's Process*

Members of the campus Japanese Culture Club frequently gave talks to one another. Eli Van Der Zee, who had a deep fascination of the *katana,* or Japanese sword, offered to speak at next month's meeting. He planned to persuade listeners of the katana's rightful place in history and its current positive reputation among Japanese enthusiasts.

Eli already knew a lot about the katana, but he wanted to use some highly credible sources to convince his listeners to value it like he did. After a few hours of research, he was able to identify three key sources.

While all three sources passed the CRAAP test to Eli's satisfaction, he realized his bigger challenge was that he would have to spend some time explaining the sources to his listeners so they, too, would see them as highly relevant and reliable sources. How could he describe each citation conversationally in a way that each would make sense to his listeners as a credible source? With that question in mind, he brainstormed a plan for how he would introduce them, which combined front-loading with internal citations:

Three main sources for katana speech:
1. *Secrets of the Samurai Sword,* a 2008 film shown on the PBS science TV show *NOVA*
2. *The Connoisseur's Book of Japanese Swords,* a 1998 book by Kokan Nagayama published by Kadansha USA
3. *The Nihonto Message Board,* dedicated to the study of Japanese swords and fittings, http://www.militaria.co.za/nmb/

Katana Speech: Strategies for Verbal Source Citation

1. I'll mention the NOVA film in the introduction. I think most people have heard of NOVA, but just in case, I'll describe it as "a multiple award-winning science television series produced at WGBH in Boston that's aired on PBS in the States and in over 100 other countries."

Source #1: Popular TV show that listeners are familiar with to be verbally referenced in speech introduction

2. My guess is that no one's heard of the Nagayama book, but it contains key information that informs multiple spots in the speech, so I'll need to work hard to make it stand out. I'll refer to it several times throughout the presentation, but the first time I'll introduce it by title and, to emphasize its significance and credibility as a supporting source, I'll explain that it's "a comprehensive and clearly written guide of Japanese swords that's a must-have for true connoisseurs. It was written in 1998 by Kokan Nagayama, a famed Japanese sword polisher, competition judge, and instructor. The book was translated into English by Kenji Mishina, another sword polishing instructor, who's worked at the British Museum and writes frequently about Japanese swords."

Source #2: Obscure source to be verbally referenced in greater detail and in multiple places to emphasize its credibility

3. My final source is the online discussion board. This is such a niche source that I doubt anyone's heard of it, so I'll need to explain why it matters and is useful as a source reference. When I refer to it, I'll tell them that Nihonto is "a highly active online discussion board that's dedicated to the study and preservation of Japanese swords and fittings. It offers links to other websites, clubs and societies, and books. It's used a lot by enthusiasts like myself."

Source #3: Online discussion board source relevance to be explained later in the speech after foundation has been laid with the other two sources

review questions

1. What mind-set is helpful to adopt prior to beginning any research? What skills should you have before starting your research?
2. Other than the web, what are some sources available for researching your speech?
3. Why is it important to assess the credibility of a research source? What is information literacy? Why is it an essential skill for modern researchers?
4. How should sources be cited in your speech? How does this differ from citing sources in written work?

key terms

connect

For online exercises, quizzes, and hands-on activities, see the Chapter 7 assignments in Connect Public Speaking.

exercises

1. Split the class into several small groups, and send each to a different part of your campus library. Have each group find at least three databases, reference materials, or research services they weren't aware of before. Ask a librarian or staff member for more information about what you find. As each group reports its findings to the rest of the class, have someone create a master list of them for everyone to share at the end of the class.

2. As a class, choose a narrowed topic you'd all like to know more about. Assess what most people already know about the topic, and decide on the relevant information you would need to research for a twenty-minute presentation to the class.

3. Choose a topic and find a website you might use for researching it. Evaluate the site according to the CRAAP test on page 157. Share your analysis with your classmates.

4. Watch a speech on video, or attend a speech on campus. Choose one whose title suggests that the speaker has done some research. Analyze the connection between how (or whether) the speaker cites research and the speaker's credibility.

Support Your Ideas

LEARNING OBJECTIVES

1 Apply the general criteria for selecting supporting material for a public speech.

2 Explain why narrative is a popular form of support.

3 Identify and provide examples of objective support.

4 Identify and provide examples of illustrative support.

5 Identify and provide examples of subjective support.

6 Explain the role of testimony as supporting material.

chapter preview

8A Select the Right Form of Support

8B Use Narrative

8C Use Objective Support

8D Use Illustrative Support

8E Use Subjective Support

8F Use Testimony as Support

Review Questions
Key Terms
Exercises

G ood presentations are not filled with aimless talk and generalizations. Listeners expect you to back up your ideas with strong supporting materials. Substantiate your ideas, and bring them to life by incorporating such material as narrative, facts, examples, testimony, and personal experience. By elaborating on your ideas with good support, you reduce your audience's need to make its own inferences (and perhaps misconstrue your intent). This chapter examines different types of supporting materials and provides some considerations to keep in mind when selecting them.

8A Select the Right Form of Support

Supporting your ideas doesn't mean incorporating just any available, random material. Look to the context, the audience, your topic, and your ideas as you decide which supporting materials are relevant and useful. For example, a simple explanation suffices when you're informing classmates about applying feng shui concepts to a living room, but convincing your coworkers to hire Interior Design Firm X for the office renovation project may require supporting recommendations from experts, examples of the firm's work, and bottom-line financial data.

Here are some selection criteria to apply to your forms of support. (Add these to what you learned about evaluating a piece of research, pp. 155–165.) These criteria are applicable to informative, persuasive, and special-occasion presentations.

1. Relevance

Arguably the most important criterion, **relevance** means that your form of support has some sensible or logical connection to the idea you're communicating. During preparation and research, you might come across intriguing examples and fascinating bits of information. But not all will be relevant to your idea. Include supporting material only if it makes a point related to your message. Resist the temptation to add an extraneous idea just because it's interesting to you.

2. Appropriateness

Your choice of supporting materials should complement the audience, topic, and occasion. For example, a final project for an advanced science class requires a great deal of solid support—facts, statistics, descriptions, and explanations—whereas a farewell speech at your favorite teacher's retirement party might include lighthearted anecdotes and admiring, emotion-laden memories from other students. Be sure to consider the appropriateness of your form of support. What supporting material is most likely to help you meet your identified communication goals and to engage your particular audience of listeners?

3. Variety

Back up each idea you communicate with multiple forms of support. Your speech quickly becomes tedious if you rely on only one or two types of support. Add variety to your presentation by including statistics, examples, emotional proof, explanations, and stories.

Before you can choose the appropriate form of support, however, you need to understand the various types—narrative, objective support, illustrative support, subjective support, and testimony.

8B Use Narrative

The use of **narrative,** or story, is a listener-friendly action. Long before the invention of written languages, humans learned, taught, and entertained themselves through narratives. They told stories to explain their origins, the weather, seasons, natural phenomena, and the rhythms of the life cycle. Cultures throughout the world have myths, legends, and folktales that have been passed down through generations, many surviving even today. Stories of heroes and gods are the foundation of many belief systems and the basis for unity and cooperation within societies.

Walter Fisher, professor emeritus at the University of Southern California's Annenberg School of Communication, asserts that people are storytelling animals; we use stories to create memory and make sense of our world. Fisher argues that we are really *Homo narrans,* narrative creatures who "experience and comprehend life as a series of ongoing narratives, as conflicts, characters, beginnings, middles, and ends."[1] His **narrative paradigm** proposes that storytelling is so central to what it means to be human that a story that rings true with listeners' experiences is often more effective than building up rational evidence or constructing a logical argument.[2]

Stories that successfully inform, persuade, or touch the emotions of other people should, according to Fisher, meet two criteria:

- With **narrative coherence** the story hangs together well and makes sense structurally. The characters, scene, and action seem to belong together, important details are present, the story logically compares to similar stories, and the characters act reliably.
- **Narrative fidelity** speaks to how true and human the story appears. Does this story sound like one the listeners might tell about their own lives?

Narratives are popular in modern public speaking; speakers know that listeners are quick to embrace a good story. Indeed, using narrative can go a long way to making your public speeches more engaging. And the conversational style of listener-centered speaking lends itself perfectly to storytelling. Audience members are more likely to find your story coherent and true when you show that you know the story, when you give them genuine eye contact, and when you speak with your own authentic voice.

You probably know from your own experience how well stories work. It's why you most likely enjoy reading novels, watching television, and going to the movies. You've also probably experienced the energy that a good story brings to a public speech. Because people are so used to thinking in narrative patterns, stories are an engaging and efficient way for you to support an idea you're communicating to an audience.

connect

For sample student videos that use narrative, see the online student speech techniques video clip "Using Narrative."

1. Reasons for using narrative

Whether running for class president, presenting to clients, or speaking to fellow parents at the local school meeting, use narratives for several reasons: because they create images that connect with listeners, they evoke images, they instruct and inspire, they entertain, they can humanize a general concept, and they benefit you as a speaker.

Narratives create images that connect with listeners

No matter how far removed your story is from listeners' current reality, it encourages them to interact, creating images from the words you use and bringing in their own experience as they mentally insert themselves in the story.

One audience will never forget the narrative about an escape from Communist Romania. Audience members listened intently as the speaker told about the night he jumped into a river while being chased by guards. He related how he struggled to swim against the current and finally made his way to the riverbanks of Yugoslavia and from there traveled by land to Hungary, Austria, Germany, and finally the United States. The listeners that day created personal images in their minds of a frightened young man literally swimming for his life in the darkness. They wondered what it would be like to face such circumstances and whether they would have had the strength and courage to do as he did.

The stories you tell need not be as dramatic as this one, but the point is the same: narratives help synthesize the complexities of life while inviting your audience to connect to your message through the creation of images.

Narratives evoke emotions

Good stories have strong emotional content, including the universal feelings of hope, fear, love, envy, or joy. Stories infused with emotion can grip an audience, keeping them engaged with the speaker, establishing a mood, and helping them remember your message long afterward. Evoking emotion is a useful strategy during all types of speeches. For example, people with something to sell (a product, a service, a belief, a place) are increasingly relying on stories to help potential "customers" see a lack in their lives or community that only these goods can fill. Narratives that bring listeners to a point of pain, embarrassment, horror, annoyance, or a need for justice, to name a few, can successfully grip the audience's attention and create a perceived need for fulfillment.

Narratives instruct and inspire

Just as the story of "Goldilocks and the Three Bears" serves to warn children about invading another person's privacy, so, too, presentation narratives serve to instruct or inspire.

Philanthropists share their own stories of giving in order to get others to make charitable contributions. Ex–gang members tell tough street stories to kids in their communities, encouraging them to stay in school and out of trouble. These compelling narratives, and others like them, encourage those in the audience to engage in constructive behavior.

Narratives entertain

Listeners like to laugh and enjoy themselves. One speaker, who presents on behalf of a local animal shelter, starts out each speech with a story about a feral orange cat. The tale centers around one evening when the speaker and two neighbors make several bumbling attempts to catch the house-invading fourteen-pound feline. The account includes a broken vase, spilled birthday flowers, a scratched back, blankets, a chimney, and a bucket of water. It ends with a wet and angry soot-covered kitty being taken away in a laundry basket to the animal shelter, and three exhausted adults tending to wounds, broken glass, blackened walls, and feelings of guilt.

The speaker's story always gets laughs until listeners realize her unfunny point—people should spay and neuter their pets to keep animal populations under control. The speaker knows that her listeners have heard this message before but finds that her entertaining story is a unique way of getting their attention. The anecdote, she feels, evokes empathy for both unwanted animals and the citizens in whose neighborhoods they live. Because people always linger after her presentations to share stories of their own, she knows they were listening.

Narratives humanize a general concept

A speaker can encourage listeners to connect with an abstract or complex idea by relating the topic to one person's experience. A politician who wants to drive home a point may tell the story of a specific citizen helped or harmed by certain policy decisions. A doctor discussing a disease may use a specific patient as a case study. Listeners can identify with these personal stories and better see the larger issues.

A specific person's story, though potentially powerful, is an example of **anecdotal evidence.** This type of evidence is often used to get listeners to draw a conclusion. But because the evidence stems from specifically chosen circumstances yet ignores others, it can't be used as your sole evidence. So, while it may be true that the new expressway through town shortened Ms. Citizen's daily commute, it may not be good policy for *all* the townspeople. The politician praising the expressway should provide additional support for his or her argument. Always identify anecdotal evidence as such for your listeners.

Narratives benefit you as the speaker

Many speakers enjoy incorporating narratives into their presentations, especially since the process of storytelling comes naturally to most people. Also, narratives are easy to remember because, in the Western tradition, there is always a beginning, middle, and end. You just have to practice your story to remember the necessary details.

The use of narrative, especially a personal one, can also increase your credibility. Speakers often preface their stories with comments like *I was at a White House dinner recently . . .* or *When I was testifying as an expert witness . . . .* Such narratives are excellent devices for increasing credibility while engaging the audience through storytelling.

Even stories that put speakers in a vulnerable position or a less-than-favorable light can add to their stature. Stories that state *When I was busted for DUI . . .* are usually told for good reason and can frame the speaker as a regular person, complete with faults and complexities, but still someone with a meaningful message to share.

2. Communicating the narrative

In order to effectively communicate a narrative within your presentation, you first need to compose the narrative itself, and then decide how best to incorporate that narrative seamlessly into the rest of the speech.

Composing the narrative

Composing the narrative involves a number of considerations: making sure you include the key components of the narrative, building a narrative structure, and when relevant, identifying the narrative as hypothetical (rather than true).

Components of the narrative Like any story, your narrative should contain the necessary components of **character** (who), **action** (what is happening), and **scene** (where and when the action is taking place). Your listeners are accustomed to hearing narratives with all these components. Use your practice sessions to ensure the components are in place.

Narrative structure Traditional Western narrative structure calls for a certain story sequence, as you may have studied in a literature class (Figure 8.1). Your narrative should contain

- the **setup,** or introduction of character and scene and the start of the action;
- a **conflict,** an event that causes the action to go in a direction toward the climax;
- **climax,** the peak of tension or the most exciting moment; and
- a **resolution,** an end to the conflict.

Your audience members expect to hear this sequence and may miss a sense of completion if your story doesn't follow it.

True or hypothetical? When you tell a story, audience members believe it to be true unless you tell them otherwise. Indeed, the ethics of public speaking require your content to be accurate and truthful. On occasion, however, a **hypothetical narrative,** or an invented story, can be of use, especially when you are conceptualizing past or future events or outcomes. For instance, none of us knows what life will be like

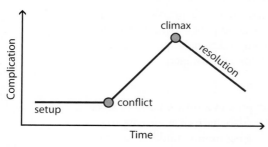

figure 8.1 Narrative Structure Western audiences expect your story to follow this narrative structure.

Storytelling in Other Cultures

Stories aren't necessarily told the same way in all cultures. If you plan to use narrative when speaking before a non-Western audience, research storytelling practices so that you can better connect with your audience. For example, if telling a story in Zimbabwe to people who speak the Shona language, you would want to begin your story with the word *paivapo,* which roughly means, "a long time ago." The audience would then answer in unison, *dzepfunde,* loosely translated as "we're ready for you." Stories end with the same words in another call-and-response.[3]

- Do you see a potential future scenario in which you would use narrative with an audience from a different culture?
- If so, where will you go for information or training on how to connect with this group?

in 2025, but that doesn't stop us from making predictions. If you use a hypothetical narrative, you have an ethical responsibility to label it as such.

Incorporating the narrative

Narratives are highly versatile and can be integrated effectively into a presentation in several ways: as an opening and/or closing device, as a supporting point, as emotional proof, or even as the primary structure for the speech.

Narrative as an opening and/or closing device The narrative structure quickly grips the audience's attention in the introduction and generates interest in your message. Completing the narrative in the conclusion brings unity to the speech.

Narrative as a supporting point Suppose, during your persuasive speech, you want to talk about glucosamine as a relief for joint pain. To support the claim, relate the story of how you experienced much less discomfort during your Zumba classes once you started taking the supplement several months ago.

Narrative as emotional proof While narratives can provide rational or logical support to a point you're trying to make, they can also convey feelings that can persuade an audience. Emotional proof is discussed in greater detail later in this chapter on page 187.

Narrative as structure A story can be the basis for the entire body of your speech. Read more about the chronological structure in Chapter 9, on pages 201–202.

SPEAK
Responsibly

Alligators Lurk in the Sewers of New York City!

Our culture is filled with stories that many or most of us believe to be true. Perhaps you know that terrorists have been buying up missing or stolen UPS uniforms. And we all know that if you leave a baby tooth in a glass of Coca-Cola overnight, it will dissolve by morning. Right? *Wrong*. These stories, or **urban legends,** are *not* true, but speakers occasionally share such legends as if they were. Don't risk your credibility by spreading urban legends as you attempt to support a point. Some quick research on an urban legend website (such as Snopes.com) can help you determine whether your planned narrative is true, unconfirmed, or false.

8C Use Objective Support

Objective support includes facts, definitions, and statistics—ideas that are, for the most part, agreed on, measurable, observable, and consistent. Objective support is based on things other than thoughts, opinions, or feelings.

1. Facts

connect

For a sample student video that uses factual support, see the online student speech techniques video clip "Informing with Facts."

Which of the following are facts, and which are not?

- Shark attacks kill hundreds of people each year.
- Nelson Mandela is a hero.
- Plastic water bottles release carcinogenic compounds when reused.

None of these is a fact. Between 2000 and 2010, sharks killed an average of five people worldwide per year.[4] While Mandela is an incredible inspiration to countless South Africans and other world citizens, to call someone a "hero" is an opinion, not a fact. The plastic-water-bottle story is a blend of fact and fiction.[5]

Idea you want to communicate	Fact to support it
Rosa Parks' refusal to move to the back of a Montgomery, Alabama, city bus was a calculated decision—not a spontaneous one.	Parks had been a local NAACP leader for twelve years, had received training in civil rights organization, and was familiar with earlier challenges to segregation.[6]
Provide shade or mud for your pigs.	Pigs have no sweat glands.

Facts can be proven to be true or to have happened. They are verifiable and consistent, not just based on opinion. Use facts to give listeners a sense of reality or to bring them to your point of view.

You have some research to do before presenting facts to your listeners. Verify the accuracy of your facts by looking at multiple sources. Don't take facts out of context. Find out whether there's ideology (opinion) behind the fact; **truthiness,** or a devotion to information one wishes were true even if it's not, is a disturbing trend. Adhere to ethical principles, and protect your credibility by fully understanding your facts and using them honestly in your presentation. Librarians, teachers, and websites like Snopes.com, FactCheck.org, and the Straight Dope can help you separate facts from fiction.

truthiness *n.*—a devotion to information one wishes were true even if it's not.

The term "truthiness" was first coined by satirist Stephen Colbert, who parodies ideologically influenced news anchors by playing a conservative one on TV. While in character on *The Colbert Report,* Colbert explains, "I'm not a fan of facts. You see, facts can change, but my opinion will never change, no matter what the facts are."

Origin of "Truthiness"

2. Definitions

Definitions explain or clarify what a word, idea, or expression means. Definitions take very little time to state and can make or break a point you are trying to communicate. (A definition may also be the foundation for your speech. See section B1 in Chapter 15.)

It is difficult for a listener to stay engaged and interact with your ideas if the terms you use are unfamiliar. Use definitions when you have even the slightest concern that some audience members might not know what a word or an expression means.

connect

For a sample student video that uses a definition, see the online student speech techniques video clip "Defining a Term for Listener Comprehension."

Idea you want to communicate	Definition to support it
New OSHA standards are intended to reduce work-related hazards in the poultry industry.	OSHA stands for the Occupational Safety and Health Administration, a governmental agency within the Department of Labor whose mission is to ensure the safety and health of U.S. workers.
U.S. citizens should look to Canada to see the advantages and disadvantages of socialized medicine.	Socialized medicine is a health care system publicly administered by a national government, unlike the U.S. system, which is mostly privately owned and managed for profit.

Whether your definition clarifies what an individual word or a larger idea means, definitions play an important role in a listenable presentation by keeping you and your audience on common ground. There are several ways to define a word or an idea: from a dictionary, by comparison, by contrast, by operation, by example, and by explanation.

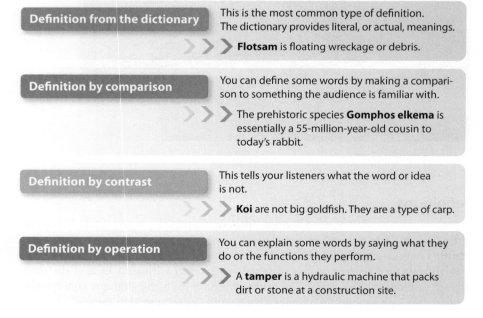

Definition from the dictionary
This is the most common type of definition. The dictionary provides literal, or actual, meanings.

>>> **Flotsam** is floating wreckage or debris.

Definition by comparison
You can define some words by making a comparison to something the audience is familiar with.

>>> The prehistoric species **Gomphos elkema** is essentially a 55-million-year-old cousin to today's rabbit.

Definition by contrast
This tells your listeners what the word or idea is not.

>>> **Koi** are not big goldfish. They are a type of carp.

Definition by operation
You can explain some words by saying what they do or the functions they perform.

>>> A **tamper** is a hydraulic machine that packs dirt or stone at a construction site.

Definition by example	These definitions explain something by providing familiar examples.

> > > **Bodily fluids** include blood, sweat, saliva, and tears.

Definition by explanation	These definitions provide extended details, helping you paint a larger picture for your listeners.

> > > **Straight edge** is an alternative lifestyle born of the punk movement. It's dedicated to clean living and advocates total abstinence from tobacco, alcohol, and recreational drugs.

3. Statistics

Statistics are numerical data that describe some sort of relationship. For example, statistics may show how attitudes have changed over time, how behaviors differ among individuals or groups, or how one thing compares to another. Use statistics when numbers will effectively draw attention to an issue, will create or reinforce a point you're trying to make, or will help listeners quickly understand a relatively complex or confusing issue.

Idea you want to communicate	Statistic to support it
Glacial melt would be bad news for many people.	Over 600 million people worldwide live in coastal areas less than ten meters above sea level.[7]
Antismoking campaigns have had an effect on U.S. adult smoking rates.	Forty-two percent of U.S. adults smoked cigarettes in the 1960s, whereas only 21 percent do so today.[8]

Statistics need special handling to be an effective form of support. Here are some concerns and potential solutions.

During your research

Throughout the course of your research process, as you encounter, gather, and evaluate statistical data, it is crucial to keep in mind that statistics are easily manipulated and context is essential; to know the source of your statistics; and to understand the process—the when, why, and how—of gathering statistics.

Know that statistics are easily manipulated; context is essential Author Aaron Levenstein once said, "Statistics are like a bikini. What they reveal is suggestive, but what they conceal is vital." And your listeners are savvy. They know that statistics can be manipulated in ways to support just about any argument or any point of view. If you are going to use statistics, you must know what they're actually saying before sharing them with your audience.

For example, say you find a statistic in a pro-environmental article reporting that 1,000 acres of old-growth forest are cut down and removed in Country X each year. Without knowing anything else about this statistic, you might conclude that 1,000 acres constitute a significant loss of trees each year. Your interpretation is that this must represent a devastating blow to Country X's environment. However, the article fails to mention that there are 1.5 *million* acres of old-growth forest in Country X and that 70 percent is protected in a national reserve. At current rates, it would take 450 years to cut down the 30 percent of trees not protected. In the meantime, Country X has a well-managed reforesting program.

The broader context makes a big difference in how we view or understand statistics. Without context, a speaker can make almost any statistic support nearly any argument. Keep digging so that you understand the larger context in which a particular statistic operates and, just as importantly, provide that greater context for your listeners.

Know the source of your statistics Many organizations—whether political, civic, ideological, for profit, or not for profit—collect statistics of their own or pay others to collect statistics for them. They might report only those statistics that support their particular missions or goals. Do your research before choosing statistics to include in your presentation. Know the source of the statistics, and understand why they were reported. In general, governments, educational bodies, and nonpartisan polling organizations generate and cite unbiased and unmanipulated statistics.

Understand the process of gathering statistics Research *when* the statistics were gathered. Are your statistics up to date, or are they already obsolete? Do they tell a current story or an old one? Are they still relevant?

Know *why* the statistics were collected. Were they collected to represent the world as it is (the bad as well as the good) or to promote a cause, elect a candidate, sell a product, or reinforce a particular outlook?

Finally, understand *how* the statistics were collected. Were people randomly polled or carefully selected to participate? Were they paid? How large is the sample number of respondents, and how does that number compare to the size of the larger population? Were questions phrased to generate certain responses? Was the research done in face-to-face interviews or behind the anonymity of a computer screen? Were data self-reported or collected by scientific means?

You may not be able to find answers to all these questions, but they affect the way we interpret the statistics and the confidence we have in them.

During the presentation

Similarly, once you have finished your research and know which statistics will best serve your presentations, you will still need to follow some guidelines in order to communicate

create
converse
connect

Don't Overuse Statistics

While statistics are a valuable way to support an idea, avoid giving your listeners too many statistics. Remember: unlike readers, listeners have to interact with numbers at your pace and discretion. They cannot stop to think about the statistic, go back to reread it, or seek to better contextualize it. Most listeners have a finite capacity for hearing numbers and making sense of them. When numbers begin to run together, few stand out and none have any significance. Choose your statistics wisely. Share those that are essential, and help your audience make sense of them.

the information effectively to your audience: explaining what the statistic means as well as simplifying the numbers for your listeners.

Explain what the statistic means Since you've researched the statistic to the best of your ability, it's now your responsibility to put it in context for the audience. For example, if you talk about the 60 percent approval rating of the current president one year into his or her presidency, contextualize it by comparing it to the ratings of past presidents one year into their presidencies. Also explain that the ratings were gathered by a nonpartisan polling organization in a phone survey of 3,500 randomly chosen U.S. adults from all fifty states.

Simplify the numbers for your listeners Numbers can be hard for listeners to keep track of. Round off numbers when speaking conversationally. For example, say *nearly 32,000* rather than *31,862*. If you give a lengthy list of numbers, summarize what they mean collectively.

connect

For a sample student video that uses statistics, see the online student speech techniques video clip "Summarizing Statistics for Listener Comprehension."

8D Use Illustrative Support

Illustrative support includes examples, descriptions, and explanations. These forms of support clarify, expand on, or provide more information for listeners. In essence, they help paint a fuller picture. Illustrative support is common in conversational interactions, where you're most likely already skilled in using it. When your public speaking is communication-oriented and listener-focused, illustrative support should come naturally. After all, you want to do everything you can to help your listeners understand what you're talking about.

1. Examples

An example provides a particular illustration of a broader concept. Listeners like to hear a speaker say *for example,* because it offers them a chance to double-check their understanding by moving from the abstract to the tangible and concrete.

Idea you want to communicate	Example to support it
Tattooing is one of the most universal means of expression through self-decoration.	Cultures throughout history have tattooed to express, for example, tribal affiliation, status, allegiance, beauty, and sexual allure.
The rise of social media is changing what information is sought during the employment interview.	To better evaluate applicants, some employers are requesting job seekers' user names and passwords for Facebook, Twitter, and other social media sites during the interview.

Examples come in several forms: they are either brief or extended, and they are either real or hypothetical.

Brief or extended examples

Brief examples A **brief example** is one or two sentences that provide an instance of the larger idea being communicated. It's useful only when the audience can quickly understand or already understands the reference from prior experience. When touting the benefits of a particular laundry chemical, sharing the brief example of *its power in removing red spaghetti sauce stains* is meaningful because it is common knowledge that red spaghetti sauce is difficult to remove from clothes. On the other hand, in your speech on the improprieties of state officials, the brief example *just recall the case of Rod Blagojevich* might mystify many listeners. Most likely, only some would know and remember that he was found guilty of a wide range of corruption charges while governor of Illinois.

Extended examples An **extended example** is a mini-narrative; it has a plot and some characters, and something happens. It draws your audience in and keeps them listening. In your presentation advocating the advantages of the Taser (a type of gun using an electric shock rather than a bullet), use the extended example of the police force in City X that recently added Tasers to its regular weaponry. You could share the results of the first six months of Taser use by mentioning how shooting deaths by police dropped, how suspect-apprehension rates increased, and how officers reported feeling just as safe and competent in their jobs carrying Tasers as when they had carried guns.

Real or hypothetical examples

Real examples Real examples are just that—real. Most examples used in presentations come from real experience, real research, real cases, real history, and real knowledge.

Hypothetical examples If no real example exists to support your idea or if your idea looks into an unknown future, a **hypothetical example** can show what could be. In a presentation on wind farms, you could use a hypothetical example of a community powered by electricity gathered solely from wind turbines. As you ask listeners to envision this potential future, describe the oddly pleasing look of the spinning turbine towers, the lack of overhead electric lines, and the lower prices paid for electricity. If you use a hypothetical example, you are ethically obligated to cite it as such. Otherwise, your listeners assume that all examples you use are real.

2. Descriptions

A description can bring an idea to life or create an image through expanded details. You may need to describe what something looks like, how something happens, how something works, how someone feels, or how we experience something. Descriptions create visual images or feelings in your listeners, allowing them to interact with your message by bringing in their own experiences.

connect

For sample student videos that use imagery, see the online student speech techniques video clip "Using a Vivid Image."

Idea you want to communicate	Description to support it
Wind can damage orange crops.	The tough branches of the orange tree whip against each other, putting minute scratches on a new, tiny orange. That small scratch develops into a larger blemish that covers a significant part of the mature fruit.[9]
Spend your next summer vacation in Ireland.	You'll find endless grass trails in the countryside, enclosed by moss-covered stone walls. The pink, purple, and yellow wildflowers contrast with the green grass and blue sky.

3. Explanations

Explanations provide background or additional, detailed information. They go beyond definition or description. Explanations look behind the scenes, telling listeners why things exist, how things came to be, why something is done in a particular way, or why certain behaviors occur. Explanations help listeners "catch up" to where you are so that they are ready to move on to the next idea with you.

Idea you want to communicate	Explanation to support it
Today, most people believe that dreams reflect unconscious desires.	Before Sigmund Freud, most dreams were understood to be a type of supernatural experience. Freud was the first to offer a new idea that dreams were the unconscious surfacing of buried or repressed emotions.[10]
Some Muslim women cover their heads, a practice called *hijab*.	*Hijab* shows submission to God and the woman's willingness to follow the guidance of the prophet Muhammad. It also shows her disinterest in receiving attention from someone other than her husband.

8E Use Subjective Support

Subjective support is based on thoughts, opinions, experience, or feelings. It includes emotional proof and personal experience. These forms of support are not based on facts and are not measurable, observable, or consistent.

You may be wondering: *If these forms of support are not based on fact, how can I include them in a presentation? What could they possibly be worth?* Subjective support is worth a great deal, but in different ways than objective and illustrative evidence. Though listeners respect factual support that appeals to their minds, they are also capable of learning and being convinced through emotions and experience. Recall Fisher's research on narratives, discussed earlier in the chapter.

SPEAK Responsibly

Use Subjective Support—to a Degree

Some may argue that subjective support is the easiest type of support to use in a speech. It's relatively simple to collect, and we know from experience that people are attracted to it. Use it, but don't overuse it. Think critically about your ideas and evaluate which ones are better backed up with objective and other forms of support discussed throughout this chapter.

Be Emotionally Generous

During everyday interaction, it's natural when speaking of something exciting or sad to reflect the emotion in your face, voice, and body. Some public speakers, however, hold back their emotional display in deference to some imagined propriety or set of rules. But there's no need to be formal and unemotional throughout the speech. Instead, be yourself and let authentic emotion show through—be emotionally generous. Are you talking about an injustice or a joy? Something funny or disgusting? Then show it. Identify the emotional rhythms of your presentation and communicate them meaningfully.

1. Emotional proof

Emotional proof is not based on fact and is not necessarily logical; it supports your point by referencing human emotions. These emotions are real and genuine to those who experience them, and they can alter and define interactions and events in instructive or meaningful ways. It usually takes a skilled writer, visual artist, or performing artist to successfully evoke emotion in readers and viewers, but a public speech is a powerful delivery system, and even novice public speakers can use emotional proof to persuade audiences.

Idea you want to communicate	Emotional proof to support it
Children in poorer school districts should receive state-funded equipment equal to that available to children in richer districts.	It is not fair to deprive children of needed school equipment because of where their parents choose or can afford to live.
Consider getting a worm composting system for your house or apartment.	My roommates and I thoroughly enjoyed watching the worms turn our food scraps into rich soil. We got attached to them and even named them Wally and Wanda.

2. Personal experience

A personal experience relates a circumstance from the speaker's or someone else's life. Like emotional proof, personal experience is real and genuine and can alter and define interactions and events, thereby providing meaning.

Idea you want to communicate	Personal experience to support it
Morbidly obese adults should consider stomach-reduction surgery.	My friend Frank weighed over 300 pounds when he had the surgery two years ago. He's now down to a healthy 175 pounds and considers the surgery one of the best decisions he's ever made.
Costa Rica is rich in colorful bird life.	I was there for two weeks last year and saw more species than you can imagine: electric green quetzals, iridescent blue motmots, and bright yellow toucans. Scarlet macaws were everywhere.

connect

For a sample student video that uses personal experience, see the online student speech techniques video clip "Using a Personal Example."

When offering personal experience, be sure to introduce it as such. Personal experience is a type of anecdotal evidence, meaning it is only one case in point and does not necessarily prove a larger point or support a larger body of evidence. Personal experience is usually too weak to act as your only form of support, but it can add richness to an idea when combined with other supporting material. Also, many listeners just like to learn a little bit about speakers' personal lives.

8F Use Testimony as Support

Testimony, quoted words that support an idea, can be objective, illustrative, or subjective. It's a useful form of support for catching listeners' attention and convincing them of the importance of your ideas.

1. Reasons for using testimony

Use testimony for several reasons. First, testimony backs up your own idea by showing how another credible person supports or agrees with it. If you claim that identity theft is on the rise, providing testimony from an official in the fraud division of the U.S. Department of Justice will strengthen your point.

Second, testimony offers your listeners a glimpse into worlds they may otherwise be unable to access. Though neither you nor your listeners, for example, could ever know what it was like to be a child conscripted into a rebel African army, testimony from one of the Lost Boys of Sudan regarding his plight offers powerful firsthand evidence for your presentation. Few people will ever experience space flight, but testimony from someone who has been on a mission in space adds unique insight to your speech.

Finally, testimony can show the wide range of reactions and views people have on a given issue. In your informative speech on current measures in border security in Texas,

Idea you want to communicate	Testimony to support it
Shark attacks are infrequent, but humans have an inordinate fear of and fascination with them.	Naturalist, Pulitzer Prize winner, and retired Harvard professor E. O. Wilson once said of sharks, "We are not just afraid of predators, we are transfixed by them, prone to weave stories and fables and chatter endlessly about them, because fascination creates prepared-ness, and preparedness, survival. In a deeply tribal sense, we love our predators."[11]
Actors who play real-life characters feel more confident when they can identify with the real person on some personal level.	"He was the last private man," Leonardo DiCaprio said of playing Howard Hughes in *The Aviator.* "He was one of the most iconic men the country has ever seen, but he had a strong need for privacy. I can empathize with that."[12]

providing testimony from law enforcement officials, ranchers living near the border, and even those who have crossed the border helps your listeners understand the many perspectives and experiences surrounding this complicated issue.

2. Types of testimony

The two basic types of testimony are expert testimony and lay testimony.

Expert testimony

Expert testimony comes from people with authority on a topic or in a field. It carries clout, especially if the expert has impressive qualifications and is unbiased.

Lay testimony

Lay testimony comes from people, including you, who have firsthand knowledge of or experience in a particular area. Your sister may not be an expert in race-car driving, but her testimony about her year of race-car driving lessons can lend credence to your ideas.

3. General tips for using testimony

As with other forms of support, testimony can be utilized most effectively in your presentation if you give listeners context about the person whose words you are using, ensure the testimony is relevant to your point, know the source of the testimony, and use the testimony in its context.

Give listeners some context about the person whose words you are using

Unless the person is well known, his or her name alone tells your listeners little. Supply identifying information such as the person's title, occupation, degree, years of experience, or societal role. In essence, explain "who" this person is that makes his or her testimony valuable.

Ensure that the testimony is relevant to your point

You want to share only material that strengthens the idea you're communicating. Don't use testimony just because someone famous said it or it's uniquely phrased.

Know the source of the testimony

If you find a quote by a Dr. Alexander McCormick that perfectly supports your point, research his background. Is he a medical doctor or a PhD? Did he earn his degree from an accredited institution? Is he an independent researcher or a spokesperson for a drug company? Use the CRAAP test, presented in Chapter 7 (p. 157), to evaluate the credibility of any source of testimony you use.

Use the testimony in its context

It's unethical to take words out of context to try to support a point. For example, suppose you want to highlight the tensions between China and the United States and you find some testimony from the Secretary of State regarding recent interactions with her Chinese counterpart. Suppose the Secretary actually said, "While we had some significant differences, overall the meeting was productive and we found several areas of common ground from which to move forward in our talks." You cannot select the first half of her sentence and tell listeners, "In her meeting with her Chinese counterpart last week, the Secretary stated that there were 'significant differences between the two countries.'" Such a sentence would misrepresent the overall meaning of her original testimony.

4. Communicating the testimony

Testimony can be communicated within a presentation either through quoting or paraphrasing.

Quoting

You can quote some testimony directly, especially if it is brief (one or two sentences) or if it is essential to communicate every word exactly as the speaker said it. As always, acknowledge the source. Use a full quotation when

- the language is memorable or is phrased in such a way that it uniquely reflects the person's perspective or time in history;
- it is difficult to summarize the testimony without changing its meaning;
- it would take much longer to put the idea into your own words; or
- you want to comment on the words themselves.

Even though you are relying on a conversational style throughout your presentation, it is acceptable to write down and read quoted testimony verbatim.

Paraphrasing

Though direct quotations work well in the situations just discussed, **paraphrasing,** or putting the testimony into your own words, is acceptable in others. Paraphrase when

- the idea communicated in the testimony is more important than the wording of the testimony;
- the idea in the testimony is too complex to quote verbatim; or
- the person's words are too specialized, too inappropriate, or too long to quote verbatim.

Not only is paraphrasing good for maintaining a conversational style and increasing audience comprehension of your ideas, it also shows your ability to simplify ideas, thereby enhancing your credibility. When paraphrasing, tell the audience what you're doing ("let me paraphrase"), indicate the source, and be ethical by not veering from the meaning of the testimony.

Supporting Your Ideas in Action *A Student's Process*

In her History of Television college course, Chyna Green was assigned to do a presentation on the growth of The Weather Channel, as a company, from inception to present. While she initially thought it a strange topic, she was fascinated once she got into her research. She soon identified her central idea.

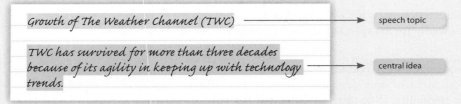

> *Growth of The Weather Channel (TWC)* ——————→ speech topic
>
> *TWC has survived for more than three decades because of its agility in keeping up with technology trends.* ——————→ central idea

Researching, choosing, and analyzing types of support

Chyna's research yielded mostly objective forms of support: factual company information, some from The Weather Channel website itself and some from a number of news articles charting the company's expansions and forays into new technology—particularly its moves to create interactive TV apps for both SD and HD versions of the channel. After researching, Chyna analyzed the kinds of support she had gathered in terms of the criteria of relevance, appropriateness, and variety that she remembered from her public speaking course.

> *Relevance: I'm confident here. The information I've gathered is about The Weather Channel's technology and how it has generated continued user engagement and support. I'm certainly not straying into other topics, and I resisted the temptation to include some tangential information such as its international channels and movies that TWC's been featured in.*
>
> *Appropriateness: The information I've gathered is of interest and at an appropriate level for my college classmates taking this History of Television course with me. I'll define any jargon or technical terms that I'll use that we haven't studied yet in class, and I'll be sure to explain and emphasize the credibility of my sources.*
>
> *Variety: Problem here—I have mostly facts and statistics, and an endless string of these can make listening more of a challenge for my audience. I need a new plan for more source variety, perhaps a narrative, some explanations, and maybe even some testimony.*

primary types of support

Chyna decided to craft her history as a *narrative* around the expanding technology The Weather Channel used, telling the story from its use of the original WeatherStar technology in the early 1980s to its upgrades to IntelliStar, and its expansion to radio, newspaper, and online services such as desktop widgets and personalized texts to mobile phones. She also planned to provide some quick *explanations* of what some of the technologies were capable of and finally, to round things out, she also got some *testimony* from a midlevel manager at corporate headquarters in Georgia when he replied to her e-mail inquiry.

Chyna felt confident that the variety of her forms of support would better engage her audience and keep them listening.

additional types of support

review questions

1. What are the three general criteria for selecting supporting material for a speech?
2. Why is narrative such a popular way to support your message?
3. What is objective support? What are some examples of it?
4. What is illustrative support? What are some examples of it?
5. What is subjective support? What are some examples of it?
6. What is testimony? What role does it play in your speech?

key terms

relevance 172
narrative 173
narrative paradigm 173
narrative coherence 173
narrative fidelity 173
anecdotal evidence 175
character 176
action 176
scene 176
setup 176

conflict 176
climax 176
resolution 176
hypothetical
   narrative 176
urban legend 178
objective support 178
truthiness 179
statistics 181
illustrative support 183

brief example 184
extended example 184
hypothetical example 185
subjective support 186
emotional proof 187
testimony 188
expert testimony 189
lay testimony 189
paraphrasing 191

exercises

1. With a group of classmates, decide what types of support (facts, explanations, personal experience, or other) would be best for the following presentations. Be prepared to defend your answers to the class.

   • Celebrating the hundredth anniversary of the founding of your school

connect

For online exercises, quizzes, and hands-on activities, see the Chapter 8 assignments in Connect Public Speaking.

- Persuading listeners to register to vote
- Informing listeners on the benefits of potassium

2. Interview a well-known storyteller in your community or someone who teaches storytelling at your school. What insights can he or she share with you about effective storytelling?

3. Look at the types of definitions on pages 180–181. Be prepared to define six terms, one from each category, to your classmates. Find words that you think they will benefit from learning.

4. Find a statistic of interest. Thoroughly research its origin, purpose, and context. As a class, discuss what you have learned.

5. Watch the video or read the transcript of the speech given by George W. Bush during "The World Will Always Remember September 11th" ceremony on December 11, 2001. With a group or as a class, note any instances of emotional proof and discuss their effectiveness.

Developing Your Message

Developing Your Message

It's now time to organize your ideas into a coherent whole. A well-structured message is important because it sets a clear path for your ideas. Only when you know where you're going, can you take listeners with you. These three chapters offer rationales and tips on structuring speeches in ways that allow listeners to better follow your train of thought. You'll then learn how to introduce and summarize your ideas, and create transitions.

•   •   •

Organize Your Ideas

LEARNING OBJECTIVES

1 Understand the relationship between your thesis and its main points.

2 Know the patterns for developing and arranging your main points.

By this point in the speechmaking process, you have your topic firmly in place and have narrowed that topic into a thesis. The thesis now needs to be supported by main points (also called main supporting points) that relate to one another and are arranged logically. Organizing your ideas helps you focus and, just as important, helps your audience stay with you. This chapter first discusses the importance of having a thesis statement and main supporting points that work together to create a coherent organizational whole. You'll then learn several patterns of organization for arranging the body of your speech. It's your responsibility to give your listeners a well-organized message—they expect and deserve it.

9A Build Main Points That Support Your Thesis

This is a good time to review the discussion from Chapter 6 (pp. 133–136) about the thesis statement—the one main idea to which everything else in your presentation connects. In that chapter, you read about the important distinction between a true and a false thesis.

- When a speaker employs a false thesis, he or she explores a topic from several random angles yet leaves listeners with no single new perception of the world. The use of a false thesis is a common error among beginning speakers.
- In a true thesis, you narrow your topic into one central idea, and the main points that support it are predictable and not easily substituted. Listeners leave the presentation seeing the world in one new way.

Obviously, as a listener-centered speaker, you are seeking to develop a true thesis. But *how* do you make that happen? You've got to have a thesis and main supporting points that work together to achieve either your informative or persuasive purpose. You'll notice from Table 6.1 (p. 134) that each sample thesis has a word (or two) that suggests or acts as a stepping-stone to the main supporting points in the speech body.

Topic	True thesis	Predictable main supporting points, not easily substituted
Mythology	While details differ, all mythic heroes follow the same stages in their quest.	The **stages** include selection from the general populace, the fulfillment of the quest, and the return as a hero.
Beef	Several types of bacteria can be found in poorly processed beef.	The **types** include salmonella, *E. coli* O157:H7, campylobacter, and listeria.

The word that generates the main supporting points is called the **organizing term.** In the two examples above, the nouns *stages* and *types* tell the audience how the speaker plans to develop the narrowed topic in the speech body. There are innumerable organizing terms. You get your organizing term (which will always be a noun) from one of the many patterns of organization.

A **pattern of organization** is just that—a pattern you use to arrange your main supporting points in the body of your speech. A clear pattern tells your audience how your main points support the thesis and how they are related to one another. Following a pattern is also helpful to you as a speaker. Here's what one speaker said:

> In my first few speeches, I wasted a lot of time going from one scenario to another, and this created a situation that made my audience work hard to listen and follow me. It also made it difficult for me, because I spent so much time thinking about what I was going to say next that I lost any audience connection I had tried to create. By learning how to follow a pattern of organization, I was able to create an ordered situation in which I could successfully operate. Instead of my focus being inward, it was now outward, directed at my audience.

The next section of this chapter discusses seven patterns of organization—topical, chronological, causal, comparison or contrast, spatial, problem-solution, and Monroe's motivated sequence. Most of these patterns can be used for either informative or persuasive speech purposes (as well as for special-occasion speeches and other communication needs such as writing an essay or answering an interview question). Choose only one pattern of organization for any given speech, but be familiar with them all. A knowledge of all the patterns helps you decide which one works best for your particular topic, audience, and occasion.

connect

For sample student videos that highlight of the spoken thesis and main points preview, see the online student speech techniques video clip "Stating the Thesis and Previewing the Main Points."

9B   Arrange Your Main Points

In each section that follows, we'll use the topic of "elephants" as an example for each pattern of organization, using two to five main supporting points for any given example. Note that each example creates a thesis by using one organizing term and one narrowed topic. Table 9.1 (p. 211) summarizes the patterns.

1. Topical pattern

Sometimes known as classification or division, the **topical pattern** divides the topic into subclasses or subtopics based on their similarity.

connect

For a sample student video that relies on the topical pattern, see the online student speech techniques video clip "Using a Topical Pattern."

Organizing Terms for Topical Pattern

Terms include *kinds, classes, reasons, varieties, brands, breeds, features, categories, methods, techniques, schemes, strategies, groupings, policies, tactics, shapes, levels, sizes, theories, assumptions, actions, measures, procedures, legacies*

Special consideration: Avoid the terms *aspects* and *things*, which are too vague to be useful. (Almost anything can qualify as an aspect of something else.) These two terms do not help you narrow and focus your speech.

Sample topic and idea you want to communicate (informative)

While researching elephants for an informative speech,[1] you learn that these great beasts don't just hang around randomly within their herd. Instead, the members are grouped in what ecologists call social circles. An elephant's lineage on its mother's side determines its standing within the herd and thus its social circle. You think this topic is of potential interest because people are social animals, too. Not only will your audience learn about elephant society, they may also reflect on how status operates within human society.

Draft of Thesis Statement with Organizing Term

> Organizing term
>
> Narrowed topic

I want to inform my audience about the *categories* of elephant social circles.

Draft of Main Supporting Points

The *categories* are

> Main point #1
>
> Main point #2
>
> Main point #3

- the central structure (composed of the matriarch and her calf)
- the main family unit (the matriarch's other offspring and her sisters)
- the bond group (other relatives with their own families)

Moving the thesis from written to verbal form You are now done with your draft; your structure is working on paper. In your actual speech, however, you want to use language and syntax (sentence structure) that's natural to the way you speak.

> Written syntax sounds too stiff for a speech.

Revised written thesis: There are three categories of elephant social circles.

Your spoken thesis, then, may sound like this:

> Spoken thesis uses natural language and syntax.

Final spoken thesis: An elephant's place within the herd is determined by which category of social circle it belongs to.

If you succeed in communicating your idea and the main points that support it, your audience will understand the world in this one new way:

> Spoken thesis
>
> Organizing term
>
> Main point #1 preview

Using the Thesis and a Preview of the Main Points in the Speech

An elephant's place within the herd is determined by which category of social circle it belongs to. You'll learn first about the social circle known as the central structure, composed of the matriarch and her calf; second, the main family unit, containing the matriarch's other offspring and her sisters; and finally, the bond group, encompassing the matriarch's other relatives and their own families.

Main point #2 preview

Main point #3 preview

2. Chronological pattern

In the **chronological pattern,** the thesis follows a time arrangement and shows how events or ideas occur over time, either forward or backward; the relationships between the main points are based on time or sequence. Narratives, for example, are told chronologically.

connect

For a sample student video that relies on the chronological pattern, see the online student speech techniques video clip "Using a Chronological Pattern."

Organizing Terms for Chronological Pattern

Terms that refer to the passing of time, including *steps, stages, periods, phases, chapters, epochs, historical eras*

Special consideration: It's tempting to use the word *history* as an organizing term for the chronological pattern, but it doesn't work. To say something has "four histories" makes no grammatical sense. Instead, use *historical eras* or *historical phases* as your organizing term.

Sample topic and idea you want to communicate (persuasive)

You discover in your research for a persuasive presentation that, though elephants are a big draw for many circuses, the way they're trained for performing is controversial. The more you read and discover, the more you agree with those critics who contend these methods are unnecessarily harsh. You research a series of steps that elephant trainers use in their work[2] and believe that if people knew about these steps, they may not like what they've learned.

Draft of Thesis Statement with Organizing Term

I want to convince my audience that the *steps* used in training an elephant for circus performance are cruel.

Organizing term

Narrowed topic

Draft of Main Supporting Points

The *steps* are

- separating a young elephant from its mother
- "breaking" the elephant (training it to be submissive to people)
- teaching it elementary performing tricks
- teaching it advanced performing tricks

Main point #1

Main point #2

Main point #3

Main point #4

Moving the thesis from written to verbal form Again, small changes in the language bring the thesis statement from draft written form to a final thesis that sounds natural when spoken.

Revised written thesis: The steps used in training an elephant for circus performance are cruel.

Final spoken thesis: The training steps elephants endure in order to prepare for circus performance are against their nature.

Spoken thesis uses natural language and syntax.

Using the Thesis and a Preview of the Main Points in the Speech

The training steps elephants endure in order to prepare for circus performance are against their nature. First, we'll talk about how the baby elephant is weaned, or separated from its mother. Next, you'll hear how the elephant is broken, or made submissive to a trainer. Only after this can the elephant be taught performance tricks, from elementary ones like raising a foot to advanced ones such as doing a handstand.

Spoken thesis

Organizing term

Main point #1 preview

Main point #2 preview

Main point #3 preview

Main point #4 preview

3. Causal pattern

The thesis in a **causal pattern** focuses on either the causes or effects of something. When using this pattern informatively, you explain what the cause/effect link is. When using the pattern persuasively, you make a claim about the link—whether it exists, is true, or is valuable.

Special consideration for causal pattern Another option in this pattern is to take a chain-of-events approach and explain or argue a direct cause-and-effect relationship. In this instance, your first main point would describe the cause, and the second would explore the effect. You may even have a third point explaining or arguing a subsequent effect of the first effect. In some instances, as in the case of a historical topic, you'd first look at a situation (the effect) and then work backward to explain or argue what led to it.

Organizing Terms for Causal Pattern

For a cause speech—*causes, reasons, grounds, motives, sources, roots, antecedents, explanations, determinants*

For an effect speech—*effects, results, consequences, impacts, outcomes, upshots, end results*

Sample topic and idea you want to communicate (informative)

Your research for an informative speech shows that African elephant populations have decreased. There is no single reason for the population decline; instead, it's a complicated and multilayered problem, much of which stems from increasing human populations in the elephants' habitat.[3] You want to give your audience a sense of the complex interplay between people and elephants, and explain why the animals often lose out.

Draft of Thesis Statement with Organizing Term

I want to inform my audience about the human-related *causes* of declining elephant populations in Africa.

Organizing term

Narrowed topic

Draft of Main Supporting Points

The *causes* are

- habitat destruction and degradation
- retaliation for human-elephant conflict
- hunting elephants for meat
- continued ivory poaching

Main point #1

Main point #2

Main point #3

Main point #4

Moving the thesis from written to verbal form How will you change the language of your written thesis to sound more natural to your listeners?

> **Revised written thesis:** Human-related activities are among the causes behind Africa's declining elephant populations.

SPEAK
Responsibly

Cause or Contributing Factor?

It's easy to suppose cause-and-effect relationships:

Overstated Cause-and-Effect Statements

- *The family survived the house fire because of the smoke alarm installed that afternoon.*
- *Too many hours playing video games causes depression.*
- *The elm trees died because of a fast-spreading fungal infection.*

On occasion, such a direct relationship may be true, but more frequently, your "cause" may simply be one of several contributing factors. Single causes are difficult to determine (and, if you're speaking persuasively, claiming just one may weaken your argument). More often, several factors, in complex interplay, lead to a given outcome. For example, while the smoke alarm no doubt played a role in the family's escape from the house fire, the facts that the fire started near the parents' bedroom and that one parent is a very light sleeper and therefore smelled the smoke right away can't be overlooked as contributing factors to the family's survival.

You owe it to your audience to dig deep into your research and convey to them the quality and quantity of the links between your cause-and-effect discussions.

Final spoken thesis: African elephant populations are declining, and you'll learn several human-related causes behind this development.

Using the Thesis and a Preview of the Main Points in the Speech

African elephant populations are declining, and you'll learn several human-related causes behind this development. These causes include, first, the destruction and degradation of the elephants' traditional habitats; second, the frequent retaliation for human-elephant conflict; next, hunting them for their meat; and finally, the continued practice of ivory poaching.

> Spoken thesis relies on conversational style (e.g., use of second-person *you*).
>
> Spoken thesis
>
> Organizing term
>
> Main point #1 preview
>
> Main point #2 preview
>
> Main point #3 preview
>
> Main point #4 preview

4. Comparison or contrast pattern

The **comparison pattern** addresses a new idea by showing the similarities between two *seemingly unlike* things, one of which is typically already familiar to the audience. The **contrast pattern** points out the differences between two *seemingly similar* things, one of which is typically already familiar to the audience. Avoid a presentation that both compares and contrasts; the speech will veer off in two major directions instead of remaining focused on just one.

Organizing Terms for Comparison or Contrast Pattern

For a comparison speech—*similarities, parallels, resemblances, analogies, correlations*

For a contrast speech—*differences, dissimilarities, distinctions, disparities, variations*

Special consideration: When using this pattern, you must have at least two items—connected by an *and*—in your narrowed topic (e.g., "the similarities between the elephant *and* other animals"). In other words, it makes no sense to discuss, for example, "the similarities between the elephant."

> Organizing term

Sample topic and idea you want to communicate (informative)

In this example, your research is again for an informative presentation, but based on your audience analysis work, you know your listeners are already familiar with the idea of people putting horses to work. They may not know that people in other parts of the world put elephants to work in many of the same ways. That is the new idea you want to teach this audience.

> Narrowed topic. Note: This pattern requires two items connected by *and* in your narrowed topic. While the *and* may not appear in the final spoken thesis, it needs to be in your written draft to ensure a full comparison or contrast message.

Draft of Thesis Statement with Organizing Term

I want to inform my audience about the *similarities* between the working elephant and the working horse.

Draft of Main Supporting Points

The *similarities* are

- their use as an agricultural assistant .... Main point #1
- their use in ceremony and tourism .... Main point #2

Moving the thesis from written to verbal form Your job is now to take what's working on paper and revise it into word choice and syntax more natural to the way you speak.

Revised written thesis: Some cultures put elephants to work in ways that are similar to the ways we put horses to work.

Final spoken thesis: Here in the West, we are used to seeing horses at work, but you'll see that some cultures put elephants to work in similar ways.

> Spoken thesis relies on a conversational, listener-centered style (referring to the West and using the first-person plural *we* and the second-person *you*).

Using the Thesis and a Preview of the Main Points in the Speech

Here in the West, we are used to seeing horses at work, but you'll see that some cultures put elephants to work in similar ways. Much like horses, elephants are used as assistants in agriculture and also as props in ceremonies and tourism-related activities.

> Spoken thesis
>
> Organizing term
>
> Main point #1 preview
>
> Main point #2 preview

5. Spatial pattern

The **spatial pattern** discusses the topic according to the way things fit together in a physical space of any size. The supporting points relate to one another according to a geographical pattern or a relative physical relationship, such as top to bottom, east to west, inside to outside. This pattern works well when you want to create a mental picture of something whole that is made of various elements set apart by physical location. Note the root word *space* in the term "spatial."

Organizing Terms for Spatial Pattern

districts	*areas*	*layers*
sections	*segments*	*strata*
boroughs	*sectors*	*components*
regions	*divisions*	*zones*

Sample topic and idea you want to communicate (informative)

Many people know that there are two major species of elephants—Asian and African. But there's really no such thing as a "pure" Asian elephant. Instead, there are several recognized subspecies, distinguished by region. This informative approach helps audience members better understand the role geography plays in species differentiation—in this case, among Asian elephants.

Draft of Thesis Statement with Organizing Term

I want to inform my audience about the *regions* of Asian elephant subspecies.

Draft of Main Supporting Points

The *regions* are

- southern India and Sri Lanka (where you find *Elephas maximus maximus*)
- Southeast Asia (*Elephas maximus indicus*)
- Malaysia and Sumatra (*Elephas maximus sumatrensis*)

Moving the thesis from written to verbal form Once again, use natural language and syntax to give voice to the idea that's working on paper.

Revised written thesis: Geographic regions determine Asian elephant subspecies.

Final spoken thesis: There is no such thing as a "pure" Asian elephant. Rather, you'll learn that Asian elephants belong to one of many subspecies, each tied to a specific geographical region.

Using the Thesis and a Preview of the Main Points in the Speech

There is no such thing as a "pure" Asian elephant. Rather, you'll learn that Asian elephants belong to one of many subspecies, each tied to a specific geographical region. Let's look first at the Asian elephant subspecies *Elephas maximus maximus,* found in southern India and Sri Lanka. We'll then look at *Elephas maximus indicus,* found in Southeast Asia, and lastly at *Elephas maximus sumatrensis,* from Malaysia and Sumatra.

6. Problem-solution pattern

The **problem-solution pattern,** most commonly used for persuasive speeches, defines a problem and offers a feasible solution for it. Related to this is the **problem-cause-solution pattern,** in which the first point defines a problem, the second argues the causes for this problem, and the third proposes a solution that lessens or eliminates the cause. This pattern can also be used informatively should you need or want to *explain* how a problem was solved (rather than argue how it should be solved).

Special consideration for problem-solution pattern Narrow the problem to something specific. For example, the problem of "orphaned baby elephants in Africa" is easier to focus on than "the threat to elephants worldwide through ivory poaching." Also, be sure that your solution addresses or solves the specific problem you cite.

Margin labels:

Organizing term

Narrowed topic

Main point #1

Main point #2

Main point #3

Spoken thesis relies on a more conversational, listener-centered style, using the second-person "you."

Spoken thesis

Organizing term

Main point #1 preview

Main point #2 preview

Main point #3 preview

Use Tandem Power

Take a look at the list of organizing terms under the causal pattern on page 202. You may ask why there are six additional synonyms for *effects*. Won't just *effects* do? Not necessarily. Many languages, including English, contain words that, while similar, have slightly different meanings.

As you develop your thesis, use a thesaurus to find a list of words similar to your potential organizing term (or type "visual thesaurus" into your favorite search engine if you prefer that method). However, turn to a dictionary to determine meaning. Words are not necessarily interchangeable; the subtle nuances of meaning are what make a language rich. So, while *effects* may convey your meaning if your main points are simply results of a certain cause, *consequences* may be the better option for a message focusing on the relationship of the cause to the effect. Keep looking until you find the right organizing term for your thesis.

Organizing Terms for Problem-Solution Pattern

Other terms for *problem*—*challenge, obstruction, difficulty, crisis, predicament, dilemma, question, uncertainty, reservation*

Other terms for *solution*—*answer, key, resolution, response, cure, antidote, way out, escape, rescue*

Sample topic and idea you want to communicate (persuasive)

During research for a persuasive speech on the consequences of ivory poaching, you discover a program in Kenya for fostering baby elephants that are orphaned in poaching incidents. The organization has a good reputation and the cost of fostering is affordable. You believe this is an attractive and meaningful way for people in the United States to get involved in helping African elephants.

Draft of Thesis Statement with Organizing Terms

I want to persuade my audience to combat the *problem* of orphaned baby elephants in Africa through the *solution* of fostering.

Narrowed topic

Organizing terms

Draft of Main Supporting Points

The first task in the speech body is to address the problem. Second, you provide the solution.

Main point #1 (problem)

Main point #2 (solution)

- A baby elephant needs milk for the first two to three years of life. When orphaned through poaching, the baby will most likely die.
- One feasible response is to foster a baby elephant for $50 through the David Sheldrick Wildlife Trust in Kenya.

Moving the thesis from written to verbal form   Be sure to "translate" the thesis from its written form into your own language and syntax.

Revised written thesis: Get involved in helping orphaned African elephants.

Spoken thesis relies on concrete, listener-centered language.

Final spoken thesis: Baby elephants are at risk in Africa, and your financial donation to an excellent program in Kenya can help answer this challenge.

Using the Thesis and a Preview of the Main Points in the Speech

Spoken thesis

Organizing terms

Main point #1 preview (problem)

Main point #2 preview (solution)

Baby elephants are at risk in Africa, and your direct financial donation to an excellent program in Kenya can help answer this challenge. After learning about the peril faced by elephants orphaned through ivory poaching, I know you'll want to send an affordable amount of money to the David Sheldrick Wildlife Trust to foster one of these young creatures.

7. Monroe's motivated sequence

Alan Monroe, a pioneer in the field of communication, developed a variation on the problem-solution pattern in the mid-1930s.[4] **Monroe's motivated sequence**—used only in persuasive speeches—is widely adopted by public speakers who want listeners to reconsider a predisposition, firm up a present commitment, or move to action. Politicians frequently use the pattern (e.g., *Get out the vote!*), and you've undoubtedly seen it used in many television commercials (e.g., *Want to attract a date? Buy our aftershave.*).

The sequence is inherently listener-centered—it emphasizes what the audience members can do and decreases the chance that they'll view a situation as hopeless. Speakers who want to incorporate a narrative in their speech or make a call to action may prefer Monroe's motivated sequence to the basic problem-solution pattern.

The motivated sequence relies on five steps:

1. attention
2. need
3. satisfaction
4. visualization
5. action

You'll still need to craft a thesis statement and establish credibility at the beginning of the speech. You'll also want to stress the transition between each step in the sequence.

Attention

The first step is to gain your audience's attention. Use one or more of the attention-getting strategies (pp. 241–244), including startling statistics, an engaging anecdote, or a relevant quotation. The attention step should not only gain the audience's attention, but also prepare listeners for the upcoming discussion, just as any good introduction would do.

Sample topic and Monroe's motivated-sequence attention step (persuasive) Continuing with the theme of elephants, here's an example, in outline form, of how a speech on the need for improved elephant-conservation management[5] would be developed under the motivated sequence:

- *The culling (killing) of adult elephants in Kruger National Park, South Africa, in the name of herd management, has had apparent negative physical and psychological effects on the young elephants left in the herd.*
- *Better options must exist.*
- *Elephant contraception provides a better alternative to the culling of excess elephant populations.*

Thesis

Organizing terms

Need

Once you have the audience's attention, you establish the existence of the need or problem. Use objective evidence, illustrations, and stories to describe the problem and to convince listeners that it exists, that it's significant, and that it's likely to persist if no action is taken to combat or satisfy it. Most importantly, show how the problem affects, influences, or shapes the lives of your listeners. Take the time here to convince them that they should care enough to take action.

Sample topic and Monroe's motivated-sequence need step (persuasive)

This step establishes the problem

- *South Africa is the native range for elephants.*
- *Human encroachment on this land led to a reduction of the elephants' range.*
- *Establishment of Kruger National Park allowed for increased protection of elephant populations, and this protection has created a current overpopulation of elephants.*
- *The consequences of this overpopulation affect people, elephants, the land, and the ecosystem.*
- *Culling of herds is the existing preferred mode of population management because it is relatively easy and provides meat to many processing plants built just outside park boundaries.*
- *Culling is cruel, morally wrong, and psychologically damaging to young elephants that have lost their families to this way of controlling the population.*
- *Elephants are a major draw of safaris, which support South Africa's tourist industry. We may not live in South Africa and depend on elephants for our livelihood, but we should take a moral stand on a beloved, environmentally important creature.*

Satisfaction

The main function of the third step, satisfaction, is to present a solution to the need. Here, you not only outline the answer to the need, but also convince the audience that the solution is realistic, feasible, and better than other alternatives. If you know that listeners will have objections or counterarguments to your proposed solution, you should be prepared to answer them. For instance, in this example, you may need to address those who say that culling is needed to prevent the damage to the ecosystem caused by the overpopulation of elephants.

This step proposes and discusses the solution

Sample topic and Monroe's motivated-sequence satisfaction step (persuasive)

- *Some may say that we need to cull the elephant herds to prevent irreparable damage to the ecosystem.*
- *Elephant birth control, however, is a better answer to overpopulation than culling.*
- *Audrey Delsink's research and results on pachyderm contraception is showing feasibility and success.*
- *The same contraception has shown success in wild horse and deer populations in the United States.*

Visualization

The main purpose of visualization is to intensify your listeners' desire to see the proposed solution work by having them visualize the future. There are two versions of the future you can describe: one in which your solution has been implemented and one in which it has not. Depending on your topic, you may choose to discuss only one version of the future, or you may choose to discuss both. Again, be sure to discuss relevance. Show your listeners how they stand to lose or benefit from the future you describe.

Sample topic and Monroe's motivated sequence visualization step (persuasive)

Positive Visualization

Possible future #1 (with solution implemented)

- *population growth under control*
- *elephant families together*
- *elephants supporting the ecosystem in a healthy way*
- *elephants available to support tourism interests*

Negative Visualization

Possible future #2 (with solution not implemented)

- *population out of control*
- *ecosystem damaged*
- *culling on the increase*
- *damaged elephants becoming more aggressive*
- *an increase in elephant meat-processing plants, resulting in even more culling and orphaned elephants*

Action

The final step in the motivated sequence provides ways for the audience to get involved in meeting the need or solving the problem. Involvement can mean taking direct action, altering a predisposition, or firming up a way of thinking. If you ask your listeners to take direct action, be specific and realistic. Add to your persuasion by telling the audience that you have taken the same action (or are taking steps to do so); convince them you "walk your talk." Summarize your ideas, make your call to action, and finish with a statement that lets your listeners know your talk is completed.

Sample topic and Monroe's motivated-sequence action step (persuasive)
- *Results from Delsink's studies show that pachyderm contraception works.*
- *Taking no action means supporting those who want to cull herds to supply meat-processing plants, because that's what is happening now.*
- *Join me in making donations to Delsink's project via the Makalali Game Reserve.*   Call to action
- *If you're interested in a safari, research management practices before you commit. Don't support those organizations that cull herds.*   Call to action
- *Contraception works for all kinds of species and can work for elephants, too.*

Time management and motivated sequence steps

Depending on your topic and audience, some steps in the motivated sequence may require more time and effort than others. For example, if your audience is already convinced of the need, quickly highlight that step and spend more time on the last three steps. If your audience is gathered because they believe in one particular solution, skim the first three steps and help them visualize an outcome, but spend the majority of your time on the action step. If your audience is unaware of the need or hostile toward your proposed solution, action might be less important than focusing on some of the earlier steps. In other words, the motivated sequence is not an inflexible set of steps. Instead, it provides guidelines for persuading a particular audience on a particular occasion.

table **9.1** Patterns of Organization for a Public Speech

Each pattern below can be used for informative, persuasive, or special- occasion speeches, except for Monroe's motivated sequence, used for persuasive speaking only. The topic of "Italy" provides the examples.

Pattern	Explanation	Potential organizing terms	Example of a thesis and main points
Topical	Main points are based on some sort of classification system or identifiable grouping.	kinds, classes, varieties, brands, breeds, features, legacies, categories, techniques, schemes	Italy deserves its reputation as one of the Western world's greatest cultures because of its *legacies* in art, music, and science.

(continued)

table **9.1** *(continued)*

Pattern	Explanation	Potential organizing terms	Example of a thesis and main points
Chronological	Main points relate to each other according to time.	steps, stages, periods, phases, chapters, epochs, historical eras	Italy's history over the last 150 years is often divided into the three *eras* of the Kingdom, the Fascist era, and the Republic.
Causal	Main points show the causes or the effects of something.	*For a cause speech*: causes, reasons, grounds, sources, roots *For an effect speech*: effects, results, consequences, impacts, outcomes, upshots, end results	Its rich soil and the moderate climate in which the grapes are grown are among the *reasons* Italy enjoys its reputation as a producer of world-renowned wines.
Comparison or contrast	Main points show how one idea compares or contrasts with another idea.	*For a comparison speech*: similarities, parallels, resemblances, analogies *For a contrast speech*: differences, dissimilarities, distinctions, disparities	Ancient Rome and ancient Greece share many *similarities* in their architecture, political systems, and contributions to the art of public speaking.
Spatial	Main points relate to each other according to placement or location.	districts, sections, boroughs, neighborhoods, regions, areas, cities, segments, sectors, divisions, layers, strata, components	When visiting Rome, be sure to visit its distinct *neighborhoods*, including the religiously significant area of the Vatican, the tourist area of Piazza Navona, and the older, quieter areas of Trastevere.
Problem-solution	Main points consist of a problem and a proposed solution for the problem.	*Other terms for problem*: challenge, obstruction, difficulty, crisis, predicament, dilemma, question, uncertainty, reservation *Other terms for solution*: answer, key, resolution, response, cure, antidote, way out, escape	Italy could face the *challenge* of cleaning up the Po River if Milan would *resolve* to implement modern systems to treat sewage and wastewater.
Monroe's motivated sequence	Relies on five steps: attention, need, satisfaction, visualization, and action.	Use similar organizing terms to a problem-solution pattern	Visit Italy's Amalfi coast on your next vacation. [Use the five steps to motivate your audience to action.]

Organizing Ideas in Action *Two Students' Processes*

Cynthia Parks and Devin Coats were each tasked with creating a color concept for a remodel of a student space on campus and then sharing it with their peers through an interior design presentation. They both had taken public speaking, so they understood the many different patterns of organization they could use to arrange their ideas for this interior design project.

Cynthia's process for choosing an organizing pattern: Topical

Cynthia started with research on color theory, learning that human beings respond best to environments that have color, but not overwhelmingly powerful color, and she soon envisioned the space in a palette of bright oranges and soft greens. She thought it would be best to argue these choices using a topical pattern, using *reasons* as her organizing term.

Draft of thesis statement with organizing term
I want to persuade my audience that orange and green are the best color choices for the new student space for reasons based on color theory.

Thesis

Organizing term

Thesis and preview of main points:

Based on color theory, I'm suggesting designing the new student space in a palette of oranges and greens for the following three reasons:

1. Richly pigmented or very bright colors tend to close in the sense of space while lighter and more delicate hues can enhance the feeling of spaciousness in a room.

2. Warm hues such as red, yellow, and orange are enlivening. Green is seen as close to the earth and comforting.

3. Equal values in different hues are harmonious.

Spoken thesis

Organizing term

Main point #1 preview

Main point #2 preview

Main point #3 preview

Devin's process for choosing an organizing pattern: Contrast

Devin spent some time in the student space that was being remodeled, studying the current (and outdated) look of pink and mauve and imagining what colors would give it a dramatic new feel. He contended that his choice of bold gray, cream, and peacock blue was effective by contrasting it with the current color scheme, using *differences* as his organizing term.

Draft of thesis statement with organizing term

I want to persuade my audience that my suggested color scheme of bold gray, cream, and peacock for the new student space is an improvement by contrasting the differences with the current interior design.

> Thesis

> Organizing term

Thesis and preview of main points

The differences you'll feel in the remodeled space if you go with my suggestions of gray, cream, and peacock blue are significant.

> Organizing term

> Spoken thesis

1. The new look will say "we're contemporary" as opposed to the sense of "we're so yesterday" conveyed in the old look.

> Main point #1 preview

2. The new look will appeal to women and men more than the old look, which was more appealing to women—and even then, just a few of them.

> Main point #2 preview

review questions

1. What is the relationship between a thesis statement and its main supporting points?
2. What are the seven patterns for developing and arranging your main supporting points for a speech? Which pattern might you use for your next speech and why?

key terms

organizing term 199
pattern of
    organization 199
topical pattern 199
chronological pattern 201
causal pattern 202

comparison pattern 204
contrast pattern 204
spatial pattern 205
problem-solution
    pattern 206

problem-cause-solution
    pattern 206
Monroe's motivated
    sequence 208

exercises

1. Select a topic and outline three informative speeches from it (thesis and main points only), one from the topical, chronological, and contrast patterns of organization. Choose a topic (e.g., cars, gum, music, fairy tales) for which you don't need to do any research.

2. Use the same topic (or choose a new one), and now create three persuasive speeches (thesis and main points only), one each from the same three patterns as in the first exercise.

3. Get in a circle with several others and create a chain-of-events story that will illustrate the causal pattern. Have one person come up with an event. The next person creates an event that would "logically" result from the first, and so on. How many times around the circle can you go?

4. As a group, describe a problem that interests everyone. For five minutes, brainstorm as many potential solutions as possible (no matter how ridiculous they seem). Narrow down the list to three solutions using whatever criteria you all would like. Have three students argue each of the chosen solutions to the problem in an impromptu persuasive speech.

connect

For online exercises, quizzes, and hands-on activities, see the Chapter 9 assignments in Connect Public Speaking.

10

Outline Your Speech

LEARNING OBJECTIVES

1 Explain the reasons speakers create a preparation outline.

2 List the guidelines for creating a preparation outline.

3 Contrast your preparation outline with your speaking notes.

chapter preview

10A Understand the Role of the Preparation Outline

10B Create the Preparation Outline

10C Turn Your Preparation Outline into Speaking Notes

Review Questions
Key Terms
Exercises

You've learned how to narrow your topic into a thesis and organize your main supporting ideas according to a pattern, thereby creating the foundation of your speech. You're now ready to prepare an outline of your ideas that assures you of a complete and cohesive message. Creating a comprehensive outline is a key speaking responsibility—only when you know exactly where you're going with your message can you take your listeners with you. This chapter details the purpose of the outline and provides guidelines for creating a strong preparation outline for the body of your speech. It also shows you the difference between a preparation outline and a set of speaking notes and gives you insight and advice on preparing and using those notes.

10A Understand the Role of the Preparation Outline

A successful speech begins with the building of a **preparation outline** that presents your major thoughts—each written as a full sentence to express a complete idea—in one place. This outline (also known as a working outline) allows you to plan the order of your ideas. More importantly, it ensures that your ideas relate to one another logically, are well balanced, and have adequate support. These essential speechmaking steps will give you—and, in turn, your listeners—confidence in your structure. As one student noted:

> *The act of sitting down to outline my message was actually a relief. I had done so much research that my head was spinning with ideas. I couldn't see how I was going to make sense of it all. Having all my ideas there, on one page, helped me focus and move forward.*

Be flexible while building your preparation outline. The outline is usually in a constant state of flux as you perform relevant research and think about what you want to say; it's rare for a preparation outline to be "perfect" on the first draft. You'll most likely rework yours several times as you arrange, rearrange, add, and delete ideas. Finally, not only is the preparation outline essential for your own speech success, it also lets you communicate your speech plan to others such as your instructor, supervisor, or speaking host.

Let's now look at the many ways the outline is important for your speech structure.

1. The outline shows the relationships among your ideas

An effective presentation aims to communicate one new idea to your listeners. Therefore, you need to highlight that one major idea—the thesis—and make sure that all the other ideas in the presentation relate to it. Those other ideas are known as:

- **Main points**—the larger ideas that support the thesis. Most speeches have two to five main points.
- **Subpoints**—ideas that support a main point. Nearly all main points have subpoints, typically two or more of them.
- **Sub-subpoints**—ideas that support a subpoint. Not all subpoints have sub-subpoints, but when they do, there are usually two to four of them for each subpoint.

A typical outline of ideas looks like this:

THESIS
MAIN POINT #1
    Subpoint A
    Subpoint B
       Sub-subpoint 1
       Sub-subpoint 2
    Subpoint C
MAIN POINT #2
    Subpoint A
       Sub-subpoint 1
       Sub-subpoint 2
    Subpoint B

connect

To view the final version of the student informative speech shown in preparation outline form below, see the online speech video "All Eyes on Saturn."

Here is a sample preparation outline of a speech. (Chapter 11 presents a full discussion of introductions, conclusions, and transitions, but they have been included here to show what a complete outline looks like.)

Speech title: "All Eyes on Saturn"

Speech purpose: To inform

Thesis: Saturn's distinctive features make it one of the more unusual planets.

Introduction

Attention-getting opener
- The broad expanse of light in the night sky has long captured the human imagination.

Creates audience connection
- You, too, have probably gazed up on a clear night and wondered what those individual specks are like up close.
- Luckily, scientific inventions and theories have allowed us to "visit" some stars and planets, talk about them here on earth, and better understand our place in the larger universe.

Establishes personal connection and credibility
- Saturn has long been a planet of interest to me. With some solid research behind me, including an article in *National Geographic*, NASA's website, and an interview with one of our campus' astronomy professors, I'd like to share with you some of the more fascinating things I learned.

Thesis
Organizing term
- Saturn has a variety of distinctive features that make it one of the more unusual planets in our solar system.

Preview of main points
- Those distinctive features include Saturn's composition, its rings, and its moons.

Transition: Let's look first at Saturn's unique composition.

I. THE COMPOSITION OF THE PLANET ITSELF IS UNIQUE.

    A. Unlike the terrestrial planets, Saturn has an interior of mostly simple molecules such as hydrogen and helium.

        1. It also has traces of water, ammonia, ice, and methane.

        2. It is the least dense of all the planets and would float in water.

    B. Its interior core is very hot.

        1. Saturn's temperature is 12,000 Kelvin (11,700° Celsius) at the core.

        2. Saturn radiates more energy into space than it receives from the sun.

        3. This heat contributes to the unusual motions of its atmosphere.

| Main point #1 |
| Subpoint A |
| Sub-subpoints 1 and 2 |
| Subpoint B |
| Sub-subpoints 1, 2, and 3 |

Transition: Let's now move outward from the planet itself to one of Saturn's most attention-demanding features, its rings.

II. SATURN IS PROBABLY BEST KNOWN FOR ITS RINGS.

    A. Saturn is not the only planet with rings, but it is the most famous.

    B. The rings are multifaceted.

        1. They are composed of silica rock, iron oxide, and ice particles.

        2. Individual particles range in size from specks of dust to chunks the size of small automobiles.

        3. Rings can measure up to thousands of kilometers in diameter.

        4. Rings average close to one kilometer in thickness.

    C. In 1610 Galileo was the first to record observation of the rings.

        1. He couldn't explain them.

        2. Thanks to the work of astronomers ever since, we now have a greater, yet not complete, understanding of these rings.

| Main point #2 |
| Subpoint A |
| Subpoint B |
| Sub-subpoints 1, 2, 3, and 4 |
| Subpoint C |
| Sub-subpoints 1 and 2 |

Transition: Saturn's third distinctive feature is found yet farther away from the planet—its many moons.

III. SATURN'S MOONS ARE ANOTHER NOTEWORTHY FEATURE.

    A. NASA reports that fifty-three satellites (moons) have been observed.

    B. The moons vary in composition.

        1. They vary in material.

        2. They also vary in size.

    C. Their orbital planes differ.

        1. Two moons orbit within the gaps between the main rings.

        2. Some moons interact with the rings.

| Main point #3 |
| Subpoint A |
| Subpoint B |
| Sub-subpoints 1 and 2 |
| Subpoint C |
| Sub-subpoints 1 and 2 |

Subpoint D

D. Some of the moons have distinctive characteristics.

Sub-subpoints 1, 2, and 3

1. Titan, the second-largest moon in the solar system, is so large that it affects the orbits of nearby moons.

2. Iapetus has one bright side and one dark side, with a huge ridge running around most of its dark-side equator.

3. Phoebe orbits the planet in a direction opposite that of Saturn's larger moons.

Conclusion

Signpost to conclusion

- It's time to wrap up our tour of Saturn.

Review of main points

Recap of thesis

- You've learned that its composition, its rings, and its many moons make Saturn one of our most intriguing planets.

Take-away idea for listeners

- Scientists continue exploring Saturn and, if your ears and eyes are open, it's highly likely you'll learn a lot more about Saturn in years to come.

Closing material

- Our understanding of our neighbor, three planets away, is just beginning.

Bibliography

Douthitt, B. (2006, December). Beautiful stranger: Saturn's mysteries come to light. *National Geographic*, 38–57.

Lovett, L., Horvath, J., Cuzzi, J., & Robinson, K. S. (2006). *Saturn: A new view.* New York: Harry N. Abrams.

National Aeronautics and Space Administration. Solar system exploration: Planets: Saturn. Retrieved April 19, 2012, from http://solarsystem.nasa.gov/planets/profile.cfm?Object=Saturn&Display=Overview.

Dr. Peter Etsitty, astronomy professor. Personal interview. April 19, 2012.

2. The outline shows superior, subordinate, and parallel ideas

In an outline, ideas relate to one another in one of three ways: they are superior, subordinate, or parallel to other ideas in the outline. Look at the Saturn example to see these relationships in action.

Superior ideas

A **superior idea** is an idea that has other ideas supporting it; it is superior to (or more important than) other ideas.

- The thesis is superior to the main points.
- Main points are superior to subpoints.
- Within a main point, subpoints are superior to sub-subpoints.

Subordinate ideas

A **subordinate idea** supports other ideas and is less important than them.

- Main points are subordinate to the thesis.
- Subpoints are subordinate to a main point.

Parallel ideas

A **parallel idea** is equal to other ideas in importance.

- Main points are parallel to other main points.
- Subpoints are parallel to other subpoints.
- The thesis, the "most superior" idea in the outline, has no parallel idea.

3. The outline ensures adequate support for each idea

A good outline ensures that each idea has a sufficient amount of support. In the Saturn example, the thesis has three solid main points. The first main point has two clear subpoints, both of which have some sub-subpoints.

As you prepare an outline for your presentation, make sure that your thesis has at least two main points. If you have just one, chances are your only main point is the same as (or very close to) your thesis, which means you do not have full support for your thesis. You'll need to go back to your research to rethink and broaden your message.

As a general rule, each main point for your presentation has at least two subpoints. A subpoint frequently has a few sub-subpoints and, on rare occasions, a few sub-sub-subpoints, but that is about as "low" as you want your outline to go. The more levels of ideas you have, the greater the likelihood that you—and your listeners—will get lost in a structural maze.

Some examples of inadequate support are shown on page 222. Where does the mistake occur in each example? The answers are also provided.

Every 1 Needs a 2

Each speech expresses a sole central idea. Another way to say this is that the thesis has no counterpart, or parallel idea. *All* other items, including main points, subpoints, and subsubpoints, must appear in your outline, at minimum, in pairs (as parallel ideas). Remember these rules:

- If you have a **1,** you've got to have at least a **2.**
- If you have an **a,** you've got to have at least a **b.**
- If you have a **i,** you've got to have at least a **ii.**

Example 1

<u>THESIS</u>

MAIN POINT #1

Example 2

<u>THESIS</u>

MAIN POINT #1

    Subpoint A

    Subpoint B

    Subpoint C

MAIN POINT #2

    Subpoint A

    Subpoint B

    Subpoint C

    Subpoint D

MAIN POINT #3

    Subpoint A

Example 3

<u>THESIS</u>

MAIN POINT #1

    Subpoint A

    Subpoint B

        Sub-subpoint 1

        Sub-subpoint 2

            Sub-sub-subpoint a

            Sub-sub-subpoint b

                Sub-sub-sub-subpoint i

                Sub-sub-sub-subpoint ii

            Sub-sub-subpoint c

            Sub-sub-subpoint d

    Subpoint C

Answers:

1. Too few main points to back up the thesis (MAIN POINT #1 only; the thesis needs at least two main points).
2. Too few subpoints to back up MAIN POINT #3 (Subpoint A only; if you have a Subpoint A, you must have at least a Subpoint B).

3. Too many lower-level ideas (Sub-sub-sub-subpoints i and ii), increasing the chances that the speaker and audience will get structurally confused.

4. The outline ensures a balance of ideas

Finally, the outline helps you see whether you have a relatively good balance of ideas. In the Saturn example, each main point, with its varying number of subpoints and sub-subpoints, gets roughly equal "playing time." As you prepare your own outline, ensure that you give each main idea approximately equal attention—a quick visual scan does the trick. While you certainly don't need to calculate this balance exactly, listeners may begin questioning your planning if you spend six minutes on the first main point, five on the second, and only one on the third.

Where is the balance error in this example?

<u>**THESIS**</u>
MAIN POINT #1
    Subpoint A
    Subpoint B
        Sub-subpoint 1
        Sub-subpoint 2
    Subpoint C
MAIN POINT #2
    Subpoint A
    Subpoint B
    Subpoint C
    Subpoint D
MAIN POINT #3

Answer: There is an improper balance of support for MAIN POINT #3.

10B Create the Preparation Outline

Here are some general guidelines for creating your preparation outline. If your instructor requires a typed preparation outline from you prior to your speech, he or she may have a preferred format; be sure to follow it.

1. Be consistent in your numbering, lettering, symbols, and indentation

Visual consistency helps you *see* the relationship of ideas quickly. You achieve consistency by building in similarities and variation in numbering, lettering, indentation, and symbols such as typeface (italics, boldface, etc.), capitalization, type size, and perhaps even font color. Here are two examples:

Visually Inconsistent	Visually Consistent
Thesis	<u>THESIS</u>
I. First main point	I. FIRST MAIN POINT
A. First subpoint	A. First Subpoint
B. Second subpoint	B. Second Subpoint
1. First sub-subpoint	1. First sub-subpoint
a. First sub-sub-subpoint	a. First sub-sub-subpoint
b. Second sub-sub-subpoint	b. Second sub-sub-subpoint
2. Second sub-subpoint	2. Second sub-subpoint
C. Third subpoint	C. Third Subpoint
II. Second main point	II. SECOND MAIN POINT
A. First subpoint	A. First Subpoint
1. First sub-subpoint	1. First sub-subpoint
2. Second sub-subpoint	2. Second sub-subpoint
B. Second subpoint	B. Second Subpoint

2. Use complete sentences

Key words and trigger phrases are all you need for speaking conversationally from your notes during the speech delivery (as you'll see later in the chapter). Preparation outlines, however, require full sentences to ensure that each part of the outline expresses a complete idea. Here are some examples:

Less Effective	More Effective
II. RINGS	II. SATURN IS PROBABLY BEST KNOWN FOR ITS RINGS.
A. Most famous	A. Saturn is not the only planet with rings, but it is the most famous.
B. Composition	B. The rings are multifaceted.
1. Silica rock, iron oxide, and ice particles	1. They are composed of silica rock, iron oxide, and ice particles.
2. Size range	2. Individual particles range in size from specks of dust to chunks the size of small automobiles.
3. Diameter	3. Rings can measure up to thousands of kilometers in diameter.
4. Thickness	4. Rings average close to one kilometer in thickness.

SPEAK
Responsibly

Alternate Formats for Outlining

Not everyone's mind works best with the standard linear outline format that we've discussed so far. You can outline your speech ideas in a variety of visual formats. Figures 10.1 and 10.2 show two formats, the mind map and the organizational chart. We also discussed the mind map in Chapter 6 as a way to generate topic ideas (p. 130). Chapter 12 (p. 281) also introduces the concept of the visual storyboard.

Figure **10.1** **The Mind Map, an Alternate Format for Your Preparation Outline**

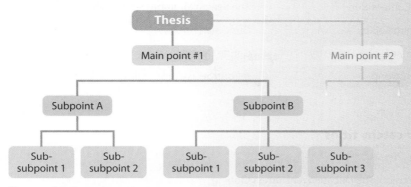

Figure **10.2** **The Organizational Chart, an Alternate Format for Your Preparation Outline**

- What is another system(s) for outlining your ideas?
- What advantages would that system have over a standard outline?

3. Label the speech parts

To make sure that all the necessary components are present, many speakers like to label the parts of their speeches (introduction, thesis, audience relevance, main points, transitions, etc.) after they've incorporated everything into the outline. See the earlier Saturn outline as an example. If you're labeling, ask your instructor whether he or she prefers using parenthetical or marginal annotations (or some other format) to label the parts.

4. Title the speech

You may not need a title for your in-class presentations, but if the speech is going to be publicized or published, a title is required. Spend some time thinking about your title. Try to create one that both communicates your topic and attracts audience attention.

The first box below shows some examples of titles that are either clear or catchy, but not both. Which is better? Both approaches have advantages and disadvantages. Often the answer depends on how formal the speaking situation is and on your personality. One option is to blend the two approaches by including the clever or catchy part as the main title and the communicative, utilitarian part as the subtitle. Connect the two parts with a colon, as in the examples in the second box below.

Clear *or* catchy titles

Clear title (though not catchy)	Catchy title (though not clear)
Mango Production in the Caribbean	Orange Orbs in a Palm-Tree Paradise
Google's Competition	The Search for Improved Search
The Saguaro Cactus	Our Green Amigos
The History of Laser Dentistry	Gentle Dental
Lance Armstrong	A Controversy in Spandex

Clear *and* catchy titles

Flying Rats: The Problem with Pigeons
A Split Decision: The Debate over Human Cloning
Big Business: Breast Implants and the Plastic Surgery Industry
Fur Crazy: Join the New Anti-Fur Campaign
Staged Rage: A Look Behind the Success of Xtreme Cage Fighting

SPEAK
Responsibly

Works Cited, References, Bibliography . . . Which Term When?

It's your job to know the differences between these terms and to know which type is preferred for any speech (or paper) you're working on.

- **"Works Cited"** and **"References"** both list, in alphabetical order by last name of author, editor, etc., full citations to any work—including Internet sources—you have cited, referenced, or paraphrased in your speech. Generally you use "Works Cited" when using the MLA (Modern Language Association) style and "References" when using APA (American Psychological Association) style.
- **"Bibliography,"** by contrast, refers to an alphabetized list of *all* works you consulted, whether or not you used the work in your speech. It is the preferred term for this type of list in both MLA and APA styles.

The academic discipline in which you're giving the speech determines the reference style you'll follow. In general, the APA style is preferred in the social sciences whereas MLA is the style of choice in literature, the arts, and the humanities. Many other disciplines follow more specialized styles. For example, works in chemistry follow a style guide published by the American Chemical Society whereas historians tend to use the *Chicago Manual of Style*.

Always check with your teacher as to the preferred style.

5. Attach a list of research sources used

As you read in Chapter 7, it's your ethical responsibility to provide an account of the sources you used while researching. Add the references list to your outline under the heading "Works Cited," "References," or "Bibliography." The heading "Notes" or "Research Citations" may also work. These various terms actually have distinctive uses. They're explained in the "Speak Responsibly" box above.

10C Turn Your Preparation Outline into Speaking Notes

Your preparation outline is not what you use to practice and deliver your presentation. If you took your preparation outline with you to the front of the room, you would undoubtedly get distracted by its wordiness. Worse, you'd be tempted to read from it, hampering

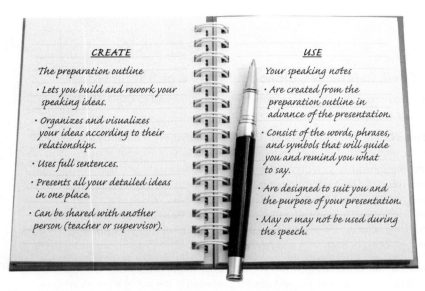

CREATE

The preparation outline

- Lets you build and rework your speaking ideas.
- Organizes and visualizes your ideas according to their relationships.
- Uses full sentences.
- Presents all your detailed ideas in one place.
- Can be shared with another person (teacher or supervisor).

USE

Your speaking notes

- Are created from the preparation outline in advance of the presentation.
- Consist of the words, phrases, and symbols that will guide you and remind you what to say.
- Are designed to suit you and the purpose of your presentation.
- May or may not be used during the speech.

Figure **10.3** **Turning a Preparation Outline into Speaking Notes**

your ability to speak conversationally with your audience. Effective practice and delivery instead require a set of speaking notes (sometimes referred to as a speaking outline).

Your **speaking notes** consist of the words, phrases, and symbols you need as a reminder of what you want to say during your presentation. Create these notes from your preparation outline at least a few days before the presentation, as you begin to practice your presentation. They act as your guide, so they need please no one but you. But their quality can make or break your speech. Figure 10.3 shows the different characteristics of the preparation outline and speaking notes.

Below are some tips for preparing and using your speaking notes.

1. Create your speaking notes to complement your method of delivery

The kind of speaking notes you create depends on your method of delivery. (Chapter 13 discusses these methods in detail.) Speakers using two of the styles of delivery—extemporaneous and manuscript—typically use notes. Impromptu speakers use notes only once in a while, and memorized delivery, as its name implies, requires no notes.

Speaking notes for an extemporaneous, or conversational, delivery

The most conversational—and therefore the most listenable—speeches are given extemporaneously, meaning they flow from speaking notes containing only key words and phrases that trigger the ideas you plan to communicate. Your practice sessions give you the opportunity to organize your ideas, figure out what you want to say, and ensure that you can say it all within the speaking time frame. You know your message. You own it. The trigger words and phrases are all you need to activate those ideas, speak naturally, and keep yourself on message. They allow you to focus your eye contact on your audience instead of on your notes. See Figure 10.4 for an example.

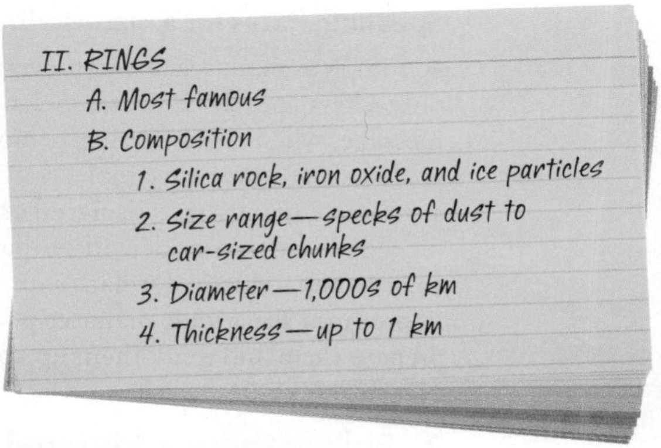

Speaking notes for an impromptu delivery

Impromptu speeches, or those given with little to no preparation, allow little if any time for making speaking notes. If there is time, some quick notes on a piece of scratch paper are sufficient reminders of your main points. As you'll read in Chapter 13, in impromptu speaking, no one expects you to have a fully researched presentation, organized in a complex fashion. Listeners do, however, expect you to make a point and to make it briefly.

Figure 10.4 Speaking Notes for Conversational Delivery Earlier in the chapter (p. 224), these words were correctly labeled as "less effective" for creating your preparation outline. They're all the notes you need, however, for speaking conversationally during delivery.

Some quick notes can help you meet those goals. If you're attending a city planning meeting, for example, and the topic is the future of the city's freeway system, you may be inspired to offer some input from an article you read recently about the many benefits of rubberized asphalt. The set of notes in Figure 10.5 could be made in well under a minute and would be sufficient to keep you focused.

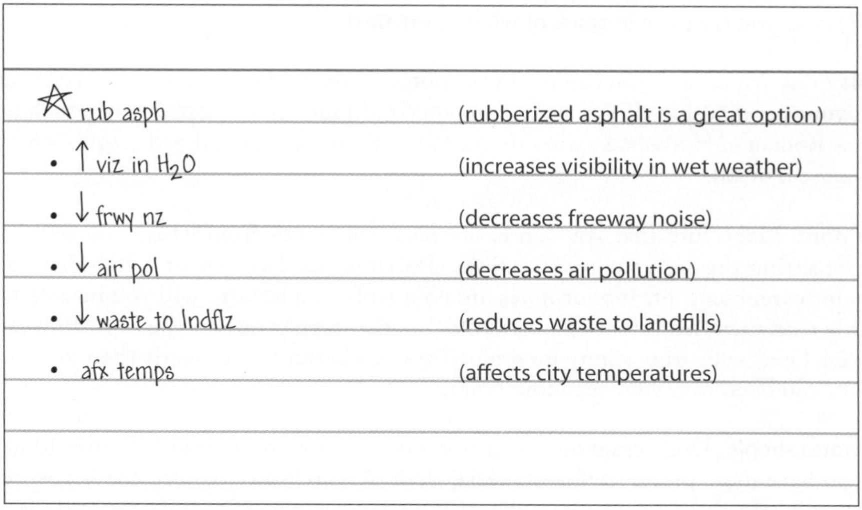

Figure **10.5** **Impromptu Notes on the Benefits of Rubberized Asphalt**

Speaking notes for a manuscript delivery

A complete manuscript (with every planned word visible on the page) is appropriate in only a few speech contexts, including instances when you must communicate a precise message, when there is a high emotional content, or when the text is to be published or analyzed. To take an example, consider the State of the Union Address: the president uses a complete manuscript displayed on a teleprompter screen.

If your manuscript will be published, hand in a neatly typed, formally structured copy (comparable in format to an essay). But, similar to notes for extemporaneous and impromptu situations, manuscripts used during delivery are for your eyes only; you may prepare them and mark them up any way you like.

2. Follow these additional tips for preparing your speaking notes for conversational delivery

Best practices for preparing speaking notes for conversational delivery include making your speaking notes user-friendly, preparing your speaking notes early, and using the right material for your speaking notes.

Make your speaking notes user-friendly

Experiment with your speaking notes for the first few presentations until you find the method that works for you. Even though they need not please anyone but you, you still should create your notes purposefully and treat them with care. Here are some tips and suggestions:

Use only one side of the notecard or paper It's confusing to turn cards and sheets of paper over and over as you try to keep track of what to say next.

Use legible print Make sure you can read your notes. If your notes are handwritten, take care with your penmanship. If you use a computerized font, choose a plain style such as Times New Roman or Helvetica rather than a loopy, tight, or over-stylized script such as *Snell Roundhand* or Onyx.

Use large print Make sure that you can easily read your notes from where you will be standing or sitting during your presentation. Use large handwriting or a fourteen- or sixteen-point computer font. If your notes are on a table or a lectern, will you be able to comfortably read them from that distance? Despite the large print, do you need to wear your glasses? Don't substitute vanity for credibility—it's better to see clearly than to hesitate, squint, and bend over your speaking notes.

Keep the notes simple Don't cram too many notes on one page or notecard (Figure 10.6). It's better to have more pieces of note material than to search the page for the key word or phrase you need.

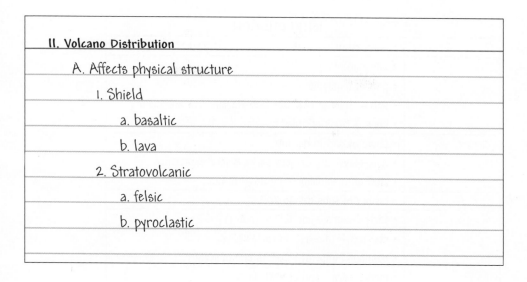

II. Volcano Distribution

    A. Affects physical structure

        1. Shield

           a. basaltic

           b. lava

        2. Stratovolcanic

           a. felsic

           b. pyroclastic

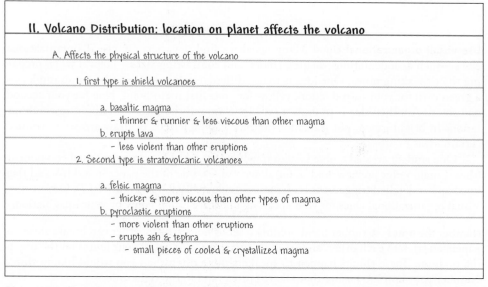

II. Volcano Distribution: location on planet affects the volcano

    A. Affects the physical structure of the volcano

        1. first type is shield volcanoes

           a. basaltic magma
              - thinner & runnier & less viscous than other magma
           b. erupts lava
               - less violent than other eruptions
        2. Second type is stratovolcanic volcanoes

           a. felsic magma
               - thicker & more viscous than other types of magma
           b. pyroclastic eruptions
               - more violent than other eruptions
               - erupts ash & tephra
                  - small pieces of cooled & crystallized magma

Figure **10.6** **Simple Notes Are More Effective Notes** The clean and simple card on the top is more likely to effectively support you during your speech. The card on the bottom is crammed with too many ideas and written in print too small to easily read.

INTRODUCTION	
Attn material	• Navy Brat
Credibility	• father in Navy • part of family life • web = Chief of Nav Ops Sub Warfare Div; sub history • book = *Book of Subs*, Brayton Harris
Picture	• photo of dad in his sub
Aud. connection	• non-Navy? amusement parks is your experience • stuff of imagination—movies, intrigue
Thesis	• history of subs 16th to 20th C
Preview	• early designs—late 16th to mid-19th C • new tech—mid-19th to early 20th C • continued impvmt—20th to end of WWII • modern era—end of WWII to now

Figure 10.7 Personalize the Format for Your Notes Some speakers create their own visual formats for their notes. This speaker identified the structural components in the left column and put her corresponding notes in the right column.

Use visual organizational clues Many speakers find a variety of visual organizational clues—such as indentations, shapes, colors, and contrasting sizes—helpful when preparing their speaking notes. One idea is to use different-colored notecards. For example, use a green card for your introduction, yellow for your first main point, blue for your second, and so on. Another idea is to draw a red circle around the thesis, highlight research notations in bright green, put transitions in blue capital letters, or draw arrows to connect certain ideas to others.

One student created a note system in which she listed her organizational components (thesis, main point preview, and so on) down the left side of the paper in red ink and then lined up her detailed trigger words on the right side in black ink (Figure 10.7). Get creative. Visual organizational clues for your speaking notes are limited only by your imagination.

Number the notes A rubber band holding a set of notecards together can break, sheets of paper can stick to each other, and speaking notes can slip out of your hands on the way to the podium. These things happen to speakers more often than you would like to think. Number your notes to ensure that all are present and in the right order.

Add personal notations and images Your speaking notes can act as personal reminders during the presentation. Little bubbles off to the side of the page saying *breathe, smile,* and *almost done!* can support you in beneficial ways. Draw some eyes on your notes to remind

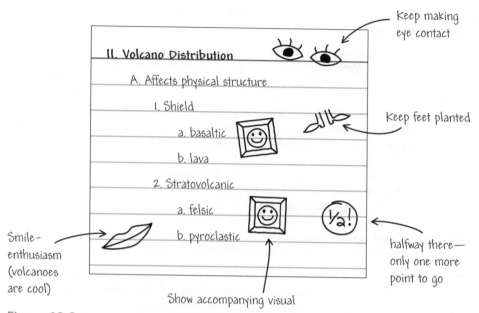

Figure 10.8 Notes with Personal Reminders Are there any personal notations and images you can use to help you during your speech?

yourself to make more eye contact, or draw a picture frame to cue yourself that it's time to incorporate visual support into your presentation (Figure 10.8).

Prepare your speaking notes early to become familiar with them

Prepare your first set of speaking notes as you begin practicing your presentation, but expect those notes to undergo changes. As you practice, you're bound to find that you're trying to accomplish too much or that an idea would be better placed somewhere else or needs more support. Keep a pen handy, and remember that being flexible in the early stages of practice is a good thing.

As your speaking day approaches, stop making drastic changes to your notes. Adding a key word here and there is fine, but by this time in the process, despite additions, deletions, circles, arrows, and underlines, you should be familiar with the location of the ideas and the overall look of your speaking notes. Resist the temptation to change their appearance right before your speech—the new look of the notes may distract you. Use the notes you *know*, the ones you practiced with.

Use the right material for your speaking notes

There are a number of note-making materials to choose from. For classroom speaking, always check with your instructor for any unique note requirements he or she may have.

Notecards Notecards are a good choice. Speakers of all kinds use them in classroom, workplace, and community presentations.

- Notecards are inexpensive to purchase and easy to write on.
- Notecards that are three-by-five or four-by-six inches are easy to hold.
- Notecards come in different colors and can add an element of visual organization.
- If no lectern is available or you choose not to use one, notecards are a smart choice. They're small and don't create a visual barrier between you and your audience.
- One drawback of notecards, because they're small, is legibility. Use careful penmanship. Don't tarnish your credibility by struggling to read a small font or your own messy handwriting.
- A second drawback is bulkiness. A huge stack of notecards is hard to handle and can easily slip from your hands. Aim for two to ten cards. If you're using key words and phrases only, you should need no more than that anyway.

Computer-generated notes Many speakers like the convenience of creating notes on the computer and printing them with one click of the print button.

- Use computer-generated notes only if you're sure you can place your notes on a lectern or table, in a notebook, or somewhere else out of the audience's view. Holding sheets of paper can be awkward and raise a visual barrier between you and your listeners.
- You can still add some handwritten notes ("bring out graph here," "make eye contact") or other visual marks like arrows, dashes, or stars if needed.

Slideware Use presentational slideware such as PowerPoint, Prezi, or Keynote only for the visual representation of ideas, not for sharing your outline or speaking notes with your audience. Show the audience only slides of visual importance. Put speaking notes in a sidebar or window visible only to you. (See Chapter 12, pages 271–284, for a full discussion of slideware.)

Notebook paper Notebook paper can be a tricky choice for making notes. Use it with caution.

- Most notebook paper is relatively thin and transparent. Frayed edges and pen marks bleeding through to the other side look unprofessional.
- Notebook paper is flimsy, folds over easily, and makes crinkly noises when you shuffle it.
- Use notebook paper if—and only if—you are absolutely sure the notes will remain out of the audience's view.

Other technological devices Tablets, phones, and other handheld devices that store digital notes are an increasingly popular choice for speakers. Follow many of the rules you've already learned, such as those about font size, visual notations, and simplicity. Also, be sure that your device has a full charge on speaking day; batteries die when you least expect it.

3. Determine whether (or not) to use your speaking notes for the presentation

At some point, you'll want to decide whether or not to use speaking notes. It's perfectly acceptable to use notes; both novice and experienced speakers use them. Notes provide a desirable sense of direction and measure of security.

As you become an experienced speaker, your relationship with your notes will probably change. Some speakers use visual cues on presentational slides to trigger ideas. Experience with particular ideas—even complex ones—allows you to rely on your notes less and less. While going without notes isn't necessarily a goal, many speakers do reach the point of speaking this way. Speaking without notes is about trying new things and having confidence in yourself. If you believe in your ideas, own them, and want to communicate them, you can learn to speak without notes, freeing yourself up for even more immediate interaction with your listeners.

If you decide to use notes in your delivery, here are a few guidelines:

Practice with your notes

This advice can't be stressed enough. You must be familiar with your notes in order for them to support you on speech day.

Look at your audience, not your notes

The greatest temptation for beginning speakers is to look down at their notes more than they need to. But it's easy to use speaking notes as a reference to keep you focused rather than as a document to be followed verbatim. You'll soon find it natural to look down briefly at your notes, find the next key word or trigger phrase, and then lift your eyes up again to continue communicating with your listeners, just as you did during practice.

Be familiar with your notes

Looking at your audience instead of your speaking notes allows you to gauge whether and when you should deviate from your notes. On occasion, you'll find you need to enhance an idea, repeat a point, or go off on a brief tangent. The greater your familiarity with your notes, the more you can leave them yet get right back to your planned ideas when you need to.

Use notes discreetly

Move from one note to another discreetly and smoothly. Speakers who shuffle notes loudly and obviously in search of a particular note or reference create a distraction and lose credibility with their listeners.

Outlining in Action *A Student's Process*

Like millions of people around the world, Olivia Carson listened with increasing irritation to the incessant and monotonous sound of the vuvuzela (a type of plastic horn) during South Africa's hosting of the 2010 FIFA World Cup. She was later relieved to learn that many sporting organizations around the world—from baseball to cricket to soccer—have since banned the horn. She planned to give a persuasive speech supporting the ban.

Olivia's Speech Preparation Outline: Draft 1

Olivia's first main point in her speech preparation outline, which laid out the problem, evolved like this:

A. *The vuvuzela is a problem.*

    1. The noise bothers the athletes.

    2. The noise bothers the commentators.

    3. The noise bothers the other spectators.

> Outline Draft 1: One week before the speech

Olivia's Speech Preparation Outline: Draft 2

Olivia spent a few more days doing research and thinking further about her thesis and main points and then went back to her outline to revise it:

A. *The vuvuzela, the plastic horn that caused a worldwide controversy during the 2010 World Cup, is a problem.*

    1. The noise bothers the athletes on the playing field or court.

        a. The players had trouble concentrating.

        b. They had trouble communicating with one another during the game.

    ~~*2. The noise bothers the commentators.*~~ *[I'm going to delete this subpoint as I couldn't find sufficient research.]*

    2/3. The noise bothers the other spectators who are trying to enjoy the game and participate in traditional ways.

        a. Unprotected exposure to the horn can cause damage to ears.

        b. Those watching on TV or listening on the radio reported a lot of annoyance, too.

> Outline Draft 2: Five days before the speech, after more thought and research. Additions Olivia made to her previous outline are highlighted.

Olivia's Speech Preparation Outline: Draft 3, Final Draft

Olivia felt that the second draft was a huge improvement over the first, but the more she researched, the more additional useful supporting information she found. She had also begun to practice her speech, which helped her identify places where the sequence of ideas and supporting materials wasn't as effective as it might be.

A. The vuvuzela, the plastic horn that caused a worldwide controversy during the 2010 FIFA World Cup, created a problem that demanded attention.

   1. The noise was a real concern for the athletes on the playing field or court.

      a. They had trouble communicating with one another during the match.

      b. The players couldn't get their rest.

      c. The players had trouble concentrating on their job.

   2. The noise bothered the other spectators who were trying to enjoy the match and participate in traditional ways.

      a. Unprotected exposure to the horn can cause damage to ears.

      b. They can be potential weapons for those wanting to cause trouble.

      c. Those watching on TV or listening on the radio reported a lot of annoyance too.

         i. Filters were tried but affected the clarity of the TV and radio audio commentary.

         ii. Some people had to watch with no sound, thereby lessening the enjoyment of the match.

         iii. Radio listeners were left with only one choice, listen to the vuvuzela or not listen to the matches at all.

      d. Doctors warned that diseases were likely to be spread through the droplets of saliva coming out of the horn.

> Outline Draft 3: Three days before the speech, after more thought, research, and practice. Additions Olivia made to her previous outline are highlighted.

review questions

1. What is the purpose of a preparation outline?
2. What are some of the major guidelines for creating a preparation outline?
3. How does your preparation outline differ from your speaking notes?

key terms

preparation outline 217
main points 217
subpoints 217
sub-subpoints 217

superior idea 220
subordinate idea 221
parallel idea 221
Works Cited 227

References 227
Bibliography 227
speaking notes 228

connect

For online exercises, quizzes, and hands-on activities, see the Chapter 10 assignments in Connect Public Speaking.

exercises

1. Copy a transcript of a speech. Cut the copy up paragraph-by-paragraph, and mix up the pieces of paper. Then try to put the speech back together. Determine the reasons for your success or lack thereof.

2. With a partner, find a three- to five-minute recorded speech in the library or on the web. While you listen, reconstruct the speaker's preparation outline. Was it easy or difficult to do this? Why or why not?

3. Consider your last speech or your next speech. Come up with at least five titles for it. Analyze the strengths and weaknesses of each choice.

4. As a class, right before (or right after) your next round of speeches, bring in your speaking notes—no matter what they look like to others. Place all the notes (no names attached) on a table in front of the classroom and take a look at all of them. What did this tell you about the individual nature of notes? Did you pick up any tips you can apply next time you prepare speaking notes?

5. You have one minute to create a set of speaking notes (thesis and main points) for the following impromptu speaking situations. Compare your notes with those from some of your classmates. What did you learn from one another?

   • During the staff meeting, your boss asks for someone to train the new employees on the latest upgrade to the office computer system. Make your case that you're the best "someone" for the job.

   • Your class is discussing the end-of-the-year party. Present your three ideas.

11

Create Introductions, Conclusions, and Transitions

chapter preview

11A Introduce Your Ideas

11B Conclude Your Ideas

11C Transition between Ideas

LEARNING OBJECTIVES

1 Explain the role of the introduction and describe its components.

2 Explain the role of the conclusion and describe its components.

3 Define "transitions" and convey why you would use them.

Awell-developed and engagingly delivered introduction makes your presentation more listener-centered by providing audience members with a bright and colorful road map for the approaching speech body. In your conclusion at the end of your talk, you want to create a sense of closure and help your audience put together everything they've learned into a meaningful whole. You'll also learn about your responsibility to use transitions, those words and phrases that help your audience follow the progression and relationship of your ideas. This chapter identifies the purpose of the introduction, the conclusion, and transitions and provides guidance on developing and communicating these important speech parts to your audience. It also provides guidelines for handling a question-and-answer session.

11A Introduce Your Ideas

Though the introduction is the first part of the speech you'll present, you prepare it *after* you've organized and outlined the body (see Chapters 9 and 10). If the introduction is indeed the road map to the body, the body is the road, and you must build that first.

1. The role of the introduction

Like a memorable film or a gripping novel, a presentation needs to start somewhere; the introduction is a place to launch what is to follow. While the introduction is a relatively brief portion of the speech, comprising 10 to 20 percent of the presentation, it performs several essential functions: it creates a relationship with your audience, introduces your communication style, fulfills listener expectations, and orients your audience for the upcoming message.

The introduction creates a relationship with your audience

As you'll soon learn, the individual parts of the introduction help create social bonds between the speaker and the audience, even while conveying important content.

The introduction introduces your communication style

Your listeners typically take some time to get used to your voice, your speaking style, and your appearance before they interact with the heart of your message. The introduction gives them the opportunity to do so.

The introduction fulfills listener expectations

An effective presentation has a kind of expected rhythm. It begins in some identified place, takes listeners somewhere meaningful, and then looks back, reflecting on the ideas covered. Audience members, nearly all of whom have experience with previous presentations, therefore anticipate your introduction.

The introduction orients your audience for the upcoming message

Most importantly, your introduction prepares your listeners for the ideas you'll be expressing in the body of your speech. Your introduction tells them whether they'll be listening, for example, to be informed or persuaded. It also provides any historical or psychological context needed to prepare them for your message.

2. Develop the introduction

Developing an introduction follows no firm rules. This chapter provides some time-tested suggestions, but no two introductions need be alike. Critically examine the specifics of your topic, audience, and occasion when developing your introduction. For example, if you're speaking to inform or persuade a new audience, you'll want an introduction containing most or all of the components described below, but if you're speaking to a group you know well about a topic familiar and relevant to everyone gathered, you may only need to provide a warm greeting, stress the thesis, preview your main points, and get right into the body.

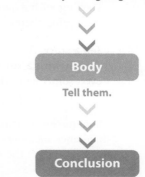

Nonetheless, take your introduction seriously. One student described discovering the importance of introductions the hard way:

> *That intro is the first impression the audience has of you. A light and unimaginative intro gets you nowhere, because you're likely to lose your listeners even before you begin. I know—I thought I could wing my first intro. But take it from me: you definitely want to have a plan for what you're going to say, because it makes a difference. I now know that, too.*

In addition, most effective introductions, despite their differences in structure and style, accomplish the following common aims: they capture the audience's attention, introduce the topic and thesis, preview the main points, create a connection between your listeners and your ideas, build initial speaker credibility, and provide other orienting material.

Capture the audience's attention

You must capture and hold the audience members' attention before they will listen. Plan some **attention material** that will intrigue them and make them want to keep listening to you. Apply your creativity to the list of traditional strategies below, or come up with something unique.

Whatever approach you take to this opening material, make sure its content is appropriate and relevant to your topic, audience, and occasion. For example, it makes sense to begin your presentation on the musician Beck with an interesting anecdote about his pre-stardom years. On the other hand, it makes little sense to open that speech with a joke about a chicken—no matter how attention getting. Showing a shocking photo of earthquake devastation would misdirect the audience's mood at a ceremony meant to honor those killed in the catastrophe. People in attendance would know how the victims died; such pictures would be gratuitous.

Many traditional strategies for catching your audience's attention can be effective, including telling a story; directly engaging the audience; making reference to the audience, occasion, or moment in time; asking a question; using images or sound; using humor; starting with a quotation; surprising or startling listeners; or even puzzling your listeners or piquing their curiosity. Each of these strategies is described below.

Tell a story Audiences like narratives and almost always tune in to a story. Open your speech with a story from the past, present, or future about yourself, another person, or even someone in the audience. Because introductions are brief, offer a shortened version, or tell part of the story at the beginning and other parts of it later in the speech.

Engage the audience Audiences are generally happy to get involved in a presentation. Ask audience members for a show of hands, request that they write something down to refer to later, or get them to participate through a relevant action.

A **literal question** is concrete and looks for an actual answer from the audience.

- *How many of you have been to Niagara Falls?*
- *Can anyone give me a definition of the word* ennui?

A **rhetorical question** doesn't require an actual answer but instead invites the audience to respond silently.

- *What's your first reaction when you think of Hollywood?*
- *Which side of the term limits debate are you on?*

Make a reference to the audience, occasion, or moment in time Audiences like to be referenced. Many speakers open their presentations with a specific reference to the geographical location (*here in the Lone Star State*), the purpose for gathering (*we are gathered to celebrate the union of our dear friends*), or the moment in time (*as we come to the end of the fiscal year*). Such references help create a common bond between speaker and audience.

Ask a question Audiences will respond to questions. Asking one is an effective way to start your presentation. Questions may be literal or rhetorical.

While a question serves as valid opening material, beware of overusing it. Because questions are relatively easy to prepare, many novice speakers rely on them for every speech. Challenge yourself to think beyond questions. What else can you do to open up your presentation?

Also, if you ask a question at any point in your presentation, whether at the beginning or in the middle, make it quick and easy to answer. Be sure to provide a moment for the audience to offer a response, whether literal or silent. Asking a question and then immediately going on to your next sentence can call into question the sincerity of your communication.

Use images or sound Audiences are naturally drawn to these. Incorporating one or more into your opening is a great way to gain attention. Project a big picture of Mark Zuckerberg for your speech on Facebook, display a model as you open your talk about a new commercial jet, or play a brief clip of Cajun music to begin your discussion on that disappearing musical language.

Use humor If it's appropriate for your topic, nothing breaks the ice like humor. Humor, however, is tricky. First, you must be believable as a funny person, and not everyone is. More importantly, though, humor can sometimes offend, tarnishing your credibility and distancing your audience from you just when you want to connect with them. It is not appropriate to use humor that has as its target race, ethnicity, culture, sexual orientation, body parts, body shape, religion, occupation, or even hair color. Most of the "humor" in such jokes relies on stereotypes, which says more about the speaker than it does about anyone being targeted by the stereotyping. Irony, wit, puns, and unique observations can be successful. Of course, as always, examine your topic, audience, and occasion before deciding how—or whether—to use any type of humor.

Using quotations in introductions

- **For your speech on memory:** *Comedian Ellen DeGeneres once pointed out, "I have the worst memory ever so no matter who comes up to me— they're just, like, 'I can't believe you don't remember me!' I'm like, 'Oh, Dad, I'm sorry!'"*

- **For your presentation on the necessity for free speech:** *Eleanor Holmes Norton, a congressional delegate representing Washington, DC, once said, "The only way to make sure people you agree with can speak, is to support the rights of people you don't agree with."*

Start with a quotation Quotations, or quotes, are pithy statements carrying a memorable punch. If using a quote, give the name of the author. You might need to briefly identify the author if the name is not widely known. Numerous books and websites compile quotes of all kinds.

Surprise, shock, or startle the audience Another way to grab your listeners' attention and make them want to hear more is to startle them. Many surprising or startling pieces of information come in the form of statistics, stories, statements, and hard-to-believe facts. If you choose this attention-getting method, the content must be ethical and relevant to your topic; don't shock people just for the sake of shocking them.

Puzzle listeners or pique their curiosity Putting something out there that attracts the natural curiosity of your audience is an effective way to open your speech. Mention the fact that the average human nose remembers 50,000 scents. Say that a new device has been invented that

Examples of how to surprise the audience

- **For your speech about child-rearing costs:** *The U.S. Department of Agriculture says it takes more than a quarter of a million dollars to raise a middle-class child born in 2010 to age 18.*

- **For your speech on the history of the U.S. flag:** *Our national anthem, which was inspired from an image of the flag after a battle, is actually set to the tune of an English drinking song called "To Anacreon in Heaven."*

Saving Your Thesis for the Conclusion

While most informative and persuasive presentations benefit from communicating a thesis early, on some occasions you'll want to communicate it later in the speech. With-holding the thesis until the conclusion may create an atmosphere of suspense and drama in some special-occasion speeches. For example, at your boss' retirement party, you may recount several memorable stories in the body of the speech and then conclude with the thesis: *It's for all of these reasons that Norma is so deserving of the honor we pay her this afternoon.*

Saving the thesis for the end of your speech may also work in a persuasive presenta-tion with an especially controversial central idea. Rather than risk losing listeners early on with a potentially divisive message, you can use the introduction and speech body to create goodwill, build a strong factual case, and establish an emotional connection to the topic. By the conclusion, the audience should be more receptive to considering your point.

- Can you think of a persuasive speech topic where it might be effective to save your thesis for the conclusion?
- Have you ever listened to a speech where the speaker chose to save the thesis for the end? If so, did the strategy keep you effectively engaging with the speaker's message?

may revolutionize human transportation. Chances are good your audience will continue listening to hear you reveal more.

Introduce the topic and the thesis

You'll generally communicate the thesis, the structural core of your presentation, in the introduction. The thesis prepares your audience to listen to the upcoming body. Overtly placing a main idea is simply smart speaking.

Your thesis must make sense to your listeners at the time you communicate it. In the example below, listeners would sense a large gap between the intriguing attention material and the equally interesting thesis. They would inevitably be distracted from listening, de-spite their interest, because they would be busy wondering how those two ideas connect to one another. It is your job to create a logical flow of information from one idea to the next.

Introduction with Misplaced, Disconnected Thesis

Attention material   *People are often surprised that there are twenty-six identified spe-*
cies and at least eighty-five subspecies of rattlesnakes. Some have
exotic names like the Oaxacan blacktail rattlesnake, the Tamauli-
pan rock rattlesnake, and the Central Plateau pygmy rattlesnake.

↓

Thesis   *Today, you'll learn about several treatments for rattlesnake bites.*

> Gap in the logical flow of information creates a listening distraction and a misplaced, disconnected thesis.

Many presenters like to discuss the topic briefly in a broad fashion and then work their way toward a narrower thesis. In the improved example below, the thesis, "There are several treatments for rattlesnake bites," will now make sense for your listeners when you all arrive there together because it has a logical platform on which to stand.

Revised Introduction with Logical Progression from Topic to Thesis

Attention material   *People are often surprised that there are thirty-two identified spe-*
cies and at least sixty-seven subspecies of rattlesnakes. Some have
exotic names like the Oaxacan blacktail rattlesnake, the Tamauli-
pan rock rattlesnake, and the Central Plateau pygmy rattlesnake.

↓

Whatever the species, all rattlesnakes have venomous bites.

↓

Rattlesnake habitats are found around the world.

↓

Humans are increasingly venturing into those habitats.

↓

Bites are more likely to occur with increased human-rattlesnake
interaction.

↓

Thesis   *Today, you'll learn about several treatments for rattlesnake bites.*

> Broad topic is narrowed in subsequent statements, creating a logical, natural progression between the attention-getting material that introduces the topic and the thesis that makes a point about the topic.

Preview the main points

Previewing the main points sets up a mental road map, preparing listeners for the main stops they can expect along the upcoming tour of ideas in the body of the speech. Many

SPEAK Responsibly

Speaker as Tour Guide

Melinda Womack, professor of communication at Santiago Community College, says to "consider the metaphor of the 'tour guide.' [It] is your task to take us, your audience, on a 'tour' of your idea. We are ready to be guided along a 'mind trip.' You have the responsibility to be prepared to introduce the 'tour,' lead us [along the path of your] main ideas, relate to our needs, keep us interested, motivate us to participate actively in the 'idea tour,' [and summarize where we've 'been']."[1]

It is easy to relate to the tour-guide metaphor. Think about tours you've taken at a museum, a factory, or a national park. The tour guide probably spent some time welcoming you and explaining what would happen on the tour. After the tour began, your guide stopped and talked in depth about certain features and then moved on to the next point of interest. At the last stop, the guide most likely gave some concluding remarks and provided an opportunity for questions. The metaphor ends here, because tour guides have a way of steering you in the direction of the gift shop (their "call to action," so to speak). But the point is well taken—your tour is one of ideas, and it's your responsibility to lead your listeners along the path of those ideas.

- Do you agree with Womack's metaphor? Why or why not?

speakers like to communicate the preview soon after the thesis because these two introductory components are closely connected. It's helpful to use signposts (which you'll read about later in the chapter) such as *first*, *second*, *next*, and *finally* to let the listeners know you're previewing the main points. Here is an example of the speaker's preview for the informational speech on rattlesnake-bite treatments:

> *The main treatments we'll cover today include, first, washing and cleaning the bitten area; second, immobilizing the bitten area and keeping it lower than the heart; next, using a suction device; and finally, counteracting the venom with an antivenin.*

Signposts

Main points preview

connect

For a sample student video on creating a connection between your audience and your ideas, see the online techniques video clip "Connecting the Thesis to the Listener."

Create a connection between your audience and your ideas

The introduction is your first opportunity to create a connection between your audience and the ideas you plan to communicate (see Chapter 5, pages 111–116, for more on connecting with the audience throughout the presentation). When you create **audience connection** in the introduction, you relate to your listeners' needs and wants by convincing them that your tour of ideas is relevant and worth their listening time.

The topic, audience, and occasion determine how much audience connection you need to make. Some connections are easier to create than others. For example, a speaker giving a presentation on "how to write a winning college scholarship application" before a group of high school seniors does not have to work hard at establishing a connection. The listeners are probably attending the presentation because they *want* the information. Nonetheless, a brief connection should be made.

A speaker sharing material without obvious relevance to the audience may face more of a challenge to create a connection. For an informative speech on "China's taste for ice swimming," for example, a speaker would have to think more abstractly and look beyond the specific topic. This speaker could appeal to listeners' desire for offbeat party-conversation topics, to their general taste for human eccentricities, or to their wish to know more about an increasingly important country with a traditionally private past.

Whatever the situation, don't presume the link between your listeners and your ideas. However you choose to establish the connection, you need to verbalize it. *You* may be passionate about the topic, but there's no guarantee your audience members share your fascination. It may be obvious to *you* how the topic relates to your listeners, but they may not see it in the same way. Emphasize the connection between the topic and your audience. Use listener-centered pronouns like *we*, *you*, and *us*. Be open and obvious. Establish the connection from more than one angle if you can. Try making connections on an intellectual, social, emotional, psychological, and interpersonal level.

Build initial speaker credibility

The introduction is also your first opportunity to begin building your speaker credibility. (See Chapter 4, pages 82–89, for more on creating credibility throughout the presentation.) Audience members want to know that they're about to give their listening energy to someone sufficiently knowledgeable and prepared to lead the talk. Building speaker credibility is not about bragging and boasting; instead, it objectively assures your audience that you are the right person to provide information on this topic. You can build this trust and credibility in the introduction of your speech in a number of ways: by communicating your interest in the topic, by describing your research, and by mentioning any other personal information that's relevant to your topic and thesis.

Communicate your interest in the topic Listeners are curious about why you chose your topic. For example, in your persuasive speech arguing a theory about why Machu Picchu was abandoned, mention how the Peruvian Lost City has intrigued you ever since you first learned about it in fifth grade. The more passionate and personal a connection you can show toward your ideas as you introduce them, the more likely your audience is to view them in the same way and stay engaged and enthusiastic about your topic.

Describe your research into credible sources Another great way to build trust with listeners is to link yourself to material or people your listeners already consider credible. The *Journal of the American Medical Association*, for example, is widely known for its relevant,

connect

For a sample student video example, see the online techniques video clip "Establishing Your Personal Interest in the Topic."

well-researched, and peer-reviewed medical information. Using information from one of its articles for a speech on experimental cancer treatments doesn't just enhance the credibility of your content; it also makes you look good for finding the material, making sense of it, and communicating it. When you demonstrate your ethical obligation to do credible research, you increase the confidence your listeners have in you.

Mention other relevant personal information If you have any personal information that is relevant to your topic, mentioning it can lend you credibility. Your accounting degree, for example, will give your audience confidence in your presentation on tax preparation, though it's less relevant for your speech outlining the success of your city's graffiti task force. Your age, personal connections, credentials, membership in a group, or specific education or training can all increase your credibility—when they're relevant to the topic you are discussing.

Provide other orienting material

Your speech may require you to add some other orienting material in your introduction. To fully prepare your audience for the development of the main idea in the body of the speech, you may need to

- define terms,
- show a location on a map,
- briefly explain a concept,
- explain who someone is, and/or
- provide some brief history or context.

The introduction is the place to provide any kind of "knowledge boost" that will prepare your audience for listening to your larger message. For example, in his informative speech on the political tensions between India and Pakistan, one student showed a map of the region during his introduction so that listeners could see the length of their shared border and better appreciate the role geography plays in the countries' strained relations.

3. Communicate the introduction

The introduction is important because you want to get your tour of ideas off to a good start. *How* you deliver the introduction is as important as what you say. Techniques and tips to consider during practice sessions include customizing the order of the introductory speech components, refining these components, signaling the thesis, using a confident and warm delivery, not announcing your name and topic, and last but not least, practicing the full introduction several times.

Customize the order of the introductory components

While it's customary to begin by capturing the audience's attention and to finish with a preview of the main points, thereby creating a natural bridge to the body of your speech,

Examples of possible sequences of introductory components

Capture attention	**1**	Capture attention
Introduce topic	**2**	Connect with audience
Narrow topic and state thesis	**3**	Introduce topic
Connect with audience	**4**	Narrow topic and state thesis
Begin building credibility	**5**	Preview main points
Provide some other orienting material	**6**	Begin building credibility
Rephrase thesis and preview main points	**7**	Provide some other orienting material

the other components of your introduction can be communicated in any order that works for your presentation. Experiment with the order of your introductory components until it makes sense for your purpose.

Refine the introductory components

Even though you are, in essence, completing a checklist of the introductory components, avoid the checklist sound and feel. Smooth out the components using conversational language to create a natural, seamless flow from one component to the next. Some components may require just one sentence, whereas others may need a few. Be thorough. It can help to view the introduction as a self-contained "pre-story" to the "story" that is the speech body.

Signal the thesis

Phrases such as *the focus of my presentation will be* . . . or *after hearing my talk this morning, I hope you'll be inspired to* . . . get an audience's attention and tell them "Listen up. Something important is coming."

Use a confident and warm delivery

Stand confidently but naturally. Smile and use a friendly, normal tone of voice. Look at your audience. Show them through your body language and tone that you're a knowledgeable person with interesting and worthwhile ideas to share. Communicate through your words and actions your genuine interest in your ideas.

Avoid announcing your name and topic

On occasion, a new speaker feels the need to announce his or her name and topic before beginning the presentation. Pre-speech proclamations such as *My name is Benny Franklin, and my speech is about electricity* are not necessary. In many of your speaking contexts, the audience already knows who you are, and your topic becomes evident once you start talking. In speaking situations in which the audience does not know you, you can count on being introduced by someone.

Practice your full introduction in detail several times

By now, you should sense the importance of the introduction. Practice your introduction several times to ensure that your presentation will get off to a good start. Practice (fully discussed in Chapter 13) gives you a general sense of what you want to say and builds up confidence as you go into the actual presentation.

11B Conclude Your Ideas

As with your introduction, craft your conclusion *after* you have prepared the body of your speech. Because the introduction and the conclusion contain several of the same components and perhaps some similar ideas, it makes sense to create these two parts of your speech structure in tandem.

Student speakers often admit to not giving as much attention to the conclusion as they do to other parts of the speech because they assume *something will come to me while I'm up there.* But most quickly see this error. Chances are slim that a meaningful speech ending will suddenly come to you. Plan to spend time creating your conclusion.

1. The role of the conclusion

Like a good story—whether it's written, told verbally, or conveyed on-screen—a speech needs a place where the experience culminates in a meaningful way. The conclusion provides a sense of closure, fulfills listener expectations, encourages future listener interaction with your ideas, and ties up any loose ends.

The conclusion provides a sense of closure

Comprising 5 to 10 percent of the presentation, your conclusion is the place where you *tell them what you've told them.* It helps your listeners make sense of what they've just seen and heard. The conclusion is not the place to introduce and explain new ideas even if they are related to your topic. Save those new ideas for your next speech.

The conclusion fulfills listener expectations

Just as listeners expect an introduction to your presentation, they also expect a summary. If you stop speaking during what appears to be the body of the speech, you catch the audience off guard and leave them feeling unfulfilled. Instead of interacting with the ideas they have just heard, these listeners are jarred by your abrupt ending and become distracted with questions such as *Why didn't he conclude his ideas?* or *So what does this all mean?* Fulfill your listeners' expectations by giving them a conclusion.

The conclusion encourages future listener interaction with your ideas

What should your listeners do with all your ideas? Take advantage of the conclusion to state your own preferred outcomes. Also, tell your audience how the ideas you've shared have made an impact in your life. You might talk about how you now see things differently and what you plan to do in the future. Your listeners may be inspired to do the same.

The conclusion ties up any loose ends

Depending on what you said in the introduction or body, you may need to provide epilogues to stories or mention follow-up events. You may also want to encourage further research or speeches on the topic. For instance, in his speech on new veterinary techniques for treating internal hemorrhaging in dogs, one speaker had referenced a boxer that had been hit by a car and needed emergency care. In the conclusion, the speaker assured the audience that the dog was alive and well—the new techniques had worked in this case.

2. Develop the conclusion

A conclusion makes sense only in relation to the material it follows. Most informative and persuasive speeches benefit from conclusions containing most or all of the components listed in this chapter. Special-occasion speeches are more flexible by nature and may contain only one or two components. Time-tested components of a valuable conclusion include using a key phrase that links the body to the conclusion, reiterating the thesis, reinforcing and reviewing the main points, providing listeners with a take-away, and finishing with strong closing material.

Use a key phrase that takes listeners from the body to the conclusion

You need to let your listeners know that the tour of the main ideas is done and about to be summarized. You can use a variety of key phrases to do so. Audiences listen for these phrases, which put them in the proper frame of mind to begin summarizing with you. While you want to use words natural to your vocabulary, here are some common phrases that indicate the start of the conclusion:

- *In summary . . .*
- *To conclude my thoughts . . .*
- *To recap . . .*
- *I'll finish by saying . . .*
- *To wrap things up . . .*
- *Let's review what we've discussed today . . .*

connect

For a sample student video example, see the online techniques video clip "Concluding a Speech."

Reiterate the thesis

connect

For a sample student video example, see the online techniques video clip "Linking the Conclusion to the Introduction."

Summarizing your central idea one last time increases the chances that your listeners will leave your presentation seeing the world in that one new way you intended. Here are a few examples:

- *In summary, we've looked today at the fascinating history of the machine gun.*
- *If you leave my presentation with one idea this afternoon, let it be this: paying now for preservation of the manatee is a far superior option to paying later in the form of a forever-altered ecosystem.*

Keep in mind that in your conclusion you will need to reinforce your thesis using language that's different from how you introduced it. Repeating the exact phrasing you used earlier would sound awkward. Rely on natural conversational speech patterns and communicate your thesis with similar but not identical phrasing.

Reinforce and review the main points

Remind your audience again how you supported your thesis by reviewing the main points. A quick summary is all that's needed. Here's an example:

> *In summary, we've looked today at the fascinating history of the machine gun. We started with its invention in the United States in the late nineteenth century. We then looked at its adoption by the British Army, its military relevance to Germany in both world wars, and finally, its modern applications.*

Connect with the audience by providing a take-away

connect

For a sample student video example, see the online techniques video clip "Providing a Take-Away."

Though you've already made your ideas relevant to listeners at several points in the speech, make a connection one more time. A **take-away** suggests what your audience can think about or do with your ideas after leaving your speech. When speaking to inform, your take-away encourages listeners to keep engaging with your ideas in ways that benefit them or others. In a persuasive speech, the take-away often endorses action by audience members—how they can put your ideas to use, or create something new from them, or communicate them to others. Here's an example for your speech about preserving the manatee:

> *Consider joining the Save the Manatee Club, a nonprofit organization co-founded by singer Jimmy Buffet and Bob Graham while he was governor of Florida. Your donation will help SMC reach its goals, including public education campaigns and advocating for manatee protection measures, such as establishing sanctuaries and lowering speed limits for boats.*

Finish with strong closing material

There are as many ways to end a presentation as there are ways to begin one. In all cases, however, the last words you leave with your audience should be memorable. Plan them in advance and deliver them with warmth and confidence. It's not necessary to script this material word-for-word, but it's helpful to know, in general, what you want to say. Here are some suggestions:

- **Make use of attention-getting techniques.** Many of the kinds of attention-getting devices you read about earlier in the chapter—stories, references to the audience or occasion, questions, images, and quotations—also work well for a closing statement.

- **Refer to a previous statement.** Create a connection to your specific opening material or to something you said earlier in your presentation. This helps bring your speech full circle.

- **End with a thought-provoking idea.** Make a provocative comment so that listeners leave the presentation thinking about your message.

- **Conclude with a take-away.** If appropriate, use your well-planned take-away as your final statement.

The following do *not* suffice as closing statements:

- *Thank you.* You may choose to add a genuine thank you after your final sentence, but these two words do not replace a well-crafted ending.
- *Are there any questions?* Nothing kills the rising energy of a conclusion like this question. Now the audience members, who no doubt want to applaud, must instead remain quiet to see whether there are indeed any questions. If you plan to have a question-and-answer session after your presentation, see the later section of this chapter for guidelines.
- *That's it,* or *Uh, I'm done.* New speakers sometimes feel compelled to add one of these unnecessary taglines. Your well-prepared and delivered closer makes them unnecessary. Strong closing material stands on its own.

3. Communicate the conclusion

A strong conclusion leaves your audience with a positive impression. As with the introduction, *how* you deliver the conclusion is as important as what you say and practice sessions are vital. Some of the tips and techniques for delivering your conclusion described below are similar to those for communicating the introduction while others are unique to the conclusion:

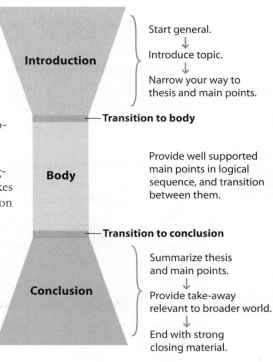

Introduction
Start general.
↓
Introduce topic.
↓
Narrow your way to thesis and main points.

— **Transition to body**

Body
Provide well supported main points in logical sequence, and transition between them.

— **Transition to conclusion**

Conclusion
Summarize thesis and main points.
↓
Provide take-away relevant to broader world.
↓
End with strong closing material.

figure **11.1** **Visual Summary of the Speech Structure**

customize the order of the concluding speech components, refine these components, maintain confidence, create a sense of rising action, and avoid rushing the conclusion.

Customize the order of the concluding components

As with introductions, the structure of conclusions follows no firm rules or patterns. Though your conclusion should begin with a transitional marker and end with memorable closing material, what you say in between and the order in which you say it are determined by the content and formality of your presentation and your own speaking preferences.

Refine the concluding components

Again, you want to avoid sounding like a checklist. As you did with your introductory components, speak conversationally, and let your listeners hear a natural flow from one concluding component to the next. It may help to see the conclusion as the "post-story" to the "story" that is the speech body.

Maintain confidence

Avoid relaxing your posture too much and/or speeding up your speaking pace in a way that shows your relief that the conclusion has finally arrived. Maintain your self-assurance. Let the listeners see, hear, and feel your passion for the ideas you have just expressed.

Create a sense of rising action

A listenable conclusion moves its energy upward and forward. You've just spent a good deal of time communicating valuable, meaningful ideas to your listeners. Don't lose them here. Maintain momentum by having a plan for your conclusion and knowing what ideas you want to share and in what order.

Avoid rushing the conclusion

Even though you and your audience know you are about to conclude, take your time. Speak at your natural pace. On occasion, a novice speaker—usually out of both anxiety and relief at the speech being almost over—makes the mistake of starting back to his or her seat while still delivering the final sentence. Stay where you are until you are finished speaking. Audiences want to applaud. It's your job to remain in front of the audience and graciously accept your listeners' gratitude.

4. The question-and-answer session

If time allows, question-and-answer sessions, often called **Q&A,** are a dynamic part of any informative or persuasive presentation. Traditionally, most Q&A sessions take place at the end of a speech. On some occasions, however, such as informal business meetings or classroom presentations, audiences are invited to ask questions during the presentation.

table **11.1** Why It's Good to Take Questions

For you	For listeners
Listeners are more likely to keep interacting with your ideas.	They get a genuine, personalized answer. For example, perhaps a listener wants a word defined, an answer for a current project, a connection made between two ideas, or some background on an issue you raised.
Listeners are less likely to leave your presentation with misconceptions about your ideas.	Many audience members enjoy intellectual exchange and use your speech ideas to inspire their own thinking or to challenge yours.
When listeners realize you know more about your topic than you had time to discuss in the speech, your perceived credibility increases.	Some questioners want to practice their own public communication skills and see whether they can compose and confidently deliver a few sentences in front of a room full of people.
Questions can alert you to any ideas you missed, hadn't considered, or didn't convey with enough clarity. That helps you learn how to more effectively convey your ideas next time.	Some people ask a question for other listeners who may not be in a position to ask for themselves. Or the questioner might want to elicit information from you that he or she thinks another person needs to hear.

Many speakers look forward to the Q&A. It's an opportunity to shine in the eyes of your audience, show respect for the listeners, and create a richer communication experience for all in attendance. When you offer a Q&A, the audience gets two messages—you are open to new perspectives, and you value the input of others (See Table 11.1).

Managing typical questions

The tips described below offer guidance for handling the actual Q&A session: how to explain the format, call on people, and comment on the question; when to repeat the question; when and how to listen during Q&A; how to handle multipart questions; when and how to make eye contact; and how to answer questions, signal the end of the Q&A session, and manage potential rough spots.

Explain the format ahead of time Ground rules for the Q&A help everyone know what to expect. Tell listeners how long you will take questions. If necessary, indicate microphones where people can line up, or just say you will call on people as hands are raised. Some speakers like to alert the audience to a post-speech Q&A before beginning their presentation so that listeners can jot down questions and avoid interrupting during the speech.

Call on people in order Try to keep track of when people raise their hands for questions, and call on them in that order.

If warranted, make a positive statement about the question before answering it Examples include *Yes, that's a very important point* or *I'm glad you asked that.* Be careful not to overdo your praise. Listeners quickly recognize that some questions are better than others, and you don't want to be accused of patronizing anyone or being disingenuous.

Repeat the question if you suspect other audience members could not hear it It's your responsibility to ensure that all in attendance know the content of the question.

Listen attentively without interrupting It's civil and ethical to give your full attention to the questioner. Let the person ask the full question without interruption. Try to hear what he or she is really asking, and if you're unsure, ask for clarification.

SPEAK
Responsibly

Are There Any Questions?

Your presentation concludes. You call for questions. You anxiously wait. Yet despite your terrific topic, thorough research, sound organization, and your enthusiastic and confident delivery, you're met with silence. *No one seems to have a question.* A careful read of the audience can tell you which of these two options is better:

- If attention still seems to be focused on you and your message, you can get things started by pointing out a question you had while doing your research, or one that's arisen since you've been immersed in the topic. Answering this "question" may spark others (perhaps those who are shy, or just need more time to think) to ask questions of their own.
- On occasion, your audience may just be done listening. If people begin to gather personal belongings, check their phones, or converse with each other about non-speech-related topics, it's time to end your presentation. People may be pressed for time or perhaps your speech—despite your best efforts—didn't resonate as you had hoped. Accept the audience's response, thank them for their attention, and, with a genuine smile, bid them goodbye.

Tips for listeners: you can help increase a speaker's confidence (especially a novice speaker) by asking a question. It shows you were listening.

Acknowledge multipart questions and answer each part separately Acknowledging each segment of a multipart question serves two purposes—it tells the questioner that you understand what is being asked, and it helps other audience members follow your answer. Explain which part of the question you'll answer first. Once you've completed that answer, alert listeners that you're now going to answer the next part.

In answering, look at everyone, not just the questioner It's natural and polite to give eye contact to the questioner for the first few moments of your answer, but after that, answer to the whole audience.

Answer briefly, specifically, and clearly The point of Q&A is to answer audience questions, not to showcase your knowledge on unrelated points. Answer questions concisely and succinctly. Avoid the temptation to go off on tangents. Some speakers like to follow a formula: provide a concise answer, support it, repeat the answer, and ask whether the question was satisfactorily answered.

Signal when the Q&A session is nearing its end Alert the audience by saying, for instance, you'll be accepting just two more questions. Many speakers like to take back the floor to make a final statement, allowing them to end on a strong, memorable note. Thank the audience for their participation, and let them know if you'll be available for further interaction.

Managing potential rough spots

Some questions can mess with the best-laid Q&A plans. Rough spots like the ones in Table 11.2 (page 258) are rare, but it's good to be prepared for them.

11C Transition between Ideas

The final steps in the building of your speech structure are **transitions,** obvious verbal clues to help your listeners follow the progression and relationship of ideas. Transitions are your focus once you've created a thesis and developed your main points, introduction, and conclusion.

1. The role of transitions

In composition classes, where we create written messages, we're taught to build in subtle transitions between ideas. In speaking, however, we need to be more obvious with the words and phrases that link our ideas. While presenting, you know exactly where you are in the overall structure of your talk. For example, you know when you've completed the introduction and are moving into the first main point, and you know that this first main point includes a description of a three-step process. No matter how simple or complicated your structure, you understand it as a speaker. Listeners, however, don't automatically

table **11.2** Managing Q&A Rough Spots

Potential trouble spot	Navigating it
The question is long or complicated.	Paraphrase or reword the question in simpler terms to ensure accuracy and help other listeners follow the exchange.
You don't understand the question.	Politely ask the person to rephrase the question another way. Once you think you understand it, paraphrase it to be sure you have it right before you answer.
You can't think of an answer right away.	It's perfectly acceptable to take a few moments to formulate an answer.
You don't know the answer.	Let someone else answer the question, or if it's appropriate, tell the audience you'll research the question and get back to them with an answer.
The question is actually a comment.	Thank the participant for the comment and let it stand as is, or respond with a related comment before taking the next question.
The question is irrelevant.	Assure the questioner you will be available after the presentation to address his or her particular concerns, but that you don't want to take up the audience's time right now.
You feel attacked.	The average speaker rarely faces hecklers; it's more likely to happen if you are in a high-profile position or speaking on a highly controversial topic. Nonetheless, keep to the high road, and don't fall prey to the heckler; you don't have to answer.

know where you're going; you have to show them the way with your transitions. You are the tour guide. Nathan, an English major, says this:

> I have to admit that I was resistant, at first, to adopt really overt transitions while speaking. Especially for someone used to writing, it seemed rather unsophisticated. But it works. One of the most important things I have learned this semester is to communicate a speech to someone's ear. In order to do this, you simply must be obvious about your intentions and very clear in your progression of ideas.

connect

For a sample student video example, see the online techniques video clip "Using Transitions and Signposts."

2. Develop transitions

There are four major types of transitions: linking transitions, internal previews, internal summaries, and signposts.

Linking transition

A **linking transition,** sometimes known as a bridge, is a phrase that takes your listeners from one part of your speech structure to the next, such as from your introduction to the body or from one main point to the next. Linking transitions are the most common type used in a presentation:

- *To begin, let's look at Penelope Cruz's childhood.*
- *Another reason farmers and scientists are joining forces is to explore new crops that will tolerate the higher salt content found in the local water.*

Internal preview

An **internal preview** provides your audience an advance look into the next idea you are about to discuss. Internal previews are appropriately named. They take place, after all, in the body—the internal portion—of the speech.

An internal preview is similar to the preview of the main points you include in your introduction, but an internal preview forecasts only the next idea in the body. You won't need an internal preview for every upcoming idea. Use these previews instead to help your listeners keep track of upcoming multipart, abstract, or complicated ideas.

> *Photo radar is one solution many cities are using to stop speeding.* — Linking transition to main point
>
> *Photo radar collects three kinds of data—the car's speed, license-plate information, and a photo of the driver. Let's talk about each of these in turn.* — Internal preview of subpoints

In the example below, you're in the middle of your second main point, in which you're discussing the NBA's lockout of players during contract negotiations:

> *Let me share with you the responses to the lockout from two groups—the players and the owners.* — Internal preview of sub-subpoints

Internal summary

The opposite of an internal preview, an **internal summary** helps listeners make sense of an idea they have just heard. Not every idea needs an internal summary. It's a handy device to use when wrapping up a multipart, abstract, or complicated idea. Internal summaries point to the importance of an idea and help the audience remember it before moving on with you to your next idea.

> *We've seen how water differs from most bottled sports drinks in calorie content, "energy" delivered, and cost,* — Internal summary — *but did you also know that pure water provides other benefits that bottled sports drinks can't replicate?* — Next idea
>
> *Before moving on, here's the bottom line with this body of research: there are too few studies to draw firm conclusions about the relationship between dairy intake and prostate cancer.* — Internal summary

connect

For a sample student video example, see the online techniques video clip "Using an Internal Preview."

Some speakers like to use both an internal summary and an internal preview in one sentence. That's an appropriate option for creating a linking transition between two ideas.

Internal summary / **Internal preview**

Now that we've looked at the world's second tallest building, Taipei 101, let's go to the top and tour Dubai's Burj Khalifa.

Internal summary / **Internal preview**

So the rising costs of gasoline are clearly an issue. Let me show you how, in our city in particular, light rail can be part of the solution.

Signpost

A **signpost** is a word or brief phrase alerting your listeners where you are in the speech or indicating the relationship of one idea to the next. Signposts come in the form of numbers, common transition words, short phrases, and even questions. Some speakers get stuck using one kind of signpost, starting every new idea with an *Okay, all right, so,* or *next*. Pay attention to signposts as you practice and deliver your speech, or have others listen and comment. Being aware of a repeated (and therefore potentially distracting) signpost is the first step to eliminating it and finding a new one to use. Table 11.3 shows some common signposts.

table **11.3** Common Signposts and Their Purposes

Move to a new idea	Expand on an idea	Show how ideas relate to each other, sequentially	Show how ideas contrast	Show how ideas are similar	Show how an idea causes or affects another
Let's move on	Another reason/ problem/ benefit, etc.	First, second, third, etc.	Nevertheless	Similarly	Consequently
After that	Moreover	Next	Still	Likewise	As a result
Following that	Furthermore	Afterward	Even so	In the same way	So
Then	In addition	Later	But	Along the same lines	For that reason
Subsequently	What's more	Finally	However	Equally	Therefore

3. Use transitions during the presentation

Transitions need not be fancy, formal sentences. Whether you realize it or not, you're already used to providing transitions during everyday conversations:

- *You won't believe what happened to me yesterday. OK, the story goes like this . . .*
- *Oh yeah, that reminds me of the next thing I wanted to tell you.*

Rely on this familiar experience of using everyday conversational transitions when speaking with your audiences. While the language style of public presentation is certainly not as casual as that of everyday conversation, the *idea* of transition use is the same—you're helping listeners follow you. At the same time, use language and a tone of voice that are natural for you. For example, if words like *subsequently* and *heretofore* aren't part of your natural vocabulary, don't use them. Perhaps *after that* or *before that* fits your conversational style.

Any transition is fine as long as it serves its purpose. A good transition smoothly performs its function, and its wording will come naturally if your true intention is to guide and lead your listeners along the tour of your ideas.

Plan your transitions in your preparation outline. As you practice, listen for places where an internal summary or a signpost would be helpful. If you're practicing in front of other people, ask them for feedback about your use of transitions.

Audience Connection in a Speech Introduction in Action *A Student's Process*

Clinton Cody's informative speech was coming up. He had already decided on his thesis and main supporting points:

<u>Speech purpose</u>: to inform
<u>Topic</u>: Peculiarity of celebrities' kids' names
<u>Thesis</u>: Psychologists say there are a few logical reasons that celebrities give their children off-beat names.
<u>Main supporting points</u>: The <u>reasons</u> are:
1. Many celebrities tend to be non-conventional thinkers to begin with.
2. Unique baby names are a way for famous people to keep attention focused on themselves.

Clinton was also confident about how he would open the speech. He would begin his introduction by piquing listeners' curiosity with a list of some of the weirder names celebrities had chosen for their kids, including Audio Science, Moxie Crimefighter, and Ocean. Likewise, he had planned out how he would establish credibility in his introduction—among other things, he would make a point of referencing the 2005 Three Rivers Press book, *Baby Name Wizard*, by Laura Wattenberg.

Using audience analysis to assess audience relevance

The rest of Clinton's introduction components were in good shape, but he was having trouble creating clear audience relevance. *Why should his listeners care about celebrity baby names?* To better analyze his audience, which would help him create that audience relevance, he sat down with a couple of classmates and performed a demographic scan of the group.

> *Reasons my listeners may not care about my topic or think it's relevant:*
> - *Most audience members are too young to have kids of their own yet; naming kids is not necessarily on their radar.*
> - *Some pay attention to pop culture, but not all.*
> - *Most people just dismiss these names with a laugh when they hear them.*

Audience analysis

It was this third audience analysis item—the laughing—that finally gave Clinton his connection idea. Critical thinking is a focused college skill. If he could take listeners beyond the laughter to a place of deeper, abstract thought, then maybe he could appeal to everyone, no matter their age, parental status, or attraction to pop culture.

Clinton's final introduction

> *Are people in your social network named Audio Science, Moxie Crimefighter, or Ocean? Or, like me, are they named Jason, Rosa, and Suzanne?*
> *There's probably a reason for that. Audio Science, Moxie Crimefighter, and Ocean were born to celebrities. And yes, celebrities* are *different than you and me. While they probably attend more parties than we do, and have more fabulous clothes, they also frequently give their kids weird names. Most of us laugh when we hear a weird celebrity baby name like Kyd, Rocket, or Diva Thin Muffin, and sure, go ahead and join in. I've done my share of jokes. But my speech today is going to invite you to dig deeper and ask yourself critically what these names say about the nature of celebrity itself. You should find the exploration pretty intriguing.*

Opening rhetorical question piques the audience's curiosity and begins to engage them.

Clinton begins narrowing the topic and building the platform for his thesis. He also works to build a relationship with his listeners while creating an audience connection between his listeners and his ideas. Listener-centered pronouns help here.

(student paper continues on next page)

We should bear in mind that a child's name is often more about the parents than it is about the child. This is true for those of us, like me, named after a cherished grandparent or for those of us named after a famous person the parents admire, like my friend Atticus who was named after the father in <u>To Kill a Mockingbird</u>. *Laura Wattenberg, in her 2005 book,* <u>Baby Name Wizard</u>, *published by Three Rivers Press, tells us that it's also true for celebrities.*

> **Establishing of credibility and personal interest.** He also continues using listener-centered pronouns to keep strengthening audience connection.

Psychologists say there are a few logical reasons that celebrities give their children off-beat names.

> **Thesis** with its organizing term

We're going to explore those reasons in this presentation. You'll see, first, that many celebrities tend to be nonconventional thinkers to begin with. Also, unique baby names are a way for famous people to keep attention focused on themselves.

> **Preview of main points** that includes signposts. And, of course, he continues using listener-centered pronouns.

review questions

1. Why does a speech need a strong introduction? What parts should you include in your introduction?
2. How does a conclusion complete a speech? What parts should you include in your conclusion?
3. What are transitions? What role do they play in your speech?

connect

For online exercises, quizzes, and hands-on activities, see the Chapter 11 assignments in Connect Public Speaking.

key terms

attention material 241
literal question 242
rhetorical question 242
audience connection 246

take-away 252
Q&A 254
transitions 257
linking transition 259

internal preview 259
internal summary 259
signpost 260

exercises

1. Find a transcript of a speech in a book or on the web. On a separate piece of paper, outline the ideas in the introduction according to their functions. What sort of

attention material did the speaker use? Can you spot the thesis? The initial attempts at audience connection and credibility? Keep trying to find these.

2. Consider your last speech. Come up with five alternate types of attention-getting material. Would one of these have been more effective than the one you used?

3. Watch a video of a speech. As soon as you sense that the conclusion is beginning, stop the video. Develop a possible conclusion of your own.

4. Attend a speech in your community or on campus. Typically, these speeches have a question-and-answer session. Keeping the chapter information about Q&A sessions in mind (bring notes if you must), analyze how well the speaker handled that part of the presentation. Report your findings in class.

5. During one of your classes this week, pay attention to how your instructor employs transitions between ideas. First, if you hear transitions, identify the method your instructor uses to move from idea to idea. Do you hear internal previews or summaries? Second, analyze the effectiveness of these transitions. How did they help you as a listener? If you heard no transitions, what effect did that have on your listening?

4
Presenting Your Speech

Presenting Your Speech

S peech day is approaching and you are now ready to deliver your message to others. In these three chapters, you'll learn how to enhance your message with visual support, understand and appreciate the connection between practice and responsible public communication, and discover how to keep your listeners involved in your messages by using your language, body, and voice for positive communicative effect.

•   •   •

CHAPTER **12**

Select and Incorporate Visual Support

LEARNING OBJECTIVES

1 Explain why speakers use visual support in their presentations.

2 List the best practices for using presentation software in your speech.

3 Describe the types of presentational support.

4 List the guidelines for using visual support during your presentation.

chapter preview

12A Understand the Role of Visual Support

12B Understand the Role of Presentation Software

12C Know the Types of Presentational Support

12D Know How to Use Your Visual Support

Review Questions
Key Terms
Exercises

267

Speakers even a few decades ago never could have imagined the technology we can use today to create images quickly, inexpensively, and creatively. Effective, well-developed visual support, also known as presentational support, makes a speech more listener-centered by attracting audience attention and encouraging interaction through sight as well as hearing. Many speeches greatly benefit from some sort of visual support, but not all talks need it. This chapter first explores the role of visual support in your speeches. Next, we look at presentation software and other types of visual support. You'll also learn how to use any type of presentational support.

12A Understand the Role of Visual Support

Think about the last speech that you attended or watched online. Chances are good that the speaker—no matter how powerful the words in the message—used some sort of **visual support,** material like images, animations, charts, and models, to enhance his or her ideas. Today business, community, and classroom speaking frequently includes the integration of visual support. If you want to reach audiences in these contexts, it's your responsibility to learn and practice the principles of **visual literacy,** defined as effectively understanding and conveying ideas through visual means.

On occasion, speakers use other forms of presentational support, such as playing sound clips or asking audience members to touch, taste, or smell something. These types of support can be quite effective at helping listeners stay focused on your message. But because visuals are the primary form of presentational support, they are our focus.

According to communication scholar Dale Cyphert, we can no longer relegate visual support to being an afterthought to the verbal message. Instead, we must "broaden and deepen our understanding of visual presentation" and, in many cases, consider our visual communication as part of our greater message.[1] Keep Cyphert's message in mind as you read this chapter and consider and create your visual support.

Communication, as you know, is about choice—and some choices are better and more effective than others. Think critically about the consequences your visual support will have on your message, your audience, and yourself. For example, is that photo truly informative or will it promote stereotypes? Does that graph genuinely help you with your persuasive message or is it just showing off your software skills? Think and then make responsible choices.

Let's look now at some ways visual support helps you in your presentation.

1. Visual support connects with the audience

Nothing grabs your audience's attention and (if necessary) redirects it toward you and your message like the unveiling of a visual. Your use of visual support sustains your speech in several ways: it increases understanding, influences opinion, and creates memories; it stimulates audience interaction; and it helps make abstract concepts concrete.

connect

For sample student videos that use different types of visuals, see the online student speech techniques clip "Using Visual Support."

Visual support increases understanding, influences opinion, and creates memories

Cognitive scientists say that your audience may learn better from words and pictures than from words alone.[2] They'll remember that picture of the woman's leg damaged by flesh-eating bacteria; they'll better understand the water cycle after seeing your animated sequence illustrating evaporation, condensation, precipitation, and collection; and they'll talk later about the before and after photographs of your friend who lost 150 pounds after lap band surgery. Many images also allow those with language differences to better interact with your message.

Visual support stimulates audience interaction

Visual support provides your audience with something else to do while interacting with your ideas. A map arouses spatial thinking and takes listeners to a particular place; a photograph evokes emotion; an animated sequence answers a long-held question. The more you can do to keep your listeners engaged, the less time they have to get distracted.

Visual support helps make abstract concepts concrete

Visuals can "give a face to" or "prove" abstract ideas. One student, while talking about the brutality of Mexico's drug war, showed several photos that got his previously unaware classmates to see the reality of the country's violence. "Mexico's drug war" was no longer an abstract notion—the visuals had proved that—and listeners were now more open to the speaker's persuasive message as to how Americans can help end or at least reduce the problem.

2. Visual support benefits the speaker

Visual support strengthens your speech by helping *you* in the following ways: to help you make a point, to help you convey emotion, to provide a shortcut, to increase your credibility, to keep you engaged, and to keep you on message.

Visual support helps you make a point

Well-designed visual support can help you indelibly make a point in a way that your listeners will remember. Convince your audience of the increasing air-pollution levels in your area by showing a photo of the thick brown cloud hanging over your fair city. By performing a quick demonstration, show your listeners how easy it is to merge digital files.

Visual support helps you convey emotion

Some visuals convey emotional rhythms and undertones that help you communicate your ideas. As you discuss the consequences of poverty in India, display an image of children sifting through mountains of garbage. During your speech promoting animal adoption, project an image of someone hugging her new dog.

Visual support helps

to make a point.	to convey emotion.	to provide a shortcut.
		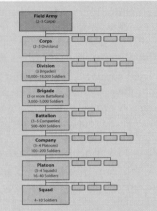
Showing the photo as you talk about air pollution in your city reinforces your point.	A speech promoting animal adoption gains emotional power and support from a visual of a joyful owner and adopted dog.	An organization chart explains the setup of U.S. Army units more quickly than a complete verbal explanation.

Visual support provides a shortcut

Almost all ideas can be communicated through language, but some are more quickly communicated through visual means. You could talk at length about how a tadpole turns into a frog, but showing its stages of development as you discuss them lets your audience quickly visualize what you are describing. You could explain the hierarchical structure of the United States Army with words, but showing an organizational chart helps your audience grasp the chain of command in much less time.

Visual support increases your credibility

Emerging norms for an "eloquent" public speaker include the ability to incorporate effective visual support.[3] Audiences today are exposed to an increasing number of multimedia presentations and therefore bring expectations to your public speech and may use them to determine your credibility.[4] Well-designed visual support, used effectively, also tells your audience that you have thought deeply about your ideas and that you respect your listeners enough to create visual support that will help them grasp your message more quickly.

SPEAK
Responsibly

Do You Fully Understand Your Visual?

All the widely available digital and print images today make it easy to find and use ready-made visual support. It's fine to use a found image as long as you fully understand what it represents. (Also, don't forget to cite it.) Some speakers, especially those who procrastinate or are pressed for time, make the mistake of using a piece of visual support without examining or understanding it. For example, a speaker discussing United Nations food programs in Africa once displayed a graph showing UN food-program statistics in Iraq. This weak display of visual literacy confused listeners and distracted them from the message, and it lessened the speaker's credibility—both major concerns. Remember: choose or create a visual because you need to support an idea, not just because the visual is appealing, available, or slightly related to your idea.

- What questions do you ask yourself when selecting a found piece of visual support?
- Are these informed questions? Why or why not?

Visual support keeps you engaged

Many speakers take pleasure in designing visual support. Others enjoy picking things up with their hands, pointing, demonstrating, and pressing buttons during their presentations, all with the goal of communicating ideas. Most speakers report that visual support channels their energy in a positive way, giving them "something to do other than stand there."

Visual support keeps you on message

An increasing number of speakers choose to use visual cues instead of notes when presenting. These speakers practice connecting ideas to images and then, during the presentation, use the images to cue what they want to say when. Some presentation software systems like PowerPoint and Keynote have a presenter view, allowing you but not the audience to see things such as notes, cues, and the next slide in line.

12B Understand the Role of Presentation Software

Presentation software, also known as **slideware,** has revolutionized the use of visual support in speeches. Invented in Silicon Valley in 1987 as an application for the Macintosh computer and later sold to and popularized by Microsoft, presentation software has become commonplace, if not expected, in presentations in business, military, government,

connect

For a sample
student speech
that uses Prezi, see
the online speech
techniques video
clip "Using Prezi."

connect

For a sample stu-
dent speech that
uses PowerPoint,
see the online
speech videos "All
Eyes on Saturn"
and "Energy or
Anathema?"

community, and academic contexts. Some popular presentation software programs include PowerPoint, Prezi, and Keynote.

Remember, however, that slideware is a tool—not the substance of your talk. It's not a replacement for what you do as the public speaker. Each presentation is different and will have its own visual considerations. One frequent presenter who uses slideware describes it this way:

> *My slides do not tell nearly the complete story. If you attended one of my presentations, you would see that the slides serve to reinforce my points and my connection to the audience. But on their own, aside from being interesting and perhaps nice to look at, they serve no real utility outside my presentation. And that's OK. Presentations are ephemeral, a unique moment in time to connect, to teach, persuade, sell, or whatever your purpose of the talk may be. Once it's over, it's over.[5]*

When you use slideware, you'll want to use it effectively. All too often, the potential of slideware is not realized. For instance, how many of us have had to endure a deck of slides containing full-sentence bullet points that the speaker read aloud word-for-word? The good news is that people in many areas, including marketing, design, cognitive science, and communication, are thinking well beyond bullet points, redefining contemporary visual presentation, and offering new kinds of advice.[6] This section of the chapter presents some of what they're saying. Learn best practices in digital visual communication and then put them to use during your presentations.

1. When to use presentation software

You can use presentation software for any or all the following reasons: when it's right for your message, when it's right for your audience, when it's right for your speaking context, and/or when it's right for you.

When it's right for your message

Think about the ideas you're communicating and consider which ones could be more easily conveyed with an accompanying visual. Here are some ideas that work well in visual form. Of course, you could describe these ideas through language, but showing them is a more efficient and effective means of communication.

- **Relationships of size:** how big a certain jungle leaf is in relation to a 10-year-old boy, how small the Smart car is, how similar in size human and dolphin brains are.

- **Relationships of time:** before and after reconstructive facial surgery, the Roman Coliseum then and now, a photo of you as a baby and one as a high school senior.

Use visual support to show relationships of size.

Use visual support to show relationships of time. For example, these fresco images of the prophet David from Michelangelo's *Sistine Chapel,* before (left) and after (right) restoration help listeners see the effect of the art restoration process.

- **Relationships of space:** maps, charting movement from one place to another, a mock-up of the solar system.

- **Unique or unfamiliar objects or features:** Chilean arpilleras (cloth tapestries created as an act of political resistance), a new species of mushroom, Cy the one-eyed kitten.

- **Things difficult to describe:** a certain kind of cloud, a weird shape, a style of artwork, an older style of clothing, relationships within an organization.

- **Complex objects:** an architectural blueprint, a wiring system, a chemical compound.

- **Small things enlarged for understanding:** a hair follicle, a microchip, a tooth.

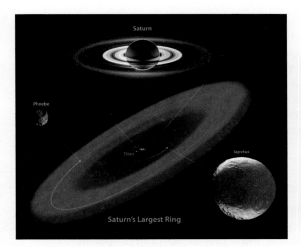

Use visual support to show relationships of space.

Use visual support to show things that are difficult to describe, such as a cirrus cloud.

When it's right for your audience

Use slideware when it is right for your audience, not just for you. Some speakers rely on presentation software for their *own* needs.[7] After all, the built-in bullet-pointed templates encourage them to focus their ideas, help them with their outlines, and compel them to be prepared for upcoming speeches. This focus on the self results in the single most common and most egregious error—using slides to display your speaking notes (also called a speaking outline). (Outlines are discussed in detail in Chapter 10.)

Your speaking notes are for your eyes only. Listeners want to interact with you and your ideas, not follow along you read words off a screen. In fact, research suggests that the human brain more effectively processes and retains verbal and written information separately than it does simultaneously.[8] Your slides should accompany your message, visually enhancing your information, substituting for it, or adding atmosphere, *but they do not need to repeat what you're already saying.*

Use slides to draw your listeners in, keep them connected, and allow them to interact with and remember your ideas. A great listener-centered slide presentation does all that and more, but speaker-focused slides of your speaking notes do not.

When it's right for your speaking context

You can't easily use slides with a speech in a courtyard, on a touring bus, or at a scenic overlook. Not all speaking situations are right for slides. Presentation software requires a wall or screen, electricity, a projector, and a functioning computer that you know how to use. Are all of these readily available to you? In some spaces, you need to dim or turn off the lights for the slides to be seen well. No matter how engaging your presentation, a dark or semidark room can be the wrong environment for drowsy audience members who have just eaten lunch or are at the end of a long day.

When it's right for you

Slideware doesn't guarantee an effective speech. Speakers who use slideware give both good and bad presentations. So do speakers who don't use it. There is no consensus on whether using PowerPoint improves a speaker's ability to communicate or an audience's ability to understand the speech content.[9] Slideware is merely a supporting tool, one of many. Use it if your ideas benefit from the additional visual angle (see page 268) and if you feel comfortable using it. Of course, your instructor, supervisor, or the speaking host may require presentation software for a variety of reasons. You'll certainly need to learn to use it in these situations.

2. Advantages of presentation software

Once you've decided that presentation software is right for your message, your audience, the speaking context, and for you, you can confidently use it for its many advantages: it unifies a lot of material, looks professional, and is easy to learn and to operate.

Presentation software unifies a lot of material

Good slide design, which you'll soon read about, unifies multiple pieces of visual content (photos, tables, video, lists, charts) into one visual piece.

Presentation software looks professional

Crisp, colorful slides are a pleasure to view, and when designed effectively, they tend to be easier for an entire audience to see than some of the other visual options. Audience members are spared the flimsy poster board filled with ink smudges or the monochromatic transparency with that distracting white strip down the side.

Presentation software is easy to learn

You no longer need specialized training in graphic design and computers to create a superb visual presentation. It's likely that you already have a degree of skill in using presentation software programs. If not, use this course as a good opportunity to increase your digital literacy. Ask an instructor, classmate, or worker at a campus computer lab for a quick lesson. Look in the software program itself for built-in tutorials or find them on the web. Check out a training class in your community; these classes are widely available.

Presentation software is easy to operate

When all is running smoothly, slideware is simple to operate. You can use a remote-control device, ask someone else to run it for you, or stand by the computer and run the program yourself. Operating commands are simple and quick and won't distract you from your main task of communicating your ideas to your listeners.

3. Disadvantages of presentation software

Even if you have decided that presentation software is a good choice for your upcoming speech, you need to be aware of its disadvantages: it can conceal complex ideas, dumb down your speech, disconnect you from your listeners, and the software itself can fail.

Presentation software can conceal complex ideas

The built-in outline templates that most users of presentation software employ to create a series of bullet-pointed slides may conceal complex ideas you need to communicate.[10] Some ideas are too multilayered, nonlinear, or intricate to format within the constraints of some software templates, especially PowerPoint.

For example, after the loss of the space shuttle *Columbia*, investigators attributed part of the disaster to the presentation software used within NASA during the crisis.[11] Though the engineers knew that the foam that hit *Columbia*'s left wing at liftoff was potentially damaging, their ambiguously-worded PowerPoint slides led decision makers higher up in the organization to perceive the situation as much less dangerous (see Figure 12.1, p. 276). Face-to-face communication among NASA employees, rather than minimal, text-only

figure **12.1** **A PowerPoint Slide's Dire Consequences** NASA's reliance on confusing slides overloaded with text like this one diminished the potential dangers in the *Columbia* space shuttle aircraft design and structure. Investigators later decided these slides were one of the causes of the *Columbia* crash.

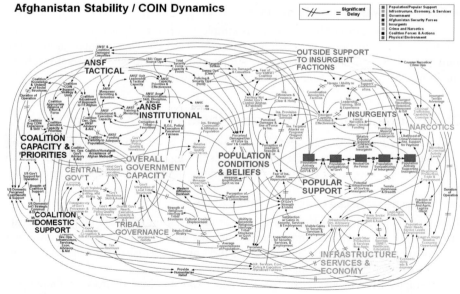

This almost unintelligible Pentagon briefing slide made headlines in Spring 2010. Designed to convey the complexity of the Afghanistan military conflict, the slide ended up making the Pentagon look bad. It seemed an apt illustration of the shortcomings of the military action itself, and it also underscored how reductive PowerPoint can be.

outlines, was needed to fully relate the nuances and uncertainties of the crisis up the chain of command.

People have had the ability to communicate complex ideas for centuries—well before the invention of presentation software—and many of our contemporary ideas can still be communicated without it.

Presentation software can dumb down your speech

The built-in templates can reduce the intellectual impact of your content and presentation.[12] Bulleted lists and brief outlines limit what you can say and may have the overall effect of making your presentation look as if it's geared toward the least knowledgeable listener. Goofy clip art and dancing sentences, accompanied by silly noises, quickly grow old and may result in your losing credibility.

Presentation software can disconnect you from your listeners

A heavy reliance on presentation software can create a disconnect between you and your listeners just when connection and interaction are your goals. The low lighting required for some slideshows minimizes eye contact. The allure of the colorful slides draws listeners' eyes to an inanimate screen. The disconnect increases if you need to stand in the back of the room to operate the software program.

Presentation software can fail

Technology and equipment can and will fail at times. (Causes can be anything from the computer or software freezing to a dead laptop battery.) Some speakers like to bring in printed backups of their important slides or an essential chart. Others practice giving the speech with and without presentation software. Whatever your strategy, have a backup plan for your slide presentation. See pages 282–284 for tips on avoiding technology and equipment failure.

4. Making a great slideshow

Figure 12.2 clearly illustrates the top three common annoyances about ineffective slideshows, according to a survey summarized in a paper at the 2009 National Communication Association conference.[13] Would you have answered the same way as the survey respondents? Regardless, the more important related point is that there are other ways of presenting your slides that can help you avoid these familiar pitfalls, and most pertain to following design-based guidelines.

1 The speaker read the slides to us

67.4%

2 The slides showed full sentences instead of bullet points

45.4%

3 The text was so small, we couldn't read it

45%

Figure **12.2** **Top Three Slideshow Annoyances**[14]

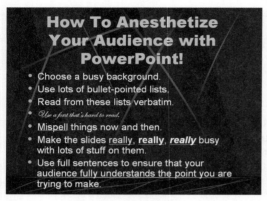

Figure 12.3 **Slide Design Problems to Avoid**

Learn the design principles[15] of simplicity, visual impact, relationships of ideas, color and contrast, and credibility, and then, using your critical-thinking skills, apply them to each visual presentation. (These same principles can work for poster boards or any other two-dimensional type of visual.) As design expert Garr Reynolds says, "Design matters. But design is not about decoration or about ornamentation. Design is about making communication as easy and clear for the viewer as possible."[16] Figure 12.3 presents a mock-up of an ineffective slide that visually summarizes many of the missteps people tend to make. Figure 12.4 (p. 280) shows the design principles described below in action, via an ineffective first-draft slide for an informative speech on energy drinks and the more effective revised version of the same slide.

Principle one: Simplicity

- Each slide should communicate one idea only. Don't ask your listeners to make sense of a slide that contains a complicated numerical chart with seven columns and thirteen rows, or eighteen photographic angles of a particular object.
- A busy slide is not a better slide; less is almost always more effective.
- On each slide, include areas of visual rest, also known as white space or negative space.
- Aim for only necessary, communicative elements on each slide. It's fine to have an occasional decorative picture or a modestly designed background, but avoid irrelevant elements such as unnecessary information, an over-stylized font, Roman (III, IX) instead of Arabic (3, 9) numerals, or extraneous icons or shapes.
- Keep asking yourself: will it compromise my message if I remove or alter this word, or line, or icon? Get the slide down to essential words and images.

Principle two: Visual impact

- Find or create big, colorful, clear images including photographs, charts, maps, or drawings, and place these prominently—one idea at a time—on a slide. Bright, simple visual imagery can grab people's attention and make your message more memorable.
- If you add text to the slide, the words should act as a title, a prompt, or an abbreviated summary of the single point you're trying to communicate with the image.
- On occasion, text is essential—it's the very point you're trying to make. Try to avoid long lists, though. Put your one idea, in words, prominently on the slide.

Principle three: Relationships of ideas

- Show through visual means which ideas are more important than or equal to others.
- Draw attention to the most important idea on your slide through prominent placement, contrasting color, or larger size.

SPEAK
Responsibly

Collecting and Citing Your Images

Making or collecting images for your slideshow is easier than ever. Numerous websites contain huge image databases, categorized every imaginable way. Some sites charge a small fee, or you can type "free images" into your favorite search engine. Google Images is a popular place to start your search.

Just as you do with any idea you borrow for your speech, ethics require you to cite the source of the image, whether it is the photographer, an agency, the database, or a website. One common practice is to cite the source in a small font, below or to the side of the image.

- Group relevant elements together. For example, showing equally sized swatches of red, blue, and yellow would emphasize their parallel relationship to one another as "three primary colors."
- Help direct viewers' eyes to the most important element on your slide through such devices as arrows or lines.
- Display a blank slide (all white, gray, or blue) during moments in your presentation when you're communicating ideas that need no visual support. The visual break also helps separate ideas from one another. Additionally, a blank slide at the end of your speech helps keep attention on you and your final ideas. The "End of slideshow" screen that pops up automatically in some programs may suggest "End of speech" to some listeners.

Principle four: Color and contrast

- Color can attract attention, separate ideas, and even evoke emotion.
- Unify your slides by using a consistent color palette and pattern for your background and font. Some colors—such as blue and white, or yellow-gold and dark brown—work well together whereas others—like orange and black or lavender on blue—do not.
- Colors can affect our moods and behavior. Understanding the basics of color psychology allows you to use the power of color to communicate. Examples include using green for the environment, red for danger, or white for purity.
- Contrast is especially important. Use differing colors, sizes, groupings, shapes, and placement to help your audience better access and understand the ideas you're communicating. For example, larger images get attention before smaller ones and dark text shows up better against a light background (like the black on yellow of many traffic signs).

Ineffective, first-draft slide

Principle 1
Simplicity:
Too many words create a busy look.

Principle 2
Visual impact:
No idea stands out, and the single image, too small and poorly placed, adds little.

Sugar in Energy Drinks

divide grams by 4.2 to get teaspoons

- Redbull
  - 27 grams in 8.4-ounce can = 6 teaspoons
- Rockstar
  - 66 grams in 16-ounce can = 16 teaspoons
- Monster
  - 54 grams in 16-ounce can = 13 teaspoons

Principle 3
Relationship of ideas:
It's hard to determine the differences in sugar, yet that is the purpose of the slide.

Principle 4
Color and contrast:
The use of all black lettering, with little to no font size difference, means no one point stands out.

Principle 5
Credibility:
A brand name (Red Bull) is misspelled.

Effective, final slide

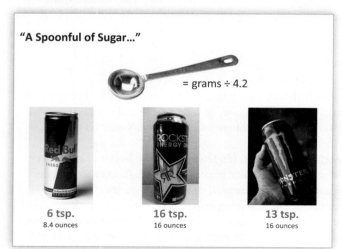

"A Spoonful of Sugar…"

= grams ÷ 4.2

6 tsp.
8.4 ounces

16 tsp.
16 ounces

13 tsp.
16 ounces

Principle 1
Simplicity:
The slide displays one idea only.

Principles 2–4
Visual impact, Relationship of ideas, and Color and contrast:
The three photos and red numbers stand out and make a point about sugar quantities.

Principle 5
Credibility:
The photos have enough pixels to be clear, and the slide text uses proper spelling.

connect
To view the final slideshow featured in Figure 12.4, see the online student speech video "Energy or Anathema?"

Figure **12.4** **Design Principles in Action**

How Many Slides Should I Have?

There are no rules for the number of slides you should have in any given presentation. A thirty-minute presentation with five slides can be just as effective as a five-minute talk with fifteen pieces or a twenty-minute speech with none. Consider your specific topic, its suitability for visual support, and your audience's needs for understanding your ideas.

If you're showing slides, you've created them for a reason and want to use them. Remember that each visual takes up time in your presentation—probably more than you think. A novice speaker frequently makes the common mistake of having too many slides. Listeners watch helplessly while the speaker, suddenly aware of the remaining time, rushes through the rest of the slides without describing what's in them. Timed practice sessions help determine the realistic number of slides you can show and discuss.

Principle five: Credibility

- Your images are a direct reflection of your thinking and consideration for the audience.
- Make sure that all fonts are large enough and that there are enough pixels in your pictures to ensure consistent clarity.
- Double-check your slides for grammar and spelling. The slide spelling "poker" with an extra *r* evoked laughter as the audience imagined a game called "porker." Do you mean *there, their,* or *they're*? Don't let grammatical or spelling errors distract from your message and lead to embarrassment.
- Avoid gimmicks. Presentation software gives you the ability to incorporate a lot of attention-grabbing tricks. Don't be tempted by a sound effect or a too-busy background effect whose only purpose is to draw attention to itself. Also avoid setting the automatic advance on the slideshow settings. These settings don't take into account the spontaneity you may need to discuss a slide or interact with a quick audience question.
- Practice good time management. You need more time than you think to design and create professional-looking support. Don't wait until the last minute.

5. Storyboarding as an option

Storyboarding, a practice traditionally used to plot out a film or commercial, is a visual thinking process that involves sequencing a series of images to tell a story.

Communication scholar Walter Fisher reminds us that we are fundamentally storytellers (review his narrative paradigm in Chapter 8, pages 173–174), so it's natural to think of our speech as a story. Rather than planning out your speech with an outline, storyboarding invites you to "name a scene or situation, identify the point of view or hero of the story, present a crisis or conflict that will become the point of the story, and create a storyline that will be considered coherent and plausible by the audience."[17]

When you storyboard your ideas, you create a visual narrative for the audience to absorb while they hear your verbal message. Your visuals are planned as integral to the message and the listeners' experience, creating a complete, multichanneled communication event.[18]

Storyboarding is an option embraced by an increasing number of speakers. Watch Al Gore's Academy Award–winning film *An Inconvenient Truth* (2006) or nearly any TED Talk (www.ted.com) to see storyboarding in action.

If you want to experiment with storyboarding, here are some tips and guidelines to follow:

connect

For a sample student speech that relies on storyboarding, see the online speech video "Good *E. Coli* Gone Bad."

- Start by envisioning the "story" of your speech (see above).
- Sketch out visual ideas by hand or use a software application. The individual images, created on paper, software applications, or Post-its, can be continually reshuffled as you work to tell your story.
- Create or locate the images and put them onto digital slides. Some software applications even supply storyboard-specific images.
- Build the slideshow in a way that you can connect with the audience. Work to create a moment of shared perception with your listeners with the goal of creating new meaning.[19] You can rework the images in the slide sorter until you create the desired story.
- Practice (and practice again) with the slideshow, knowing what you'll say as you show each slide. The point is not to memorize, but to familiarize yourself with your verbal narrative as it accompanies the visual narrative.
- During the presentation, your slides not only provide meaning for your audience, but they also now act as visual cues for you—when you see image X, you're prompted to talk about Y, just as you practiced. Using this technique can lessen or eliminate your need for speaking notes.
- It's natural to gain more comfort with each storyboarded presentation you give. At first, you may only want to experiment with a few slides and still use notes during delivery. Eventually, it's likely that you'll find yourself creating visual narratives with ease and feeling fully confident in using the slides as cues for your speech.

6. Guidelines for using technology in your presentation

Technology empowers us in wonderful ways, but equipment is not always reliable or perfect. Use the checklist in Figure 12.5 to ensure that using technology makes sense for your particular presentation.

Also, clearly communicate your technology/equipment needs to your contact at the speaking site prior to your presentation. Speaking hosts and technicians may downplay your questions, assuring you, "Yeah, we've got everything you need, don't worry." Do worry. Be reasonable in your technological requests, and then politely and firmly state

Experience

___ Do you confidently know how to work the particular version of the hardware, the software, or the electronic device?

___ Do you need additional training? If so, is there enough time for you to get it?

Equipment and Accessories

___ If you plan to use live web pages, does the presentation room have Internet access? If so, is it cable or wireless?

___ Does the computer have the right application(s) loaded?

___ Does the computer or electronic device have the right ports for any data-storage devices or cables you'll be bringing?

Compatibility

___ Does the program you need work only on a PC, or will it also work on a Mac? Which format is available at the speaking site?

___ Is the right port available for your flash drive or other data-storage device?

Plugs and Electricity

___ Are there enough working electrical outlets nearby?

___ Do you need a three-pronged outlet?

Practice and Preparation

___ Does your schedule allow you to get to the speaking location well before your audience on the day of the presentation (at least thirty minutes ahead of time, though preferably more) to make sure that all necessary equipment is present and in working order?

___ Have you located operating buttons and dials, like volume control and mute?

Cues

___ If you are using a video or audio clip, is it cued to the exact spot you need?

___ If you need to show a web page, is it already opened?

Have a Backup Plan

___ If the flash drive is not working, can you access a backup copy of your data from your e-mail account or other online location?

___ Use a practice session or two to see what technology-supported images you could do without if necessary. Can you communicate the idea without such support?

Figure **12.5 Technology Checklist**

your needs. You cannot afford the negative impact on your credibility when the available technology/equipment doesn't meet your presentation needs.

12C Know the Types of Presentational Support

Digital slides are the most popular delivery systems for presentational support, but other methods include poster boards, display boards, transparencies, and flip charts. These low-tech materials helped speakers communicate ideas very well before the invention of presentation software slides—and they still work. Photos and photo illustrations, video and animation, charts and graphs, and maps are the most common types of two-dimensional visual support. Other types of presentational support, such as people, animals, and objects and models, are presented in full 3-D in the speaking space.

1. Photos and photo illustrations

connect

For a sample student speech that uses photographs effectively to tell a narrative and support an argument, see the online speech video "Benefits of Organic Milk."

Photographs show your audience what something looks like or evoke an emotion. Use photographs to show exactly how bizarre-looking some deep-sea creatures are. Use a photograph of police officers attending a colleague's funeral to make your point about the need for increased use of police body armor.

Technology has made it possible for nearly anyone to manipulate photographs. A **photo illustration** does not record the real world as a photograph would; instead, it is a created image that looks like it *could* be a photograph. Use a photo illustration to show what your new city plaza might look like upon completion. Stage or build a photo illustration of a harried individual being pulled in all directions by children, pets, friends, and coworkers. If there might be any confusion among your listeners, you are ethically obliged to point out that your visual is a photo illustration, not a photograph.

Photo illustration.

2. Video and animation

Video starts with the power of a photograph and adds sound and action. Use a video to show the incredible force of a volcanic explosion or to support your opinion that Lady Gaga deserves her reputation as an outrageous performer. An animated sequence (one that has movement) is also helpful in communicating ideas—find one or make your own. Use one to take your audience on a "three-dimensional" tour of a theatre set. Show an animated sequence of a mutated gene affecting a normal cell cycle.

SPEAK Responsibly

3. Charts and graphs

A **chart** is a diagram that groups detailed information in one place. A **graph,** sometimes called a **data-driven graph,** helps you communicate numerical relationships. Some of the most common types of charts and graphs are defined and described below.

Flow chart

A **flow chart** shows the sequence of operations in a process. For example, use a flow chart to show how scholarship applications are collected, processed, and ranked.

Organizational chart

An **organizational chart** shows how authority and supervision are distributed within a company or an organization. Use an organizational chart to explain the structure of a new company you are launching.

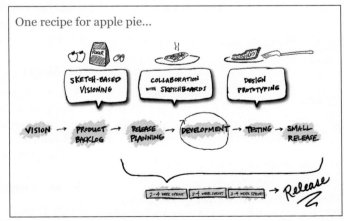

A flow chart shows the sequence of steps in a process, as in this overview of the design process from a user-experience conference presentation.

A timeline shows the chronology of events.

Timeline

A **timeline** shows key events arranged chronologically. Use a timeline to show important dates and events leading up to and following the Prohibition Amendment or to show key deadlines for an upcoming group project.

Pie graph

A **pie graph** shows how 100 percent of something is broken down into smaller segments; the segments of the pie always add up to 100 percent. Use a pie graph to show that 47 percent of your classmates work full-time, 33 percent work part-time, and 20 percent do not work at all.

Bar graph

A **bar graph** uses bars of varying lengths, oriented vertically or horizontally, to illustrate comparisons of two or more values; numerical data and explanatory labels are arranged along the x- and y-axes.

Line graph

A **line graph** uses single or multiple lines to show trends over time. Use a line graph to show winter-holiday sales figures at your company over the last fifty years.

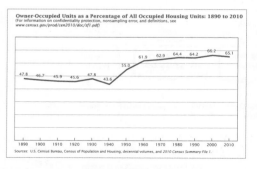

A line graph shows trends over time, as in this U.S. Census Bureau graph charting home ownership rates over more than a century.

4. Maps

A map is a great way to show spatial relationships and involve your audience. Not only do maps help orient those who are geographically challenged, but they also are big and colorful and can take your listeners on a journey to another part of the city, state, region, country, or world.

5. Multimedia

Many presentations today combine the power of images, animation, video, data, and sound all in one place. Soft-

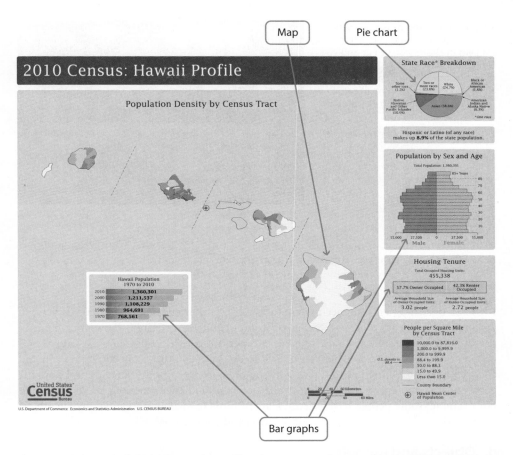

The 2010 U.S. Census included demographic profiles of every state, using a combination of visuals: a color-coded map, bar graphs, and a pie chart.

ware allows you to create exciting multimedia presentations, but it will take extra time. Plan accordingly.

6. People

Speakers sometimes use themselves or others as visual support to attract an audience's attention and encourage interaction. Most people like to watch other people doing or demonstrating things. Show how to wrap a sari by putting one on. Use an assistant as you demonstrate self-defense techniques. Ask for volunteers as you teach your audience the trick of guessing someone's weight within three pounds. If you are using other people

This U.S. Army speech, from the series "Preserving the Sounds of Liberty," explains the history of the Fife and Drum Corps instruments. The speaker relies on both 3-D visual support and audio support—in the form of corps musicians in uniform who play during parts of the presentation.

to assist you, share your plan with them ahead of time. Ensure that your "visual-support person" enhances your presentation rather than distracts from it.

7. Animals

If there's one thing an audience prefers to watching other people, it's animals. If you get permission, bring in your dog to demonstrate obedience training. Show your colorful parrot while discussing its characteristics as a pet. Of course, make sure the animal will cooperate with you and do what you need it to do. Will your dog concentrate on you and the trick you are asking her to do, or will she be more interested in getting to know the people in the audience? Also, consider the potential audience reactions to your animal. For example, some people have intense fears of birds or snakes, and some people are allergic to dogs. Try to ensure that your listeners and your animal will remain safe.

8. Objects and models

Nearly all objects attract attention, but they make a bigger impact when they are novel to the majority of your audience. Everyone has seen a cell phone, but how many people have seen a kidney stone? Demonstrate the advanced technology of a titanium knee by bringing in an example. Show your audience how exotically cool a didgeridoo is by giving a mini-concert with this primitive Australian instrument.

One veterinarian who often speaks on career days at local schools likes to bring in cat X-rays and her stethoscope. She says that these items get the children's attention and help keep their interest while she talks about the world of veterinary medicine. You can also use objects for their value as metaphors. Show a pair of champagne glasses to symbolize a couple's commitment. Light a candle to represent an "eternal flame of hope" in the search for a cure for multiple sclerosis.

A **model** is a three-dimensional scaled-down version of an object too large or too dangerous to bring to your presentation. Architects build models to show clients their vision of a new park or building. A replica of an eighteenth-century sailing ship helps your

Creating a Meaningful Handout

Handouts are appropriate for some speaking situations and may be expected in some business contexts. Here are some guidelines for creating a meaningful handout:

- A good handout is not a copy of your speaking outline or your PowerPoint slides—these often lose their meaning once your presentation is over.
- Instead, a good handout provides your audience members with additional information you don't have time to cover, reviews the relationships between the ideas you shared, or gives your listeners something to follow, such as a complicated chart or series of statistics, at some point during your presentation.
- If the handout contains data you'll be talking about, project an enlargement of the data for easy audience reference.
- Unless your handout contains something listeners need to follow during the presentation, provide your handout afterward so that your audience won't be distracted while you're still speaking.
- If you're required to provide the handout before or at the beginning of your talk, consider asking listeners to put it aside for now, and assure them that you'll review it with them at the appropriate time in your presentation.
- If the handout has multiple pages, number them for easy reference.

audience gain an appreciation for its grace and complexity. A model of a weapon allows you to demonstrate, in a safe and nonthreatening way, how it is used. When using objects or models, ask yourself: Do the sight lines in the room let those on the sides or in the back see? Can everyone observe the details on that Fabergé egg, or do you need a projection device like a document camera or an Elmo Visual Presenter to magnify them? If you have to manipulate a small part of your model, will your hands be steady enough to do it?

connect
For a sample student speech that uses objects, see the online demonstration speech video "Pool Cleaning."

12D Know How to Use Your Visual Support

You already know the importance of having enough time to prepare your presentational support. You also need sufficient time to practice with it. Though you don't need to work out the exact steps of using your visual, familiarize yourself with its details so that it looks and feels natural when the time comes to use it in front of your audience. You want your visual support—be it high-tech, low-tech, or no-tech—to enhance your presentation, not detract from it. Here are some guidelines for using your visual support during your presentation.

1. Presenting your visual

Your audience must be able to easily see, understand, and interact with your visual. Follow these recommendations:

Introduce the visual

Provide your audience with a few words of orientation prior to showing and discussing your visual support. Explain what the audience is about to experience by saying, "Here's a chart to help you see exactly where the money we raised last year went to help the children in our community," or "I'm showing you this map of South America so that you can see how many countries contain at least a portion of the Andean mountain chain."

Know what you want to say

You should be familiar enough with your visual that you don't have to study it to think of something to say during the presentation. (Many speakers make little notations on their notecards about when to show a visual and what to say about it.) Don't be like the speaker who not only failed to label the x- and y-axes on her graph but also had no clue what they were measuring. This speaker soon got so frustrated that she just stopped interacting with the visual, leaving it there as a reminder of her lack of preparation. Have a plan for what you are going to say, practice it, and then convey it to your audience.

Point to the spot of reference

Don't assume that your audience can locate the exact spot of reference on the visual even if it's obvious to you. Use a laser pointer or another pointing device (a metal pointer, a pencil, your finger) to draw your audience's attention to that exact slice of the pie graph or that particular visual characteristic you're discussing.

Allow time for the audience to absorb the material

Despite your visual's simplicity, your audience needs time to make sense of and interact with the visual. Allow enough time for them to do so.

Speak to the audience, not to the visual

It's common for novice speakers to get too absorbed in a visual. While showing your visual, keep your face, eyes, and body oriented toward the audience, as you were doing earlier in the speech. It's perfectly acceptable to look at your visual when pointing to a spot of reference, but don't let your eyes stay there.

Cite the content of the visual

You often need to cite a reference, especially if your visual is a data-driven graph. For example, point out that "this is a 2011 chart from the Centers for Disease Control and Prevention." See page 165–168 for a full discussion on citing research sources and pages 79–80 for guidelines regarding fair use of another person's creative work.

2. Avoiding distraction

Visual support gives your listeners something to do, but that's both an advantage and a disadvantage. It's a disadvantage because audience members can get distracted and lose track of your message. Use the following strategies to keep audiences appropriately focused on your ideas:

Show the visual only as needed

Keep your iguana in the terrarium under a sheet until it's time to show off his beautiful beaded pattern; keep your poster-board chart turned around or flat on the table until you need to discuss it; show a blank slide until you're ready to show one with content. Once you've finished discussing the visual, remove it to redirect your audience's attention back to you and your continuing message.

connect

For a sample student speech that uses a poster-board chart, see the online speech video "Fair Trade."

Beware of putting things in your audience's hands

People are naturally curious. Once something is given to them, they pay attention to it, not the person who gave it to them. Display your photo on a screen rather than passing it around the room. Project your pie graph rather than giving a copy to each audience member. If you want to give people something to take home, it's usually best to wait until the end of the presentation to do this.

Consider legality, safety, and propriety

Presentations suffer when speakers use illegal, unsafe, or improper visual support. For example, one classroom audience was rightfully shaken when a student brought in a gun to demonstrate how to clean it. The speaker's message would have worked well at a meeting of gun owners in a private club, but the mere presence of a weapon in a public classroom created an enormous distraction for the majority of the listeners.

Check with your speaking host if you are thinking of using anything that may not be legal, such as alcohol in the hands of a minor, drugs on campus, or weapons in public buildings. Ask yourself whether your visual—knives, dogs, or needles—could cause you or someone else harm or is in questionable taste in your speaking context. You want your audience to remember your speech for its ideas, not its inappropriate visual support.

Choosing Images in Action *A Student's Process*

Sara Jordan's speech assignment was to teach listeners about a piece of work designed by an architect, designer, or artist. Sara had learned about German artist Käthe Kollwitz in her art history course and had been drawn to Kollwitz's powerful and dark images of the less fortunate—victims of poverty, war, and hunger. She chose Kollwitz's 1903 etching, *Woman with Dead Child,* as her topic.

Integrating accompanying images

Sara chose only a few images for her slideshow, carefully considering what she wanted each to communicate. To ensure each image served a specific, relevant function, Sara drafted a document for her own reference that included each slide image, accompanied by notes to herself on how and why she would use that image in her presentation.

Slide 1: Full image of Käthe Kollwitz's <u>Woman with Dead Child</u>, 1903

How I'll use the image:

I want to give the audience a full view of the piece before I talk about it in depth. The idea is to give the audience time to explore their own ideas, thoughts, and feelings about loss and sadness. So, I'll start off with a question: "What do you feel when you look at this piece?" Though not everyone will answer, it should push them to really look and explore those feelings on their own— thus introducing both the piece and the overall idea I hope to communicate by the end of my speech.

(student sample continues on next page)

Slides 2 and 3: Close-up of mother, close-up of child

How I'll use the images:

This is when I go into depth about the feelings expressed in the piece. I'll focus on only a few things—the mother in one image and the child in another. I think I can keep the audience more focused on my message by closing in on smaller parts of the whole. You need to really look at the mother, to see the harsh lines used to draw her, along with the darker values that create a sense of despair and darkness. I want my audience to then concentrate on only the child's face, to see the light reflected there, symbolizing the child's innocence and contrasting so sadly with the mother's darkness.

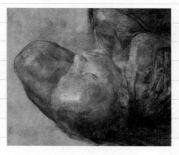

Slide 4: Return to full image of piece

How I'll use the image:

I want to show the full image one last time. My hope is that the piece is now not just a "gloomy" image, but one that holds depth and meaning. At this point, I want my peers to take away with them some understanding about the darker feelings we choose to hide away, when, really, we must face them and even express them in our own way, just as Kollwitz did with her artwork.

review questions

1. What are the reasons for using visual support in your speech? How does a visual connect to the audience? How does using visuals help you as the speaker?
2. When should you use presentation software? What are some of the advantages and disadvantages of using it? What are some best practices for creating an effective slideshow?
3. What are some of the types of visual support you can use in your speech?
4. How do you best use your presentational support during the speech?

key terms

visual support 268
visual literacy 268
slideware 271
storyboarding 282
photo illustration 284
gratuitous image 285

chart 285
graph, or data-driven
   graph 285
flow chart 285
organizational chart 285
timeline 286

pie graph 286
bar graph 286
line graph 286
model 288

connect

For online exercises, quizzes, and hands-on activities, see the Chapter 12 assignments in Connect Public Speaking.

exercises

1. Pick up a copy of *USA Today*. On your own or with a classmate, analyze its use of visual support—charts, graphs, and so on. How does a given piece of visual support help you better understand the article it's connected to? Present a summary of your analysis to your classmates or your instructor.
2. Go to a magazine or the web (Google Images is a good place to start), and bring in six examples of visuals, one each that shows:
   - a relationship of size
   - a relationship of time
   - a relationship of space
   - a unique or unfamiliar object or feature
   - something that is difficult to describe
   - something small that needs to be enlarged for understanding
3. As a class, discuss the advantages and disadvantages—from a listener's point of view—of the slideware presentations you have seen.
4. You're giving an informative presentation on the four major blood types (O, A, B, and AB). With some classmates, brainstorm potential visual support to support your speech.

CHAPTER 13

Practice Your Presentation

LEARNING OBJECTIVES

1 Explain why practice is a critical responsibility for speakers.

2 List the tips for effective practice.

3 Identify the four methods of delivery, and explain how practice factors into each of them.

Basketball Hall of Fame player and coach John Wooden once said, "Failure to prepare is preparing to fail." His point applies to endeavors of all sorts—public speaking included. One of the most important ways a public speaker prepares is through the exercise and art of practice. Whether your presentation is a two-minute personal introduction or a forty-five-minute keynote address, practice serves to familiarize you with your ideas, reinforce technique, build confidence, and help you meet your goal of communicating your ideas effectively to your listeners. This chapter demonstrates why practice is one of a speaker's most important responsibilities. It also provides tips for effective practice and shows ways to practice with your chosen method of delivery.

13A Achieve Speaking Success through Practice

You've spent a good deal of time choosing and researching a topic, organizing your ideas, and preparing support for them—your speech content is solid. But your language, voice, and body movements must complement the content for the presentation to be effective. Practice is the key to achieving this alignment.

The term *rehearse* is sometimes confused with *practice*. *Rehearse*, however, better applies to choreographed performance. Actors, directors, and technicians, for example, must rehearse together to block out action, memorize lines, and hit light and sound cues. Night after night, the stage production must look and sound predictably the same.

But *practice,* the verb of choice for public speakers, refers to getting experience that you can draw on in your presentation. Athletes, for example, practice to familiarize themselves with skills, plays, theory, equipment, and other teams. The practice does not give a predictable result in the athletic event, but it provides the athlete experience to make informed choices at critical points during the competition.

Your speech practice does the same for you. While you cannot foresee exactly what will happen during your presentation, practice gives you a good idea of what to expect. Familiarizing yourself with the structure and organization of your ideas, your examples, your visual support, your audience-connection techniques, and your notes gives you experience and confidence to draw upon as you make decisions during your presentation. In fact, research shows a positive correlation between speech preparation time—including the number of oral practice sessions—and speech success.[1]

Practice can also create **muscle memory,** a kind of procedural memory that gets stored in your brain through repetition. The *act* of physical practice (out loud, as opposed to "practicing" silently in your mind) is what stores the material in your brain, helping you remember what you want to say and do while presenting. It's also the most efficient way to identify potential rough spots. For example, many sentences that read well and make sense written on a page prove difficult to say out loud, and likewise, certain transitions, especially those that involve integrating visual support, will be delivered best if you have practiced them physically rather than mentally.

Let's now look at three main ways that practice helps you achieve speaking success.

1. Practice enhances your ownership of your material

Practice creates **ownership,** or an intimacy between you and your ideas. This owner-ship establishes familiarity with your material and confidence for the upcoming presenta-tion. The more you practice, the better. If your speaking notes somehow vanished a few minutes into your presentation, your ownership of the ideas, obtained through practice, would allow you to keep speaking and your listeners to keep perceiving you as genuinely knowing or believing the ideas you're expressing.

2. Practice builds confidence and increases your positive speaker's energy

Practice that leads to a sense of ownership provides an additional reward—a sense of control over any anxiety or excess adrenaline created by the upcoming presentation. Though you want some adrenaline to give you speaker's energy, fear of not knowing how your speech will go is one of the greatest contributors to excess adrenaline in novice speakers. Practice reduces this fear. It builds confidence by ensuring that you know what you're doing.

3. Practice prepares for your time limit

Practice sessions ensure that your material fits within your **time limit,** your allotted window of time to present. No matter how compelling your ideas or engaging your delivery, you must respect any time limits given by your instructor, your supervisor, or the speaking host.

Reasons for time constraints

Time constraints generally are related either to speaking logistics or to audience expectations.

Logistical reasons The person who has asked you to speak or who is managing the **speak-ing logistics,** or the details of the event, has a schedule to adhere to. If you've been given seven to ten minutes to speak, it means the other fifty to fifty-three minutes of the hour are accounted for. Make the job of the speaking host an easier one by staying within your time limit.

Audience reasons Most audiences know in advance about how long a speaker plans to present, and this announced time frame creates an expectation. Your audience members are willing to give you their listening energy for that expected time frame, but rarely will they give you more.

Audiences in the United States, who are culturally socialized to see time as a com-modity, are especially time conscious.[2] They want to hear you speak, but they've most likely fit your presentation into what is otherwise a full day. Speaking for a little less than your allotted time usually pleases an audience because it allows extra time for questions, discussion, and restroom breaks. But once you've gone over the expected time limit with no indication of concluding your presentation, all sorts of internal messages come into play.

SPEAK
Responsibly

Timing Is Everything

As a speaker, you have the responsibility to respect the time limit you've been allotted. Here are some tips to use during practice for meeting speech time constraints:

- The introduction will comprise roughly 10 to 20 percent of the total speech time, the body 75 to 80 percent, and the conclusion 5 to 10 percent. Figure out how much time to devote to each section. For example, for a 6- to 8-minute speech, time the intro at about a minute to a minute and a half, the body at five to six minutes, and the conclusion at about a minute.
- With these proportions in mind, use a timer as you practice. Another option is to have a friend monitor the timing device and give you visual or audio cues as you reach certain timing goals. If you have an Apple- or Android-based smartphone or tablet, check out the McGraw-Hill SpeechPrep app, a mobile tool designed to help you create and organize notecards, as well as practice, record, time, and review your speech. To learn more or download the app, search "Speech Prep" in iTunes, the App Store, or the Android Market.
- Set the timer at the maximum time allowed by the assignment and count down. Begin to practice the speech and add or cut material if you're far off your timing goals.

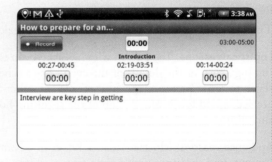

Knowing that you'll be able to deliver your message within the allotted time helps build confidence that you'll be ready for the actual presentation.

Listeners start thinking: *When is the conclusion going to start?* or *Doesn't this person realize there are three others waiting to speak?* At this point, they are no longer fully listening to you.

The importance of timed practice

Like nearly all speakers, you're bound to experience time in a new way during your public presentation. Sometimes, excess speaker's energy causes many of us to speak more quickly than usual. Likewise, some of us tend to go off on tangents and speak too long, forcing us to rush at the end. It may take a speech or two to figure out whether your actual presentations tend to run shorter than, longer than, or roughly equal to your practice sessions. The timed practice sessions go a long way toward figuring that out.

Running long during practice

Running long during your practice sessions is more common than running short. For most people, time goes by faster than anticipated. Alyssa's experience is typical:

> *The first time I clocked a practice session for my six- to eight-minute informative speech, I came in at thirteen minutes. It hurt, but I had to cut information. The next time I timed it, I was down to ten. I cut some more. I finally got it down to a little more than eight minutes. I knew from experience that I tended to speak more quickly during my presentations than I did during my practice sessions, so I thought I would be okay, and I was. My actual speech time was just under eight. The practice helped me get a feel for the real thing.*

If you're like Alyssa, how do you know what material to cut? See Table 13.1 (p. 300) for some tips.

Running short during practice

It's less common for speakers to run short during practice, but it does happen. Don't worry if you run somewhat shorter than your given time limit, but if you're running significantly shorter during practice (one-half of the time limit, for example), consider adding material. However, if you've said all that you need to say, don't add material simply to pad the speech. Instead, stay with the short speech. In general, though, speakers who come up very short have not explained, enhanced, or supported their ideas well enough.

Many of the tips for adding are the opposite of the tips for cutting in Table 13.1. See Table 13.2 (p. 301) for some additional tips.

13B Use These Tips for Effective Practice

Eight simple tips will make your practice worth your time and effort: starting early, practicing aloud, practicing everything, practicing the presentation in parts, practicing in front of trusted listeners, evaluating your progress during and after each practice session, giving practice your undivided attention, and finding the right amount of practice.

table **13.1**　What to Do if You're Running Long during Timed Practice

Approaches to trimming a speech	Related tips and examples
Prioritize your ideas.	**Tip:** Accept that it's common to share only 5 to 20 percent of your knowledge about a topic.
Look for areas of repetition.	**Tip:** One example is probably enough to communicate your idea.
Consider combining two separate, overlapping ideas into one.	**Example:** Combine "grizzly bear habitat" and "black bear habitat" into one larger category of "bear habitat in general."
Provide a general sense of your idea rather than sharing all the intricacies.	**Tip:** This approach integrates idea prioritization with combining ideas. **Example:** Instead of discussing all nine "identified problematic emotions" in your speech on troubled relationships, mention that there are nine, quickly list the top five, and discuss only the most significant one or two. Your audience still gets the general idea that "certain emotions tend to create problems for couples."
Look for unnecessary background material.	**Example:** In your speech on "the most recently discovered Egyptian mummy," the *what, when,* and *where* will suffice; you can cut the details about *who* discovered it and *how*.
Prioritize the details in a story.	**Tip:** Most stories are intelligible from their essentials—character description, setup, conflict, climax, and resolution.

1. Start early

Making effective use of your time, or employing good **time management,** is key for speakers. As we saw above, you need time to gain ownership of your material, build speaking confidence, and ensure that speech time constraints are met. Don't wait until the last minute to begin your practice. Even if your schedule is busy, find some time to practice, even if you have only five minutes one day and ten minutes the next. Once you start, you should be motivated to continue and make time for longer practice sessions.

2. Practice aloud

You may be able to work silently with your ideas at first, but as your presentation nears, as noted earlier in this chapter, *you must practice your material aloud*. Practicing aloud lets

table **13.2** What to Do if You're Running Short during Timed Practice

Approaches for adding to a speech	Related tips and examples
Find more research sources.	**Tip:** It's likely that at least one more useful source contains some additional information on your topic.
Assess the balance of your ideas and look for weak links.	**Tip:** Perhaps one of your three main points is not as well supported as the others.
Provide definitions and descriptions.	**Tip:** Ask yourself whether listeners could benefit from enhanced definitions or descriptions of words, people, places, or concepts. **Example:** Don't assume that all listeners know who Richard Avedon was or why the Chinese city of Xi'an is famous.
Give a quick demonstration.	**Tip:** A quick demonstration helps your audience visualize and better understand an idea. **Examples:** Show an example of how to use the FOIL trick for multiplying binomials. Demonstrate the correct stance for a free throw.

you hear your ideas and decide whether they make sense when spoken. Practicing aloud also helps your presentation evolve; you learn better ways to present your material each time you go over it.

It's common for your first few oral practice sessions to not go smoothly. This was Daniel's experience:

> *I couldn't believe what happened in my first practice session. I tripped over words, stumbled over ideas, went off on irrelevant tangents, and forgot to define technical terms. My brain knew my material, but the connection to my mouth had not yet been made. How was my audience ever going to understand me if I couldn't express myself? I'm glad I gave myself time for practice—out loud practice. My speech came off really well.*

Some speakers say they don't practice aloud because they're embarrassed to be seen or heard talking to themselves. Don't let this stop you. Even some experienced speakers practice aloud anywhere and everywhere one last time before they go into the speaking space—to walls, to trees and shrubbery, and on the street outside the venue. If you're speaking on campus, practice in an empty classroom, an individual study room at the library, or better still, the actual speaking space if it's available. Most people who overhear you practicing aloud will quickly realize and accept what you are doing.

connect

For a sample student video example that illustrates how practice can help you work through trouble spots in a speech, including words that are hard to say, see the online techniques video clip "Pronouncing a Difficult Word."

Record yourself in private on your phone or webcam and learn from the playback. Seeing and hearing yourself in action lets you know how you'll look and sound in front of your listeners. Video recordings have the obvious advantage of enabling you to evaluate physical and visual trouble spots as well as audial ones, but if you don't have the setup to create a practice video, an audio recording is still useful. (Again, if you have a smartphone or tablet, experiment with the McGraw-Hill SpeechPrep app, which was designed for speech practice and records and times your audio practice sessions, among other features. Search for "Speech Prep" in iTunes, the App Store, or the Android Market to learn more or to download the app.)

3. Practice everything

Besides practicing aloud, be sure to practice all components of your presentation. It can be tempting to save time during your practice sessions by saying to yourself:

- *I'll just come up with an example or two at this point to show what I mean.*
- *I'll tell the story that supports that point here.*
- *I'll show that visual during that moment.*
- *And then I'll find a way to wrap up the speech when I get to the conclusion.*

Wrong. *Having* a plan and *practicing* it are quite different. It's difficult to "come up with an example" and make it meaningful when you are under pressure during the actual presentation. Stories don't always come out the way you want them to the first time they're told. Again, practice *all* components of your speech.

4. Practice the presentation in parts

In your early practice sessions, break your speech into small, manageable parts. Spend your first practice session on just the introduction, the next one on just one of the main points in the body, and so on. In the final practice sessions, practice all the parts, in the correct order.

5. Practice in front of a trusted listener or two

To test your goal of successfully communicating an idea, practice at least once in front of a friend, classmate, or family member. These listeners can be

---

What you can ask trusted listeners to do during your practice sessions

- Paraphrase your ideas back to you, especially the central idea and main points.

- Evaluate if you move between speech components clearly (e.g., from the introduction to the body, from one main idea to the next, and from the body to the conclusion).

- Tell you if a particular idea, example, or story makes sense or is confusing—and why.

- Assess whether your visuals enhance your ideas, and convey what they like or don't like about them.

- Comment on your delivery style (do you appear natural? nervous? robotic?).

create
converse
connect

Public Speaking Myths

Here are some common myths concerning public speaking practice and delivery:

"The goal of practice is to memorize everything I will say." The goal of practice is to familiarize yourself with your ideas and the order in which you'll communicate them. (You'll read more about the role of memorization later in the chapter.)

"It's a short speech. I don't need much practice." All speeches need a thesis, need to be organized, and need to have supporting material. Practice ensures that all these elements are in place—even for speeches that are planned to last only two minutes.

"I must choreograph my body movements." You're not an actor, and you are not playing a memorized role. Let your body move naturally—just like you've been doing your whole life.

"I'll picture the audience naked." This "hint" only creates an uneven relationship of power between those who are dressed (you) and those who aren't (the listeners). It's better to want to communicate to equals.

"I can just look over audience members' heads." People can tell when you're not looking them in the eye. If you're not showing interest in them, why should they show interest in you?

- Have you heard any other myths about practicing for or delivering a public speech? If so, why do you think these myths persist in our culture?

an excellent source of feedback, which will let you know whether and where there are areas that need improvement.

Practicing in front of family and friends can have drawbacks, however. You need to identify the right listeners, those who can be honest with you and provide constructive criticism. It's not helpful to practice in front of listeners who may like anything and everything you do. Conversely, people who are exceptionally critical are of little benefit.

Also, beware of self-proclaimed experts. Some listeners may not be able to provide the relevant feedback you need for your kind of public speaking. What Uncle Joe learned in that public speaking workshop thirty years ago may not be consistent with the modern theory and skills you're learning in your course. The assignment for the informative speech your roommate gave last year may be different from the project your instructor is assigning this term. Accept feedback and advice from these listeners, but ultimately follow the specifics of your assignment.

6. Evaluate your progress during and after each practice session

Learn from each practice session. If you are confusing yourself or your practice listeners while giving an example or describing a certain concept, stop, rethink, and start from the beginning.

Listen to the tone you're using to ensure that it's conversational. One student speaker noted, *When I was practicing my informative speech, I was telling myself, "Stop sounding like you're reading an essay!" I thought if I sounded like that when I was by myself, I was going to sound worse on the day of my speech.*

As noted earlier, many speakers like to record their practice sessions for further self-evaluation. Practice recordings—video, audio, or both—can uncover things you were unaware of, helping you focus on needed skills and concepts during subsequent practices.

7. Give practice your undivided attention

Practicing your material takes full concentration. Make sure you are in an appropriate, safe space. For example, don't practice while driving. One public speaking student rear-ended someone at a stoplight on his way to class and later admitted that he had been practicing aloud to himself in his car. He was so distracted by his practice that he failed to see the red light, much less the other car. Use common sense.

8. Find the right amount of practice

How much practice is enough? There's no amount that suits every speech. Manage your time to get in at least three to five full practices; eventually, you'll see what amount of practice is best for you. Ask your instructor or a trusted classmate whether he or she thinks your last speech sounded unprepared, over-rehearsed, or practiced just about right. If your last speech was recorded, listen objectively for yourself.

Pitfalls of too little practice

Many speakers don't practice enough. That is especially true of college students facing a busy schedule—or falling prey to distraction, overconfidence, or procrastination. A speaker who does not practice enough, especially on a researched presentation, pays for it with increased stress, a lower grade, and more importantly, a failure in speech purpose.

Jordan, one overconfident procrastinator, serves as an example. Jordan would rush into the room at the last minute on the day of his speech, scribbling things on his speaking notes and digging in his backpack for his required outline. When he stepped to the front of the room, he needed time to arrange all his notes, tuck in his shirt, remove his

create
converse
connect

My Best Practice Advice . . . International Style

International speakers face additional public speaking challenges. Here are some of their recommendations:

- *First, international students should find native English speakers to practice with. Sad but true, I realized that your English does not improve if you continue to speak your native language often or if you talk mainly with other international students—both of you make similar mistakes and lack deep information about English. Also, examine U.S. culture and try to attend other public speaking events so you can have models.* Hasan (Turkey)

- *We have a saying in my part of Russia. The English translation would be, "It's easier to act yourself into a new way of thinking than to think yourself into a new way of acting." In other words, don't think too long about trying something new. Jump right in and practice it! It surprised me that I took to American-styled public speaking so easily.* Alex (Russia)

- *Be persistent in your practice, even if you get frustrated—which you will. Give your best, and learn from your mistakes. The United States is a safe place to make mistakes. I don't mind making them, because it's the only way I learn.* Arelí (Mexico)

hat, and smooth his hair. He got the basics of each assignment, but inevitably, something significant was missing. He failed to produce a required visual for one speech, had no identifiable thesis for another, and lacked some essential background material on yet another. He used a conversational tone of voice, but it was often *too* informal, containing distracting mild obscenities and inappropriate slang.

At the end of the course, Jordan wrote about how the course humbled him. He confessed to practicing minimally or not at all for the first several presentations, thinking he could get by on his high school speaking experience and his wit. While the coursework was within his capabilities, his procrastination and overconfidence ultimately offset his speaking effectiveness. Jordan wrote that he was glad to have taken the class even though a good grade was well out of reach by the time he realized he should have had more practice sessions.

Pitfalls of too much practice

A presentation in a conversational style may contain minor flaws, such as a mispronounced word, a repetition or two, or an idea not fully explained, but a speech with a few momentary imperfections is preferable to a presentation that sounds over-rehearsed. That style of speaking distances the speaker from the audience, leading to a less listenable speech.

Patricia, an admitted overachiever, was one such speaker. Though her topics were compelling, her speech structure perfect, and her support well developed, her delivery on her first few speeches was exceedingly overpracticed. Every gesture appeared stiff and planned, every sentence sounded memorized, and every pause seemed choreographed. This delivery style was in stark contrast to the everyday style she used outside her presentations, so it was clear she was capable of being conversational and using natural gestures.

Patricia and her instructor finally struck an agreement that she would prepare as usual but would practice aloud only twice. And what a different speaker she was. Most significantly, her relaxed style in turn relaxed her audience. Rather than sitting back, watching "The Patricia Show," and then politely applauding, they actually listened and asked questions at the end.

Patricia enjoyed those results. She reported that it was the first time she found herself being "mindful and present" during a speech. She liked looking at the audience, actually thinking about what she wanted to tell them, and processing their feedback. She liked the challenge of knowing her material yet getting to be a bit impromptu at times. She could now see that her overly practiced "speeches" had become inwardly focused exercises in checking off a list of planned activities and phrases; they were not exercises in communication.

If you're like Patricia, it may be disconcerting to hear someone telling you not to practice as much as you can. That's not the underlying message. You must practice, but you also need to know that less can be enough. Too much practice can quash the freshness and spontaneity you need and want during your presentation. Trust yourself that a few practice sessions, maybe only two to five, are sufficient for you to learn your material and know how to communicate it effectively.

13C Practice for Your Chosen Delivery Method

Speeches can vary in the style or manner of delivery. There are four basic methods. You can speak conversationally from notes (extemporaneous speaking) or spontaneously with or without notes (impromptu speaking), or you can speak from a fully written-out text (manuscript speaking) or from memory (memorized speaking). The conversational style is the most common, but we'll also discuss situations when a different delivery method may be appropriate.

Extemporaneous speaking and its advantages get emphasized below because this method complements the listener-centered approach to public speaking especially well. Keep in mind, however, that few real-life speeches are purely extemporaneous. Any given speech may contain elements of all four methods. For example, you may deliver most of a speech conversationally from key words and phrases, but you might memorize the opening statement, closing lines, and thesis. You might write out expert testimony used to support an idea and read it word-for-word. At the same time, if you think of a fresh example while speaking, you'd communicate it spontaneously.

Your first few speeches provide an opportunity to find which delivery method works best for you. Consider your method of delivery as an art to be learned and practiced. Think primarily extemporaneous, but allow yourself to incorporate the other methods if and when you need them.

1. Extemporaneous speaking: Using the style of important conversation

The **extemporaneous method** entails presenting conversationally from prepared key words and phrases in your speaking notes. These key words and phrases, also known as **triggers,** act as prompts to remind you what you want to say about a particular idea. There's no written text with every *a, and,* and *the* planned out.

You've read throughout this book about the benefits of speaking in a conversational—or extemporaneous—style of speaking for the majority of your public presentations. It is the most listenable style when speaking in your classes, at work, in your community, or in your various organizations.

An example of extemporaneous speaking

The following two paragraphs illustrate the contrast between a written or memorized text and extemporaneous speaking. The first example is a fully written text, and the second is a transcript of the same ideas as they were communicated extemporaneously, or conversationally. The extemporaneous language is not as grammatical as that of the written text, but it's closer to the way most people talk. More importantly, the language patterns are familiar to listeners.

A sample of extemporaneous speaking notes, with triggers only, follows the transcript. You would practice with these notes and use them during delivery. (More sample notes for this and other methods of delivery are found in Chapter 10, pages 228–230.) Some speakers use the extemporaneous method but no notes: they memorize their key words and then speak conversationally from them.

Fully Written Text

Bodies need calcium daily to keep bones and teeth strong, to ensure proper function-ing of muscles and nerves, and to facilitate the clotting of blood. Most U.S. adults assume that they get a sufficient amount of calcium in their diet, but chances are they do not. When blood-calcium levels drop markedly low, this vital mineral is "bor-rowed" from the bones.

The Same Idea Communicated Extemporaneously, or Conversationally

Calcium is an amazing mineral. It keeps our bones and teeth strong. It makes sure our muscles and nerves work properly, and it even helps our blood clot—all good things. If you're like most adults in the U.S., you think you're getting enough calcium, but you're probably not. After doing my research, I'm pretty sure I don't. And it got me worried, because when we're calcium deficient—meaning we don't get enough calcium from our diet—our bodies have to get that calcium from somewhere else, and as it happens, that somewhere is often our bones. So our bones get weak and are more likely to break and then take longer to heal when they do break.

Speaking Notes with Key Words and Phrases Only

- *Calcium plays impt. role*
- *= bones, teeth, muscles, nerves, clotting*
- *U.S. adults ≠ calcium*
- *When deficient, takes from bones . . .*
  dangerous . . . weak, break, longer to heal

Other advantages of extemporaneous speaking

- Time to research, organize, and practice your ideas

- A greater ability to make eye contact because you're not reading a script

- The ability to adapt and/or respond to feedback because your eyes are on your listeners and not focused on a text

- A sense of security because you have speaking notes

- Increased credibility because a conversational style shows you own your material

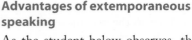

Advantages of extemporaneous speaking

As the student below observes, the advantages of the extemporaneous method greatly outweigh the advantages of the other three styles of delivery, especially the appeal of conversation to the listener's ear:

After one speech, I was complimented for my conversational tone and for "knowing my stuff." I realized then that it was okay to not have something written out word-for-word. All along I had been apprehensive about losing my train of thought, but it's much easier to interact with your listeners when you prepare—but don't script—what you are going to say. I like the audience focus of extemporaneous speaking.

2. Impromptu speaking: Delivering a message off the cuff

The **impromptu method** involves speaking with little to no preparation. The need or desire to speak in public on an impromptu basis occurs more often than you may think. Also known as improvising, ad-libbing, or speaking off the cuff, impromptu speaking is common in educational, business, civic, and ceremonial contexts.

> ### Examples of impromptu speaking situations
>
> **At work or in your community, you might**
>
>
>
> - introduce a new coworker or member.
> - present project updates.
> - report on last month's progress.
> - share a relevant, new idea.
>
>
>
> - voice support of or opposition to an idea or another speaker.
> - give a toast at a party.
> - be recognized for a job well done and be asked to say a few words.
>
>

The fear of sounding unprepared causes some people to dread impromptu speaking, but you need not fear or avoid it. Understanding what an impromptu speech is and learning some tips can give you confidence to deliver one. Your impromptu speech may not be as articulate or detailed as a well-prepared speech, but few listeners expect it to be. Your impromptu audience is not counting on you to provide profound statistics and thoroughly structured arguments. They're not expecting a detailed introduction, an exceptionally graceful delivery, or enhancing visual support. Instead, they want you to briefly make a point. If you can do that, your impromptu presentation can reach your audience in a meaningful way.

Make your impromptu point in organized fashion

Best practices for on-the-spot speeches are simplified versions of many of the same preparation techniques used at earlier stages of the speechmaking process and with the other delivery methods.

Focus on a central idea Even with minimal preparation time, you can quickly assess the situation and your listeners and come up with the single key point you want to make.

Organize your thoughts Once you've chosen the main idea you want to communicate, quickly decide how you want to organize your thoughts. Figure 13.1 (p. 310) offers some suggestions, abbreviated versions of the patterns of organization you learned about in Chapter 9.

Other tips for preparing an impromptu presentation

Following a few other tips will make for an effective impromptu speech.

Problem/Solution

What you might say
- *I see two main problems with that proposal.*
- *Here's my proposed solution.*

Cause/Effect

What you might say
- *I think I know the reason(s) why this has happened.*
- *There may be a few unwanted consequences if we adopt this plan.*

Past/Present/Future

What you might say
- *Though it's been done that way in the past, may I propose we do it this way in the future?*
- *Here's how I see our present situation.*

Pros/Cons

What you might say
- *Let me summarize the advantages I've been hearing around the office about the relocation proposal.*
- *The cons are many if we go that route.*

One theme

What you might say
- *The film's overriding theme, to me, was how large cities ultimately create a sense of loneliness.*
- *I will always remember Maggie for her offbeat sense of humor.*

figure **13.1** **Using Patterns of Organization in Impromptu Speaking** Support your main idea by adhering to an obvious speech structure.

Jot down notes It's always good to have something with you on which to take notes. That way, you are always prepared to write or type a few key ideas before speaking.

Time your impromptu comments appropriately Raise your hand or, if it suits the speaking situation, begin to speak as soon as an impromptu comment comes to mind; your comments have less impact if someone else has already made them or if the group has moved beyond that particular discussion. If your comment comes to mind after the topic has shifted, wait until a question-and-answer period has been called. Discussion leaders often ask things like "Are there any further questions or comments on this issue before we move forward?" If your comment is still relevant, it may be acceptable to politely bring the conversation back by preceding it with a comment such as "I'd actually like to respond to the point Andrew made a few minutes ago." Groups often provide an opportunity for open discussion or new business at the end of a gathering; use this time for impromptu comments as well.

SPEAK Responsibly

Impromptu Speaking Errors

Avoid the common mistakes that impromptu speakers often make:

- **Don't apologize or keep reminding people that you are unprepared.** Listeners are more interested in your message than in the fact that you're speaking off the cuff.
- **Don't talk just to hear yourself speak.** Be sure that you have an audience-relevant point to make.
- **Don't ramble.** Impromptu comments quickly lose their impact when you've made your point but then add *and then . . .* or *and another thing I've been meaning to say . . .* .
- **Don't make a point that has already been made.** On occasion, a point is important enough to be made again by another person. Just be clear that you're reiterating or supporting a previously made point.
- **Don't use the impromptu method for speeches that demand more preparation time.** The impromptu method doesn't suit all speaking situations. It can't make up for more extensive practice and planning you should have done.

Be brief Impromptu presentations should not be long. One point, clearly made in a minute or so, has more impact on an audience than a long, rambling dissertation. Say only what you need to say.

3. Manuscript speaking: Reading from a prepared text

The **manuscript method** of delivery, or reading verbatim (word-for-word) from a fully prepared text, is difficult to do well. Why? Because it takes great skill and experience to read complete sentences and paragraphs in a way that looks and sounds truly conversational. Public speakers who rely on a manuscript may get too involved in what they think is the "security" of their text. They spend countless hours writing out their words only to deliver them verbatim with a lack of enthusiasm and poor eye contact with their audience. This "easy way out" usually leads to presentations with a low degree of listenability. Listen to what Mandee, a college sophomore, said:

> *During my first speech, I suffered a big misconnect between being a good writer and being a good speaker. I spent hours writing what I thought was going to be a clever piece of work. I did not realize I would have a hard time translating all the elaborate and detail-rich sentences to something my listeners could access, much less appreciate. I was so intent on wowing my crowd with my "amazing" writing abilities that I forgot the most important fundamental public speaking lesson—that it's not about me, it's about them.*

Avoid the manuscript method for all but a few speaking situations, which we'll discuss shortly. Don't be tempted to adopt the speaking method of public officials or politicians who often speak from a full text on a **teleprompter,** a device that displays a prepared text on a transparent screen at the speaker's eye level, giving the audience the impression of eye contact. This style of speaking might be what you encounter when you listen to famous speeches, but it is not the way most people speak in everyday academic, business, and community contexts. Resist the perceived safety net of a manuscript; it is a false sense of security because that's what these speeches often sound like—false. It's better to have a few incomplete sentences, forget one minor detail, or trip over a word now and then, as may happen while you are learning to speak extemporaneously, than to numb your audience with a stilted delivery and a monotone reading voice. You have enrolled in a course about public speaking, not one called "Written Essays Read Aloud."

Pitfalls of the manuscript method

An over-reliance on the manuscript method can yield a number of problems during a speech; the most common pitfalls are described below.

The patterns of written language are hard on listeners' ears Audience members may not be willing to expend the energy to listen to you read your text and may instead stop listening.

Eye contact is compromised Because you have to read the text, there is little opportunity to look at your audience.

Most speakers struggle with syntax, word pronunciation, and verbal emphasis and inflections These missteps, which happen to most speakers at some point when reading a manuscript, are not noticed by listeners when the speech is delivered conversationally— because conversational speaking is not about perfect speaking. Written language emphasizes correct syntax and perfect pronunciation and inflection, so the inevitable minor slip that happens to almost everyone becomes more pronounced in the manuscript method. Credibility suffers when listeners begin to wonder why you cannot read your own writing.

The audience perceives that you lack ownership of your ideas Listeners may question whether you really know or believe in what you're saying.

You can't easily adapt to the audience or occasion When you are using the manuscript method of delivery, it's difficult to stray from the text to include a last-minute example, to clarify a difficult concept the audience is struggling to understand, to insert some appropriate humor, or to refer to a previous speaker. If you deviate from the text to include such additions, the change from written to spoken patterns is often abrupt and awkward.

When to use the manuscript method

The manuscript method is appropriate for you to use in several specialized contexts, described below.

Tips for Using a Manuscript

With the exception of ceremonial speaking, it is doubtful you will need to use the manuscript method very often. If you must, however, here are some tips to follow:

- Give yourself plenty of time to prepare your manuscript. You need time for research, organization of ideas, word choice, and revisions.
- Write your manuscript using patterns of language that are relatively conversational. As you write, read sentences and paragraphs aloud to hear how they sound.
- Prepare a manuscript you can easily read from. Use a large font; double- or triple-space the lines; use a slash mark to indicate a pause or a double slash to indicate a stop.
- Prepare a manuscript for easy page turning. Don't let a paragraph continue from one page to the next; start each page with a new paragraph. Also, help prevent pages from getting stuck to one another by dog-earring the corners or by putting each sheet in a plastic sleeve.
- Practice until you can deliver the text as conversationally as possible. Then practice again. Practice until you can comfortably look up from the text on several occasions during the reading.
- If applicable, practice with a teleprompter. These are becoming increasingly popular at large-scale meetings. If you are using a teleprompter, spend some time learning how to use it.

When it's essential to communicate a precise message Speakers who make presentations during legal proceedings, congressional hearings, or times of emergency, when the specificity of the words and facts is critical, often use detailed manuscripts.

When the highly emotional nature of the occasion calls for a speaker to stay focused A prepared script allows you to organize your thoughts and choose your language in the calmer moments before a highly emotional event, such as a tribute to your father or a memorial service for a good friend. Having the text with you keeps you focused during the delivery.

When exact timing is essential A few situations require adherence to an inflexible time schedule: for example, the room is available for only a short time, or the speech is being broadcast.

When the text is to be published or analyzed It would be atypical, for example, for the president of the United States to extemporize a speech about American foreign policy.

create
converse
connect

Mnemonic Devices

Memorization can serve a small role in the public speech. Many speakers use **mnemonic devices**—memory tricks—to memorize the speaking outline. Don't worry about how inane these mnemonic devices may sound to an outsider; they need only make sense to you. Here are some examples:

- **Use an acronym.** For example, a speech about the five steps of firing a rifle might use the acronym BRASS to remember the main ideas (breathe, relax, aim, sight, squeeze).
- **Use or create a clever saying (also known as an acrostic).** "Kings play chess on fine green silk" can help you remember the taxonomic hierarchy (kingdom, phylum, class, order, family, genus, species).
- **Use or create rhymes.** "Divorced, beheaded, died. Divorced, beheaded, survived" recalls the fate of each of Henry VIII's six wives in the order he married them.
- **Invent stories.** "The island gear adventurously met a fish." The story makes no sense, but it does help you remember the main ideas in your speech on the joys of scuba diving (traveling to exotic locations, using the latest equipment, meeting other adventurous people, encountering amazing sea life).
- **Construct a memory palace or mental walk.** Referred to as the method of loci by the ancient Greeks and Romans, this technique visually places ideas in various spots around a familiar or imaginary physical space.[3] You "see" the ideas in certain locations and remember to talk about them as you mentally walk a pre-planned route around your house, building, or palace.

This important speech has implications for international relations, military strategy, and economic action that affect a great many people. The president needs to use carefully scripted language that everyone around the world can understand and analyze.

4. Memorized speaking: Reciting from recall

The **memorized method** of speaking, committing a prepared manuscript to memory, is the most difficult of the four delivery styles. Only a few people are adept at it. If you're familiar with the embarrassment of watching an inexperienced actor struggle with lines, imagine the frustrations of listening to an inexperienced speaker try the memorized method.

Reasons to rely on memorized speaking sparingly

When most speakers use the memorized method, the unnatural words, halting delivery, and obvious facial and gestural choreography quickly make it clear that a performance is under way. While you may occasionally want to memorize an opening line, a short quotation, or a short acceptance speech (like the ones you see people give at the Golden Globes), refrain from memorization as your delivery method.

Disadvantages of memorized speaking

The problems with the memorized method are the same as those for the manuscript method. There are, however, some additional disadvantages:

Communication is compromised The memorized speech runs the risk of becoming an exercise in recitation and losing its main purpose of communicating an idea.

Train of thought is lost The slightest gap in memory can cause you to panic and your speech to fall apart. You don't want your audience to endure awkwardly long pauses while you mentally hunt down the next sentence.

Steady eye contact is difficult It's a challenge to maintain direct eye contact with your listeners while recalling things from memory. Think about how your eyes roll upward when you're trying to recall something.

Speech Practice in Action *A Student's Changed Habits*

Tomas Garza was a serious student with a high incentive to do well in his public speaking course. He approached his practice sessions with good intentions and focus from the very beginning of the term. However, as he reflected on his speechmaking choices as the term progressed, he was able to identify what he tended to do well instinctively, and he also changed his practice habits to improve on some of his weaknesses.

Tomas' practice habits at the start of the school term

In practice sessions. Tomas found it very helpful at the start of the term to practice sharing his ideas aloud with friends. He wouldn't talk to them using a full speech format, with an introduction and visuals, but he would convey the thesis and the main points in full as he was planning to do in the speech body. He did this so he could practice sharing his ideas in a conversational way. He could also gauge listeners' responses and answer any questions they had about the clarity of his ideas. This practice really helped his focus.

Benefits of Tomas' practice habits

Right before the actual speech. Prior to the real presentation, Tomas would prepare the full introduction and conclusion and his visuals, but he just practiced once or twice in his head, feeling confident that he could deliver the speech effectively.

Weaknesses of Tomas' practice habits

During and after the speech. Tomas was a strong speaker because he engaged his audience and knew his content. However, based on his practice habits and his first few speeches, he began to notice some consistent problems and tendencies, and he wrote them down to make sure he remembered to address them in future presentations.

> *Recurrent problems to work on in future speeches:*
> · *I consistently go over in time.*
> · *I tend to ramble while figuring out how to convey some finer points.*
> · *I add new things that come to my mind while speaking, which only adds to the two problems already mentioned.*

I'd give this advice to other speakers: Play around with your practice habits. What you do now may be helpful but keep talking to other speakers you admire, and ask them what they do. There may be some great ideas that you can beg, borrow, and steal—and make into your own for the better.

Tomas' practice habits today

Tomas continued talking his ideas out to his friends as he had done before because he found the feedback to be amazingly helpful. However, to solve the problems he had identified over time, he added one more step to his practice habits: after integrating the feedback from his trusted listeners, Tomas would then practice—seriously practice— aloud, by himself, multiple times, and with a timer. Adding that second step created a world of difference in Tomas' confidence and in his ability to address his complex ideas within the time frame he was given.

Tomas' retained practice habits

Tomas' new practice habit

Benefits of Tomas' new and improved practice sessions

review questions

1. Why is practicing for a public speech so critical?
2. What are the tips for effective practice? Which are the most important for you and why?
3. How does your practice for extemporaneous speaking differ from that for impromptu speaking, manuscript speaking, or memorized speaking?

key terms

muscle memory 296
ownership 297
time limit 297
speaking logistics 297
time management 300

extemporaneous
   method 307
triggers 307
impromptu method 309
manuscript method 311

teleprompter 312
mnemonic devices 314
memorized method 314

exercises

connect

FOr online exer-
cises, quizzes, and
hands-on activities,
see the Chapter 13
assignments in
Connect Public
Speaking.

1. Interview someone who regularly gives presentations to find out about his or her practice habits. (Your instructor or boss may be able to recommend someone to interview.) Afterward, share what you learned with your classmates. Questions to ask may include:
   - Can you walk me through one of your practice sessions?
   - What are your best practice tips?
   - Is there a time you wished you had practiced a speech more?
   - How has your practice changed since you were a novice speaker?

2. Consider your last speech or the one you're working on now. Invent a mnemonic device to keep track of the order of the ideas in one part of the speech body or the speech body as a whole. As a class, list the mnemonic devices on the board.

3. For your next speech, record your first practice—mistakes and all. Then record one of your final practices. Write a short report on the differences.

4. Get together with a few classmates before your next speech, and take turns practicing in front of one another. As each speaker practices, each listener must give at least three pieces of feedback, pointing out a combination of strengths and weaknesses. After all the speakers have had a practice session, take a break and repeat the process.

5. With a few other students, watch two memorized versions of the Gettysburg Address on YouTube:
   - Evan Sweet (search words: Evan Sweet Gettysburg Address)
   - A Lincoln impersonator (Barry Production Gettysburg Address)

   Disregarding the obvious disparity of the production quality of the two videos, discuss how each speaker's memorization helps or hinders the communication of the content of Abraham Lincoln's famous speech.

CHAPTER 14

Communicate with Your Language, Body, and Voice

LEARNING OBJECTIVES

1 Describe how the language of your speech can affect your message and your relationship with listeners.

2 Categorize the ways your body "speaks" during your public speech.

3 Describe the ways your voice—*how* you say what you say—supports or diminishes your message during your speech.

chapter preview

14A Use the Power of Your Words

14B Support Your Message with Your Body

14C Support Your Message with Your Voice

Review Questions
Key Terms
Exercises

udience members use their ears and eyes to engage with you and your message. Their ears pick up your language, tone of voice, and any supporting sound you use, and their eyes take in everything your body and visuals are doing and showing. Ideally, your delivery attracts and includes others in your message. But it can also divert attention and exclude—and profoundly affect your credibility. This chapter looks at the influence your language, body, and voice have on your ability to deliver a listener-centered speech that supports the message you want to convey.

14A Use the Power of Your Words

Language has tremendous power. It not only determines our perception of the world and shapes relationships, but it also influences our ability to communicate with others. The words and phrases we choose to use while speaking have real meaning for our listeners. This section looks at three primary goals to strive for, through language, in your presentation.

connect

For a sample student video example, see the online techniques video clip "Using Vivid Language."

1. Be inclusive

You want to invite your audience into your presentations to interact with the ideas you're discussing. **Inclusive language** acts as a bridge to an audience, increasing your chances of making a connection. It tells an audience that all potential listeners are welcome and respected. Conversely, **noninclusive language,** relying on negative stereotypes, derogatory remarks, or offensive terms, acts as a barrier, pushing the audience away and making listeners feel inferior.

Your choice of language *is* a message. It speaks volumes about your thinking, your integrity, and your esteem for the audience. Effective speakers aim for inclusiveness in their language choices. Few people use noninclusive language intentionally; fewer still want to antagonize or alienate an audience. Some people, however, purposefully use language in public contexts to gain attention and/or to shock, typically for political purposes. For example, Malcolm X spoke forcefully against white exploitation in the 1960s during his call for political empowerment for blacks, and some people in the gay community use the potent term *queer*, reclaiming a word once used against them in the quest for political and social equality. But, in general, most speakers use inclusive language to keep audiences engaged and listening.

We'll now look at several styles of language: some with the ability to draw an audience in, some with the ability to push an audience away, and some—depending on the speaker, the audience, and the occasion—with the ability to do both.

"-isms"

As you scan the next few pages and see words like *sexism, racism,* and *heterosexism,* images of the political-correctness police may come to mind. These paragraphs, however, are not about political correctness; they're about consequences. Though some people neither notice nor care what gender pronoun, racial descriptor, or sexist or homophobic comment a speaker uses, many do care. Don't let stereotypical comments or inappropriate words draw needless attention, creating a barrier between you and your listeners and diminishing your communication effectiveness.

Sexism Sexist language tells a listener that a speaker organizes the world according to sex or gender, most often in reference to occupation, ability, or behavior. The examples below highlight common instances of sexist language along with alternative nonsexist language choices.

- Everyone knows that not every doctor and executive is *he* and not every teacher and nurse is *she,* yet some speakers still use these gender-specific third-person pronouns. Instead, you can say, *When you see your doctor about these symptoms, he or she should be able to make a quick diagnosis.* The other option is to pluralize the noun: *When you see your doctors about these symptoms, they should be able to . . .*
- Females play basketball, and males cook and go grocery shopping. Use gender-neutral terminology when making references to occupations and activities. Describe a man as a *nurse* (just as you would do for a female in the occupation), not a *male nurse.* Refer to a woman as a *business owner* (just as you would do for a male), not a *female business owner.*
- When referring to people 18 years of age and older, use the terms *women* and *men. Girls* and *boys* typically refer to people 17 and younger.

Racism Racist language tells a listener that a speaker organizes the world according to race, most often in reference to ability, occupation, behavior, and preferences. Unless it's essential to the idea you're trying to convey, why label the student Latina or the lawyer Korean? Here are some examples of ways to avoid racist language:

- If a person's race is crucial to the point you're communicating, find and use the most accepted term. The evolving nature of language makes it difficult to know all the preferred terms, but some are more acceptable than others (for example, *Asian* is more acceptable than *Oriental*). You, your audience, and the occasion may all influence the appropriateness of a certain term (*African American* or *Black? Indian* or *Native American?*). Check with the speaking host, an instructor, or trusted friend prior to the speech to find the most acceptable words to use for your specific audience.
- Be careful of the phrase *those people.* Although few intend it, speakers using this phrase immediately erect a barrier between *us* and *them,* giving the impression that the *we* are superior to whoever *those people* might be.
- English contains phrases with roots in ethnic or racial stereotypes. Although they may be in common use, they reflect poorly on speakers who say them. Avoid phrases such as
  - to get *gypped* (the term is related to gypsy),
  - to *jew* someone down, and
  - *too many chiefs and not enough Indians.*

Heterosexism **Heterosexist language** tells a listener that the speaker is acting on the premise that all people are heterosexual. In addition, **homophobic language,** or words that use homosexuality as a target of humor or disapproval, reflects poorly on the speaker. Here are some common heterosexist assumptions and ways heterosexism can infiltrate a speech, along with ways to avoid it:

- Not all women are looking to marry men, and not all men are always checking out women. Avoid using sweeping statements about male-female attraction unless that type of attraction is the topic of your speech and your audience has voluntarily come to hear it. Consider discussing person-to-person attraction instead.
- When speaking in general terms about relationships, use *partner* or *significant other.* Save terms like *husband* and *girlfriend* for examples about specific people who may have those significant others.
- If the idea you are communicating requires a reference to a person's sexual identity, use the generally preferred terms *gay* (for men), *lesbian* or *gay* (for women), *bisexual man* or *bisexual woman,* and *transgendered person. Same-sex couple* is typically used to refer to two people in a same-sex relationship.
- Be wary of making stereotypical comments about sexual orientation. Obviously, only a small percentage of lesbians ride motorcycles (as do only a small percentage of heterosexual women).

Other kinds of linguistic barriers

Category	Keep in mind
Religion	• Not everyone celebrates Christmas. • Only a tiny fraction of Muslims support acts of terrorism. • Most mainstream or mixed audiences don't respond well to hearing about your religious beliefs (unless your speech is promoted as religious in nature and the audience is voluntary).
Age	• Not all teenagers are wild and experimental. • Many middle-aged people never have a midlife crisis. • Many older people (the term preferred to *elderly, aged,* or *gramps*) are strong and active, not weak and feeble-minded.
Occupation	• Lawyer jokes usually fall flat. • Not all corporate executives are greedy. • *Geek* is not descriptive of most computer experts.
Weight	• Obesity is a severe problem and not something to stereotype or ridicule. • Not all overweight people eat a lot and fail to exercise.

Slang

Slang is best described as words used and immediately understood within a specific group. That specific group can be a small collection of friends, a city, a region, a culture, or a country. There is skateboard slang, military slang, California slang, Puerto Rican slang, and slang spawned by particular television shows. Within a group, slang may be used quite freely, but when slang is used between communities, the consequences can range from perplexity to serious misunderstanding.[1]

Is slang an appropriate language style for public speakers? It depends on these factors:

The occasion Slang is rarely suitable for formal presentations at work or school. Informal speeches, however, sometimes benefit from the use of slang, because it can encourage the audience to relax, participate, and enjoy the presentation.

The audience Slang can serve as a bridge or a barrier between you and your listeners. A speaker who uses the right slang terms in front of the right audience immediately communicates a shared outlook. But slang that's inappropriate, misunderstood, or not understood at all only draws needless attention away from your message.

The speaker Not everyone can use slang productively. Your audience must believe that you are a genuine user of a slang term for it to be effective. Are you the right age (or hip enough) to use the term? Are you a member of the group or culture that uses it? Do you know the term's correct pronunciation and intonation? Your slang should reflect your status as an insider, not an outsider, to be well received by your audience.

The slang Your decision to use slang depends on the slang itself. Certain categories of slang, such as toilet slang, sex slang, or cultural slurs, are rarely appropriate in any sort of public speaking context; they hurt your credibility and risk offense. Other slang terms are short-lived (*rents* for parents, *bug out* for leave the premises) or so specific to a particular group (*puppy feet* for a poker player's hand consisting of a flush of clubs) that they only confuse most listeners. On the other hand, some slang terms are so common and innocuous (such as *cool*, *sweet*, or *no worries*) that most people don't even regard them as slang; these are more likely to be appropriate in most speaking situations.

Jargon

Language of a technical nature, specific to a profession or hobby, is known as **jargon.** People working in the medical field have jargon (e.g., *bagging, DNR, MVA*), as do those who breed Bengal cats (e.g., *homozygous, back crossing, whisker pads*). When you choose an academic major, part of what you learn is the jargon of the discipline. For example, by the time communication majors earn their degrees, terms such as *immediacy, org com*, and *proxemics* are a regular part of their vocabularies.

Jargon can be appropriate in public speaking, but as with slang, you must analyze the occasion, the audience, and the jargon itself before deciding whether or not to use it. For example, using jargon with others in your field while presenting in class or at a conference not only provides a shortcut to communication but also bonds you and your listeners through shared language. If you are speaking before a mainstream audience, jargon can enhance your perceived professional status, but take the time to quickly define or explain such terms to ensure that everyone in your audience understands them.

Obscenities

"Four-letter" words may be a part of your daily or occasional vocabulary, but they are mostly off-limits in public speeches. Even though only a few obscenities still carry the power to shock, anger, or incite, obscene words and phrases have a way of unnecessarily drawing attention to themselves in formal or even informal presentations. Why raise a linguistic red flag and jeopardize your credibility when you would rather have your audience focus on your ideas?

Obscenities range from hard to mild. Most public speakers have little trouble avoiding hard-core obscenities. Even mild obscenities, such as *screwed up, that sucks,* and *pissed off,* can have a negative impact on many listeners. It's not worth risking your credibility and your audience's goodwill with unnecessary words.

If you must use obscenities, do so for valid reasons. For example, one speaker, discussing discriminatory behaviors toward racial minorities, quoted obscene remarks others had made toward him over the years. The obscenities were shocking, but they supported his point that such discriminatory behavior exists. Obscenities may also serve a purpose in specific speaking contexts—a coach giving a pep talk to the team before a game or military superiors addressing their troops. In these situations, the obscenities are meant to motivate the listeners, uniting them in their common goal.

"Big" or cultural vocabulary words

Does your vocabulary contain words like *guile, unctuous,* or *catapedaphobia*? Terms like these are often referred to as "big" or "fancy" vocabulary words. Cultural vocabulary words are specific to a particular culture or language, and many of these have worked or are working their way into U.S. English. Film, theatre, and television, for instance, have popularized the Yiddish word *shlep,* meaning to pull or carry with effort. Most cultural words, however, remain unfamiliar to those outside the cultural community of their origin.

Both big and cultural vocabulary words are acceptable in a public speech—as long as they're used in the right context, with the right audience, for the right reason (showing off is not one of them), and defined when necessary. Increasing your vocabulary is a lifelong task, but the payoff is considerable: it adds greatly to your speaking credibility and allows you to express yourself more clearly and more precisely; you'll know, for instance, the nuanced difference between *predicament* and *plight.* As a public listener, a large vocabulary provides you with a framework for interpreting the messages you hear. For example, you can more easily engage with the speaker who refers to *the Zeitgeist* (the ideas or trends characteristic of a time and place) when you know the word.

2. Be credible

The accuracy of your language affects how audiences perceive your competence, especially in formal contexts. One successful software sales representative who often speaks to large groups understands the importance of accurate grammar and pronunciation. He says, "We are talking large sums of money, and I cannot afford to look the least bit amateurish. The way I talk is a significant part of the whole sales package."

While conveying ideas to others is your overall goal, you want your use of language to reflect positively on your knowledge, your values, and the time you've spent thinking about your message. Monitor your own language style on a daily basis. The more you use

Linguistically Diverse Audiences

When you are a native speaker of a language, or you speak it very well, it's easy to forget that your language contains words, phrases, references, and even intonations that can confuse those still learning the language. Here are a few strategies for building understanding and relationships with diverse linguistic audiences:

- During your practice sessions, look out for words that your listeners might misunderstand. If you use slang, jargon, or "big" vocabulary words, take time to define them.
- If possible, practice with a listener who doesn't speak the language as well as you do. Ask him or her to let you know should a misunderstanding occur.
- On occasion, it's a good idea to visually display an unfamiliar word, or an image symbolizing or explaining a word or concept. This would work well, for instance, in your speech on the steampunk movement.
- Consider your use of cultural references. For example, using *white picket fence* as a substitute for "middle-class suburban life" may confuse some listeners.

credible language in your everyday interactions the more likely you are to use it during your public presentations.

There is no need to be perfect in your use of language, however. Most of us make errors while speaking; we're human. The key is in how we manage them. Should you catch an error during your presentation, simply go back and correct the mistake, much as you would do in everyday conversation. Your audience will understand and not judge you disapprovingly. Not correcting the error, however, may lead your listeners to question your competence, and thus your credibility.

Grammar

English, like most other languages, is constantly evolving. Words and phrases once considered grammatically incorrect are today often uttered without notice. While "proper" grammar (adherence to a dialect called Standard American English) is still expected in most business and academic contexts, grammar rules may be relaxed in other settings, such as informal community events. Moreover, the conversational patterns you rely on as a public speaker allow you to be more casual with your grammar than you are in your writing. Dangling modifiers and incomplete sentences, for example, will not usually be noticed when spoken. What's ultimately important is that your language communicates to your specific audience.

table **14.1** **Correcting Common Grammatical Mistakes**

Error in grammar	Better choice
Using *good* and *well* interchangeably	*Good* is an adjective; it modifies a noun. *Well* is an adverb; it modifies a verb (and adjectives and other adverbs). **Correct:** "The licorice tastes *good*." **Correct:** "He skates really *well*."
Using words that sound like other words but have different meanings	Use a dictionary to know the difference between words that sound similar. **Examples:** *Sympathy* means sorrow for another's pain whereas *empathy* refers to the understanding of another's feelings; *afflict* means to cause distress or anguish, and *inflict* means to cause something unpleasant to be endured by another.
Misuse of *fewer* and *less*	Use *fewer* to refer to amounts you can count and *less* to refer to proportions or degrees. **Example:** "She likes you *less* [in regard to degree] because you have *fewer* [countable] attributes than her last date."
Improper pronoun placement—*him and me, him and I,* or *me and him?*	You wouldn't say, "Here's a picture of *I*," so it's incorrect to say, "Here's a picture of *him and I*." **Correct:** "Here's a picture of *him and me*." When including yourself in a list of pronouns, always put yourself last. **Incorrect:** "Here's a picture of me and him." **Correct:** "Here's a picture of him and me."
Using words that don't exist	Make sure your words are indeed words. **Incorrect:** *heighth* **Correct:** *height* **Incorrect:** *unconscience* **Correct:** *unconscious*

Still, you want to be perceived as a competent speaker. Some instances of incorrect grammar should be avoided. You may want to check with your instructor, a mentor, or a supervisor for guidance on your grammatical accuracy. See Table 14.1 above for some common grammatical errors and alternative choices.

Pronunciation

I was admiring her volumptuous *shape from* acrost *the room when she obviously* mis-interpretated *my glance and went totally* nucular!

connect

For a sample student video example that illustrates how practice can help you work through new words or words that are hard to say, see the online techniques video clip "Pronouncing a Difficult Word."

This sentence humorously highlights poor pronunciation (or, as some people mistakenly say, *pronounciation*), but correct pronunciation is a critical matter for public speakers. **Pronunciation** is the way you form the sound of a word—including where the stress is and how many syllables there are. Like incorrect grammar, incorrect or sloppy pronunciation draws undue attention, creates a distraction, and diminishes your credibility, affecting the overall quality of your presentation. For most people, correcting mispronunciations is just a matter of realizing their mistakes and fixing them.

Mispronouncing unfamiliar words and proper nouns can undermine your credibility. If, during research, you come upon an unfamiliar word like *inchoate, archipelago,* or *equivocal,* what are you doing to do? How about names for specific people such as *Claude Debussy* or *Mahmoud Ahmadinejad* and locations such as *Nasiriyah* in Iraq or the Welsh region of *Bwlch*?

Whether your incorrect pronunciation comes from habit or unfamiliarity, it's your responsibility to take the time required to learn correct pronunciation—and there are plenty of helpful resources available. Ask trusted friends, mentors, or instructors to point out any pronunciation errors you make and then make corrections. Numerous websites feature commonly mispronounced words and their correct pronunciations, and many online dictionaries contain an audio pronunciation for each entry. Also, pay attention to the way respected media figures pronounce their words. For the names of specific people, do a basic YouTube search to find a credible interview, a public speech, an award ceremony, or any video segment in which the person in question says his or her own name or is introduced. It's also worthwhile to check more than one source to confirm that both use the same pronunciation.

If you're a non-native speaker, English pronunciation may be a challenge for you. If possible, practice your speech in front of a native speaker and learn from the feedback. Also, take comfort that most listeners will quickly understand the source of your pronunciation errors and will give you a greater listening effort.

SPEAK
Responsibly

Own Your Words

Consider this scenario: a speaker is smoothly presenting ideas. But after a quick glance at the notes, the speaker hesitates and then haltingly mispronounces *incorrigible* as "in-ko-RIG-i-ble." Most likely this speaker, rather than conveying an idea he or she owns, has lifted—plagiarized—the word from somewhere without mastering its use.

Speakers who use words with no personal meaning to them create communication problems and commit a breach of ethics. If you come across a new word in your research, look up its definition and pronunciation and begin to practice with it. Once the word becomes part of your vocabulary—which will happen quickly—you own it and can use it in your speeches with confidence.

3. Be personable

While inclusive and credible language is critical to your speaking effectiveness, your personality can emerge from your language and play a positive role in your presentations. One way to add individual vibrancy is to incorporate figures of speech such as metaphors, similes, and alliteration. (These terms are defined and discussed in Chapter 18 on page 400.) Another way is to lend your own cultural and personal style to your speeches. Part of our national richness comes from the wide range of ways that people use language. Not only are most of the world's languages spoken here among families and communities, but the styles of English—our common language—vary as well.

Dialects

Technically, each of us speaks a dialect of English.[2] Sometimes mistakenly referred to as an accent, a **dialect** is a version of a language made up of variations in syntax (sentence structure), pronunciation, grammar rules, pacing, rhythm, word choice, and expressions. The dialect you speak derives from a complex combination of your geography, social class, culture, and family influences. Some people speak one dialect throughout their lives, while others adopt a new one after moving to a new place, entering a different social network, or joining an occupational field. Many people are bi- or multidialectal, able to switch between dialects depending on the place, occasion, or audience.

Considerations about dialects and public speaking

Reliance on a dialect can be a speaking strength, but it can also be a weakness. As with all your other public speaking choices and decisions, it is essential to consider the context, speaking situation, and your audience. Most of all, it is crucial to be genuine and natural in your presentations.

Sharing a dialect with your listeners can be an advantage Some dialects, even nonstandard ones, can be used successfully by the right person in a particular context. Your ability to use a dialect brands you as an insider, in tune with the people in the audience and the ideas they care about. Former President Bill Clinton did this with great success by strengthening his native Southern dialect while speaking in the American South.[3]

Dialects are effective only if they are genuine Your ability to communicate and your credibility suffer when you are perceived to be trying too hard to use a dialect. You also run the risk of offending true speakers of the dialect.

Criticism may be tied to how well you are understood Because dialects are directly tied to our identity, emotions can run high when others make subjective judgments about the way we speak. If instructors, supervisors, or evaluators give you such feedback, they are usually sharing with you an impression of how well you are meeting the principles of "proper" English, also known as the Standard American English dialect; it is not a critique of you or your dialect.

14B Support Your Message with Your Body

Nonverbal communication is communication without words.[4] *What* you say when presenting is obviously important, but listeners interpret as much (if not more) meaning from *how* you say what you say with your body and with your vocal qualities (discussed later in the chapter). In fact, studies show that anywhere from 65 to 93 percent of a sender's message is conveyed and interpreted through nonverbal channels.[5]

The good news is that even novice speakers can hold their bodies comfortably, naturally, and effectively. All you need to do is rely on what you already do well. For example, in your everyday interactions you know how to look others in the eye when you speak, animate your hands for emphasis, and freely express emotions on your face. If you concentrate on communicating your important message during your speech, your body should naturally follow along.[6]

Nonetheless, it's helpful to analyze what your body is saying and doing, intentionally or otherwise. Sometimes, excessive speaker's energy causes you to do things like repeatedly scratch your arm, smack your notes into your hand, or flick your hair from your face. You are probably unaware of these movements when you're speaking, but they send contradictory messages or distract your audience. A visual recording of your speech is a good way to check what you were doing—and not doing—during your presentation. Your instructor may point out these behaviors, too. Once you are aware of the messages your body is sending, you can make adjustments if necessary.

Sustained eye contact says to your listeners

- You are prepared
- You own your material and want to communicate it to them
- You're interested in your listeners and respect them
- You want to convey your sincerity, honesty, and confidence

Maybe these people do care about what I have to say.

Eye contact helps you as the speaker because

- It allows you to read your audience for feedback
- It reduces your excess speaker's energy

1. Eye contact

The human eye possesses great communicative power. Indeed, your audience interprets things about you and your message based in part on what you do and say with your eyes.

Novice public speakers often struggle with eye contact, but with conscious intent most people acquire this skill. To improve your own eye contact, be aware of some common errors. Then you can more easily detect them in your own speaking and make any necessary adjustments. See Table 14.2 (p. 330) for some common eye contact problems and how you can address them.

2. Facial expressions

Your facial expressions create a rich palette for communication; they get your listeners' attention and convey your emotions about your ideas. Showing concern on your face when discussing a somber and serious issue is natural, but it's also natural to reenact

SPEAK
Responsibly

Adapt to Cultural Differences

Mimi, an international student studying in the United States, struggled with eye contact throughout most of her speech course. In her home culture, eye contact between men and women is considered inappropriate. Intellectually, she knew that her U.S. audience of men and women expected eye contact, yet making it happen required great conscious effort.

Mimi's experience illustrates how people from different cultures use and interpret nonverbal behaviors differently. From hand gestures to eye contact to the distance we stand from others, our own culture provides us with a vocabulary of silent behaviors that speak loudly during our communication interactions.

If you are presenting before audiences who share your culture, you shouldn't have many problems with misinterpretations of nonverbal behavior. However, if you need to present in front of an audience from a culture different from your own, research appropriate nonverbal behaviors beforehand. You not only want to increase the chance of your message reaching your listeners as you intend it, but you also want to save yourself and your audience from potential confusion or embarrassment. Many books, websites, consultants, and other resources exist for researching the nonverbal behaviors of other cultures.

- Had you been in Mimi's audience when she was struggling with eye contact, would you have thought her ill-prepared or would you have realized culture may have been a factor in her reluctance to look at you?
- As a speaker, are you trying to overcome any culturally influenced nonverbal behaviors that are different from those of your audience?

with a facial expression the sudden surprise you felt when you learned something unexpected or your euphoria when you experienced something wonderful.

Don't choreograph your facial expressions ahead of time. Use your practice sessions to familiarize yourself with the emotional rhythms of your presentation so that by the time the speaking day arrives, your face moves in ways that naturally complement the words you are saying.

One facial expression is appealing to nearly all listeners—the smile. When appropriate to the topic being discussed, your smile helps you connect with your audience. Show genuine positive feelings toward those people who have taken time out of their day to listen to what you have to say by expressing those sentiments on your face.

3. Posture

Your body should move naturally and support your message. Nonetheless, because audiences interpret meaning from the way you hold and move your body, it can be helpful to

connect

For a sample student video example, see the online techniques video clip "Using Facial Expressions."

table **14.2** Mastering Eye Contact

Common eye-contact problem	Why it's a communication problem	Solution
Getting lost in your notes or visual support	Listeners question your ownership, preparation, and sincerity.	Practice so that your notes and visuals support you instead of distracting or confusing you during the speech.
Looking at only one person (usually a supportive and friendly face)	Staring makes that one person self-conscious and others feel unimportant.	Distribute your eye contact, as you do while talking to a group of friends during everyday conversation.
Looking at your evaluator	You have a room full of listeners who want to hear your ideas, not an audience of one.	Treat your evaluator as a regular member of the audience; there is no need to pay him or her special attention.
Favoring a particular section of the room	Those you're not favoring feel ignored.	Respect all listeners, know where they are (even the lone person in the back), and distribute your eye contact accordingly.
Looking above the heads of your listeners or at the floor	Listeners can tell when your eyes are fixed six inches above their heads or two feet below them on the floor, especially in a smaller room.	Let your gaze fall naturally on the faces of your listeners as you look around the room. Human connections are made there.

analyze your posture in your post-speech evaluation and make any needed modifications for your next presentation.

Standing shows respect for the audience and your ideas, so if you are able to stand, you should. This allows you freedom to gesture and use visual support, and it lets all members of the audience comfortably see you. Your clothing also typically hangs better on your body when you stand. If physical or medical reasons prevent you from standing or if the informality of the event lends itself better to sitting in a chair or on the edge of a desk, sit up as tall as possible and position yourself in such a way that all audience members can see you.

On occasion, though, when we are in front of an audience, the bodies we have been using comfortably our entire lives can suddenly feel awkward and clumsy. See Figure 14.1 for some common issues with arms, hands, legs, and feet. But if you use the same body posture you use during important personal conversations, you should be fine.

4. Gestures

Human gestures fall into two main categories. **Illustrators** are natural movements of the hands, head, and other body parts that accompany speech but have no meaning in

**Person A:
Positions that don't read well**

**Person B:
Positions that read well**

 Arms and hands clasped behind your back, hanging straight down at your sides, or crossed in front of your chest (you look rigid and closed off)

 Hands on hips (can suggest boredom or sarcasm)

 Hands in your pockets (uncomfortable or too relaxed)

 Playing with your hair, jewelry, pen, or notes, or repeatedly scratching your arms or neck (distracting)

 Toe tapping or "happy feet" (you look anxious)

Shoulders back and square to the audience

Arms hanging loosely and naturally, elbows bent somewhat

Strong and stable lower half to support a confident upper half

Hands available for holding notes or for gesturing

figure **14.1** **Using Your Body Well during Presentations**

themselves. When we say that "Jonathan likes to talk with his hands," for example, we are referring to the many illustrators he uses. When he makes a chopping movement to emphasize a particular point, he's using a specific illustrator. While illustrators have no inherent meaning, they do clarify, complement, or reinforce a verbalized message.

Emblems are movements or positions of the body that have precise meaning and are immediately understood by others in the communicator's culture. Among the most commonly used U.S. emblems are hand gestures for *okay, thumbs up,* and *stop;* a shoulder shrug for *I don't know;* and a head nod for *yes.* However, these are not universal gestures. Emblems are also popular in many co-cultures, or smaller cultures within a larger culture, such as a sport team, dance community, or particular neighborhood. Emblems used in these contexts may mean something completely different or nothing at all to your particular audience, so monitor your use of them.

connect

For a sample student video example, see the online techniques video clip "Using Gestures."

SPEAK
Responsibly

To Use or Not to Use . . . the Lectern

Lecterns can lend formality to a speech and provide a place to put your notes. They can, however, also be a source of distraction.

- If you have a choice, use the slender lectern shaped like a "music stand." The "big box" lecterns (also known as a "coffin" style) block your body, creating a barrier to communication.
- If you're going to use a lectern, stand comfortably behind or next to it. Standing too close to or too far from it or holding it tightly sends out messages that audiences notice and interpret negatively.
- Most speakers enjoy the freedom they feel without a lectern. You may feel vulnerable at first, but you'll probably come to like the closer proximity to your audience, the freedom to move around, and the confidence you can convey with your body without any barrier in front of you.

Your use of gestures is often influenced by personality. If you are physically expressive during everyday conversation, then be expressive during your presentations. On the other hand, if you are typically reserved with your gestures, you may want to experiment. You don't want to be someone you're not, but most audiences respond positively to animated speakers, and your gestures help you appear animated.[7]

Gestures are also often influenced by the message:

- Some *topics* inspire gestures more than others. Most people limit their gestures when discussing something serious or somber but gesture more when the topic is lighter.
- Some *explanations* are better conveyed through gestures. Imagine not using your hands when trying to describe the size and shape of a particular object, such as a tightly wound spiral; a long, narrow rectangular pool; or a three-tiered birthday cake.
- Gestures also frequently accompany the description of certain *actions*, such as climbing a ladder or running in a darting fashion.

5. Physical distance

The concept of interpersonal distance is a specific category of nonverbal communication called **proxemics.** As a public speaker, consider the context (and perhaps the culture, since the meaning of interpersonal distances is not universal) and determine how much space you should maintain between yourself and your audience; you want this distance to be appropriate.

Proxemics

Determined by room	Often you can move furniture to better work with your speech goals. Can you create a more intimate atmosphere by moving the lectern off to the side, moving a big table out of the way, or rearranging the chairs into a horseshoe shape?
Accentuated by elevation	At times, you need to be on a stage or platform for better audience sight lines. If not, place yourself at the same level as your audience to show your preference for communicating on a literally equal level.
Affected by movement	Pacing about the room for no apparent reason is distracting to your audience. Moving a few steps toward your listeners (while making an especially important point, for instance) can engage and intrigue them.

create
converse
connect

Establish Relationships without Saying a Word

One of the messages we convey through our nonverbal communication is **immediacy,** or the degree of liking we feel toward others. Take a moment to envision a speaker with a high degree of immediacy. Chances are good that you pictured things like *sustained eye contact, a smile, a close proximity,* and *a relaxed and comfortable posture.* What else did you see? And what was your impression about this speaker?

When you're the speaker, having a positive mind-set will increase your perceived degree of immediacy. Own your message and genuinely want to convey your ideas to the group of people gathered before you. Let the passion you feel toward your ideas be expressed in your body. Move naturally, in pleasing ways, and you'll enjoy the benefits of establishing warm relationships with your audience.

Adapting for Speakers with Disabilities

When people with disabilities speak in public, a few extra issues arise:

Tips for the speaker with a disability You may need to do some additional work during pre-speech planning, especially in checking on equipment availability and room setup. Request any type of extra assistance or accommodation you may need, such as a ramp to a stage, an interpreter, an adjustable lectern, a reconfiguration of the seats for better sight lines, or someone to assist you with your visual support. Communicate with the speech host early enough for your needs to be met.

Tips for audience members Interact with the speaker in the same ways you would with a speaker without a physical disability.

- Give eye contact to the speaker who is blind.
- If a speaker is communicating in American Sign Language, look at the speaker's face rather than at his or her hands or at the interpreter who is voicing.
- If possible, arrange your seat so that you can comfortably see the face of a speaker who uses a wheelchair.
- Don't patronize a speaker who has a physical disability by responding to him or her differently than you would a speaker without a disability.

Tips for the speech host Ask every speaker when the speech is arranged whether any extra assistance or accommodation will be required during the presentation. Even if you know that a speaker has a disability, don't assume that you know what he or she needs—always ask. The Americans with Disabilities Act mandates certain accommodations, but your personal attention to each individual speaker's needs is appreciated. If you are hosting a slate of speakers, be sure to treat each equally. If all speakers will use a lectern or microphone, make sure it's adjustable. If all speakers will sit at a table in the front of the room, make sure the table can accommodate each person equally well.

14C Support Your Message with Your Voice

Your listeners are skilled at decoding the messages conveyed in your speaking voice, even if they aren't always doing it consciously. The qualities of your voice, including emotional tone, volume, flow, articulation, pitch, and pace, are a type of nonverbal communication because they, in combination with your words—the verbal message—create meaning. Collectively, these nonverbal vocal qualities are known as **paralanguage.** The prefix *para* here means "to assist." Much like a paralegal assists lawyers, paralanguage assists in the creation of meaning in your language.

As the members of your audience listen to the ways you vocalize your messages in your presentation, they interpret things about you, your ideas, and the way you feel about them as an audience. The most listenable vocal qualities for public presentations are those you use naturally in important conversations. Though every individual communicator is different, chances are you speak confidently, clearly, and with varied inflection when speaking to someone you respect. These are the qualities you want in your speeches.

Your instructor can point out the qualities of your voice that enhance

How listeners perceive your vocal qualities

Speaker		Listeners
Speakers with vocal qualities that support and complement the words in their presentations elicit these kinds of responses	>>>	*Listen to that animated tone and upbeat pace. This sounds like a fun topic.*
	>>>	*Her angry voice is genuine. Maybe I should look twice at that situation she's talking about.*
	>>>	*He definitely did his research. He sounds so confident when talking about those sources.*
Speakers with vocal qualities that contradict or lessen the effectiveness of their words can trigger incorrect interpretations and unintended consequences	>>>	*That's so sarcastic. Does she even care about that person she's referring to?*
	>>>	*Did he practice? All those uhs and long pauses make me question it.*
	>>>	*I can barely hear. She's asking me to do what?*

your message and those that distract or give out contradictory messages. Your own post-speech self-evaluation is also beneficial. You need to be aware of any distracting vocal tendencies before you can make the right adjustments. It's your responsibility to control the way you sound to others. The major vocal qualities that carry meaning are discussed in greater detail below: emotional tone, volume, speech flow, articulation, pitch and inflection, and pace.

1. Emotional tone

Be mindful of your **emotional tone,** that powerful and wide-ranging quality of your voice that communicates emotions. Be generous with your emotional tone. If you're discussing something that frustrates, saddens, or exhilarates you, let that emotion be heard. But don't choreograph or overact your emotions. When you aren't conveying a strong emotion, use a tone of confidence, friendliness, openness, and respect while speaking. Your listeners should respond positively.

Your practice sessions are the place to get in tune with the emotional rhythms of your ideas. Identify the varying emotions in the different passages of your speech, and communicate those emotions honestly and generously during delivery.

2. Volume

Volume, the loudness or softness of your voice, is one of the most important vocal qualities. The medium range of volume is usually the most effective when speaking to an audience.

connect

For a sample student video example, see the online techniques video clip "Maintaining Your Composure at the Finish."

Receiving feedback about your volume from a trusted listener is helpful because you can sound different to yourself than you do to others.

For a variety of biological or cultural reasons, some people have soft voices, but a low volume creates *access* issues. Listeners may be willing initially to work at hearing you if you're a quiet speaker, but after a while, many will give up trying. If people can't hear your message, they cannot understand and interact with you. While less common, some voices boom out and make listeners uneasy.

In adjusting your volume, you also need to consider the speaking space. Find a volume loud enough to be heard but not so loud that your listeners shrink back in their seats. What works in a small conference room may not work in a larger lecture hall and vice versa.

Finally, maintain your volume as you near the ends of your sentences. Some speakers begin their sentences in a strong voice, only to finish them weakly or even inaudibly.

3. Speech flow

You want your words and sentences to flow as smoothly as possible. Most people have some natural pauses and hesitations in their speech, but an excessively uneven and jerky delivery leads to an awkward, choppy presentation. When your words come out in chunks . . . a few at a time . . . with lots of verbal trips and . . . delays in between, your listeners may wonder whether you gave much prior thought to what you wanted to say. They may question whether you own the message.

Your practice sessions go a long way toward smoothing your delivery. Familiarizing yourself with your ideas through practice helps them flow gracefully during your actual presentation. That increases your credibility.

Two common speech flow issues to consider as you assess your own speech flow are verbal junk and the silent pause.

Verbal junk

Also known as fillers or disfluencies, **verbal junk**—sounds or words like *um* and *y'know*—are a problem for many speakers. Your instructor and your own self-evaluations are helpful in pointing out use of verbal junk. A few *uh*s and an occasional *okay* are rarely noticed—many communicators commonly use them—but if you use excessive *um*s or *yeah*s and/or pronounce them with intensity, then you need to work on decreasing, if not eliminating, them. Be mindful of your fillers during your personal conversations and work to correct them. That will lessen your chance of using them during your presentations.

The silent pause

Learn to embrace the silent pause rather than fear it. Many speakers pause momentarily while thinking of a word or deliberating how to phrase an idea—and this brief silence is usually preferable to filling that thinking time with the verbal junk described above. In addition to giving you time to think, pauses can add drama to a presentation. Your listeners may even appreciate a pause, as it gives them time to catch up, think about your ideas,

SPEAK
Responsibly

Using a Microphone

Some speaking spaces will offer or require the use of a microphone, which many speakers welcome because it allows for normal intonation and expression. Here are some general guidelines for confidently and credibly using a microphone:

- **Get to the room early for a sound check.** Microphones come in many styles—lectern, wireless, handheld, and lavalier (or lapel)—and each kind behaves differently depending on the technology and the speaking space. During the sound check, the technician or a trusted friend can help you find the proper distance from the microphone to achieve an appropriate speaking volume and to avoid "popping" sounds that may occur with sharp consonants.
- **Know how it works.** Where's the on-off or mute switch? If it's a lectern mic, how do you adjust it to your height? Are there wires you could trip on? How much can you move your head and still be heard?
- **Beware of amplifying unintentional sounds.** Don't get caught saying something into the microphone you didn't intend for the audience to hear. Also, long hair or jewelry can rub up against or get too close to a microphone and create a sound distraction.

add an internal comment, or jot down notes. Of course, too many long and extended pauses throughout a speech can be interpreted as a lack of preparation, but a silent pause now and then is a natural part of communicating.

4. Articulation

Articulation refers to how clearly you produce individual speech sounds. Some common examples of poor articulation are *didja* instead of *did you* and *wanna* instead of *want to*.

Some poor articulation is biologically related. When these speakers present to an audience, most listeners are understanding and accepting. But most poor articulation is heard from those who *can* articulate but, through habit or laziness, choose not to. Unlike a conversational partner who can interrupt to clarify what you are saying, your listening audience has only one opportunity to hear your words.

Here are some tips for improving your articulation:

- Pay attention to your articulation during your everyday conversations as this will translate into better articulation for your presentations. Ask a trusted friend to point out sloppy articulation habits—and accept these as constructive criticism.

- Check the way you position the speech-producing parts of your body. Are you opening your mouth wide enough to get out that *ow* sound to make *our* sound different from *are*? Are your lips rounded forward enough to make a nice *sh*?
- Study the speech habits of news reporters and announcers. They rely on clear articulation for their livelihood and make great role models for this purpose. Stage actors and narrators who do advertising voice-overs are other good examples.

5. Pitch and inflection

connect

For a sample student video example, see the online techniques video clip "Using Vocal Variety."

Your **pitch** refers to the highness or lowness of your voice, as on a musical scale, whereas **inflection** refers to the manipulation of that pitch to communicate a specific meaning. To get a better understanding of the power of inflection, manipulate the word "so" in a way that communicates the following messages in parentheses:

- So. ("That's where you've been all this time!")
- So. ("Who cares?")
- So. ("And what comes after that? Go ahead, I want to know.")

Most speakers in everyday conversation use a comfortable, medium pitch and vary their inflection in appropriately communicative ways. Do the same during your presentations. A common pitch and inflection issue to consider, however, is a narrow pitch range. A **monopitch,** or **monotone,** is a voice with little to no variety of inflection, in which every word sounds the same. Listening to a speaker with a narrow pitch range is a challenge, no matter how riveting the message. The monotone is more likely to result when you read your speech (one more reason not to rely on manuscript speaking). Find your internal energy, and let the natural communicative lilt, or "sing song," of your voice come through while speaking.

Another distracting inflection is choppiness, when a speaker ends every sentence curtly, as if chopping off the end of every idea. **Uptalk,** in which speakers end statements with an upward inflection as if it were a question—you know, like this?—is another such problem.

6. Pace

Pace is the speed at which you produce language. You naturally alter your pace, depending on the topic and the listener. Beware of pacing extremes, however, because you can lose your audience. An overly slow pace invites your listeners to let their mind wander or start thinking about other things. Or they feel patronized; you don't want listeners thinking, *Why is she speaking to me as if I were a child?* On the other hand, an overly fast pace can cause listeners to not be able to keep up with your message.

Take note of the degree of difficulty of your material and use a pace appropriate to helping the audience understand it. The average speaker in normal conversation uses roughly 125 to 150 words per minute. This is a good pace for presentations, too, as listeners are used to it. Again, relying on a trusted listener or recording your practice sessions can be useful in assessing your typical speaking pace and in identifying particular spots in your presentation where you may tend to speed up or slow down too much.

Language, Body, and Voice in Action
A Student's Process

After his first speech, Henry Duong completed a self-analysis project that required him to watch a video of his talk and carefully read his instructor's evaluation. Using the data he gathered from these sources, he needed to make a concrete plan for delivery improvement.

DELIVERY CONCERN	PLAN FOR IMPROVEMENT
I said "crap" twice and 'STFU' once. Obscenities (even soft ones) and text-speak are inappropriate to use while speaking formally, even when I'm in front of peers.	*I need to practice more so that, among other things, I can plan better word choice. Also, if I can stop using these speech styles in everyday conversation (which I really need to anyhow), I'll be less likely to use them while speaking.*
My eyes were too tied to the screen behind me that held my visuals. My audience, I think, felt left out.	*I have to trust myself that I've prepared my visuals well and that I know what's on them. I need to "be there" when my audience looks from my visuals back to me. My eye contact with them will show that I know what I'm talking about and that I'm prepared.*
My body was too tied to the lectern, and I was standing too stiffly behind it. It's true that I had some speaker's energy going on, but my stance made me look <u>really</u> nervous, like I didn't know what I was doing.	*Though it's going to feel weird, I'm not going to use the lectern next time. It might help me look more relaxed and open. I'm also going to take a step or two closer to my listeners to let them know I want to establish a friendlier connection with them.*
My voice had a monotone quality that made it a challenge for <u>me</u> to listen to <u>myself</u> during the playback. I was talking about something personally stressful (my younger brother's motorcycle accident) but you'd never know it from hearing me that day. I sounded like a robot with no soul.	*I've got to drop this perception I have about public speaking being this serious thing and be freer with my emotions. I hear those emotions in other speakers— and I always like it—so why can't I do it myself? I'm a pretty animated guy with my friends. I can do it while speaking, too. I know it.*

Critical Thinking Question: If you analyzed your word choice from your last speech, what would you find?

Critical Thinking Question: What were your eyes doing and "saying" in your last speech? Did these eye behaviors help or detract from your message?

Critical Thinking Question: Did your body placement and movements enhance or distract from your verbal message? Give examples.

Critical Thinking Question: Were any vocal qualities in your last speech distracting? Did any contradict your speaking intentions? If so, how might you change this for your next talk?

review questions

1. How can you use your language to include others? to increase your credibility? to be personable?
2. What are the many ways your body supports your message while speaking in public? Conversely, how can your body distract from your message?
3. Why are the qualities of your voice considered a form of nonverbal communication? What are the vocal qualities that support the words you use? What qualities can distract?

key terms

inclusive language 319
noninclusive
   language 319
sexist language 320
racist language 320
heterosexist language 321
homophobic
   language 321
slang 321
jargon 322

pronunciation 326
dialect 327
nonverbal
   communication 328
illustrators 330
emblems 331
proxemics 332
immediacy 333
paralanguage 334
emotional tone 335

volume 335
verbal junk 336
articulation 337
pitch 338
inflection 338
monopitch, or
   monotone 338
uptalk 338
pace 338

connect

For online exercises, quizzes, and hands-on activities, see the Chapter 14 assignments in Connect Public Speaking.

exercises

1. Spend some time with a thesaurus before your next speech. Did you find any new words that more precisely communicate your ideas? Leave room for practice to attain ownership of your new vocabulary. Do you think you'll have to define the words for your audience?

2. If applicable, watch a video of your last speech with the sound off. What message is your body giving your listeners? Share your insights with classmates or your instructor.

3. Put the lectern off to the side for your next speech. Write a brief response paper about how it felt and whether you plan to do it again in the future.

4. During the next round of speeches, choose one speaker and focus specifically on his or her use of emotional tone. Take notes on the speaker's ability to communicate his or her natural emotions as they relate to the ideas being shared. Were the emotions apparent? appropriate? genuinely communicated? effective? Write up a brief post-speech analysis, and give it to the speaker.

Types of Public Speaking

Speeches come in many flavors, and each type requires a different mind-set and unique strategies to effectively reach your group of listeners. These final four chapters look at the major types of public speeches. You'll learn about the skills needed when speaking to inform, speaking to persuade, speaking during special occasions, and speaking in a group.

• • •

Speak to Inform

LEARNING OBJECTIVES

1 Define informative speaking, and contrast it with persuasive speaking.

2 Describe the larger purposes for speaking informatively.

3 Distinguish between the types of informative topics.

4 List the common strategies you can use to help people learn.

Information is everywhere—we're sending and receiving seemingly endless pieces of it at school, at work, in our communities, among our family and friends, and through the media. As a public speaker, you want your informative messages to stand out and for your listeners to easily access, understand, and interact with them. This chapter will help you communicate those informative messages effectively and responsibly by first focusing on what informative speaking is and how it differs from persuasive speaking. You'll then learn about the larger purposes for speaking informatively, the major types of informative speeches, and how you can develop your messages geared to the ways that people learn.

15A Understand the Role of Informative Speaking

1. Informative speaking is a common practice

Informative speaking, or speaking to enhance the knowledge of others, is a relatively new phenomenon. The ancient art of **oratory,** studied and practiced by Greek and Roman scholars, focused only on speaking with competence, style, and grace for persuasive purposes. While twenty-first-century citizens still do plenty of persuasive speaking, it's an equally common practice to speak informatively—to teach others something new, to update current knowledge levels, to correct misperceptions, and to disseminate knowledge within a society or an organization.

There are endless occasions for which objective and factual presentations are appropriate and necessary.

Examples of informative speaking in action

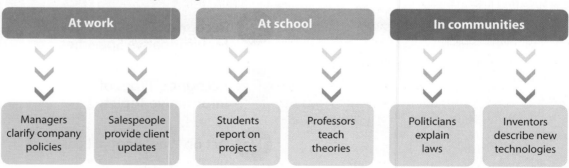

At work	At school	In communities
Managers clarify company policies	Salespeople provide client updates	Students report on projects	Professors teach theories	Politicians explain laws	Inventors describe new technologies

Indeed, we live in a time and participate in a global economy where seemingly infinite pieces of information can be shared and disseminated. A listenable, effective informative public speech occurs when you succeed in conveying your information in ways that allow the audience members to access it, understand it, and interact with it.

While it's a bonus if others subsequently choose to act on your information, that's not the point of informative speaking. On the contrary, to encourage them to do so in your speech would be an example of persuasive speaking.

2. Differences between information and persuasion

You could argue that any time people share information they're actually attempting to persuade. Because it's impossible to tell everything about a topic, intentionally or unintentionally, speakers inevitably share some facts while withholding others, thereby painting only a partial picture. Savvy listeners recognize that speakers can easily manipulate statistics, carefully select anecdotes, and control visuals—all to support a particular point of view. As a result, the lines between information and persuasion *can* get fuzzy. For example, your choice of a topic often says something about the value you place on it.

To determine your primary speech purpose, look ethically and honestly at your *intention:* If your genuine goal is to give audiences information they need, to teach your audience what you know, to convey what you have learned in your research, or to describe the world as it is, your purpose is informative. But if your goal is to share information in order to lead your listeners to a specific conclusion or to modify their values, beliefs, attitudes, or

SPEAK
Responsibly

Speaking Informatively—and Ethically

When we offer, are asked, or agree to convey information to others in a public setting, we take on ethical responsibilities, including the following rules of thumb:

- **Choose a relevant topic.** Perform a thorough audience and context analysis and be sure you're sharing knowledge that is helpful to *this* specific group of people.
- **Be up front about your intentions.** If relevant, acknowledge the potential for bias in your topic, but assure listeners that your motivation is to teach, and that you will be giving the most credible and unbiased information possible.
- **Include credible sources.** Spend the necessary time assessing the accuracy and timeliness of your research. Know who created the information and why they published it. Use only the most unbiased and credible sources you can find, and remember to cite them correctly.
- **Use concrete language.** Define terms when necessary, use words your specific audience can understand, and avoid language that excludes or offends some or all listeners.
- **Manage your speech preparation time.** People are relying on you for meaningful information. Researching, organizing your ideas, preparing visual support, and practicing all take time.

Ethical speaking is covered in greater depth in Chapter 4.

actions, then your goal is persuasive. You need to recognize and acknowledge the difference. One student described the distinction between informing and persuading this way:

> *Informative speaking was difficult for me. I'm a very opinionated person, and I didn't like not being able to spout off about what I think and feel. But on the other hand, I can now see the need for knowing how to speak informatively—and just informatively. I realize that when I'm in the audience, I sometimes just want to get right to the information without having it tied up in the speaker's messy opinions. "Just the facts, ma'am," you know? There's a time and place for everything. I've come to accept that.*

Speaker as *teacher* and *reporter* are two helpful metaphors when it comes to speaking informatively. Teachers consider their audiences and impart knowledge that's new and/or useful. Reporters find a good story, research it, and then explain to others the way things are. For example, telling your listeners how the human body processes a fat calorie is informative; telling them they should reduce their consumption of fat calories is persuasive. Teaching the historical facts about Christopher Columbus' voyages to the Americas is informative; taking a stand on whether we should recognize those voyages with a national holiday is persuasive. Figure 15.1 provides more examples.

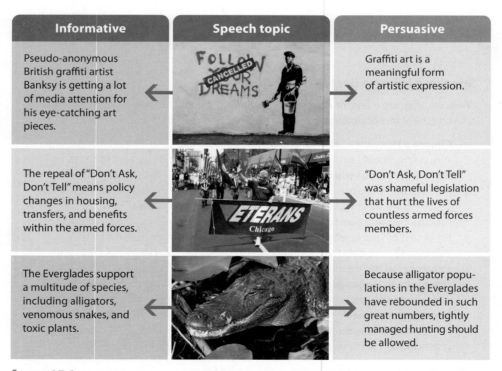

Informative	Speech topic	Persuasive
Pseudo-anonymous British graffiti artist Banksy is getting a lot of media attention for his eye-catching art pieces.		Graffiti art is a meaningful form of artistic expression.
The repeal of "Don't Ask, Don't Tell" means policy changes in housing, transfers, and benefits within the armed forces.		"Don't Ask, Don't Tell" was shameful legislation that hurt the lives of countless armed forces members.
The Everglades support a multitude of species, including alligators, venomous snakes, and toxic plants.		Because alligator populations in the Everglades have rebounded in such great numbers, tightly managed hunting should be allowed.

figure **15.1** **Recognize the Difference between Informative and Persuasive Speaking**
Source: Top image: Banksy, Boston, 2012.

Informative speeches broaden the intellectual horizons of audience members. Listeners learn about the past, present, and future. They learn how things function, gain insight into the relationships between ideas, and discover the mysteries of the greater world around them. Audience members leave the informative presentation with a wider understanding of their world. No matter how big or small this new knowledge, they see things differently once you've successfully communicated your informative ideas.

15B Recognize Larger Purposes for Informative Speeches

Throughout your informative speech, you may relay information in a number of ways: You may provide a definition or two, briefly demonstrate a process, or explain a larger phenomenon. Many informative speeches call on you to use more than one of these approaches in different segments of one speech. However, just as every speech can be classified as one primary type or genre even if it makes use of other speech types and purposes—such as a persuasive speech that includes some informative sections—every informative speech should have one larger purpose. What is the primary reason you are speaking informatively? In all likelihood, the answer will fall among the categories that follow.

1. To define

The purpose of a **speech of definition** is to give a fuller understanding of a term, typically one that refers to an object or a concept. As a result of your speech of definition, any term's meaning should be deepened and enriched for audience members—both when they use the term and when they hear someone else use it.

In many instances, in defining the term, you're answering questions like *I've heard of that, but what exactly is it?* or *What do people mean by that?* However, a speech of definition can also be about putting a closer lens on a term that audience members may have thought they understood. For example, many definitions change and evolve over time and place, and their precise meaning is specific to particular contexts and time periods.

Here are some examples that demonstrate how an effective speech of definition does far more than give a dictionary entry for a term:

- While your listeners may have heard of the term *green building,* after your speech, they'll know the specific criteria a building must meet in order to be labeled *green* and what benefits the label brings for the building's owners.
- In a speech about *entomophagy,* a term unknown to most listeners, you will, of course, first explain that it refers to the eating of insects. Even more important, however, as a result of the main points in your speech, your audience will better understand the cultural, culinary, and sustainability issues that surround it.
- By explaining the evolving legal definition of *family* over the last one hundred years, your listeners will have a better sense of its legal definition today.

connect

For a sample student speech of definition, see the online speech video "Fair Trade."

2. To demonstrate or instruct

connect

For a sample student demonstration speech, see the online speech video "Pool Cleaning."

Some occasions require teaching how to use or do something, or teaching how something works or is done. In a **demonstration speech,** you walk your audience through a specific step-by-step process, modeling the steps while you talk about them. Turn on the TV and you'll find endless examples of people demonstrating—how to cook, how to repair, how to craft. Even without the benefits of a fancy set and a production crew to help you, with some simple props, pictures, and a clear set of instructions, you can effectively teach others how to do any number of things through a demonstration.

A critical first step in this particular speech type is to avoid choosing a common process most audience members are likely to know how to do already as your topic—wrapping a gift, ironing a shirt, using a word processor program. Unless you have a genuinely new spin on the procedure, listeners will get bored or resent you for wasting their time. To avoid this pitfall, analyze your audience and answer their *How do you do that?* questions in as specific and focused a way as possible.

Overly general or common process	→	More specific, listener-centered process
How to play poker	→	How to increase your chances of beating the house at poker
How to care for a garden	→	How to properly prune a shade tree
How to train your dog	→	How to train your puppy to heel while on the leash

The **speech to instruct** is a close relative of a demonstration speech; the main difference is that you typically just talk about the procedure or task (rather than also demonstrating it). Used most frequently with concepts, this speech provides tips, pointers, and directions on how listeners can achieve better results in the future, such as effectively confronting a neighbor whose dog barks incessantly, avoiding tourist-trap restaurants, or saving time during research by using the campus library databases.

Sample topics for speeches of Explanation

1. Why leap years occur

February **29**

2. Why the mortgage industry crashed

HOME FOR SALE

3. Why wild jaguars are rarely found in the U.S.

3. To explain

People frequently ask, *why is that so, what happened,* or *what then?* Your **speech of explanation** begins with something that is or was—an event, an object, a theory, a process, a situation, a fact—and provides reasons or causes for its existence or looks at potential consequences of its existence. Speeches of explanation provide background information, clarify confusing concepts, demonstrate relationships, describe procedures, show how things work, and offer interpretation of difficult ideas.

connect

For a sample student informative speech of explanation, see the online speech video "Deaf Culture."

4. To describe

The island of Fiji . . . tell me more. People frequently want to know, in more detail, how a place, an object, a situation, or an event relates to the senses—what something looks, tastes, sounds, feels, or smells like. In cases like these, offer a **speech of description.** In this type of speech, you provide a collection of details, use vivid words, and show pictures that allow others to "see" something in a new way. Your description paints a mental image they can hang on to and have for future use.

5. To report

Newspaper reporters collect information from various sources and combine it in easily understood packages to allow others to better understand situations. Your **speech to report** does the same thing by addressing such questions as *what's going on, what are people talking about,* or *what are people saying or doing about that?* Students are frequently asked to report on something they've read or done. Members of an organization report on recent activities or surveys. Community members report on new town initiatives. These reports look to the past and summarize what's been occurring or what's been learned. This information is frequently discussed by the larger group and taken into consideration as the group decides on next steps.

Sample topics for speeches of Description

1 The trademark features of a classic, elegant Vera Wang gown

2 How it feels to be on a space shuttle

3 The historically important elements of Chartres Cathedral

Sample topics for Reports

1 Travel committee update on the upcoming trip to Puerto Rico

2  Autopsy results

3 Synopsis of the main points in Malcolm Gladwell's *Outliers*

15C Recognize Types of Informative Topics

What topic will you define, demonstrate, explain, describe, or report on? Informative speeches typically fall into one of five topic classifications—they are about an object, a person, a process, an event, or a concept. Some speeches can fit two or more of these types simultaneously. For example, a presentation on how players' heights factor into the final standings of an NBA season examines an event, but from a larger conceptual framework. Nevertheless, identifying one dominant topic classification for your speech makes for clearer communication to your listeners.

connect

For a sample student object speech, see the online speech video "All Eyes on Saturn."

1. Speaking about objects

An **object speech** teaches the audience about something visible, audible, or tangible. Think nouns: An animal, vegetable, mineral, place, or thing that is new or otherwise meaningful for the audience is the main focus in an object speech.

Sample object speeches
- Newest smartphone features
- Jupiter's moon Io
- Balinese shadow puppets
- Gregorian chants

2. Speaking about people

Most listeners like to learn about other people, including people who have significantly shaped our collective past, creating (for better or worse) the society we inhabit today. Who were they? In what historical and societal context did they live? What motivated them to act and think as they did? What challenges did they face? What is their legacy? We also like to learn about people in our present day as well as people who are poised to have an impact on our collective future—leaders, artists, inventors, policy makers, pioneers, revolutionaries, and builders—as they give us insights into what's to come.

Speeches about people can also broaden our understanding of our global community by teaching us about the way other people live. They may come from a certain place (e.g., the Minnesota Somali community), believe certain things (e.g., Mennonites), be oppressed by others (e.g., the Uighur people of China's Xinjiang region), or adopt intriguing cultural behaviors (e.g., Tonga's fakaleiti—boys raised as girls).

Typically, the goal in speeches about people is to explain or report. When sharing information about a group or another person's biography, provide concrete imagery and tell stories. These specifics help listeners see the people or the person through an objective lens rather than through the abstract lens of fame, celebrity, or history. Above all, tell your audience why they should care to know about this individual or group. Reinforce the idea that learning about the stories, struggles, insights, and achievements of others helps us better understand ourselves and the greater human condition.

Sample speeches about people

Historical figures:
- Sacagawea
- The nineteenth-century Whig party
- U.N. secretary-general Ban Ki-moon

Inventors (past or present):
- Windshield wiper inventor Mary Anderson
- Post-it Note inventor Art Fry

Modern-day figures:
- Peace activist Rachel Corrie
- Journalist Maria Shriver
- Talent-show producer and judge Simon Cowell

3. Speaking about a process

A **process speech** describes a series of actions or events that result in a specific outcome or end product. Process speeches

- provide a step-by-step explanation of how something came to be, such as how saber-toothed cats became extinct or how Apple computers rose to prominence under Steve Jobs' leadership.
- describe how something relatively abstract works, such as couples counseling or a successful advertising campaign.
- demonstrate how something concrete is done, such as creating a plant hybrid or applying *feng shui* concepts to a room.

A successful process speech allows for two possible outcomes: listeners better understand the intricacies of a particular process, or they now know how to complete a process themselves.

Sample process speeches

- *How wildfires are fought*
- *How to help a child build self-esteem*
- *How to prepare for long-distance hiking*
- *How to more effectively work in teams*

Sample event speeches

- The capture of Osama bin Laden
- The birth of Louise Brown, the first test-tube baby
- The *E. coli* 0157:H7 spinach breakout
- The Summer of Love, 1967

4. Speaking about an event

An **event speech** enlightens an audience about anything that has happened, is happening or is believed to be happening, or will happen. An event speech brings to life a singular occasion, occurrence, or experience for people who were not there. The imagery you provide helps the audience stay engaged with your message.

5. Speaking about a concept

A **concept speech** looks at the intangibles of life—theories, ideas, impressions, attitudes, beliefs, and values that we cannot see or touch but nonetheless perceive, suppose, or imagine. The goal in most concept speeches is to define or explain. A successful

connect

For a sample student concept speech, see the online speech video "That's Disgusting!"

Sample concept speeches
- Influence through sexual power
- Future role of cyber-warfare
- Freakonomics used in policy making
- Philosophy of a Waldorf education

concept speech uses concrete examples and imagery to help listeners see the associations between abstractions and reality. For instance, in your speech on corporate fraud, provide legal definitions (and, if necessary, do so in nonlegal language) and share real-life stories of people who were found guilty of the offense. When talking about teenage rebellion, explain why it happens and describe common manifestations of it.

15D Act on Ways People Learn

The skills needed for successful informative speaking are covered throughout this text. Adopting the mind-set of listener-oriented public speaking, conducting a thorough audience analysis and acting appropriately on it, creating and communicating a full introduction, using narrative, being ethical and civil, fully supporting your ideas, and practicing are among the skills you'll need to achieve your informative communication goals.

But there are a few extra considerations. This section helps you recognize and act on some ways in which people learn.

1. Make it relevant

Motivation is one of the most influential keys to learning. It's difficult for listeners to maintain their attention on your presentation and benefit from it if they don't see your ideas as relevant to their own lives. Start your speech preparation with a detailed audience analysis, and use this evaluation to craft connections between your ideas and your specific listeners' wants or needs. Attach your ideas to something they already know about or is familiar to them. Establish this initial relevance in the speech introduction and then build on it throughout the presentation. Here's how one student, Kyle, approached establishing relevance:

Kyle starts on a broad scope.

He narrows the topic more. . . .

. . . and more.

With this link between data and campus life, Kyle's almost there.

Kyle is now targeting his specific audience.

In his speech to classmates on the effects of soda on the human body, Kyle began by discussing per-capita soda consumption in the United States, narrowing consumption rates by age before ending up at the age range of the typical college student. He continued creating relevance by offering statistics on soda sales from their campus and then shared his personal observation of the amount of drinks classmates tended to bring to class. "Effects of soda consumption" was no longer an abstract problem for other people; it was an issue of immediate relevance to those in the room. Kyle had created motivation to listen and learn.

2. Remember that less can be more

In this era of data overload, bear in mind the phrase "quality over quantity" when speaking informatively. It's better to state, support, and reinforce one main idea (your thesis) than to cram too many ideas into your speaking time. Fifty unrelated details about a topic may be individually interesting, but they're difficult for the average listener to retain and the sheer number of them will prevent you from being able to explore any of them in depth. Reflecting on his overpacked informative speech about the architect Félix Candela, one engineering student honestly evaluated his problem as one of focus:

> *Should the listener perceive the architect as sculptor, or should the listener recognize alternative uses for concrete? Or is the technique of using hyperbolic parabolas the wave of some undefined future, or am I providing insight into the way I choose to build? Not all these questions needed to be answered, yet I was trying to do so. I needed to focus in on one idea and stay there.*

Listeners learn better when you highlight one main idea, clearly explain it, and support it in detail. See Chapter 6 for tips to help you narrow down your topic ideas into a thesis that communicates one—and only one—main idea.

3. Organize your ideas for maximum engagement and focus

When you teach people something new, it helps to relate it to something they already know or can more easily understand. If you're talking about something *specific,* like the Pine Barrens of New Jersey, begin with information about the New Jersey landscape in *general.* When discussing something *complex,* like correcting behavioral problems in children, break it down into *simpler* parts such as biting, touching, or verbal behaviors. Begin with a *familiar* topic such as whales and then move on to the *less familiar* topic of baleen whales before focusing in on your actual and *unfamiliar* topic of the rare bowhead whale. These larger contexts will provide a foundation for understanding the unique ideas and topics that are your focus.

Also, keep in mind the need to organize the whole of your speech. See Chapter 9 for a discussion of the organizational patterns for developing and arranging your speech, including topical, chronological, causal, comparison/contrast, and spatial patterns. No informative topic comes with a built-in mandate for a particular pattern of organization. Instead, a familiarity with each of these patterns allows you to keep examining your topic from multiple angles to see which pattern works best for what you want to say to your audience. Whatever pattern you select, identify it and follow it. It's easier for your listeners to grasp your ideas when they're organized.

4. Ensure understanding—do not assume

In many speaking situations, you can't assume that you and your listeners share similar information contexts. People take different classes, have different interests and experiences,

connect

For a sample student video on defining terms in an actual speech, see the online student speech techniques video clip "Providing an Explanation."

and even have different tastes in entertainment. Don't let listeners tune out your message because of a gap in their knowledge. Work to minimize their information-processing demands and reduce their need to make inferences. Define terms (e.g., *unguent, codify*), concepts (e.g., *Pop Art Movement, the Internet's hive mentality*), or acronyms and abbreviations (e.g., *POTUS, NOAA*) that you had to learn or look up during your research and preparation; chances are, if you had to learn them, so do audience members. If you refer to a particular person, provide a brief explanation of that person's role or title unless you are positive everyone already knows who he or she is. Make sure everyone knows what you mean when you refer to "that situation we had to deal with last year."

Check for understanding in a way that requires more than a yes-or-no answer. If you ask *Does everyone understand that?*, most people will just nod politely indicating they do (even if they don't). A better idea is to use a quick, direct audience engagement technique that confirms specific listener knowledge (or its absence). Asking *Who knows what DOMA means?*, *Who's the president of Israel?*, or *The fall equinox occurs in which month?* will get others briefly involved while ensuring everyone is on the same page. If your listeners are silent when asked such specific questions, you know you need to fill in the gaps in their knowledge.

5. Use visuals

connect

For a sample student speech that uses visual support, see the online video "Good *E. Coli* Gone Bad."

As you read in Chapter 12, visual support helps you communicate in several ways. When speaking informatively, your visuals can draw listeners in and help you make a point. Your rainfall chart will help audience members see relationships of precipitation around the region, your photo illustration of the new building will show its size and scale, your animated sequence of making bony Asian carp into edible burgers can help listeners make sense of a complex process. During speech preparation, put yourself in the place of your listeners and keep asking yourself, *What would I want to see that would enhance, clarify, simplify, or explain this message even more?* Create visuals that will satisfy those answers.

6. Use repetition

A final way to help audiences learn is to repeat and reiterate key points of your message. For example, your listeners will better identify and remember your thesis when you state it first in your introduction, refer to it again during a transition between main points, and when you emphasize it a final time in your conclusion. Don't worry about using the exact same phrasing each time. In fact, you'll sound canned and robotic if you do. Use your normal conversational patterns and let the wording of the thesis—the same central message—come out differently each time.

Repeating a key point within the speech body is equally effective. When discussing safe kitchen behaviors, you may say, *Never—I repeat, never—leave a child unattended around an open flame.* Emphasizing a message through repetition draws attention to its importance.

Informative Speaking in Action *A Student's Process*

"Fair Trade" *by Stacey Turnbull*

Choosing her topic

Stacey took on the mind-set of an investigative journalist after seeing the words *fair trade* on some chocolate bars at the grocery store and on the menu at her local coffee shop. So she asked a question—*what makes these fair-trade products different?* She then researched it and came back and taught others what she'd learned.

> *Topic:* Fair trade
>
> *Larger informative purpose:* To define
>
> *Type of informative topic:* Speaking about a concept
>
> *Thesis:* A company has to engage in certain practices before it can position its products as *fair trade.*

Identifying her larger informative purpose: To define

Stacey had heard the words *fair trade* before, but she never understood what they really meant. For example, how was fair-trade chocolate different from regular chocolate? Since she didn't know, she assumed her audience didn't know either.

Identifying her type of informative topic: Speaking about a concept

Although Stacey realized that in answering what makes a product "fair trade," she might need to explore a process—how companies interact with producers—by virtue of her central question and her larger informative purpose to define, the main focus of her presentation is a concept.

The Thesis and the Main Supporting Points

Thesis

A company has to engage in certain practices before it can position its products as *fair trade*.   Topic

Organizing her main supporting points

Stacey's main supporting points would identify and explain what those *practices* are. See Chapter 9 for a review of organizing terms.

Stacey's organizing term

Main points:

1. The company has to establish a long-term purchasing agreement with the producer of the crop or product.   Company practice #1

2. The company has to provide financial assistance to the producer, such as loans.   Company practice #2

3. The company has to pay a fair price for the goods.   Company practice #3

Stacey's speaking notes for the introduction

Recall from Chapter 10 that your speaking notes can be designed in a variety of ways, including key words, bullets, pictures, annotations, and the like. What's important is that your notes work for *you* during your speech. Stacey uses this format.

Introduction

Attn and personal relevance
- *Read article … exploitation of international farmers … all in the name of low prices.*
- *End of article … mentioned fair-trade companies as alternative.*
- *I had seen <u>fair trade</u> on products … never realized what it meant.*

Audience relevance
- *Have you seen these words … coffee … chocolate … jewelry?*
- *Know what they mean? Would you like to?*

My credibility
- *I've got answers.*
  - *I read more articles.*
  - *Talked to coffee shop owner … sells fair trade coffee.*
  - *Watched documentary, <u>Black Gold</u>, about coffee production in Ethiopia.*

Thesis
- *You'll learn that there are certain practices a company has to engage in before it can position its products as <u>fair trade.</u>*

Preview
- *Long-term purchasing agreement*
- *Provide financial assistance to the producer, such as loans*
- *Pay a fair price for the goods*

Transition to body:
- *So first of all, the company has to establish a long-term….*

review questions

1. What does it mean to speak informatively?
2. How does informative speaking differ from persuasive speaking?
3. What are the five larger purposes of informative speaking?
4. What are the five types of informative topics?
5. What are some strategies that help people learn that can be used to enhance informative speaking?

key terms

informative speaking 344
oratory 344
speech of definition 347
demonstration speech 348

speech to instruct 348
speech of explanation 348
speech of description 349
speech to report 349

object speech 350
process speech 351
event speech 351
concept speech 351

exercises

1. Research an ideological organization on the web or at the library. Search for the organization's "facts and statistics" that back up its viewpoints, assertions, or stances. Take three of these "facts or statistics," and research other sources to see whether you can find opposing "facts and statistics." What does this say about the blurred lines between information and persuasion?

2. During one of your other classes over the next day or so, pay attention to how your professor approaches information and persuasion. Was the class mostly informative or mostly an argument, in which the professor was trying to get you to accept a point of view? Provide examples as you report your findings to your classmates. Do you feel that your professor's approach to informing and/or persuading you was appropriate for that course?

3. With a small group, brainstorm ten topics of interest for each of the five kinds of informative speeches—objects, people, processes, events, and concepts.

4. Create a transcript of one of your past recorded informative speeches, or find a transcript of an informative speech in a book or on the web. In the margins, identify each of the strategies used to help listeners learn. See pages 352–354 for a full list.

connect
For online exercises, quizzes, and hands-on activities, including TED Talks and video activities, see the Chapter 15 assignments in Connect Public Speaking.

16

Speak to Persuade

LEARNING OBJECTIVES

1 Explain the role of persuasion in public speaking.

2 Distinguish between the types of persuasive speeches.

3 Identify the strategies you can use to effectively persuade others.

chapter preview

16A Understand Persuasive Speaking

16B Recognize Types of Persuasive Speeches

16C Use Effective Persuasive Strategies

Review Questions
Key Terms
Exercises

You have the right to your own beliefs and ways of doing things. In your personal life, you don't have to necessarily explain why you think a particular restaurant is romantic, why you listen to country music, or why you admire Oprah Winfrey. But when it comes to getting others to consider or adopt those beliefs and behaviors—in other words, to persuade them—you are responsible for backing up what you say. Persuasive speaking is one of the three general types of public speaking. (Informative speaking is discussed in Chapter 15, and you'll read about special-occasion speaking in Chapter 18.) This chapter first explores the concept of persuasion. It then discusses types of persuasive speeches and general strategies for persuading others.

16A Understand Persuasive Speaking

Persuasion is the act of deliberately attempting to influence the thinking or actions of others. You can use a powerful and wide array of tools in a persuasive presentation, including provocative words, eye contact, dynamism, images, stories, credible sources, vocal tone, personal appearance, and forms of argumentation. These tools, combined with the immediacy of face-to-face interaction, can shape other people's thoughts about facts, values, or policies and their actions in regard to them.

1. What is a persuasive speech?

Persuasive speeches happen every day. Living, in essence, involves constant negotiation with others. Students argue points of view in theory classes and speak out in various campus venues about many different causes. Community members speak to raise funds, protect neighborhoods, elect representatives, and shape local policy. The world of work is filled with people using persuasive speaking on a daily basis. Scott J. Jones, an investment representative with Edward Jones and Co., LLP, offers an example:

> *I speak to people about the need for investing, using my presentation skills to increase audience members' knowledge and call them to action. I determine my success by how many new clients I acquire from a specific presentation. Whether or not a listener becomes a new client, I strive to connect with each person and help him or her identify the need for saving for the future.*

Ultimately, persuasive speeches focus on issues and topics that people differ on. You use persuasive speaking to achieve one of two aims: (1) to shape the listeners' thinking (sometimes to change it, other times to reinforce existing thinking) or (2) to shape the listeners' behaving options so that they respond in a desired way. For example, people handle their money in a variety of ways, so Jones, the investment representative just mentioned, has a challenge ahead of him when he attempts to persuade people not only to invest (rather than spend), but also to invest with his company (rather than another firm).

S
N
L

A persuasive speech

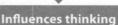

Influences thinking	Influences action
You attempt to get listeners to *adopt or shift their commitment toward* your values, attitudes, or belief system.	You attempt to influence others, either individually or as a group, *to behave* in a particular way. Assure your audience that the desired action is reasonable and achievable and that the resources exist to make it happen.
Examples	**Examples**
• *Value a college education.*	• To your film club: *Let's host an anime film festival on campus next term. We have access to the newly renovated campus theatre, a number of quality anime movies are available, and we have enough club funds to pay for public performance rights.*
• *Our town's newly elected mayor is the right man for the job.*	
• *The DREAM Act would be good national policy.*	
You *reinforce and strengthen* the values, attitudes, and beliefs a group of listeners already possesses.	• To potential customers: *This product will bring you numerous benefits, and our payment plan helps you afford to buy it.*
Examples	
• *Our company values are the right ones for success.*	
• *Let's keep forging ahead with our mission.*	
• *Our political views on this social issue are worth having.*	

2. The complex process of persuasion

Even though your persuasive messages *can* influence people, they might not always succeed in doing so. It's difficult to persuade others. Their thoughts, values, attitudes, and behaviors, just like your own, stem from a complex foundation of experience, personality, education, and socialization formed through the lifetime influence of family and culture.

Though persuasion is a challenge, it does not mean we should resist speaking persuasively. We are all affected by the words of others. Recall the conversation about dialectics from Chapter 1 and realize that the accumulation and interplay of the many messages we've received from various sources ultimately *do* affect us; none of us are exactly the same in our thoughts and actions as we were even five years ago. On a greater scale, an exchange of persuasive messages affects society as a whole. While some persuasive messages may be polarizing and confrontational, many are inclusive and nuanced, providing well-reasoned arguments for bringing people together on an issue.

So we must keep speaking to one another persuasively. The health of our democracy depends on it. Your message may be the first time your listener hears a new idea; it may be one of many messages that person hears prior to making a change; or it may be the final piece of evidence for a decision that he or she has long debated. You never know how your message will be received. But be assured that your persuasive messages, communicated effectively, *can* have impact. Don't judge the success of your persuasive speech by whether it immediately changes another person's thoughts or actions. Rather, consider your persuasive presentation effective and listenable if your audience successfully accesses, understands, and interacts with your argument.

3. Choosing your persuasive topic

For some speakers, persuasive topics rise naturally out of occupational, cultural, academic, or community interests. It's highly likely that you hold fast to certain beliefs; feel strongly about a number of local, national, or international issues; support some policies and reject others; or advocate for or disagree with a certain group, activity, or ideology. These positions may be good topic choices. Ask friends and family what issues they think you feel strongly about; sometimes others have an added perception of what matters to us more than we do.

Ultimately, you want to choose a topic that's right for your listeners and occasion. (This may be a good opportunity to review Chapter 5 on analyzing the audience and speaking situation.) For each realm of life, however—school, work, community—some basic rules apply:

- For classroom speaking, always check with your instructor for certain topics he or she prefers you focus on or avoid.
- For workplace speaking, be sure your topic connects to or furthers the mission of the organization.
- For community speaking, address topics of personal or general human interest, or current issues of local, regional, or national importance.

4. Apply persuasive principles to messages you receive

While this chapter and Chapter 17 on developing your arguments are intended to help you craft and deliver effective persuasive messages, they are also relevant to situations in which you *receive* persuasive messages. Many marketers, politicians, civic and religious leaders, and corporate spokespeople are highly skilled persuasive speakers. You need to be a critical listener. As you learn about the various types of persuasive speeches, you'll be better able to spot the types of claims and assertions you hear. As you study how to use persuasive appeals for your own presentations, you'll better recognize the strategies others use with you. As one student, Monica, sums it up, the more skilled you become

SPEAK
Responsibly

Does Your Point Have a Counterpoint?

If your topic isn't debatable, then it really doesn't qualify as a persuasive talk. Your point must have a counterpoint, or a contrasting point of view. Some speakers claim not to feel strongly about any debatable issue. Others are apprehensive about appearing rude or offensive or sparking a controversy. As a result, these speakers frequently end up choosing topics to which there's minimal or no counterpoint, stating the obvious and creating speeches that are often unengaging and ineffective. For example, persuading your audience to "be nice during the holidays" is pointless. Who (other than Scrooge) would argue that people should be mean and stingy, or worse, endorse unethical behavior like stealing from the Salvation Army's red kettles? A brainstorming session with friends, family, or your instructor should help you focus on a topic about which you *do* feel passionate—and about which people have differing points of view.

- Are you comfortable taking a side on a debatable issue? Why or why not?
- Are there any debatable topics you would especially gravitate toward? stay away from?

at effective reasoning, the more you'll demand well-reasoned arguments from others in order to be convinced:

Persuasion is everywhere in our culture. Just look and listen. I liked learning more about persuasion and applying it in my speeches, but what I'll really take away from this class is my new ability to better recognize persuasion when others use it on me, which is just about every day.

16B Recognize Types of Persuasive Speeches

When you speak persuasively, your goal is to make a claim and then argue why people should accept or reject it. Persuasive speeches argue one of three types of claims, or assertions—of fact, value, or policy.

1. Assertions of fact

When you make an **assertion of fact,** you argue whether something is true or not true, whether something happened or did not happen, or whether something exists or does

Examples of persuasive statements that assert fact

- *There is a causal link between a pregnant woman's intake of fish high in mercury and her child's risk of autism.*

- *Social Security will not go bankrupt.*
- *The Internet isolates people.*

Examples of persuasive statements that assert value

- *The United States should pursue technological progress at all costs.*
- *Spanking is an acceptable form of child discipline.*
- *We should support tourism built on sustainable resources.*

Examples of persuasive statements that assert policy

- *U.S. troops need to be provided better body armor.*
- *Protect against general antibiotic resistance by not buying antibacterial soaps.*
- *Sign up for a community-service trip to Haiti.*

not exist. Some assertions of fact are quickly answered in an encyclopedia; these are not claims of fact that interest listeners. Instead, argue assertions of fact that have not yet been definitively answered, or those on which people disagree.

Claims about past events for which the record is obscure, questionable, or nonexistent make good topics for presentations, as do claims about the present and future for which there is more than one justifiable answer. Your task is to present factual evidence and build an argument for one particular answer.

2. Assertions of value

connect

For sample student persuasive speech based on an assertion of value, see the online speech videos "Jobs: The Two Faces of Steve" or "Migrant Farm Workers."

Persuasive speeches based on an **assertion of value** argue whether something is right or wrong, whether something is good or bad, how much something is worth, how fair something is, or how important or useful something is. Assertions of value go beyond your personal preferences. You may greatly value a family heirloom, but it would be hard to provide enough evidence to make your listeners value it the same way. And, as you'll read in Chapter 17, you must support persuasive speeches with evidence. Unlike assertions of fact that require objective and verifiable evidence, claims of value are also frequently supported by subjective, personal, or emotional evidence.

3. Assertions of policy

connect

For sample student persuasive speeches based on assertions of policy, see the online speech videos "Energy or Anathema?" and "Benefits of Organic Milk."

When you give a persuasive speech based on an **assertion of policy,** you argue a program of action—how things should or should not happen, proceed, or get done for an individual or a group or at a societal level. Assertions of policy either encourage action (or non-action) on the part of listeners or seek to gain audience support (or disapproval) for courses of action that others take. As in all persuasive speeches, you must support your assertions with evidence—in this case, evidence that the course of action you're proposing will lead to desired outcomes or prevent undesired ones.

Speeches of fact, value, and policy can overlap. Value and policy are often tightly connected. For instance, if you are arguing against school uniforms, you might also argue for the value of individuality as expressed in clothing styles. Fact and value are also connected. When presenting a claim about the presence of ghosts in your town's boarded-up hotel, you may also have to persuade listeners to value unconventional forms of proof.

16C Use Effective Persuasive Strategies

Chapter 8 discusses ways to objectively and subjectively support your assertions. These include emotional proof, statistics, and examples. Chapter 17 looks at another way—reasoning. This section explores some effective general persuasive strategies you'll want to use every time you speak persuasively: knowing your audience, being realistic about your persuasive goal, organizing your argument for your listeners, making sure listeners understand, using classic and contemporary appeals, and using the power of language.

1. Know your audience

For you to succeed in persuasion, your listeners must see how they can benefit from your ideas. So, before you shape your ideas, you must know your audience. For example, a real-estate agent who specializes in helping buyers find their first homes would be wasting time trying to convince a group of well-to-do retirees to contract his or her services.

Collect audience data through research, experts, surveys, and personal observation to help you determine the demographics, values, attitudes, needs, and wants of your listeners. (See Chapter 5 for more about audience analysis.) These audience characteristics will guide your topic selection, the appropriate depth of information, the reasoning that will most likely persuade them, and the type of language that will best communicate the message.

You may face several types of audiences when speaking persuasively: an open or receptive audience, an indifferent or uninformed audience, or a closed and unreceptive audience.

An open or receptive audience

A favorable audience typically creates a pleasurable speaking situation. You can quickly get to your persuasive point, spend time elaborating on your ideas, and shape the audience's ideas and actions with relative ease. For example, during a speech to an environmentally friendly school board, your proposal for a community garden at the local middle school has a good chance of being accepted, especially if you present complete plans, outline fund-raising, and provide a list of volunteers willing to help build and maintain the garden. Follow these specific strategies when speaking to receptive audiences:

- Emphasize what you have in common.
- Give examples and tell stories that reinforce your areas of agreement.
- Be clear and open about your persuasive goal.
- Use emotional appeals that make listeners feel good about their current views.
- Encourage your audience to act immediately by providing helpful resources.

An indifferent or uninformed audience

Speaking to an audience like this, also known as a neutral audience, is a common occurrence. A variety of interests claim people's attention, and there is no guarantee that they share your interests. For example, botanist Wendy Hodgson, director of the Desert Botanical Garden Herbarium in Phoenix, speaks to numerous groups about protecting plant diversity. She often faces an uphill battle just getting people to pay attention to plants, much less be concerned about protecting them.

Like Hodgson, your main job when speaking to listeners who are indifferent or uninformed is to grab their attention and create interest in your message. Here are some strategies to use:

- Fully explain your idea. Elaborate.
- Spend extra time building the relevance of your idea. Show you have listeners' best interests in mind.
- Provide a number of good reasons they should see things your way.
- Stress audience members' commonalities; build their bonds with one another and with you.
- Highlight your credibility; show that you are trustworthy.

- Communicate your passion about your idea.
- Strongly reinforce your persuasive goal in the conclusion.

A closed and unreceptive audience

On occasion, some speakers who are especially passionate about an idea face a closed and unreceptive audience by choice. But circumstance is more likely to put speakers in this challenging situation. For example, a manager who needs to persuade a group of hostile employees to take a work furlough to improve the company's financial situation has a real challenge ahead. Here are some strategies that will increase (though certainly not guarantee) chances for persuasive success with an unreceptive audience:

- Mention the controversial nature of your idea. Ask the audience to listen, not necessarily to agree.
- Limit your persuasive goal; having the audience accept your idea *as* an idea may be your ultimate purpose.
- Emphasize areas of agreement.
- Use logical appeals rather than emotional ones.
- Use sources listeners will respect.
- Show your respect for opposing views while attempting to refute them.
- Demonstrate through your well-structured message, your clear and engaging visuals, and your confident delivery that you're well prepared.
- Reinforce your (limited) persuasive goal near the end of the presentation, but do it gently and respectfully.

2. Be realistic about your persuasive goal

Persuasive speeches rarely achieve radical shifts of commitment. You cannot persuade an audience of Republicans to become an audience of Democrats. It is nearly impossible to persuade an audience of atheists to believe in the importance of school prayer. Changes in thinking are more likely when the speaker's focus of persuasion is smaller in scope and resides in the not-so-extreme. For example, you may persuade some Republicans that a recent bill enacted by your state's majority Republican legislature was not good policy for low-income parents. You may persuade some atheists to accept a weekly minute of silence for primary-school students.

Keep in mind that when people change thought or behavior, they tend to do so a step at a time or in small increments. For example, the people in charge of the Meatless Mondays campaign are encouraging people to skip meat on Mondays so as to promote better personal health and that of the planet. They know that few meat eaters will become vegetarians overnight, but that some people will be receptive to a one-day-a-week ban. This small step is their persuasive focus, and they're gaining quite a following. When planning your speech, consider your topic and your audience, and look for the incremental steps that may work with this group. When you are attempting to persuade, small steps can be more successful than larger ones.

Consider also where your topic lies on the spectrum of generally accepted ideas. Voices promoting radical views certainly have their place in a democracy but rarely find immediate success in their persuasive efforts. To be accepted, these voices must find a way to evolve and gain wider intellectual or emotional appeal. It's the conversations taking place toward the center of an issue that tend to eventually influence public opinion and action.

This is not to say that you should target your persuasive speech only at the center of a given issue. But the more mainstream your audience, the less radical your goal should be. With middle-of-the-road listeners, it's doubtful you would succeed with *Governments should allow citizens unrestricted mobility by removing all fences, borders, and political boundaries,* or *Reduce all wages to the same amount.* Speeches like these better appeal to small segments of the population.

You need not simply tell audiences what they want to hear, however; it's good to challenge their thinking. But know your audience, and keep your persuasive goal realistic. One student, Annie, knew she was taking a risk with her thesis, *The United States Senate is an outdated institution.* Instead of trying to get her audience to agree with her, she just wanted them to be aware of her radical idea. Annie considered her speech successful because she at least got listeners to accept her idea as one to consider.

There are endless issues to discuss from a variety of angles. Speeches that argue an issue's black-and-white edges rarely persuade anyone but those already on the edges. Your persuasive ideas are more likely to appeal to larger segments of your audience when you argue ideas somewhere in the middle.

3. Organize your argument for your listeners

Organizing your ideas is key to retaining listeners' attention and helping them follow your argument. Chapter 9 covers many ways to organize your persuasive speeches, and your instructor may provide a few other persuasive arrangements, such as the comparative-advantages pattern (focuses on the advantages of your proposal to competing ones) or the refutation pattern (shows how the arguments against your claim are false). See the "Create Converse Connect" box on page 368 for another way to organize your persuasive speech. Look critically at your topic, and think about what you want your audience to do or believe. Select the pattern that works best for your persuasive goal.

There are other organizational points to consider. You may find success when you lead your listeners along the same path of your own reasoning, which you'll learn how to do in Chapter 17. Also, bear in mind that audiences are more likely to remember the points you make first (the principle of **primacy**) and last (the principle of **recency**) rather than the ones in the middle. Take the time to arrange your main points for maximum impact. If, for example, you're persuading a group to "Support the local farmer's market," you may want to arrange your five reasons like this:

1. The organic produce found there is good for you and the environment.
2. You'll find items not typically found at a grocery store.
3. The markets are convenient.

The Shape of Persuasion

Business presentation expert and trainer Nancy Duarte has identified a contour or shape of an effective persuasive presentation that she calls a Sparkline. In this format, the speaker begins with a "call to adventure" and then spends the majority of the presentation going back and forth between "what is" (the audience's current reality) and "what could be" (the speaker's vision), creating a kind of rhythm and, more importantly, a contrast that's significant and meaningful. As the conclusion nears, the speaker makes a call to action and finishes with a "new bliss," or an explanation of what the world will be like with your ideas in action. Duarte knew she had come up with a great model of persuasion when she successfully applied her Sparkline to both Martin Luther King Jr.'s "I Have A Dream" speech and Steve Jobs' launch of the iPhone in 2007.

If you would like to experiment with Duarte's Sparkline, check out her book *Resonate* (Wiley, 2010), or watch her explain the model in detail at http://www.duarte.com/books/resonate/sparkline-overview.

4. The markets are fun for the family.
5. You're supporting the local economy when you shop there.

In this example, "convenient" and "fun" are less important than the bigger issues of personal and environmental health (primacy) and boosting the local economy (recency).

4. Make sure listeners understand your position first

Persuasive speakers are often in a hurry to get to their persuasive arguments. However, listeners must first understand your position before they can be persuaded to accept your claim or point of view. Take the time to define terms, explain concepts, or describe organizations.

As an example, Claude Holmes is the founder of Desert Star, a program that empowers homeless men through community service. Wanting to grow his successful yet small nonprofit organization, Holmes created a thorough business plan and proceeded to raise funds. He designed a professional presentation that included charts, figures, photos, and other important details he expected would appeal to investors. He looked sharp and spoke enthusiastically to his audience.

Holmes quickly realized that he was in trouble, however, when the first question from an audience member was "What is it exactly that your organization does?" He had become so focused on fund-raising as his next step that he lost sight of the need to start with the basics. He had assumed that his one-sentence explanation of Desert Star would suffice. Obviously, it did not. Listeners could not make an investment decision because they were still trying to understand the organization's mission. The fund-raiser heavily revised his presentation to address this critical comprehension gap before speaking to any other investment groups.

5. Use classical appeals

The Greek philosopher Aristotle identified three broad persuasion strategies: ethos, pathos, and logos. Chapter 17 looks in depth at logos, or persuading listeners through their ability to reason. We look here at ethos and pathos.

Use the power of your character

You saw in Chapter 4 that **ethos,** or speaker credibility, is an essential tool in any presentation. But it's especially important in a persuasive speech. People are often persuaded to do or believe something based largely on the power of the personality making the request. While it's rare that you can rely solely on your ethos for effective persuasion, here are some essential behaviors and traits you should display:

Demonstrate ownership of the material with confident delivery Audiences are more likely to believe you when they think your ideas are authentically yours. If you're too dependent on your notes, or you stumble over words, hesitate, and sound uncertain, listeners may wonder whose ideas you're conveying. Communicate your genuine belief in your ideas by speaking confidently and conversationally. Listeners need to believe that *you* believe.

Communicate your genuine passion Listeners want to see and hear your passion and genuine concern for your cause. Identify the true emotions of your presentation, and communicate them naturally. Be emotionally authentic and generous. Don't hold back, but remember that displaying exaggerated expressions only distances your audience.

Be ethical and civil Coercion and persuasion share the same goal of getting people to do something, but **coercion** relies on threats, harsh displays of power, or the use of force. Unlike coercive people, who do not care if they are disrespected or feared, persuasive speakers *need* to care. Becoming convinced is a voluntary action, and thinking audiences tend to follow only those speakers they deem ethical and trustworthy. Listeners seek your commitment to positive ethical values and civility. They look to see if you are being up-front about your intentions and want to be assured that all your supporting materials are truthful and accurate. (Review Chapter 4 for the importance of ethical and civil public communication.)

Use emotional appeals

Pathos, or an appeal to your audience's emotions, is another classical persuasive strategy. People often make decisions based on emotions, ignoring or delaying logic thought about the appeal. Feelings of sympathy, anger, fear, pride, revenge, and joy are just some of the reasons people alter their predispositions or actions. You can tap into your listeners' emotions for successful persuasive effect.

connect

For a sample student video example, see the online techniques video clip "Using Pathos."

Examples of emotional appeals

- Appeal to the audience's sense of **injustice** while persuading them that telemarketers unfairly target older people.

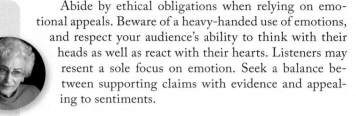

- Appeal to their belief in **sacrifice** while arguing for increased medical funding for wounded war veterans.

- Appeal to their sense of **community** while enlisting participation in a local Habitat for Humanity project.

Abide by ethical obligations when relying on emotional appeals. Beware of a heavy-handed use of emotions, and respect your audience's ability to think with their heads as well as react with their hearts. Listeners may resent a sole focus on emotion. Seek a balance between supporting claims with evidence and appealing to sentiments.

6. Use contemporary appeals

In addition to the traditional classical forms of appeal, contemporary scholars describe several other methods for persuading others: electronic eloquence, Maslow's hierarchy of needs, expectancy-outcome values, public memory, expectancy violations, and invitational rhetoric.

Electronic eloquence

Communication theorist Kathleen Hall Jamieson says that television has greatly influenced what it takes to be persuasive.[1] Jamieson notes that modern persuaders often successfully appeal to audiences through a combination of storytelling, disclosing aspects of their personality, and the integration of images—a method that has been dubbed **electronic eloquence.** Today's political campaigns, especially at the presidential level, offer good examples of Jamieson's observations in action.

You can use electronic eloquence, too. Create an opportunity to use the narrative as part of or throughout your presentation (see Chapter 8, Section B). Tell audiences why you're interested in your topic and how you got involved in it, how you use the ideas being discussed, and if appropriate, how you feel about these ideas (see Chapter 4, Section E). Make use of a variety of professional-looking informative and atmospheric visuals to support your message (see Chapter 12). The combination of these appeals can have great persuasive effect on modern audiences.

Maslow's hierarchy of needs

Psychologist Abraham Maslow developed a **hierarchy of needs,** ranging from the most basic physiological needs like food and shelter to the highest needs like creative self-expression and solving other people's problems (see Figure 16.1).[2] You can persuade others by appealing to this broad range of needs. Listeners must perceive their lower needs as filled in order to move on to meeting any higher-level needs. For instance, be sure that your listeners feel a sense of security in their jobs (safety needs) before you encourage them to participate in the company picnic (belonging needs). Encouraging people to be spontaneous while traveling (self-actualization needs) is more likely to work on a group of listeners with high levels of self-confidence (esteem needs). Maslow's theory tells us that an upward move toward higher needs is what motivates people to alter their beliefs or actions. Your audience analysis is essential in determining what needs to use as persuasive appeals.

Expectancy-outcome values

Your listeners will calculate the pros and cons of taking an action before committing themselves. **Expectancy-outcome values theory,** developed by psychology professor Icek Ajzen and communication professor Martin Fishbein, says that each of us consciously evaluates the potential costs and benefits—the value—of taking or not taking a particular action.[3] We consider the costs and benefits not only to ourselves but also to our relationships with others: *If I take this action, how will my friends/mother/ partner react?*

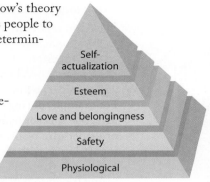

figure **16.1** **Maslow's Hierarchy of Needs**

When speaking persuasively, identify and stress the *value* of the outcome of a particular action or inaction. When recruiting people to be counselors at your summer camp for homeless kids, tell stories about the deep, authentic friendships that are made; note how such volunteer work enhances a college application; and stress the intrinsic rewards of helping others in need. Such strategies can keep your audience involved and move them in your desired direction.

Public memory

Cultural and societal groups are often invested in experiences they shared in the past—whether these experiences are serious (the September 11 attacks), eventful (the first man on the moon), or on the light side (the beanie baby craze)—and they need and desire to recall these experiences. Communication scholars describe **public memory theory** as the power that TV, music, radio, film, and other communication media have in persuading us about the way we collectively remember the past.[4] You can tap into public memories— what most people, through these media, have come to accept as true—for persuasive effect during your speeches. For example, because TV has played a key role in creating public memory of how efficiently crimes are solved, you can refer to *CSI* during your speech promoting the use of DNA evidence in court cases.

Ironically, public memory needn't be based on something that really happened to have persuasive effect. For example, most U.S. adults "remember" feminists burning their bras in the 1960s and 1970s. Yet this did not happen.[5] The public "memory" probably stems from a blending of two different, accurate events from the same time period: of women throwing bras into trash cans and of men burning their draft cards. Nonetheless, a speaker could evoke this memory during a speech on the effects of the women's movement. Keep in mind, however, that as an ethical speaker, you should rely only on public memories that are accurate, to the best of your knowledge. Once you know that the bra-burning story is false, you can no longer ethically use it as support in your argument (no more than you would use objective data that you knew to be faulty).

Expectancy violations

Have you ever been brought to attention by something unexpected a speaker said? Communication scholar Judee Burgoon's **expectancy-violation theory** notes that speakers can attract attention when their words or actions catch listeners by surprise (or violate their expectations).[6] When the outcome of the unexpected language or behavior is positive, audiences feel better about you, increasing your chances of meeting your persuasive goals. For example, during his speech encouraging others to help friends out with needed childcare, one speaker named Davin shared stories and pictures that captured his year's worth of tender care of his neighbor's two-year-old child. Since most people associate nurturing childcare with women, Davin's audience, caught off guard, embraced his message in ways—positive ways—they weren't expecting. If this man enjoyed his time with his new young friend so much, maybe they'd enjoy finding a young charge of their own.

You want to create a positive rather than a negative outcome with your expectancy violation, so check with an instructor, supervisor, or friend whose opinion you value if you have an idea about saying or doing something your audience does not expect. Poor word choice or a story that illustrates unexpected—but also unethical—behavior can cause your audience to stop listening.

Invitational rhetoric

If you are speaking in a context that allows for sustained audience interaction, consider incorporating some principles of **invitational rhetoric,** a type of speaking that's not purely informative or persuasive but, instead, finds a speaker engaging in dialogue with the audience to clarify positions, explore ideas, and express beliefs and values.[7] Initially proposed by communication scholars Sonya Foss and Cindy Griffin, invitational rhetoric aims to create mutual understanding and respect among parties who hold differing opinions, values, and beliefs. Invitational speaking requires three conditions:

- All views expressed are seen as equally valid.
- These views are seen as valuable.
- Those holding individual views have a right to know what's best for themselves and to make choices about their lives accordingly.

The idea behind invitational speaking is that once all views are expressed and understood, individuals in the dialogue may find themselves shifting their opinions but do so *on their own,* independent of another's pointed and intentional persuasive strategies. Of course, these individuals may also remain committed to their original positions.

Three strategies help you speak invitationally: knowing your position, using invitational language, and allowing time for discussion.[8] Let's say your community is deciding what to do with an old warehouse located downtown. While you'd like to see it razed and replaced with a park, you're aware that others are proposing different options. At the next community meeting, you "invite" the audience to consider all options. While you stand firmly behind your proposal and explain it well, you don't impose your position on the listeners or speak negatively about the other proposals (which would create a situation of inequality). Instead, you use invitational language such as "I came to this view because . . ." and "For me, this position makes sense because . . ." to imply respect and openness toward the other ideas, and to let listeners come to their own conclusions once they've heard all proposals and have had time for reflection.

Invitational speaking is not always easy or appropriate. If you stand so firmly on your position that you would have trouble genuinely listening with respect to opposing views, then a traditional persuasive speech is a better choice. Some topics, like those involving religion or politics, may be so inherently polarizing that finding mutual understanding is impossible.

7. Use the power of language

Persuasive speakers can purposefully use language—or more specifically, loaded language— to capitalize on **frames,** particular images or other kinds of knowledge that listeners possess. To use the term *tax relief,* for example, is to use loaded language.[9] Tax relief takes two frames (tax = "giving money to the government" and relief = "a release or a reprieve from an affliction") and combines them into a new frame ("taxes are an affliction from which we need relief"). And who doesn't want relief from something that's bad?

A powerful frame like this influences your ability to communicate. For example, those arguing for tax relief have an easy task; the evoked frame in the minds of the listeners created by the loaded word *relief* does the job for them. Those arguing against tax relief have a more difficult task. How can anyone argue against an evoked frame that sounds so appealing? Instead, those arguing "for taxes" need to rely on language evoking a different frame. Arguing for increased *tax investment,* for example, taps into the original frame for *tax,* but adds the frame for *investment*—in other words, "pay a little now, reap greater rewards in the future."

Public speakers, especially those with persuasive messages, can use loaded language to their advantage. Consider the frames evoked by the following italicized words. Each pair of terms refers to the same idea, but through language, the framing taps into different ideas the listener probably holds.

- Is the third world country you are discussing a *growing economy* or an *underdeveloped nation*?
- Is it easier to argue for or against *gay marriage* or *marriage equality*?
- Is China an *intolerant culture* or a *global force*?
- Are *undocumented workers* or *illegal aliens* the focus of your immigration discussion?
- Would the *partial-birth abortion ban* have passed if called by its medical term, *intact dilation and extraction*?

Consider the frames evoked through the use of your language. Keep a particular frame in mind as you research, create your argument, and support your idea. Who is using the frame and to what effect? What images will your words evoke? Most importantly, will the frame work for or against your persuasive goal? Remember, it is essentially a futile exercise to argue, as we saw, that your audience does not need tax relief.

Persuasive Speaking in Action *A Student's Process*

"Energy or Anathema?" *by Brandon Valdez*

Choosing his topic

While serving in the U.S. Marine Corps, Brandon, like many of his fellow Marines, consumed a lot of energy drinks. He never questioned his intake of them until he returned to school and started learning about nutrition. While studying a can of RockStar one day, he asked himself *What's in this can that's giving me energy?* He was startled by what he learned and wanted to spread the word.

Thinking about his audience and choosing his persuasive purpose: To argue an assertion of fact.

Brandon figured that most people consumed energy drinks for a variety of reasons: the burst of energy they provide, their sweet taste, because their friends drink them, and because the marketing is really slick. He assumed that, like him, they weren't questioning the ingredients in the drinks and the impact of those ingredients on their health. For this speech, he wanted to share the facts, and argue that those facts were significant enough to warrant a change in consumption habits for those who drink them, and reinforce the choice for those who already don't drink them.

> <u>Topic:</u> Energy drinks
>
> <u>Larger persuasive purpose:</u> To argue an assertion of fact.
>
> <u>Thesis:</u> The excess of ingredients used in energy drinks to "give you energy" should give you pause and make you rethink consuming them.

connect

The final video version of this persuasive student speech, "Energy or Anathema?," can be viewed online in Connect.

Research sources

Center for Science in the Public Interest
Eat This Not That, by David Zinczenko (2007)

The Thesis and the Main Supporting Points

Topic

Thesis

The excess of ingredients used in *energy drinks* to "give you energy" should give you pause and make you rethink consuming them.

Organizing his main supporting points

His organizing term

Brandon's main supporting points would focus in on the *ingredients* that are in excess. See Chapter 9 for a review of organizing terms.

Main points:

1. The excess of sugar in energy drinks is a concern.   Ingredient #1
2. The excess of caffeine is another concern.   Ingredient #2
3. The addition of taurine is unnecessary and its health consequences are still unknown.   Ingredient #3

Meanwhile, in the planning phase, Brandon pinpointed some effective general persuasive strategies to concentrate on:

- Know your audience. I started paying attention to what my classmates and others on campus were drinking. I saw a lot of energy drinks and this affirmed my decision about my topic choice. I'll also be able to use a lot of direct pronouns during the presentation.
- Be realistic about your goal. Though I stopped consuming energy drinks after doing my research, I don't expect others to do the same. Instead, I'm simply going to encourage them to rethink their consumption habits.
- Make sure listeners understand you first. I've got to spend time educating my audience before I can persuade them. Therefore, each main point will begin with strong and accurate information, complete with visuals and statistics, before I focus in on my persuasive message.

review questions

1. What is a persuasive speech? How does it differ from an informative speech? Why is it difficult to persuade others? What can we learn about receiving persuasive messages by learning how to give them?
2. What are the differences between a speech that argues an assertion of fact, an assertion of value, and an assertion of policy?
3. What are the effective general strategies you can use to persuade others? Which of these will you use for your next speech and why?

connect

For online exercises, quizzes, and hands-on activities, see the Chapter 16 assignments in Connect Public Speaking.

key terms

persuasion 359
assertion of fact 362
assertion of value 364
assertion of policy 364
primacy 367
recency 367
ethos 369

coercion 369
pathos 369
electronic eloquence 370
hierarchy of needs 370
expectancy-outcome
     values theory 371

public memory
   theory 371
expectancy-violation
   theory 372
invitational rhetoric 372
frames 373

exercises

1. With a small group, generate ten topics to alter or reinforce thinking. Generate another ten to alter or reinforce action.

2. Think of a time in your personal life when you were persuaded only by your emotions. In retrospect, was your decision a good one or not? What connections can you make between this event and the power to persuade others through the use of emotions in a public presentation?

3. Study TV advertisements for their persuasive strategies. Report on two ads, identifying the general strategies used. Is the advertiser attempting to create a belief, reinforce an existing belief, or motivate you to action? Is the advertiser using credibility or emotional appeals? Give examples.

4. Review the contemporary persuasive strategies on pages 370–373. Identify examples from your life when you used one or more of these strategies on someone else, perhaps without even knowing you were doing so. Do you see an opportunity to use one or more of these strategies in your upcoming persuasive talk? If so, which ones?

5. Research an ideological organization on the web or at the library. Search for the organization's "facts and statistics" that back up its viewpoints, assertions, or positions. Take three of these "facts or statistics," and research other sources to see whether you can find opposing "facts and statistics." What does this say about the blurred lines between information and persuasion?

Develop Your Arguments

LEARNING OBJECTIVES

1 Describe reasoning and explain its three components.

2 Identify the four patterns for arranging your reasoning.

3 List some reasoning fallacies.

H umans have long understood the reasoning power of the mind and how it can be used for making observations, testing ideas, and drawing new conclusions. In fact, we depend on our reasoning power to navigate many aspects of life, including our relationships, our work environments, and our public interactions. As someone who will give persuasive speeches, you need to develop reasoning— learning how to make logical arguments and use them convincingly. This chapter discusses the role of reasoning, provides some patterns for arranging your arguments, and highlights a number of reasoning fallacies you'll want to avoid.

(17A) Use Reasoning

You use reasoning more than you may realize. When you're low on funds and ask your parents for money, rationalizing that it's hard to study on an empty stomach, you're reasoning. When you ask your instructor to accept your paper late because your printer ran out of toner, you're reasoning. Some reasoning, as the two examples show, is more successful than others (your parents are more likely to be persuaded than your instructor). If you want to increase your chances of persuading others to think or act in a certain way, it's your responsibility to learn how to reason effectively and to do so purposefully.

While you may influence listeners through your personal appeal and appeals to their emotions (the classical strategies of ethos and pathos; see Chapter 16), you also need to acknowledge their ability to think critically. This third classical persuasive strategy identified by Aristotle is **logos,** appealing to the logical mind. As a speaker, you'll accomplish this with **reasoning,** the process of supporting a claim using sufficient, true (or probable), and relevant evidence, which is logically arranged and linked to the claim by a warrant. British philosopher Stephen Toulmin's model of a sound argument, discussed later in the chapter in the section on warrants, is helpful to use as we break down the key words—claim, evidence, and warrant— to clarify this definition of reasoning.[1]

Examples of claims

- U.S. children are fatter than ever before and will continue getting fatter in the next decade.

- Statistics 101 is a difficult course.

- The strange mutations seen in many frog species spell danger for us all.

- Sean Penn is one of the greatest actors of our time.

- All medical records should be available through a centralized electronic system.

1. State a claim

The **claim** is your statement about a fact, value, or policy— the conclusion you want your audience to draw and accept. The claim may be the focus of your entire presentation, constituting the thesis statement or central idea. Or you may use a claim in just a portion of the speech, in which you want your audience to accept a particular statement before you move forward with the rest of your persuasive presentation.

create
converse
connect

Loud Insults vs. Responsible Persuasion

You've probably seen and heard them—those television and radio personalities who rely on a booming voice, verbal interruptions, witty remarks (often written by writers behind the scenes), quoted remarks taken out of context, and verbal and pictorial insults of every kind intended to make others (who rarely get to defend themselves) look like buffoons. While some of these folks have become celebrities who wield political influence among large followings, keep in mind that the majority are actually entertainers seeking high ratings while looking to enrich themselves and their companies (and often succeeding wildly in doing so).

Don't follow their tactics when giving your own presentations. As a public speaker you want to successfully convey your message and create a positive relationship with your listeners. That means you must care about responsible persuasion, which you're learning about throughout this textbook. When speaking, separate demagoguery from argumentation, and entertainment from reality. Join the large majority of your fellow citizens who care about civil and rational discourse.

- Do you regularly watch or listen to any of these television or radio personalities?
- Why or why not?

2. Provide evidence

Evidence is the material you use to support or back up your claim. Many of the forms of support discussed in Chapter 8, including facts, statistics, and testimony, can serve as evidence in persuasive speaking. For example, to back up your claim that children are fatter than ever, use statistics from a trusted source (such as the Centers for Disease Control and Prevention, the National Institutes of Health, or WebMD) showing that only 5 percent of kids were considered obese in 1970, 7 percent in 1982, 14 percent in 1999, and nearly 20 percent today. Refer to this evidence to help listeners see that this upward trend in childhood obesity will most likely continue into the next decade if nothing is done to combat the problem.

When selecting evidence, make sure that it's sufficient, is true or probable, and is relevant to the claim.

Sufficient evidence

There should be enough evidence to back up your claim. In the child-obesity example, how large was the statistical sample of children? For instance, did the researchers look only at kids at one school in one midwestern suburb, or was the sampling from a large number of children in both urban and rural areas, from all socioeconomic classes, and from all parts of the country? To use another example: the fact that your sister got dizzy after riding the roller coaster at Amusement Park X is insufficient evidence that the roller coaster makes people dizzy. However, if ten or more people a day were complaining of dizziness after riding the roller coaster, you would have sufficient evidence.

True (or probable) evidence

Is the evidence you are using accurate and verifiable, or is it based on rumor, manipulation of statistics, or unreliable self-reporting? For example, looking again at the child-obesity claim, scientists know that people tend to underestimate their weight when interviewed on the telephone or when filling out a survey. Children tend not to even know how much they weigh. Also, actual height and weight measurements gathered by qualified personnel are more trustworthy than those obtained through self-reporting. When choosing evidence, beware of hearsay, rumor, truthiness, and urban legends. Just because you think something is or should be true does not mean it *is* true. It's your ethical responsibility to ensure that any evidence you use is reliable.

Probable evidence means that something is likely to be true, to exist, or to occur, despite insufficient evidence to prove or predict it. For example, you make a claim that bark beetles are most likely responsible for the recent dying-off of pine trees in your area. Though you have no actual evidence to prove it, you do have evidence of bark beetles causing similar damage to similar trees in nearby areas. You could use this as probable evidence.

Beware of weak probable evidence, though. To claim that the primary reason your niece did so well on her science-project presentation was that you had taken her to the science museum the day before is to use weak probable evidence. Chances are there were several other factors contributing to your niece's success. The probable link is weak, and your claim would be difficult to prove.

Relevant evidence

The evidence you use must be related to your claim. For instance, the fact that family pets have become fatter in recent decades is interesting but not relevant to your claim about the rise in childhood obesity. It could be a sign that adults in the house are feeding *all* household residents more (thus causing them to gain weight), but evidence about obesity in pets is not relevant to your claim about obesity in children. However, statistics on the decreasing number of hours devoted to recess in elementary schools may be relevant.

3. Use a warrant to link the evidence and the claim

Picture this scenario: you and your friend listen to a speaker arguing for the need to have GPS tracking units on every cell phone sold. As evidence, the speaker puts together a list of stories of people who, presumed lost, were reunited with loved ones when authorities tracked their cell phone signals. Thus, he argues for GPS tracking units on every cell phone because they serve a good purpose in finding "lost" people. While you both hear the same evidence, your friend ultimately agrees with the speaker's argument, yet you do not. This, according to philosopher Toulmin, is because of the "because"— also known as the **warrant,** or the link between the evidence and the claim.

Warrants act like perceptual filters that help make each individual interpret the connection between a claim and its evidence as effective or not. For instance, in the example above, because your friend is a new mother, she drew the conclusion that the speaker was right. If technology can play a role in finding a lost child, she's in full support. You, meanwhile, have strong beliefs about corporate intrusion on personal privacy. Thus, the speaker's examples aren't enough reason in your mind for society as a whole to give up the constitutional right to privacy.

When speaking persuasively, you'll choose warrants you hold to be true and that are personally and socially ethical. But use your audience analysis to determine whether the warrant is also effective for your specific group of listeners. Will they link the evidence to your claim with your same "because"? Will your warrant be intuitively understood (many are), or will you need to verbally express the connection between the evidence and the claim?

There are several types of warrants—authoritative, substantive, and motivational warrants.

Authoritative warant

An **authoritative warrant** relies on the credibility, acceptability, or authority of the source to link the evidence to the claim.

> Bread made with whole-wheat flour is more nutritious than bread made with refined white flour.

Claim

> My nutrition professor gave a lecture on the benefits of whole-wheat flour over refined white flour.

Evidence

> (Nutrition professors are highly credible sources in regard to food products.)

Warrant: authoritative

Substantive warrant

A **substantive warrant** uses the reliability and sometimes the quantity of the evidence to support the claim.

> Bread made with whole-wheat flour is more nutritious than bread made with refined white flour.

Claim

> A growing body of evidence in nutrition journals shows that bread made with whole-wheat flour increases the absorption of fiber, protein, and iron.

Evidence

Warrant: substantive

(Multiple medical research studies show that whole-wheat flour provides more nutritional benefits to the human body than does refined white flour.)

Motivational warrant

A **motivational warrant** connects the evidence to the claim by appealing to audience members' values, needs, desires, emotions, and aspirations.

Claim

Bread made with whole-wheat flour is more nutritious than bread made with refined white flour.

Evidence

The fiber provided by whole-wheat flour not only regulates digestion, but also lowers risks of diabetes and heart disease.

Warrant: motivational

(People enjoy the benefits of a strong and healthy body.)

17B Arrange Your Reasoning According to a Pattern

Like any listenable message, your reasoning is easier for listeners to access, understand, and interact with if it's structured in a familiar way. People commonly use four arrangements when reasoning with one another: inductive, deductive, causal, and analogical.

1. Inductive reasoning: From the specific to the general

Your significant other likes to buy you flowers, give you handmade cards, massage your neck when it's stiff, treat you to lunch, and help keep your apartment clean. Taking these behaviors into account, you conclude that this person likes you very much. Public presentations use this same pattern of **inductive reasoning,** providing several specific instances, observations, or examples in order to lead listeners to accept a general conclusion.

> **Critical Thinking Activities:**
> On the next two pages, identify the missing warrants for the corresponding pieces of evidence, and label them as authoritative, substantive, or motivational.

When you are using inductive reasoning, it does not matter whether your claim comes before or after the evidence. The important factor is for the evidence to back up the claim and to be linked by an effective warrant.

Examples of inductive reasoning

Example 1 The speaker starts with a claim and then provides the evidence to lead audiences to accept the claim:

Steig Larsson's *The Girl with the Dragon Tattoo* deserves its reputation as one of the most exciting pieces of literature of the last few years.

Claim

The novel has sold over 30 million copies.

Evidence 1

It's not common for novels to receive that much attention from so many people worldwide.

Warrant 1: substantive

Larsson won many awards for the novel, including Sweden's Glass Key Award, Britain's Galaxy National Book Award, and South Africa's Boeke Prize.

Evidence 2

Warrant 2:

Two film adaptations have been made, with the 2011 English language version starring Daniel Craig and Rooney Mara.

Evidence 3

Warrant 3:

Example 2 The speaker starts with several pieces of evidence and then takes listeners to a conclusion:

Beets contain betacyanin, a known cancer-fighting agent.

Evidence 1

Women want to do what they can to avoid cancer.

Warrant 1: motivational

Beets are a good source of potassium, which is essential for regulating water balance, levels of acidity, blood pressure, and neuromuscular function.

Evidence 2

Warrant 2:

Evidence 3

Beets are rich in vitamin C, which is essential for fighting viruses, healing wounds, and strengthening many parts of the body.

Warrant 3:

Evidence 4

Beets are rich in vitamin B folate, which is essential for a baby's normal tissue growth while in utero.

Warrant 4:

Claim (as conclusion)

Beets help maintain a woman's overall health.

Tips for using inductive reasoning

Use a sufficient amount of evidence You'll want to have at least two to three separate pieces of evidence.

Choose evidence that is true (or probable) and reliable Be sure that your research sources are credible. Remember to take full and accurate notes when doing research and know where to access your original sources.

Choose evidence that is relevant to the claim Be sure that every piece of evidence you present backs up your claim. Don't get sidetracked by some evidence that doesn't pertain to your claim and, at the same time, don't ignore evidence that disagrees with your claim. Listeners may be familiar with contradictory evidence, and even if they are not, it's unethical to overlook it.

Make sure your claim is probable based on your evidence Your claim should not seem farfetched based on the evidence you provide. You might need to narrow your claim. For example, the claim about Steig Larsson's book could be narrowed from *literature* to *crime novels*. After all, while most agree that the book is an excellent example of genre fiction, some would take issue with it being classified as good literature.

Be careful of making an absolute claim An **absolute claim** is one that asks listeners to accept that something is permanent, complete, or in no way conditional. Making such a claim is often a futile task, because few things in life meet these standards. Instead, acknowledge and communicate the degree of probability in your claim. The beet example does not claim that beets are the sole factor in a woman's good health. It claims only that beets *help maintain* good health.

2. Deductive reasoning: From the general to the specific

Deductive reasoning starts with a generally accepted larger principle that is then used as a rationale to persuade listeners to accept a claim about a specific instance. For instance, one of your brother's friends has recently been showing signs of methamphetamine abuse, and his family and friends, while fed up with his behavior, aren't sure how to get him help. You recall a paper you wrote on treatments for meth abuse, remembering especially the relative success rates of formal interventions that are timed within a few weeks after the user's last binge, when he or she may still be feeling some remorse about his or her behavior during the binge. You ask a few more questions about your brother's friend, learning that his last binge was about ten days ago and that some troubling incidents did indeed occur during it. You eventually conclude that a formal intervention might very well be appropriate in his case. Your conclusion is deductive reasoning at work.

According to the principles of logic, one form of deductive reasoning, known as a **syllogism,** follows three steps:

- **Step 1.** A syllogism states a **major premise,** defined as a statement or general principle containing an absolute relationship between two terms.

  The longest day of the year is known as the summer solstice.

  > Major premise: first term = second term

- **Step 2.** Deductive reasoning follows with a **minor premise,** defined as a specific instance about one of the terms in the major premise.

  Today is the longest day of the year.

  > Minor premise: specific instance about the first term

- **Step 3.** By combining the major and minor premises, we come to—or deduce—a conclusion:

  Today is the summer solstice.

  > The deductive conclusion

Though they're a staple of logic classes, syllogisms are uncommon in real life. In public contexts, especially, we rarely discuss things that are clear-cut or absolute. Instead, we navigate areas that are not well defined by discussing abstractions, arguing interpretations, sharing opinions, communicating values, and explaining things that *appear* to be true. In public communication, therefore, we rely on an alternate form of deductive reasoning—a syllogism known as an **enthymeme**—in which we claim probable or likely relationships between the major and minor premises, not an absolute relationship.

Example of deductive reasoning

Let's look at a real-life example of deductive reasoning in terms of probability or likelihood.

> Past reintroduction efforts for bald-eagle populations have had relative success. Two reintroduced pairs of bald eagles each recently hatched a chick on Santa Cruz Island, off the Southern California coast. The bald-eagle reintroduction efforts on Santa Cruz Island show great promise.

The major premise claims a generally accepted idea, not an absolute.

The minor premise speaks to a specific instance about *reintroduction efforts*.

The conclusion is a probability, not an absolute.

Tips for using deductive reasoning

Establish the validity of the major and minor premises Make sure that you have solid evidence to back each premise. For instance, you need to provide true, sufficient, and relevant evidence to support the claim that past reintroduction efforts for bald-eagle populations *have* had relative success. You also need to provide true, sufficient, and relevant evidence that the two recently hatched Santa Cruz Island chicks are thriving.

Establish the logical link between your major and minor premise Do not leave it up to listeners to assume what the link is or figure it out on their own. Walk them through it. For instance, talk about how Santa Cruz Island is typical of the other areas in which past reintroduction efforts of the bald eagles have been successful.

Don't insist on an absolute conclusion Instead, acknowledge and communicate its degree of probability. For example, reiterate your claim that the bald-eagle reintroduction efforts show *great promise*, not promised success.

3. Causal reasoning: From cause to effect or from effect to cause

Are some of these experiences familiar to you?

- You attempt to reason with your significant other that spending some time apart will test the strength of your love for each other.
- You convince your mom that she can work fewer hours because your leadership role on the hockey team will pay off in increased scholarship offers next year.
- Your otherwise grumpy boss has suddenly become pleasant, and you and your co-workers each suggest why.

Each of these scenarios involves **causal reasoning.** In causal reasoning, we connect two events according to a cause-and-effect relationship. One event is known, doable, or generally assumed. The other event is unknown but presumed.

The first two scenarios above argue that one event will lead to or cause another. This is **reasoning forward,** from cause to effect. In the third scenario, you observe an effect and argue its cause. This is **reasoning backward,** from effect to cause. Let's look at the scenarios again:

Reasoning Forward

Example 1. You may reason with your significant other that spending some time apart will test your love for each other.

> Doable cause
> Unknown but presumed effect

Example 2. You convince your mom that she can work fewer hours because your leadership role on the hockey team will pay off in increased scholarship offers next year.

> Generally assumed cause
> Unknown but presumed effect

Reasoning Backward

Example 3. Your otherwise grumpy boss has suddenly become pleasant, and you and your coworkers each suggest why.

> Known effect
> Unknown but presumed cause

There are many opportunities to use causal reasoning in public presentations. You may want to move audiences to action, convince them that a next step is beneficial, or persuade them to accept your explanation of why things are as they are. Arguing for cause and effect is one of the most popular patterns; there are endless opportunities to put it to work. The entire purpose of your speech may be to convince your audience of a cause-and-effect relationship, or you may need it in just a portion of the presentation.

Examples of causal reasoning

Here are some typical examples of causal reasoning you might encounter in a presentation:

Example 1. The Packers are having their best season in years. One significant reason is their conditioning coach's innovative training program.

> Effect
> Cause

Example 2. Fewer soldiers are dying in combat because of, among other reasons, tremendous advancements in blood-clotting bandages.

> Effect
> Cause

Example 3. The proposed Senate bill will stem the rising tide of illegal immigration into the United States. That will mean more jobs for legal residents.

> Cause
> Effect
> Further effect

Tips for using causal reasoning

Make sure that the known event (whether cause or effect) is true, accurate, and well supported with evidence For example, be certain that the Packers really *are* having their best season in years or that fewer soldiers really *are* dying in combat.

Link the known and the unknown events For example, provide sufficient evidence (statistics, facts, expert testimony) that the blood-clotting bandages have indeed led to fewer combat deaths. It is not enough just to say that they have. Some cause-and-effect situations are intriguing to think about but fall apart when put to the test of providing true links. For example, consider a claim that a butterfly flapping its wings in South America affects localized air patterns, which in turn affect the weather, which eventually causes a hurricane in Louisiana. Would you have the evidence to prove the links?

Make sure that the cause and the effect are close in time You have a better chance of success reasoning that the Packers' conditioning coach has made a difference if the team's improved performance occurred soon after the coach's hiring. Your chances of reasoning successfully decline as more time elapses between the cause and the effect. Was that extravagant purchase of artwork for the lobby five years ago really responsible for the company's deficit this year?

Don't overlook multiple causes or effects For instance, blood-clotting bandages are but one contributing factor in the lower number of combat deaths. Overwhelming air power, improved satellite imagery, and better combat training are also responsible. You do not need to focus on these other causes in your presentation, but you should acknowledge their contributions. Failing to do so may cause listeners to question your knowledge and preparation.

Make sure that your claimed cause or effect is likely or most likely For example, the proposed Senate bill may reduce rates of illegal immigration, but the effect on jobs should be questioned: is it possible legal residents won't want the jobs left open by undocumented workers?

4. Analogical reasoning: Reasoning through comparison

People reason by comparison all the time:

- You just met Serena at a party. She appears to have many of the same qualities as your best friend, Lorena. You invite Serena for lunch, suspecting that you and she will become good friends.
- You are offered a choice between Belgian coffee and Norwegian coffee. You have tried neither one, but you have had Belgian chocolates and consider them to be among the best you've ever tasted. You choose the Belgian coffee.
- Your new study techniques allowed you to do very well in Accounting 101. If you apply them again, you should do equally well in Accounting 102.

When engaging in **analogical reasoning,** you consider the similarities between two things and then presume an unknown quality about one of them must be true because of a known quality in the other.

Examples of analogical reasoning

Here is how analogical reasoning works for one of the preceding examples:

Unknown factor | The superiority of either Belgian coffee or Norwegian coffee

Belgium is a country known for producing many fine food items, including choco-

Consideration 1

lates. Norway is known for its friendly people and beautiful scenery, but you have

Consideration 2

not heard much about its chocolates. Many countries producing fine chocolates also

Consideration 3

produce fine coffees.

The excellence of Belgian chocolate

Known quality

The superiority of Belgian coffee

Presumed quality about the unknown

Analogical reasoning is common in public speaking. Most people are used to think-ing in analogies and can easily interact with speakers who are effectively using this type of reasoning. Your job as speaker is to show listeners how if a quality is true for one thing, then that quality is likely also to be true for a similar thing.

Example: A soccer coach motivates his team, the Thunderbolts, to believe that they

Unknown factor

can beat their upcoming rival, the Wizards. After all, the Thunderbolts unexpect-

Known to be true

edly beat the Sparks last week. The coach then proceeds to explain the many simi-

Similarities are suggested or shown between two items

larities between the Wizards and the Sparks, including their speed and defensive

techniques. The Thunderbolts eventually believe that if they play like they did last

week, they can beat the Wizards just like they beat the Sparks.

Likely to be true

Tips for using analogical reasoning

Convince your audience of the accuracy of the known quality Did the Thunderbolts beat the Sparks because they were truly the better team, or were the Sparks having a bad day because two starters were sick? If listeners doubt the accuracy of the known quality in one item, the analogy loses its power to persuade.

Show how the two items being compared are effectively alike When using relocation ef-forts in Australia among koalas to argue for similar efforts to relocate wombats, you'd need to spend a lot of time showing the similarities between koalas and wombats. At the same time, you would obviously also focus on the unique aspects of wombat relocation.

Research differences as well as similarities between the two items being compared Some differences between two items are so great or so important that they override any similari-ties, thereby significantly weakening the analogy. For example, a political science major believes that the latest foreign-policy announcement from the White House regarding Country X is a smart move. She shows how similar the current situation in Country X is to the past situation in Country Y, where the same policy was tried several decades ago. The speaker suggests to her listeners that because the policy in Country Y succeeded, the

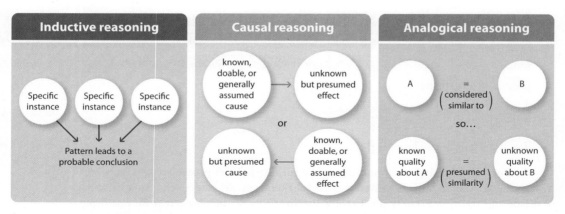

figure **17.1** **Visual Summary of Inductive, Causal, and Analogical Reasoning** Because of its many variations, deductive reasoning is difficult to depict visually and is therefore not shown here.

chances for success in Country X are high. However, the speaker may find it difficult to convince listeners of the similarities between situations in Country X and Country Y. After all, the policy was tried in Country Y back in the 1970s. The world has changed greatly since then, as has the thinking behind many U.S. foreign-policy decisions. These differences would most likely override the similarities, weakening the analogy.

17C Beware of Reasoning Fallacies

Many arguments appear logical on the surface, but deeper analysis shows the presence of a **fallacy,** an occurrence of unsound reasoning when incomplete, distracting, or irrelevant evidence is offered, language choices are weak or confusing, or the inductive, deductive, causal, or analogical reasoning itself is faulty.

There is a difference between providing incorrect facts and relating a fallacy. When a novice speaker commits a fallacy, it's usually due to poor research or poor reasoning, but it's rarely intentional. On occasion, however, people commit fallacies deliberately. Politicians, advertisers, and others who want things from you (your vote, your money, your allegiance) often provide fallacious arguments because they know that the psychological and emotional appeals in the messages can easily overpower any rational thinking the receiver of the messages might engage in (see the "Loud Insults vs. Responsible Persuasion" box earlier in the chapter). In some cases, these persuaders know that what they really have to offer could not withstand honest reasoning. If listeners detect a fallacy, deliberate or not, they are likely to question the speaker's overall intentions and credibility, making the whole presentation suspect.

SPEAK
Responsibly

Keep Learning about Fallacies

Numerous books and credible websites can help you learn more about fallacious reasoning and provide extensive examples. Before your persuasive presentation, check with your instructor or another trusted source for the presence of any fallacies in your own argument.

Another idea is to type "fallacies about [your topic]" into your favorite search engine. Depending on the topic, you may get some hits highlighting one-sided or especially ideological arguments. (As always, be sure to determine the source.) This research can teach you about the poor reasoning others use with your topic and help you avoid it in your own presentation.

An added bonus of learning to recognize fallacies is that it improves your critical listening. You are more likely to detect fallacies when others use them to try to persuade you.

Logicians describe well over one hundred fallacies. Some of the more common ones are described below: appeal to fear, slippery slope, *ad hominem*, either/or, red herring, and bandwagon.

1. Appeal to fear: Believe me or beware

Sometimes known as a scare tactic, an **appeal to fear fallacy** presents a claim intended to produce fear, thereby gaining support for a different and perhaps unrelated claim. Creating fear is not the same as providing sound evidence.

The pattern of the appeal to fear looks like this:

Claim A is presented in a way to produce fear.

Therefore, Claim B is true.

Examples of Appeal to Fear Fallacies

- *I'm sure you've heard that there are several convicted felons living in District X. You don't want your children attending school there.*
- *Car A had several rollover incidents last year. Our car is a much safer purchase.*

2. Slippery slope: You'll end up with this before you know it

The **slippery slope fallacy** occurs when you argue an inevitable connection from one event to another, bypassing links that may or may not exist. The name of this fallacy is apt: if you take a step onto a particular slippery sloping surface, there will be a progression of events and soon enough, you will find yourself at the bottom. As applied to persuasion, a slippery slope is poor reasoning because there is no guarantee that the first step will lead to all the others.

The slippery slope fallacy follows this pattern:

Event A has occurred (or will or might occur).

After A occurs, so will B, C, and so on, leading eventually to Z.

Z should not happen.

Therefore, A is bad or should not happen.

Examples of Slippery Slope Fallacies

- *If we let same-sex couples marry, what's next? first cousins? polygamists? twelve-year-olds?*
- *Security measures at airports are already an infringement on our rights. Today we need to take off our shoes. Tomorrow it will be our clothes. Body-cavity searches are sure to follow.*

3. *Ad hominem:* Attacking the person instead of the problem

An *ad hominem* **fallacy** occurs when you attack the character of the person making an opposing argument rather than address the argument. This fallacy says, in effect, that to have a legitimate claim or argument, a person must be without fault. Yet each of us has made the occasional poor choice, has fallen prey to unfavorable circumstances, or has family members whose behavior we cannot control. "Imperfect" people can still present relevant and strong arguments.

The fallacy first calls into question another person's character or irrelevant actions and then takes them as evidence that his or her argument is weak or invalid.

The *ad hominem* fallacy follows this pattern:

Person A presents an argument or makes a claim.

Person B attacks the "person" of Person A.

Therefore, Person A's argument or claim is weak or invalid.

Examples of *Ad Hominem* Fallacies

- *Mr. Y screams regularly about this problem. But he's a registered socialist. Need I say more?*
- *Senator Z's son was arrested this summer. Senator Z is obviously a poor parent and will undoubtedly make a poor legislator. She does not deserve your vote this fall.*

4. Either/or: A false dilemma

A true dilemma occurs when we are faced with a choice between two or more undesirable options. A false dilemma, or **either/or fallacy,** occurs when a speaker presents an argument that forces listeners to choose between two options when, in reality, more than two exist.

The either/or fallacy pattern looks like this:

Option A exists.

Option B exists.

The speaker advocates choosing one of the presented options (even though more options exist).

Examples of Either/Or Fallacies

- *In this fight on terrorism, you are either with us or against us.*
- *Vote for Candidate A this November; if you don't, you are choosing to see the community you know and love become a bad place to live.*

5. Red herring: A distraction from the real issue

Also known as a smoke screen, the **red herring fallacy** occurs when you raise an irrelevant topic (the red herring) in order to divert attention from an issue you're having trouble arguing or defending. The red herring is a fallacy because changing the topic does not constitute support for the original argument. When an audience detects a red herring, your credibility is questioned because it becomes clear that you have little to defend or did not plan the argument very well.

The pattern for the red herring fallacy looks like this:

Argument A is being discussed or defended.

Topic B is introduced as if relevant to Argument A, but it is not.

Argument A is abandoned.

Examples of Red Herring Fallacies

- *Yes, we probably do need to add some additional upper-division math classes, but the increasing overall dropout rate on campus really has our attention these days. And it should have yours as well.*
- *I agree that my group's findings are not complete, but other groups had great difficulty when researching this problem.*

6. Bandwagon: Everybody's doing it

The **bandwagon fallacy** says in effect that a claim or an argument should be supported or rejected based solely on peer pressure. Just because "everybody" agrees with something, is doing it, isn't doing it, or rejects it lends no credence to whatever "it" is.

This is not to say that loyalty to a group is not good policy. Sometimes conformity is the right thing to do for many reasons. The bandwagon is a fallacy, or poor reasoning, because doing (or not doing) things simply because everyone else is (or is not) does not constitute good *evidence*.

The bandwagon pattern looks like this:

Claim A is made.

"Evidence" is provided wherein "everyone" supports or rejects the claim. Therefore, the claim must be valid.

Examples of Bandwagon Fallacies

- *How can you not favor the president's recent nominee for the Supreme Court? The justice has nothing but support from Congress, and past colleagues.*
- *More than 90 percent of people who tried Product X bought it again. Don't be left out! Buy it today!*

review questions

1. What is reasoning? What three essential elements make up a reasoned argument?
2. What are the four patterns for arranging your reasoning? How does following one of these patterns help you better reach your listeners?
3. What is a reasoning fallacy? Why should it be avoided? How can you avoid making one?

connect

For online exercises, quizzes, and hands-on activities, see the Chapter 17 assignments in Connect Public Speaking.

key terms

logos 378
reasoning 378
claim 378
evidence 379
warrant 381
authoritative warrant 381
substantive warrant 381
motivational warrant 382
inductive reasoning 382

absolute claim 385
deductive reasoning 385
syllogism 385
major premise 385
minor premise 385
enthymeme 385
causal reasoning 386
reasoning forward 386
reasoning backward 386

analogical reasoning 388
fallacy 390
appeal to fear fallacy 391
slippery slope fallacy 391
ad hominem fallacy 392
either/or fallacy 392
red herring fallacy 393
bandwagon fallacy 393

exercises

1. Study again the definition for reasoning (p. 378). Write about an instance when you listened to another person's poor reasoning, and analyze why the reasoning was weak. For example, was there an insufficient amount of evidence? Was the evidence irrelevant? Was the evidence not true or probable? Was the warrant unclear?
2. With a small group, come up with two examples each of arguments that follow an inductive, deductive, causal, and analogical pattern.

3. Read this example wherein the speaker attempts analogical reasoning:

> *A recruiter from a local rural college is talking to high school seniors. She acknowledges that a lot of the seniors would like to go to the city to attend the state university, but few can afford to leave home. She spends a good amount of her speaking time showing the students how her local college is similar to the state university in course offerings, campus amenities, and quality of instruction.*

Then, deconstruct the analogical reason by answering these questions:

- Which of the speaker's statements is true?
- Which two items are argued as being similar?
- What idea is likely to be true?

4. Find three or four examples of reasoning fallacies in an article, a video, on the web, or during an interaction with someone. Explain the argument the speaker was attempting to make and in what way the argument was fallacious. What kind of fallacy was committed?

18

Speak on Special Occasions and in Groups

LEARNING OBJECTIVES

1 Explain some of the reasons we speak to mark a special occasion.

2 Describe some general strategies to use when speaking on a special occasion.

3 Identify the types of special-occasion speeches.

4 Describe some characteristics of effective group participants and leaders.

5 Identify the five steps used in small-group problem solving.

6 Explain how a group effectively plans, organizes, and gives a presentation.

chapter preview

18A Speaking on Special Occasions

18B Use General Strategies for Special-Occasion Speaking

18C Common Types of Special-Occasion Speeches

18D Value Your Job in Groups

18E Productive Group Interaction

18F Present Effectively in Groups

Review Questions
Key Terms
Exercises

This chapter looks at two more reasons you may speak in public—to mark a special occasion and to speak with others in a group. While effective and listenable special-occasion speeches may have informative and persuasive elements, they depart from the *feel* of those two types of speaking in that they tend to be shorter, more thematic in nature, and more emotionally significant to those present. Many of the public speaking skills you've learned throughout this textbook will also help you maximize your effectiveness in a group setting. This chapter first explores the reasons we speak on special occasions, provides general strategies to use when giving these speeches, and looks at the kinds of special-occasion speeches you may give. The chapter then shifts focus to speaking in small groups. It offers strategies for effective group participation and group leadership, provides a step-by-step process for successful group decision-making, and concludes with some best practices for planning, organizing, and giving a group presentation.

18A Speaking on Special Occasions

Special occasions are a part of the human experience; we often gather to celebrate, reflect, mourn, and support each other through life's milestones. More often than not, public speaking plays an essential role in these events. Imagine a graduation ceremony without its roster of optimistic speakers, a wedding without congratulatory toasts, or the Academy Awards without acceptance speeches. Without public communication, these occasions would indeed be less special—or perhaps they could not exist at all. Special-occasion speaking takes us into a separate, ceremonial space, one apart from the paces of daily life.

Your calendar is likely filled with special occasions. You may be invited to speak at one or more of them because of your role in an organization or relationship to someone. Recognize that when someone asks you to speak, they have done so for good reason. Accept the invitation graciously, and remember that even if you think you don't have anything to say at the moment, you have time to come up with something. It's also become common at many special occasions, especially weddings, parties, and funerals, for people other than the presiding speaker to have an opportunity to say a few words. If you're attending such event and have something you'd like to share, plan on participating if the opportunity arises.

Messages communicated during special occasions *are* influential; your words and actions combine with emotions to produce a memorable experience for all. To speak on a special occasion, you need not hold a prestigious title, have performed in-depth research, or be an expert on anything. You just need to be natural and gracious. When you share your words, sincerely and warmly, you give the greatest of gifts.

A special-occasion speech is, like any other speech, a listener-centered transaction. Your role is to appeal to listeners' emotions, strengthen their bonds with one another, provide them with new insights, or help them reflect, cope, celebrate, or look to the future. Today's special-occasion speakers, like those of yesterday, undertake the venerable tradition of standing out from the crowd and communicating our humanity.

Join the ranks of people of all kinds who help create special occasions, like this speaker:

I've got two weddings and one retirement party to go to this summer. After taking this class, I plan to speak at all of them. I'll be toasting the two couples and paying tribute to my boss at his retirement. I've already got a theme picked out for some of them. I want to do these, and now I know how.

18B Use General Strategies for Special-Occasion Speaking

Each type of special-occasion speech covered later in this chapter has its own strategies. Let's look first at general strategies that are appropriate for *any* special occasion—adopting them increases the listenability of your message by meeting listeners' expectations and keeping them with you in the present moment. The special-occasion speech is also the perfect opportunity to add your own creative stamp to your work. But first, know the basics of crafting and delivering this kind of speech so that you can balance your own flair with the expected fundamentals—preparing, having a clear thesis and organized message, being brief, making emotional connections, and using elevated language.

1. Prepare

While special-occasion speeches may not demand as much research as informative and persuasive speeches, you always need to do the following:

- Educate yourself about the event at which you will be speaking.
- If applicable, know how long the event has been celebrated, what its purpose is, and who will be attending.
- Find out who else will be speaking and what they are likely to cover, or look into what other speakers at similar events have presented.
- Be accurate with all your information, including names, titles, and dates.
- Gather supporting materials such as anecdotes, imagery-rich examples, and photographs.
- Practice.

Your special-occasion presentation *is* a speech, and you want to prepare for it as you would for any other speaking appearance.

2. Craft a thesis and organize your ideas

All speeches, as you know, must have a thesis, and special-occasion speeches are no exception. Also, although your special-occasion speech may or may not follow one of the patterns described in Chapter 9, it should still follow some sort of organization. Consider

table **18.1** Crafting a Thesis and Organizing a Special-Occasion Speech

Special-occasion purpose	Thesis/central idea	Pattern of organization
Speech of tribute by a grandson to his grandfather	Placed in the introduction to clearly establish the theme: *My grandfather deserves this tribute because of his dedication to his family.*	A blend of topical and chronological—using a series of stories that exemplify his grandfather's dedication, one each from his grandfather's role as a son, a father, and a grandfather.
Speech of commemoration by a university official	Placed in the introduction to ensure understanding of the day's event: *We dedicate this new fine-arts building as a space to bring out the artistic potential in our entire community.*	Causal—how the new space (cause) would allow the students, faculty, and community to create art in modern and cutting-edge ways (effects).
Speech of introduction to a fund-raising event by a local activist	Placed in the conclusion as the solution: *Your gift of time, money, and donated items for our silent auction will be felt one-hundred-fold by the earthquake survivors we are gathered here to support tonight.*	Problem-Solution—because listeners had come to the fund-raiser already motivated by a desire to donate (the solution), the speaker spent the majority of her presentation on the problems faced by the earthquake victims.

connect
For a sample student special-occasion speech that's a tribute to a grandparent, see the online speech video "Dedication."

the unique qualities of the special-occasion event before deciding where to place your thesis and how to organize your ideas. Table 18.1 provides some examples.

3. Be brief

Your special-occasion speech creates more impact when it's brief and to the point. Each speaker at the event is due his or her time, but understand that the audience wants to hear your point and then move on to the next speaker. Two to three minutes are typically used to introduce an upcoming speaker or accept an award. Five to eight minutes are sufficient to commemorate or pay tribute. Speeches to inspire may take more time, but still, brief is better when it comes to special-occasion speaking. Be succinct. Create your impact, and let the event continue.

4. Make emotional connections

Special occasions make people feel good because the speakers' words and delivery often evoke and release emotion. Use emotionally rich language, tell poignant stories, and generously share your feelings through your body and voice. Aim for authenticity and be careful not to overdo the emotional delivery in ways that would make listeners uncomfortable.

Also, consider your own emotional reactions. If the message or occasion is too emotionally charged for you, you may want to leave the speaking to others. If you choose to speak, be sure that you can maintain your composure. Practice speaking in front of others so that you can experience what it feels like to communicate your emotions and have them reflected back at you on the faces of your listeners. No matter how much they practice, some speakers are surprised to find themselves becoming overly emotional as they speak before audiences of equally emotional people. Should this happen to you, stop speaking until you feel ready to continue. Your audience will wait. On the very rare chance that you simply can't keep speaking, it's okay to stop and let the next speaker take over.

connect

For a sample student special-occasion speech in which the speaker confronts his own emotions, see the online speech video "Dedication."

create
converse
connect

Figures of Speech

Use these common figures of speech to elevate the language of your special-occasion presentations.

Alliteration is the repeated use of an initial sound in a string of words. In a tribute to her daughter, one speaker talked about how *caring, kind,* and *courageous* (note the repeated initial "k" sound) her daughter was. These three adjectives formed the main points of the tribute.

Repetition is the use of a recurring word or phrase. Martin Luther King Jr.'s repeated use of *I have a dream* is a classic example of the power of repetition.

Simile compares two things by using the word *like* or *as* in the comparison. *Their love is like sunshine, radiating out and warming all in their presence* is an example of simile.

Metaphor also compares two things, but by stating that one thing *stands for* (rather than is *like*) another. *His days of autumn* is a metaphor for the time before dying.

Onomatopoeia is the use of words that sound like what they describe. Such words enrich the imagery you can use when communicating. *Ker-plooey* sounds like an egg dropped on the floor; *squish squirsh* sounds like what happens when you walk through the mess.

SPEAK
Responsibly

Avoid Overused Phrases and Clichés

Though many special-occasion presentations have an elevated style, you still want to use language that sounds natural coming from you. Phrases like *It is with great pride and honor that I . . .* or *We are gathered here today to . . .* sound stuffy, if not corny. And clichés such as *Today is the first day of the rest of your life* or *Every cloud has a silver lining* are so familiar that they have lost their meaning and value. Consider what words *your* own heart and mind want to use to express ideas. Tap into your rich personal vocabulary. Use the words that mean something to you and will carry impact with your specific listeners.

- How do you feel when you hear clichés in a public speech?
- Can clichés serve a purpose in special occasion speaking? If so, when and why?

5. Use elevated language

Special-occasion speeches are frequently presented verbatim (word-for-word). Though the goal of any presentation is to communicate an idea to your audience, special-occasion speaking contains a secondary goal of taking your audience to a place of ceremony or ritual. A planned, dignified style of language helps you meet that secondary goal. Take time during your preparation to find the right words and phrases. Look to your dictionary and thesaurus. Listen to the rhythm of your sentences. Choose words that carry emotional impact, and practice with your delivery so that it's fluent and smooth.

Figures of speech also help elevate your language. Few speakers use figures of speech when speaking spontaneously, but you *can* include them when you have time to think about your language before the actual presentation. See the "Create Converse Connect" box on page 400 for some examples.

18C Common Types of Special-Occasion Speeches

Special-occasion speeches include toasts, speeches of introduction, speeches of tribute, speeches of commemoration, speeches of acceptance, and speeches to inspire.

1. Toast

The toast is the special occasion you're most likely to have the opportunity to deliver. A **toast** is a brief speech of honor. Toasts celebrate:

Tips for a successful toast

- **Keep it light.**
  A toast celebrates a happy occasion. Listeners are expecting to laugh and smile.

- **Prepare a theme.**
  Themes tie the words of your toast together and help listeners remember them after the celebration. Love, commitment, bravery, persistence, sacrifice, endurance, luck, and victory are all great choices.

- **Keep your wits about you.**
  Alcohol frequently accompanies events where toasts are given. If you plan on giving a toast, monitor your intake of anything that may cause you to lose your inhibitions. You don't want to embarrass yourself or the honoree.

- a person (like your brother at his graduation or a friend who just landed her dream job).
- two or more people (like a couple at their engagement or a team that has won a big contract).
- an event (like a state championship or a high school reunion).

Many people mistakenly believe that a toast is easy to give; you just get up there and say nice things about the honoree(s). While certainly not difficult, a meaningful, memorable toast requires some planning. Too many of us have experienced, for instance, the parade of unprepared speakers at a wedding who wish the couple well without saying anything meaningful—or, worse, say embarrassing and inappropriate things.

2. Speech of introduction

A **speech of introduction** prepares an audience for an upcoming speaker or event and motivates listeners to give their full attention. Below are some guidelines for the various scenarios in which a speech of introduction might be given: for introducing a speaker, for introducing an event, and for being introduced yourself.

Introducing a speaker

Check with the speaker to find out what biographical information he or she would like you to share with listeners. Double-check the pronunciation of the speaker's name, and verify his or her title. You may also conduct some research to find additional and relevant facts and stories about the speaker.

On the day of the speech, use the following best practices to guide you:

- Welcome all listeners.
- Give the speaker's credentials, including relevant details such as degrees, occupation, years of experience, and positions held. If appropriate, point out this person's speaking experience.
- Don't reveal the speaker's thesis, but prime the audience in general for what they are about to hear.
- Tell listeners how long the person plans to speak and whether a question-and-answer session will follow.
- Warmly welcome the speaker to the gathering.

Introducing an event

Do your research on the event. Find out how long the event has been taking place, why it is happening, how many people are gathered, and what the expected outcomes are. The more you know about the event, the greater your confidence is and the more interesting and meaningful you can make your speech of introduction.

On the day of the event, use the following best practices to guide you:

- Welcome all listeners.
- Establish audience connection and tell listeners what outcomes to expect from the event.
- Acknowledge any important participants.
- Preview the agenda.
- Set an appropriate emotional tone, and get the event started.

If you are introduced

If you are the person being introduced, the transition steps you should follow between the person who has introduced you and your own speech are simple but important:

- Graciously thank the person introducing you and the organization hosting you.
- Comment on the event, and mention what the speaking opportunity means for you.
- Begin your presentation.

3. Speech of tribute

When you give a **speech of tribute,** you pay honor or respect to another person, but it is more elaborate than a toast. We often hear tribute speeches at retirement parties, going-away parties, coming-of-age ceremonies, birthdays, funerals or celebrations of life, anniversaries, and award ceremonies. Here are some guidelines for giving a speech of tribute:

- **Research the person's life.** Gather stories from others who know the honoree. The richer your picture of the person, the more you have to work with and the more you can offer listeners.
- **Provide some biographical data of the person being honored.** Chances are that people in the audience know the honoree, but many will appreciate your filling in details that are new to them.
- **Give the audience an appreciation for the honoree's special qualities.** This might include his years of volunteer work or her commitment to bettering the environment.
- **Provide rich examples of things the honoree has done or accomplished.** Examples help create images for the audience to hold on to and help them better understand the person you are honoring.
- **Provide photos.** If photos of the honoree are available, consider projecting them.

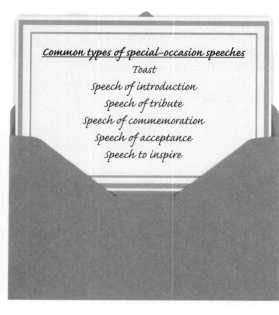

Common types of special-occasion speeches

Toast
Speech of introduction
Speech of tribute
Speech of commemoration
Speech of acceptance
Speech to inspire

- **Connect with the audience.** Tell listeners how they can be instructed or inspired from the experiences of the honoree.
- **Be positive and optimistic.** You can mention challenges and difficulties faced by the honoree, but you shouldn't dwell on them. Even if those challenges and difficulties still remain, mention how the person has positively dealt with them. At the same time, be accurate; don't make up or exaggerate stories or events to make the honoree look better.
- **Acknowledge the family and/or support network of the honoree.** It's likely that their emotions are running high, and this day is as special for them as it is for the person being honored.

4. Speech of commemoration

A **speech of commemoration** honors and recognizes an event, a place, or an idea. Commemorative speeches are given on anniversaries of historic occasions, upon completion of a major task or campaign, at the opening of a new building or monument, and at special points in a social movement. Here are some guidelines for giving a speech of commemoration:

- **Be specific about the event, place, or idea being commemorated.** Remind the audience what has occurred in the past or what is happening now.
- **Bring the audience into the present moment.** Explain why this is a unique or special occasion and why it is important for people to gather at this time and participate in this commemoration.
- **Thank stakeholders.** Honor those involved in whatever is being commemorated, and express your genuine appreciation to them.
- **Use examples.** Provide imagery-rich examples of courage, sacrifice, or hard work.
- **Use emotion.** Express the feelings this commemoration evokes in you and your audience.
- **Project to the future.** What's next? What goals are still to achieve? What can people do next? Give the audience a meaningful take-away.

5. Speech of acceptance

You give a **speech of acceptance** when you receive an award or honor. Just like the winners of a Grammy, should you receive an award, you'll be expected or perhaps even required to publicly express appreciation to the person or organization bestowing the special recognition. Here are some guidelines for giving a speech of acceptance:

- **Be prepared.** You'll often know of your award or honor ahead of time. If you know in advance only that you are a finalist, you should still prepare a speech of acceptance. It's better to have an unused speech than to win and be speechless.
- **Understand the organization bestowing the award.** Knowing what award you're being given and the meaning behind it allows you to focus your message. Speaking so attentively also increases your credibility.
- **Speak with pride and humility.** Don't let your words or body show that the award or honor is undeserved. At the same time, be gracious and humble. This is not a time for boasting, no matter how significant your accomplishment.
- **Provide rich examples.** Create images for listeners to hold on to and have a better understanding of what you have achieved.
- **Make it personal.** Describe what this award or honor means for you. Look with hope and optimism into the future.
- **Express your gratitude.** Spend time thanking others (but limit your list) for making this award or honor possible. Few people accomplish anything by themselves.
- **Stay focused.** The purpose of this speech is to accept an award or honor. It is inappropriate to take advantage of the spotlight and go off in unexpected directions, launch new ideas, or bring up grievances.
- **Be brief.** Graciously accept your award or honor, but respect the time limitations and the remaining parts of the ceremony.

6. Speech to inspire

A **speech to inspire** encourages, moves, or excites the listeners in some way. People who overcome tremendous obstacles in their own lives often speak to give others hope. Coaches speak to stimulate or revive their teams. Managers speak to motivate employees. Honored guests speak to new college graduates to inspire them to give back to their families and communities.

People who give speeches to inspire are known as motivational or aspirational speakers. Christopher Gardner is one such person. Gardner's journey from homeless single father to self-made millionaire financial broker is profiled in his book *The Pursuit of Happyness* and the film of the same name. Gardner speaks frequently, "addressing the keys to overcoming obstacles and breaking cycles."[1]

Here are some guidelines for giving a speech of inspiration:

- **Tell stories.** The narrative structure of setup, conflict, and resolution (see pages 173–177) provides a natural device for inspiring others to overcome their own challenges or difficulties.
- **Be listener-centered.** Use your own experience as an example of human capabilities, but ultimately, relate the themes of your experience to the listeners. What do they gain from hearing your story?

- **Use real examples.** The honest quality of real life carries more inspirational impact than the hypothetical.
- **Reveal your humanity.** There is no need to make your story or situation more appealing. Audiences are more likely to be inspired by your words if they sense that you are a real person, complete with complexities and frailties.
- **Be confident.** Listeners need to sense your certainty that challenges and difficulties *can* be overcome.
- **Use emotion.** Build the emotional journey, and end with high impact. Stress the optimistic future you foresee for your listeners.

18D Value Your Job in Groups

Working effectively with others is essential for success in contemporary classrooms, workplaces, and communities. In fact, more than 75 percent of employers in a recent survey listed "teamwork skills and the ability to collaborate with others in diverse group settings" as the top-ranked desirable trait for graduates entering the workforce.[2] It's in your best interest, then, to learn all you can about small group interaction including what a small group is, types of small groups, and what constitutes effective group participation and leadership.

1. Groups defined

A **small group** is a small number of individuals who work together toward an identified goal while influencing each other during the process. Let's break down this definition for clearer understanding:

People work together in groups, also known as teams, because the ability of the group to achieve something is almost always greater than that of any individual. Think about the human hand as an analogy. Though each finger has its strengths, it's ultimately limited when acting alone. When acting in concert, however, fingers can perform delicate surgery, sculpt a dramatic piece of art, create beautiful music or even, if necessary, punch a hole in the wall. By thinking and learning about group dynamics, each of us can learn to do our part and work more effectively in groups.

2. Types of small groups

It helps to understand what kind of group you're working in and its purpose. Group members may meet face-to-face in classrooms, offices, conference rooms, cafés, and living rooms. Technology allows many groups, whose members may be anywhere in the world, to meet virtually by connecting online. No matter how they communicate, here are some of the types of groups in which you may find yourself participating:

Small number— Typically three to eleven people make up a small group.

Identified goal— A small group gathers for a reason or a specific purpose. Members work to achieve a task or get something done.

Influencing each other during the process, or **interdependence—**Each member's presence affects the others in the group and shapes the outcome of the group's work.

Activity group

In an **activity group,** like a book club, hiking club, or fan club, you share an interest or hobby with other people.

Personal growth group

In a **personal growth group,** members provide support to each other as each seeks understanding, new skills, or comfort and strength during challenging times or difficult circumstances. New-parent groups, cancer-survivor groups, and Alcoholics Anonymous are examples of personal growth groups.

Educational group

In an **educational group,** you volunteer or are assigned to work with others to better understand a subject or complete an assignment. Educational groups are sometimes referred to as cooperative or collaborative learning groups.

Problem-solving group

In a **problem-solving group,** people need to address some sort of issue. Problem-solving groups often take the shape of a **committee,** a group of people brought together to perform work for a larger group or organization. Committees are either ongoing or come together to accomplish one specific task and are then disbanded.

Similarities and differences between types of small groups

Most activity groups and personal growth groups are private and self-contained, whereas educational groups and problem-solving groups must often report their findings or outcomes to other people. Some reports are written, while others are presented orally.

Here are some examples of educational or problem-solving groups presenting their work:

Examples of small group presentations

Educational group presentations

- Students team up to create a service-learning project in the community and then share the process and findings with classmates.

- A committee is convened to study gender equality in campus STEM (Science, Technology, Engineering, and Math) classes, present its findings, and make a recommendation to the campus administration.

Problem-solving group presentations

- A collaborative learning group researches health care issues relevant to the Texas-Mexico border and presents them to other learning groups.

- A work team comes up with an advertising proposal and presents it to potential clients.

Much of what you've studied throughout this book, including audience analysis, message organization, audience engagement, speaker credibility, and delivery technique, is relevant for these group presentations. However, before we discuss the group presentation in detail, let's understand a little more about how a group works and your role in it.

3. Effective group participation

While it's common for us to think of group members as two general types—participants and leaders—many groups today actually operate under the principle of **distributed leadership.** Here, despite the presence of a recognized leader, *each member* is responsible for performing the communication behaviors necessary for moving a group toward its goal.[3] Distributed leadership thus blurs the lines between participation and leadership, making it necessary for every group member to understand and value both roles.

We'll start with group participation. You can probably guess that willingness, responsibility, and a good attitude are qualities of effective group members. Here's how to capitalize on these qualities: feel a sense of responsibility for the group's success, act on that sense of responsibility, and identify and fulfill needed group roles.

Feel a sense of responsibility for the group's success

Ideally, each group member feels an equal sense of responsibility for the group's success. But this is not always easy. If you come from a **collectivistic culture,** as you do if you were born and raised in many Asian or African cultures, by definition you tend to put the good of the group ahead of your individual concerns. But if you come from an **individualistic culture,** as you do if you were born and raised in the United States, it's sometimes a challenge to give up individual needs and wants for the benefit of the group.

There are many examples of successful groups in the United States, however, so feeling that sense of communal responsibility is well within our desires and capabilities. You can increase the effectiveness of your group participation in a number of ways, described below.

Stay focused A primary ethical responsibility is to act as a **participant-observer,** someone who actively contributes to the group's purpose while reflecting on the group dynamics (and adapting when necessary). This can be difficult when you have your own agenda or are frequently distracted by your cell phone, but when each member strives to be a genuine participant-observer, the chances for the group's success rise dramatically.

Be self-reflective Expect from yourself what you expect from other group members.

Recognize that many people enjoy working in groups Group work can lead to greater learning and give people a strong sense of communal purpose. Participants value the outcomes that result when a variety of people with varying strengths come together and focus on achieving a particular goal.

Recognize that some people don't like working in groups Acknowledge, too, that some experience **grouphate,** or negative feelings toward group participation.[4] These feelings can result from prior experience where one or two group members ended up carrying the whole workload, or when the group was too easily distracted from its task, or when members felt undervalued. But remember that past experience does not necessarily dictate future experience. When you work with others who understand and value the small group process, the chances increase that you'll enjoy yourself while getting things done within a group.

Be committed to the group's success If you don't believe in the task put before the group, do what you can to change your attitude. Perhaps you can think it over and come to view the group more positively. Or talk to another group member who can help you see the group from a different angle. If in the end you still have a negative attitude, remove yourself from the group. You're doing yourself and the other group members no favor by remaining on board. If it's not possible to step aside, do your best to have a good attitude despite the circumstances, and avoid comments and actions that will interfere with other group members' ability to get the job done.

Act on that sense of responsibility

The sections below describe some responsible actions you can implement to make your group dynamics function smoothly and effectively: being dependable, speaking collectively, speaking up, managing conflict, listening well, being alert, helping others, and staying positive.[5]

Be dependable Show up on time, be prepared, and if you agree to perform a task, see it through. If something happens and you can't be present or complete a task you said you would do, alert someone else in the group as soon as possible.

Speak collectively Rather than individual pronouns like *I, me,* and *you,* use group-oriented pronouns like *we, us,* and *our* in your thinking and speaking. These inclusive group-oriented pronouns accentuate the group members' bonds with one another.

Speak up If you have helpful background information or come up with a creative idea that's relevant to the group's task, share it. If you don't feel comfortable expressing a particular idea to the entire group, share it privately with the group leader or another group member who can then communicate it to the larger group.

Manage conflict Keep your comments centered on issues and the task at hand, rather than on personalities and behaviors of other group members. Varying perspectives and disagreements are bound to occur, but when handled directly and constructively, they can propel the group forward rather than harm the group's performance. Should someone propose an idea you think doesn't belong or has little value, comments like "it figures you'd say that," or "that'll never work" only put others on the defensive. Instead, calmly and tactfully point out your concern with the *idea:* "While that's a realistic solution, it takes three days to get the test results back, so I don't see how we could accomplish that by our Thursday deadline."

Be a good listener Remain open-minded and respect what other group members say. Though you may feel strongly about the group's next step, for example, remember that others in the group may have different opinions. When you welcome new information and new ideas, remain curious, and subdue prejudice—essentially, when you're an effective listener—you contribute best to your group's success.[6] Recognize that others may have equally important and valuable things to say.

SPEAK
Responsibly

Act on Silence

Imagine the following scenario: During your group discussion, you notice that Matt is uncharacteristically silent. As an effective group listener, you know to interpret his lack of participation carefully.[7] Silence is ambiguous nonverbal behavior—it's not always clear what it means. For example, perhaps Matt doesn't understand the issue being discussed, or he disagrees with the group's direction, is apathetic, or is purposefully holding back information. The better you know Matt, the more likely you'll interpret his silence correctly, but asking him for clarification is the best way to find out. Point out the silence (*Hey Matt, I notice you're kind of quiet today*) rather than jump to conclusions (*Why are you mad?*). This allows Matt to answer in his own way, for the group to respond appropriately, and for the whole team to once again be moving together toward their shared goal.

- Do you actively monitor the communication behaviors of fellow group members? Why or why not?
- What other ambiguous nonverbal behavior might a fellow group member engage in? How would you respond if you saw it occurring?

Be alert Recognize the potential for **groupthink** and speak up if you see it occurring. Groupthink occurs when groups want to reach agreement so badly that they fail to fully analyze the situation, or they suppress confrontation and disagreement.[8] Groupthink favors harmony and cohesiveness at the expense of well-thought-out solutions.

Help others out When necessary, invite members who don't speak up that often to engage or offer assistance should another member lack time or know-how in completing a group task. Pay attention to others' strengths and weaknesses and make sure that their assigned tasks are a good fit.

Stay positive Understand that each team member contributes to the overall team morale. Be polite, make constructive comments, express confidence in the group's ability to accomplish its goals, and use positive communication behaviors including an even tone, pleasant facial expressions, and friendly body language.

Identify and fulfill needed group roles

During your group interactions, you'll most likely perform some recognized roles.[9] Two kinds—task roles and relationship-oriented roles—are required for effective group interaction. The third category, the self-serving role, is counterproductive and you should avoid it.

Task roles Roles that help the group achieve its mission are called **task roles.** When you offer to take notes, provide some needed background information, ask a clarifying question, provide an internal summary, or elaborate on a great idea you just had, you're making things happen and moving the group toward its goal.

Relationship-oriented roles Sometimes known as interpersonal roles or maintenance roles, **relationship-oriented roles** help group members work well together. Strong relationships between group members are important because they directly and indirectly affect the group's ability to achieve its task. When you express support for someone else's idea, help a quieter member take the floor, help avoid a potential conflict between other group members, recognize when everyone needs a 10-minute break, or make positive comments on the group's progress, you're facilitating relationships.

Self-serving roles Roles that serve the individual at the expense of the group are called **self-serving roles.** When a group member interrupts someone else, refuses to take a stand,

Welcoming "Newbies" to Your Group

Have you ever been the "newbie," that new person who comes into a pre-existing group? If so, did the others warmly incorporate you into the group immediately? Did you have to work your way in to finally be accepted? Did you never feel welcomed?

    If you're a group member, here are some things you can do to help a newbie feel comfortable and allow him or her to start contributing to the group's effectiveness:[10]

- **Incorporate the new member.** Be aware of the tendency to favor pre-existing group relationships. Instead, make a special effort to introduce yourself and warmly welcome the new person. A coffee or lunch invitation, and a friendly phone call, e-mail, or text can help the new member feel part of the larger group.
- **Orient the new member to the group's mission, structure, and task that needs to be accomplished.** The more the new member learns about the group's history, plans, roles of group members, timelines, outside influences, rules, limitations, and policies, the more quickly he or she can learn to navigate effectively within the group.
- **Help the new member understand the group's interactional style.** In some groups, people wait to speak until acknowledged by a leader. In other groups, members speak up whenever they want to. Does your group joke around or stick only to business? While the new group member should figure out these norms and characteristics soon enough, letting him or her know what the group's interaction style is can be helpful.

makes negative comments, talks too much, repeatedly raises objections, constantly draws undue attention, or focuses on unrelated issues, he or she negatively impacts the group's relationships and its ability to meet its goal. Obviously, these roles are undesirable during group interaction. Though it's difficult to control someone else's behavior, most people will respond positively when the negative consequence of their counterproductive behavior is pointed out. For example, instead of saying in front of the group, *You always have to dominate the conversation!* take the person aside (to help reduce defensiveness) and say, *It's difficult for quieter members to add their ideas when they sense little conversational space.*

Education is also helpful. Many group members have quickly altered their own behavior once they learn about self-serving roles and recognize that they sometimes display them.

4. Effective group leadership

While groups can operate without an identified leader, they can't operate without leadership. Leadership is a natural part of group communication. It may reside in the hands of one person or it may be distributed among several or all group members. In any case, it consists of words and actions that persuade others in positive ways and helps the group move toward its goal. Learn about the sources of leadership power, the types of leadership, and leadership responsibilities.

Sources of leadership power

Leadership is a form of power, yet successful group leaders don't seek power for its own sake. Rather, they recognize that they have talents and abilities that can help others, and they choose to use them for beneficial reasons. Your leadership power may come from one or more of the following sources: legitimate power, referent power, and expert power.

- **Legitimate power** comes from a position you hold that others acknowledge and respect. If you're a club president, a committee chairperson, or manager of an office, you hold legitimate power.
- **Referent power** comes from qualities you display that others find attractive. When you're admired and respected for being positive, charismatic, confident, and genuinely concerned for others' well-being, you hold referent power.
- **Expert power** stems from others' belief in your knowledge and abilities. When you're the only one who knows how to use a needed piece of technology, or has experience doing something the group needs done, or knows someone the group needs to talk to, you have expert power.

Types of leadership

Leaders are designated at the start of group interaction or emerge once group interaction has gotten under way.

> *Sources of leadership power*
> - *Legitimate power*
> - *Referent power*
> - *Expert power*
>
> *Types of leadership*
> - *Designated leader*
> - *Emergent leader*

Designated leader A **designated leader** is elected or appointed to the leadership position. Groups with designated leaders tend to be more stable, have fewer interpersonal conflicts, and often produce better outcomes than groups without them.[11] Should you find yourself the designated leader of your group, you'll immediately enjoy legitimate power. However, to be ultimately effective in your leadership role, you must still earn—through intentional deeds—the respect and goodwill of your group members. While all members bear responsibility for the group's success, the designated leader faces extra obligations. Group members and those outside the group often hold the designated leader accountable for the group's inner workings and final outcome. If you're the designated leader, know what makes a group function well and be confident in your abilities to provide the leadership services required (see below).

Emergent leader An **emergent leader** starts out as a group participant but, through his or her referent and/or expert power, becomes a leader. The point of emergent leadership is not to take power from the designated leader, though that could be necessary if the designated leader is unwilling or unable to perform the required leadership tasks. Instead, all group members are capable of emergent leadership when they use group-oriented communication skills. Emergent leaders are socially perceptive and able to respond flexibly to the needs of the group. They're willing to speak up early in the group interaction, helping members interpret events and their own capabilities in a positive way.[12]

Leadership responsibilities

Designated and emergent leaders alike perform these tasks of leadership: taking care of procedural needs, communicating actively and clearly, being trustworthy, understanding and communicating the group's task, facilitating interaction, respecting and supporting others, recognizing your own leadership power, and sharing credit.

Take care of procedural needs See to the logistics of group interaction, including these "housekeeping" duties:

- Secure a time and place for the group to meet and communicate that information to all group members.
- Create a list of things to be accomplished during the meeting—known as an **agenda**—and send it to all members ahead of time.
- Prepare and distribute any relevant handouts.
- Start the meeting on time.
- Take notes or ask someone else to do it.
- Summarize the meeting and lead the discussion of the group's next steps.
- If applicable, ensure all group members receive a copy of the notes taken during the meeting.

Communicate actively and clearly Be mindful and focused during the group interaction. Be an engaged listener, and speak up and out in ways that others can understand.

Be trustworthy When you're a leader, others are looking to you to be consistent, honest, loyal, and ethical. They're looking to you to follow through and to keep information confidential when necessary.

Understand and communicate the group's task Leaders must have an especially strong sense of the group's purpose, be able to communicate it clearly to the members, and inspire the group to keep moving toward its goals.

Facilitate interaction Keep the group focused on its goals, help everyone participate, recognize and handle anything that blocks the group's progress, communicate with relevant people outside the group, and make sure everyone understands the current situation before the group moves on to something else.

Respect and support others Pay attention to the interpersonal relationships among the group, make sure everyone is introduced, help members who don't speak up often to participate, stay positive, inspire confidence in the group's abilities, and help to resolve conflicts among members.

Recognize yet don't abuse leadership power Recognize the power you hold and be careful not to abuse it. Because people tend to listen when leaders talk, don't talk more than you need to, and actively encourage participation from others. Because your opinions often hold extra weight, hold back on giving them until needed. Actively seek opinions from others and express your own only as possibilities rather than as commands. Be a model of integrity.

Share credit Finally, don't take all the credit for the group's success; outwardly recognize the group's accomplishments, both to the group itself and to outside parties. If the group's outcome is not a complete success, share responsibility for this.

18E Productive Group Interaction

The ultimate goal of many educational groups and problem-solving groups is to look at a problem or an issue (what *is* happening) and make a decision about how to solve it (what *should* be happening). The decision usually involves examining data, exploring alternatives, and making recommendations for some kind of action that the group itself or someone outside the group should take. The **reflective-thinking process** offers well-defined steps for making a meaningful group decision.[13] While it may be tempting to follow your intuition and immediately start coming up with solutions for a perceived problem, groups that follow the full five-step process have higher-quality discussions and produce better decisions than those that don't.[14]

1. Identify and define the problem

Group members must first fully understand exactly what problem the group needs to solve. This step sounds obvious, but it must be done if the rest of the process is to work.

The time it takes to get everyone to fully comprehend the problem is time well spent. Ideally, the problem you address is clear, specific in scope, and allows for a variety of answers.

Here's the start of an example we'll use throughout the reflective-thinking process:

Example of Reflective Thinking in Action, Step 1

Step 1: Identify and define the problem

How should a college student group whose mission is student health and wellness respond to the increased number of vending machines on campus?

2. Analyze the problem

Once the group can identify and define the problem it faces, it's time to examine it from multiple angles. Your group may need to ask questions or conduct research to

- explore and define terms.
- question causes or effects of the problem.
- uncover the scope of the problem.
- learn some history behind the problem.
- determine who is affected by the problem.
- identify financial implications.
- consider what would happen if the problem weren't solved.

Take your time here. The more completely you analyze the problem, the greater the likelihood you'll eventually choose the best solution for it. Let's return to the group who's responding to the increased number of vending machines on campus:

Example of Reflective Thinking in Action, Step 2

The student health and wellness group responding to the increased number of vending machines on campus worked through the following analytical tasks:

Step 2: Analyze the problem

- Reviewed their mission to determine if this problem was within the scope of their purpose (it was)
- Took inventory of the vending-machine products
- Interviewed the campus dean in charge of business services to learn about the financial agreements between the campus and the vending-machine company
- Reviewed some literature on the health impacts of high-calorie and high-fat snacks
- Researched the issue on other college campuses to see if and how they've dealt with the same problem

3. Establish criteria for solving the problem

Now that your group has analyzed the problem, it's tempting to immediately start coming up with solutions. But how are you going to know which solution is best? Will it be the solution offered by the most vocal group member? the most charming? the tallest? Probably not, so you want to take some time to establish appropriate **criteria,** or measurements you'll use to evaluate the solutions once you come up with them. These criteria will help you recognize the right solution. Again, spend group time on this step. Keep working until all group members understand and feel comfortable with the criteria.

Example of Reflective Thinking in Action, Step 3

After coming up with a variety of criteria for solving the problem of the increased number of vending machines on campus, the student health and wellness group narrowed the list down to two:

1) The solution should be what's best for students' health and wellness.
2) The solution should take into consideration the need for the campus to earn outside income.

Step 3: Establish criteria for solving the problem

4. Generate potential solutions

You're now ready to brainstorm some potential solutions. This is the fun part. Here are some guidelines for effective group brainstorming[15]:

- Set aside any evaluation at this step; your goal is simply to generate as many solutions as possible. Avoiding judgment is the most important part of brainstorming.
- Be as freewheeling as possible. Every group member has permission to let his or her creativity loose and offer ideas, no matter how ridiculous they may seem at first.
- Elaborate on each other's ideas. You never know when one idea spurs another idea that spurs another idea that ends up being the perfect solution.
- Write all ideas down. You might think you'll remember them all, but you probably won't. Ask the group member who can write or type quickly to do this task.
- Keep going until your group is out of ideas.

While most brainstorming is done during a face-to-face meeting, some groups, due to geographic distance or choice, brainstorm individually and then send their ideas to a central location. This process works well, too.

Example of Reflective Thinking in Action, Step 4

The student health and wellness group enjoyed their brainstorming session.[16] They generated a number of solutions to the problem of the increasing number of vending machines on campus:

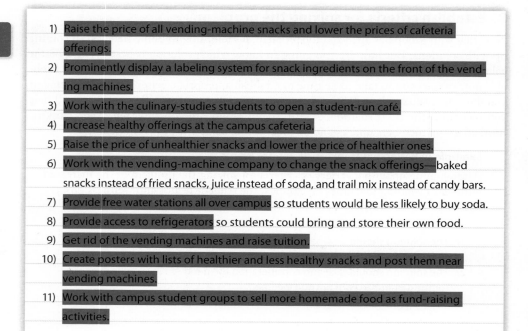

Step 4: Generate potential solutions

1) Raise the price of all vending-machine snacks and lower the prices of cafeteria offerings.
2) Prominently display a labeling system for snack ingredients on the front of the vending machines.
3) Work with the culinary-studies students to open a student-run café.
4) Increase healthy offerings at the campus cafeteria.
5) Raise the price of unhealthier snacks and lower the price of healthier ones.
6) Work with the vending-machine company to change the snack offerings—baked snacks instead of fried snacks, juice instead of soda, and trail mix instead of candy bars.
7) Provide free water stations all over campus so students would be less likely to buy soda.
8) Provide access to refrigerators so students could bring and store their own food.
9) Get rid of the vending machines and raise tuition.
10) Create posters with lists of healthier and less healthy snacks and post them near vending machines.
11) Work with campus student groups to sell more homemade food as fund-raising activities.

The reflective-thinking process

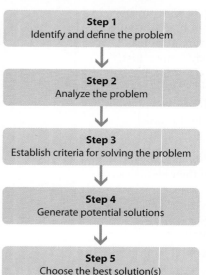

Step 1
Identify and define the problem

↓

Step 2
Analyze the problem

↓

Step 3
Establish criteria for solving the problem

↓

Step 4
Generate potential solutions

↓

Step 5
Choose the best solution(s)

5. Choose the best solution(s)

Now that your group has plenty of potential solutions, it's time to choose the best one. Many groups like to decide on a selection process before they begin evaluating. Some groups designate each solution with a *yes, maybe,* or *no* and then return to the *yes* and *maybe* lists and repeat the process as many times as necessary. Some choose to operate on a "majority rules" voting basis. Still others agree to seek **consensus,** wherein every member must agree on the final solution. Your group might use a combination of these methods or come up with one of your own.

Once all group members have agreed on the selection procedure, it's time to retrieve the list of criteria you established earlier (in Step 3) and begin using them to evaluate the potential solutions. While it can be appealing to select the first idea that meets the criteria, don't fall victim to groupthink. Give each potential solution its fair chance. As your group works through each idea—and this may take some time (perhaps even another meeting is necessary)—it should soon become clear which solution best fits your problem or, at least, is a solution every group member can accept.

Example of Reflective Thinking in Action, Step 5

After fully evaluating the potential solutions, the student health and wellness group narrowed their choices to numbers 6, 7, and 10:

1) ~~Raise the price of all vending-machine snacks and lower the prices of cafeteria offerings.~~

2) ~~Prominently display a labeling system for snack ingredients on the front of the vending machines.~~

3) ~~Work with the culinary-studies students to open a student-run café.~~

4) ~~Increase healthy offerings at the campus cafeteria.~~

5) ~~Raise the price of unhealthier snacks and lower the price of healthier ones.~~

6) Work with the vending-machine company to change the snack offerings—baked snacks instead of fried snacks, juice instead of soda, and trail mix instead of candy bars.

7) Provide free water stations all over campus so students would be less likely to buy soda.

8) ~~Provide access to refrigerators so students could bring and store their own food.~~

9) ~~Get rid of the vending machines and raise tuition.~~

10) Create posters with lists of healthier and less healthy snacks and post them near vending machines.

11) ~~Work with campus student groups to sell more homemade food as fund-raising activities.~~

Step 5: Choosing the best solution(s)

All three of the potential solutions respected the needs of the campus to earn income, the rights of the vending-machine company to do business with the college, and the students' desire for food on campus. Additionally, the student health and wellness group felt that these solutions were aligned within the scope of their mission, and most importantly, perceived these solutions as realistic and achievable.

18F Present Effectively in Groups

Now that your group has decided on a solution, there's a good chance you'll need to communicate it to other people. Your group must plan the presentation, organize it, and give it.

1. Plan the presentation

Planning the group presentation is similar to planning an individual speech.

Identify exactly what your group needs to present

Know whether the goal of the presentation is to report on your group's progress, share your findings, offer a recommendation, or some combination of these.

Analyze your audience and the occasion

You want to know as much as possible about the people in attendance and the purpose of the occasion. Know who will be there and whether there's a certain person you need to address. Identify whether this is an information-sharing session or a persuasive presentation. Find out whether money or someone's reputation will be affected by your presentation. Get a sense of whether this is a formal presentation or an informal gathering.

Identify the type of presentation

Groups present in one of several common formats: group oral reports, symposia, and panel discussions.

Group oral report In this format, the group presents findings, recommendations, or conclusions from their group work to a larger group or to another appropriate party. One member may speak as a representative of the group, or each group member may be responsible for a part of the presentation (one introduces the project, another reports on the decision-making process, another summarizes the recommendations, a final person discusses the proposed implementation of the action). The student health and wellness group (that you read about earlier) would most likely use the group oral report when presenting to the campus administration.

Symposium In a symposium, several people each give a formal presentation or oral report, each one centered on a similar topic or area of focus. A moderator introduces each speaker and shows the relationship of that speech to the greater purpose of the group.

Panel discussion Here, a moderator guides a discussion among several participants in front of an audience. Typically, each panelist makes an opening statement and then, led by the moderator, responds to the comments made by other panelists. Through this process of exploring a problem or an issue, new ways of thinking or questions about something are created for those on the panel and in the audience.

Delegate duties

Any group presentation entails some logistical decisions: Who will reserve the presentation space? Who will reserve or bring any needed technological equipment? Who best knows how to make a slideshow? Who will purchase any necessary items? Who will be the main contact person should others need to communicate with the group? If necessary, who will do the advertising for the group presentation?

SPEAK Responsibly

Managing Difficult Behaviors within the Group

Kaitlin dominates. Brady makes sexist comments. Jaime refuses to participate. Many groups have to deal with individual behaviors that create barriers for effective group interaction. Here are some ways to manage these difficult behaviors[17]:

Dominating behaviors

What you can do

Interrupting

> > >
- Speak up assertively that you're not done talking.
- If another person was interrupted, insist that you want to hear his or her complete thought.

Making authoritarian or know-it-all statements

> > >
- Politely request backup information, evidence, or justification.

Objectionable behaviors

What you can do

Making jokes at the expense of others

> > >
- Do not laugh.
- Say that those jokes bother you.

Behaving unethically or dishonestly

> > >
- Don't remain silent; it can be seen as condoning the behavior. Instead, point out the consequences the poor behavior has on the group's ability to function effectively.

Nonparticipative behaviors

What you can do

Acting disconnected

> > >
- Give a specific assignment that will make him or her feel valued and responsible.

Not doing his or her share of the work

> > >
- Mention the effect of the individual's behavior on the group.
- If the above tactic doesn't work, seek the advice of a higher authority who has other forms of leverage.
- If neither of these tactics works, you may have to ask the person to leave the group.

2. Organize the presentation

It's now time to gather supporting materials, organize the presentation, plan how to engage the audience, and ensure your group's credibility.

Gather supporting materials

If your group needs to find supporting material such as statistics, examples, or testimony, be sure to allow for additional research time. If the group chooses to incorporate visuals, ensure formatting consistency by selecting one person to whom everyone will send their images. Perhaps someone needs to prepare a handout.

Organize the presentation

Whether individual or group, each presentation needs a clear introduction, body and conclusion. Generate a thesis and organize the main points according to one of the patterns of organization discussed in Chapter 9. Remember to plan for transitions between the parts of the presentation.

Plan to engage the audience

Keep your audience engaged by relying on the audience engagement techniques you've read about throughout this textbook. Use audience-centered pronouns, consider calling for audience participation, and if appropriate, incorporate some humor.

Ensure the group's credibility

All group members have the responsibility to be prepared and be committed to an ethical presentation. If relevant, communicate the group members' education, experience, research, personal connections, and any other characteristics the audience may respect and admire. Many groups like to have a dress plan, either business attire or casual clothes.

3. Give the presentation

Use the following group presentation recommendations to your group's advantage: practice beforehand, monitor your language and nonverbal displays, and answer questions.

Practice the presentation

Practice must be part of every group presentation. Allow time for all group members to get together at least once—ideally three to five times—to go over the presentation. Repeated practice will ensure all parts of the presentation are accounted for, all visuals are prepared and relevant, and all group members know what they need to do and when. These practice sessions go a long way toward building everyone's confidence for the actual presentation.

Monitor your language and nonverbal displays

Ensure that everyone is using the same terms and defining them the same way. Have a discussion about inclusive language and encourage everyone to use it. Also encourage group members to use eye contact, and natural gestures and facial expression. Know how the group will position itself in front of the audience, and have a plan for what group members will do when they're not actively presenting. It can be distracting for an audience to watch nonspeaking group members behave self-consciously. One idea is to have them sit at a table in the speaking space or in chairs in the front row.

Answer questions

Determine ahead of time if one group representative or all group members will take questions after or during the presentation. Those selected will want to prepare accordingly. See Chapter 11, pages 254–257, for more on question and answer sessions.

Given all you've learned about group dynamics and making a good presentation, you have the tools you need to ensure enjoyable and constructive group interaction, and that the hard work of your group will be worthwhile.

Special-Occasion Speaking in Action *A Student's Process*

Ruby De Luca's grandparents' fiftieth wedding anniversary celebration was coming soon. She knew there would be an opportunity for guests to speak and wish the couple well. Ruby very much wanted to participate. She also saw the occasion as a good opportunity to try the skills she learned in her public speaking class.

Analyzing the speaking situation and audience

Ruby first analyzed the context and the audience:

- *Everyone on the guest list is a good friend of my grandparents. I don't have to spend time explaining who they are or my relationship to them.*
- *Anniversaries are about celebrating love and my theme will certainly need to reflect that. As their granddaughter who spends a lot of time at their house, I have some special insights on the way they show love to each other. Sharing these would help paint a fuller picture of them for those attending the party.*
- *About sixty people are expected at the party and there will be many who will want to speak. I'll need to make my point quickly and briefly.*

Choosing the message and delivery style

Ruby then created her message. She chose a manuscript style of delivery due to the high emotionality of the event and also so that she could get her words just right.

The Magnitude of Small Kindnesses
A Love Story
by Ruby De Luca

(Word count = 321. Most people speak roughly 125 words per minute, so my whole presentation should take somewhere between the appropriate two to three minutes.)

Bebe and Papa remind us that a successful marriage is not simply comprised of big, memorable, and expensive events, such as buying your first house, giving each other expensive jewelry, or going on a twentieth wedding anniversary trip to Paris.

While a healthy marriage certainly can contain such exciting, momentous things, Bebe and Papa have shown us that in reality, a working relationship is made up of daily kindnesses, small acts of love that reflect how two people genuinely feel about one another. These small kindnesses build up, blend together, layer upon one another, and ultimately create true happiness, trust, and security in a relationship.

Bebe and Papa, here are just a few of the small kindnesses that you give to one another that we witness and admire:

1. Bebe makes Papa healthy, delicious, and nutritious dinners every night.
2. Every morning, Papa picks fresh flowers and puts them into a bowl of water for Bebe.
3. Bebe reins in Papa's sweet tooth so he can retain his girlish figure.
4. When Bebe comes home from a trip, no matter how long she's been gone—be it a day or a few weeks—Papa always makes her a nice, romantic dinner. Usually lamb chops.
5. Bebe remembers to buy Papa new sweaters so he doesn't have to wear his old worn and torn ones.
6. Papa makes coffee for Bebe every morning.
7. Bebe chooses sophisticated foreign films for them to rent on Netflix so that Papa doesn't have to watch yet another John Wayne western, which he would do if left to his own devices.

Side annotations (left):

Ruby starts her message on a broad scope, talking about marriages in general.

Here, she begins to narrow her comments about marriage to her grandparents' marriage.

Daily kindnesses acts as the organizing term.

This brief preview tells listeners what she'll do in the main part of her presentation.

Side annotations (right):

Ruby uses her terms of endearment for her grandparents, highlighting the fact that hers is a family message.

Ruby uses audience-centered pronouns throughout the speech to connect listeners to her theme and message.

Ruby's thematic thesis is quickly stated.

Ruby uses repetition, including both honorees' names in each of her examples. She also creates a rhythm with the examples, moving between the small kindnesses her grandma does for her grandpa, and then vice versa.

(continued)

8. Every time Papa leaves Bebe alone in the house, he locks every door and window so that the night doesn't come and steal his princess away.
9. When Bebe is away, she always calls Papa to wish him goodnight.
10. Papa reminds Bebe daily that he's the luckiest man alive.

I love you both.

review questions

1. What are some of the circumstances in which you'll want to speak or be invited to speak on a special occasion?
2. What are some of the best practices you can use to ensure an effective and meaningful special-occasion speech?
3. What are the most common types of special-occasion speeches you may give?
4. What is a small group? When might you find yourself working in a small group? For what purposes?
5. What are some of the main responsibilities of a group participant? a group leader?
6. What are the five steps of productive group decision making? What are the benefits of following these five steps?
7. What are some of the best practices for planning a group presentation? organizing one? giving one?

key terms

alliteration 400
repetition 400
simile 400
metaphor 400
onomatopoeia 400
toast 401
speech of
   introduction 402
speech of tribute 403

speech of
   commemoration 404
speech of acceptance 404
speech to inspire 405
small group 406
interdependence 407
activity group 407
personal growth
   group 407

educational group 407
problem-solving
   group 407
committee 407
distributed
   leadership 408
collectivistic culture 409
individualistic
   culture 409

connect

For online exercises, quizzes, and hands-on activities, see the Chapter 18 assignments in Connect Public Speaking.

participant-observer 409

self-serving role 412

agenda 414

grouphate 409

legitimate power 413

reflective-thinking

groupthink 411

referent power 413

process 415

task role 412

expert power 413

criteria 417

relationship-oriented

designated leader 414

consensus 418

role 412

emergent leader 414

exercises

1. If you were to pay tribute to a special person in your life, what theme would you use? What five examples would you use to support the theme?

2. YouTube is filled with a variety of wedding toasts. Watch one with a partner, and analyze its effectiveness. Is the speaker prepared? Is the speaker tailoring the words to the couple or speaking about commitment in general terms? Are the words respectful or embarrassing? Is the audience responding and, if so, how? Would you want someone to speak like that at a ceremony honoring you? Report your findings to the class.

3. With a few others, individually write down positive experiences each of you has had in past groups. Share your lists. As a group, combine selected items onto a final list titled something like "Best Ever Dream Group." Reflect on the list and discuss whether a group like this could actually exist. Why or why not?

4. In a small group, review the guidelines for a successful brainstorming session. Choose from the following topics (or choose another topic that interests the group):

   • What would the world's scariest movie entail?
   • What would the best day ever be like?
   • What would the greatest college class be like for students in that class?

   Brainstorm for a minimum of five minutes. Share your list with the whole class. How were the lists different and the same? Why was this so?

Glossary

A

absolute claim An assertion that asks people to accept that something is permanent, complete or in no way conditional. (p. 385)

abstract A summary of an article or a publication. (p. 148)

action The part of a narrative that explains what is happening. (p. 176)

active listening A type of listening that requires a high level of energy to stay engaged in the communication interaction. (p. 32)

activity group A type of group in which members share an interest or a hobby. (p. 407)

ad hominem fallacy An occurrence of unsound reasoning wherein one person launches an irrelevant personal attack on the character of a person with an opposing point of view rather than addressing the competing argument itself. (p. 392)

adrenaline A natural hormone that helps the body adjust to sudden stress; increased levels of adrenaline are what make the body feel "nervous" prior to a public speech. (p. 49)

agenda A list of things to be accomplished during a group meeting. (p. 414)

alliteration A figure of speech that repeats an initial sound in a string of words. (p. 400)

analogical reasoning A form of reasoning that considers the similarities between two things and then presumes an unknown quality about one of them must be true because of a known quality in the other. (p. 388)

anecdotal evidence A kind of evidence that is only one case in point and does not necessarily support a larger body of evidence. (p. 175)

appeal to fear fallacy An occurrence of unsound reasoning that presents a claim in a way to produce fear, thereby gaining support for a different and perhaps unrelated claim. (p. 391)

appreciative listening A level of listening wherein people listen for personal pleasure. (p. 38)

articulation The clarity with which a speaker produces individual speech sounds. (p. 337)

assertion of fact The claim in a persuasive speech that argues whether something is true or not true, whether something happened or did not happen, or whether something exists or does not exist. (p. 362)

assertion of policy The claim in a persuasive speech that argues programs of action—how things should or should not happen, proceed, or get done for an individual or a group or at a societal level. (p. 364)

assertion of value The claim in a persuasive speech that argues whether something is right or wrong, whether something is good or bad, how much something is worth, how fair something is, or how important or useful something is. (p. 364)

attention material The opening words of a speech used to capture the attention of the audience and draw them into the topic; it must be appropriate and relevant to the audience, topic and occasion. (p. 241)

attitudinal information Information about listeners' attitudes, values, and beliefs that a speaker gathers prior to the speech as part of the audience analysis. (p. 103)

audience analysis The process of gathering and analyzing demographic and attitudinal information about the audience with the intention of shaping the speech for that specific group of listeners. (p. 96)

audience connection The technique of openly relating the content of a speech to the needs and wants of the listeners; it engages audience members and convinces them that the speech is worth their listening time. (p. 246)

authoritative warrant A warrant that relies on the credibility, acceptability, or authority of the source to link the evidence to the claim. (p. 381)

B

bandwagon fallacy An occurrence of unsound reasoning that relies on peer pressure as the basis for supporting or rejecting a claim. (p. 393)

bar graph A type of graph that uses vertical or horizontal lines on an x- and y-axis. (p. 286)

Bibliography An alphabetized list of all works consulted, whether or not those words are used in the speech. (p. 227)

blog   An Internet source that contains dated entries of commentary, opinion, or news on a given subject in reverse chronological order; it typically combines text, images, videos, and links to other relevant websites. (p. 149)

brainstorming   A technique for generating a large number of ideas; it can be used for finding a speech topic or a solution to a problem. (p. 128)

brief example   One or two sentences that provide an instance of a larger idea. (p. 184)

C

causal pattern   A pattern of organization that focuses on either the causes of something or its effects. (p. 202)

causal reasoning   A form of reasoning that attempts to connect two events according to a cause-and-effect relationship. One event is known, doable, or generally assumed while the other event is unknown but assumed. (p. 386)

channel   The means by which messages and feedback are transmitted between speaker and audience. (p. 19)

character   A person in a narrative who creates action or to whom action happens. (p. 176)

charisma   A speaker's great personal charm or magnetic personality that draws the attention of listeners. (p. 84)

chart   A visual display that tracks or groups detailed information in summary form using words, numbers, and figures. (p. 285)

chronological pattern   A pattern of organization that follows a time arrangement and shows how events or ideas occur over time, either forward or backward. (p. 201)

civility   A code of decency based on showing respect, honesty, fairness, and tolerance to others; it enhances the speaker's relationship with the listeners. (pp. 41, 80)

civil listener   A listener who works to suspend judgment while also giving notable feedback to the speaker. (p. 41)

claim   The statement about a fact, value, or policy—the conclusion a speaker wants his or her audience to draw and accept. (p. 378)

climax   The part of a narrative representing the peak of tension or the most exciting moment; it is followed by a resolution or conclusion. (p. 176)

closed question   A kind of question that is answered with a yes or a no. (p. 106)

coercion   Getting others to do things in a way that relies on threats, harsh displays of power, or the use of force. (p. 369)

collectivistic culture   A type of culture in which members tend to put the good of the group ahead of individual concerns. (p. 409)

committee   A group of people brought together to perform work for a larger group or organization. (p. 407)

communication orientation   An approach to public speaking that relies on the familiar goal of conveying ideas to other people; this approach is in contrast to the performance orientation, wherein speakers perceive the speech as a performance and the audience as a group of critics. (p. 51)

comparison pattern   A pattern of organization that teaches something new by showing the similarities between two seemingly unlike things, one of which is already familiar to the listener. (p. 204)

comprehensive listening   A type of listening wherein people listen to learn or understand. (p. 39)

concept speech   A speech that looks at the intangibles of life—theories, ideas, impressions, attitudes, beliefs, and values that people cannot see or touch but nonetheless perceive, suppose, or imagine. (p. 351)

conflict   The part of a narrative that introduces actions or complications leading to the climax. (p. 176)

consensus   A kind of voting in which every group member agrees on the final decision. (p. 418)

context   The specific environment or situation in which the public speaking transaction takes place. (p. 19)

contrast pattern   A pattern of organization that teaches something new by showing the differences between two seemingly similar things, one of which is typically already familiar to the audience. (p. 204)

copyright laws   Laws that protect original creative work, including music, art, graphics, and pictures from unauthorized use. (p. 79)

criteria   Measurements used by group members to evaluate potential solutions or decisions. (p. 417)

critical listening   A type of listening wherein people listen to analyze and evaluate the speaker's ideas. (p. 40)

D

database   An electronic collection of data on a single topic or variety of topics organized so that the content can be easily accessed and managed. (p. 148)

decoder   A listener who assigns and creates meaning from the speaker's words and behaviors. (p. 17)

deductive reasoning   A form of reasoning that starts with a general principle and moves toward a specific instance. (p. 385)

demographics   The characteristics of the audience, such as age, socioeconomic status, education level, and gender. (p. 96)

demonstration speech   An informative speech that contains a step-by-step process intended to teach the audience how to use or do something, or how something works or is done. (p. 348)

designated leader   A group leader who is elected or appointed to the leadership position. (p. 414)

dialect   A regional speech pattern used by a subgroup within a given population of speakers of the same language; represents a consistent pattern of pronunciation and syntax, word choice, pacing, rhythm, and expressions associated with such a subgroup. (p. 327)

dialectics   The classical Greek concept of using reasoned arguments to find a truth about a topic. (p. 12)

dialogism   Mikhail Bahktin's concept that explains that each of us becomes who we are—takes shape—based on the push and pull of discussion, exploration, and debate with others. (p. 12)

discussion group   An Internet source that allows users to discuss topics of mutual interest; discussion groups are a good first place to go for researching attitudes and opinions. (p. 148)

distributed leadership   A type of leadership that is shared by all members of the group, each potentially contributing a skill or service to further the objectives of the group. (p. 408)

doublespeak   Language that serves to intentionally hide, distort, or manipulate ideas. (p. 74)

E

educational group   A type of group in which people volunteer or are assigned to work with others to better understand a subject or complete an assignment. (p. 407)

either/or fallacy   An occurrence of unsound reasoning that forces listeners to choose between two options when, in reality, more than two exist. (p. 392)

electronic eloquence   A contemporary persuasive theory that suggests that in the electronic age (TV) successful speakers typically use narrative, self-disclosure, and visuals. (p. 370)

emblems   Movements or positions of the hands, head, and other body parts that have precise meaning and are immediately understood by others in the communicator's culture or co-culture. (p. 331)

emergent leader   A type of leader who starts out as a group participant but ultimately surfaces as a leader. (p. 414)

emotional proof   A form of support that references human emotions; it is not based on fact and is not necessarily logical. (p. 187)

emotional tone   The quality of a speaker's voice that communicates his or her feelings. (p. 335)

encoder   The speaker who creates meaning by taking ideas and translating them into various perceptible codes such as words, gestures, facial expressions, pictures, and tone of voice; the sender. (p. 17)

enthymeme   A form of deductive reasoning that claims probable or likely relationships between the major premise and the minor premise; a kind of syllogism. (p. 385)

ethical listener   A listener who engages actively to increase his or her own worldview and to hold speakers accountable to society's moral principles. (p. 43)

ethics   Standards of right and wrong, according to a particular society; a speaker who is perceived as ethical is more likely to enjoy the audience's trust, respect, and confidence. (pp. 43, 69)

ethnocentrism   Occurs when one person views his or her culture, co-culture, or viewpoints as the standard and judges others accordingly. (p. 96)

ethos   A perceived quality based on a speaker's character, it directly influences the listeners' willingness to receive and accept a speaker's ideas. It's one of three classical persuasive strategies identified by Greek philosopher Aristotle. (pp. 82, 369)

event speech   A speech describing an occasion or event that has happened, is happening, or will happen. (p. 351)

evidence   Material that supports or backs up a claim. (p. 379)

expectancy-outcome values theory   A contemporary persuasive theory that says that people consciously evaluate the potential costs and benefits—the value—of taking or not taking a particular action. (p. 371)

expectancy-violation theory   A contemporary persuasive theory that notes that people can attract attention when their words or actions catch others by surprise (or violate their expectations). (p. 372)

expert power   A type of power earned by one's knowledge and abilities. (p. 413)

expert testimony   Direct words from people with authority on a topic or in a field. (p. 189)

extemporaneous method A method of delivery wherein the speaker talks conversationally from prepared key words and phrases in his or her speaking notes. (p. 307)

extended example A well-developed and possibly lengthy illustration of a broad concept; it often has a plot and some characters. (p. 184)

F

fair use A doctrine of U.S. copyright law that permits the limited use of copyrighted materials without permission from the rights holder, as for criticism, comment, news reporting, teaching, scholarship, and research; the distinction between copyright infringement and fair use may be ambiguous and not easily defined. (p. 79)

fallacy An occurrence of unsound reasoning. (p. 390)

false thesis A sentence that appears to be a thesis statement but fails to narrow the topic and provide a clear direction for how the body of the speech will be developed. (p. 133)

feedback Verbal and nonverbal messages sent from a listener, or listeners, to the speaker. (p. 18)

fighting words Intimidating speech directed at a specific individual in a face-to-face confrontation, especially if that speech inflicts injury or incites an immediate breach of the peace. (p. 72)

First Amendment A section of the United States Constitution that provides, in part, protection for free, uncensored speech. (p. 71)

flow chart A type of chart that shows the sequence of operations in a process. (p. 285)

frame of reference An individual worldview based on background, age, education, gender, values, politics, economic status, culture, occupation, health, and ethnicity that influences the creation of the speaker's message and the listener's interpretation of the message. (p. 17)

frames Mental constructs that shape the way people see the world. (p. 373)

Freedom of Information Act Enacted in 1966, it ensures access to federal documents outside the boundaries of nine specific exemptions. (p. 152)

G

general audience An audience that is widely mixed in terms of demographics and attitudes. (p. 108)

graph or data-driven graph A diagram that communicates numerical relationships; typically a data graph calculated by a software program. (p. 285)

gratuitous image An unnecessary image, especially one that is too graphic, violent, or sexual. (p. 285)

grouphate Negative feelings toward group participation. (p. 409)

groupthink A kind of thinking in which the desire for unanimity discourages group members from taking a realistic look at a group task or problem; groupthink may cause group members to suppress confrontation, disagreement, and full analysis of the situation. (p. 411)

H

hate speech Words that harass or promote discrimination or violence against social or ethnic groups of people, or a member of such a group. (p. 71)

hearing An involuntary, biological process that occurs when a person's ears detect a sound; hearing is physiologically based. (p. 31)

heterosexist language Words that tell a listener that the speaker is acting on the premise that all people are heterosexual. (p. 321)

hierarchy of needs A theory by Abraham Maslow that says that people are motivated by a range of needs; speakers can apply this theory for persuasive effect. (p. 370)

homogeneous audience A group that has one or more important demographic or attitudinal characteristics in common. (p. 107)

homophobic language Words that use homosexuality as a target of humor or disapproval. (p. 321)

hypothetical example An illustration that looks into an unknown past or future; it shows what could have been or could be. (p. 185)

hypothetical narrative An invented story; it conceptualizes past or future events or outcomes. (p. 176)

I

illustrative support Forms of support that clarify, expand on, or provide more information for listeners; includes examples, descriptions, and explanations. (p. 183)

illustrators Movements of the hands, head, and other body parts that accompany speech, but have no meaning in and of themselves (as opposed to emblems). (p. 330)

immediacy A measure of the closeness or intimacy, displayed through nonverbal behaviors, between a speaker and the listeners. (p. 333)

important conversation The style of conversation used when talking to someone the speaker respects; it is the style of conversation preferred for most public speaking situations. (p. 11)

impromptu method   A method of delivery wherein the speaker presents with little or no preparation; also known as improvising, ad-libbing, or speaking off the cuff. (p. 309)

inclusive language   Words and phrases that act as a bridge to an audience, thereby increasing the speaker's chances of making a connection; this kind of language tells an audience that all listeners are welcomed and respected. (p. 319)

individualistic culture   A type of culture in which members tend to value the individual over the group. (p. 409)

inductive reasoning   A form of reasoning that starts with a specific instance and moves to a general principle. (p. 382)

inflection   The manipulation of vocal pitch to communicate a specific meaning. (p. 338)

information literacy   The ability to recognize the need for information and then find, understand, evaluate, and use the information in various forms for personal, social, or global purposes. (p. 155)

informative speaking   Speaking to enhance the knowledge of others. (p. 344)

interdependence   The idea that group members influence each other during the small group process. (p. 407)

internal preview   A type of transition that forecasts the next idea in the body of the speech. (p. 259)

internal summary   A type of transition that points to the importance of an idea just discussed. (p. 259)

invisible web   Also known as the deep web, it contains information that general search engines cannot access, including databases, virtual libraries, licensed information, and deliberately excluded pages. (p. 147)

invitational rhetoric   A type of speaking that is not purely informative or persuasive but, instead, finds a speaker engaging in dialogue with the audience to clarify positions, explore ideas, and express beliefs and values. (p. 372)

J

jargon   Language of a technical nature, specific to a profession or hobby, that might have little meaning outside of that group. (p. 322)

K

keyword search   The act of entering a few topic-related terms to cue a search engine to narrow down the information being sought. (p. 147)

L

lay testimony   Words from people who have firsthand knowledge or experience but are not considered experts in their field. (p. 189)

legitimate power   A type of power enjoyed when a person holds a particular position or office. (p. 413)

line graph   A type of graph that uses single or multiple lines to show trends over time. (p. 286)

linking transition   A type of transition that takes listeners from one part of the structure to the next, such as from the introduction to the body or from one idea to the next; sometimes known as a bridge. (p. 259)

listenability   The degree to which a speech is easy to listen to; achieved through speaker actions that make it easier for the audience to access, understand, and interact with the speaker's ideas. (p. 5)

listener-centered public speaker   A type of speaker who makes his or her ideas (whether simple or complex) easy for listeners to access, understand, and interact with—to listen to. (p. 4)

listening   A voluntary, mental process wherein a person receives a stimulus, chooses to attend to it, assigns it meaning, and responds to it. (p. 31)

literal question   A concrete question that requests an actual answer. (p. 242)

literate (or written) style   A style of language appropriately used when expressing ideas through the written word; this style is in contrast to the oral (or conversational) style people use when talking with one another. (p. 9)

logos   An appeal to the logical mind; one of three classical persuasive strategies identified by Greek philosopher Aristotle. (p. 378)

M

main points   The major ideas within the speech that support the thesis; main points are related to one another, are organized according to a recognizable pattern, and comprise the body of the speech. (p. 217)

major premise   A general principle containing an absolute relationship between two terms; part of a deductive argument. (p. 385)

manuscript method A method of delivery wherein the speaker reads from a fully prepared text. (p. 311)

memorized method A method of delivery wherein the speaker commits a prepared manuscript to memory and then recites it. (p. 314)

message The verbal and nonverbal content that the speaker transmits to listeners. (p. 18)

meta-listener A listener who is consciously aware of himself or herself engaging in the listening process. (p. 35)

metaphor A figure of speech that compares two things by stating or suggesting that one thing represents (rather than is like) another. (p. 400)

mind map A developmental technique for illustrating, linking, and documenting ideas and showing how they are connected. (p. 128)

minor premise A specific instance about one of the terms in the major premise; part of a deductive argument. (p. 385)

mnemonic device A memory trick or aid that need only make sense to an individual; it can help a speaker memorize key words for an outline. (p. 314)

model A three-dimensional piece of visual support that shows a scaled-down version of an object too large or too dangerous to bring to the speaking event. (p. 288)

monopitch or monotone A speaking voice with little variety in tone or inflection. (p. 338)

Monroe's motivated sequence A format for persuasive speakers who want listeners to reconsider a predisposition, firm up a present commitment or move to action; the sequence relies on five steps—attention, need, satisfaction, visualization, and action. (p. 208)

motivational warrant A warrant that connects the evidence to the claim by appealing to audience members' values, needs, desires, emotions, and aspirations. (p. 382)

muscle memory A kind of procedural memory that gets stored in the brain through repetition; it illustrates that practice binds the material to the body, helping the speaker remember what to say and do while presenting. (p. 296)

N

narrative A story that a speaker tells to engage listeners and to support a point; the narrative may be one part of the speech or may comprise the entire speech. (p. 173)

narrative coherence The quality of a story that allows it to hang together well and make sense structurally. (p. 173)

narrative fidelity The quality of a story that speaks to how true and human the story appears. (p. 173)

narrative paradigm Walter Fisher's notion that proposes that storytelling is so central to what it means to be human, a story that rings true with listeners' experiences is often more effective than building up rational evidence or constructing a logical argument. (p. 173)

noise Anything that prevents the audience and the speaker from understanding each other's messages. (p. 19)

noninclusive language Words or phrases that rely on negative stereotypes, derogatory remarks, or offensive terms; it is language that makes others feel inferior. (p. 319)

nonverbal communication A type of communication expressed without words. (p. 328)

O

object speech A speech that teaches the listeners about something visible, audible, or tangible. (p. 350)

objective support Forms of support that are, for the most part, agreed upon, measurable, observable, and consistent; includes facts, definitions, and statistics. (p. 178)

onomatopoeia A figure of speech that enriches imagery by using words that sound like what they describe. (p. 400)

open access The notion held by some in the scholarly community who consent to make their intellectual work available for free online. (p. 162)

open-ended question A type of question that allows people to elaborate (or not) as they wish. (p. 106)

open-source website (or "wiki") A type of website where any and all are invited to create or edit most entries. (p. 161)

oral (or conversational) style The style of language people rely on when talking with one another; this style is in contrast to the literate style people use when expressing ideas through the written word. (p. 9)

oratory A manner of speaking studied and practiced by Greek and Roman scholars; it focused on speaking with competence, style, and grace for persuasive purposes. Today, it refers to longer, more formal styled speeches of all kinds. (p. 344)

organizational chart A type of chart that shows how authority and supervision are distributed within a company or an organization. (p. 285)

organizing term   The word in the thesis that tells the listeners how the speaker plans to develop the narrowed topic. (p. 199)

ownership   An intimacy between the speaker and his or her ideas; it is displayed through familiarity with the content and confidence in delivery. (p. 297)

P

pace   The speed at which a speaker produces language. (p. 338)

paralanguage   The communicative qualities of the human voice; they include pace, pitch, volume, and emotional tone. (p. 334)

parallel idea   An idea within the speech that is equal in importance to another idea; main points, for example, are parallel to each other. (p. 221)

paraphrasing   Rewording another person's ideas in simpler terms. (p. 191)

participant-observer   A group member who actively contributes to the group's purpose while reflecting on the group dynamics (and adapting when necessary). (p. 409)

passive listening   A type of listening that takes relatively little energy; paying halfhearted attention to incoming stimuli either by choice or by habit. (p. 31)

pathos   An appeal to an audience's emotions; one of three classical persuasive strategies identified by Greek philosopher Aristotle. (p. 369)

pattern of organization   The arrangement of the main points in the speech body. (p. 199)

peer-reviewed article   An article in a journal that has been found acceptable by other experts in the field prior to publication. (p. 149)

performance orientation   An approach to public speaking wherein the speaker perceives the speech as a performance and the audience as a group of critics; this approach is in contrast to the communication orientation, wherein the speaker relies on the familiar goal of conveying ideas to other people. (p. 49)

personal growth group   A type of group in which members provide support to each other as each seeks understanding, new skills, comfort, or strength during a challenging time. (p. 407)

personal speaking goal   One specific, measurable skill that a speaker focuses on for a particular presentation for continued speaking improvement. (p. 61)

persuasion   The act of deliberately attempting to influence the thinking or actions of others. (p. 359)

photo illustration   A created image from one or more photographs. (p. 284)

physical context   The physical characteristics of the speaking space such as location, size, lighting, and acoustical properties. (p. 110)

pie graph   A graph that shows how 100 percent of something is broken down into smaller segments; the segments of the pie always add back up to 100 percent. (p. 286)

pitch   The high or low tone of a speaker's voice, as on a musical scale. (p. 338)

plagiarism   Attempting to pass off another's idea, or a close imitation of it, as one's own. (p. 75)

polled data   Information gathered, typically by a polling organization, about the opinions and habits of a group of people. (p. 104)

power of the podium   A symbol of truth and authority that speakers enjoy; speakers have a responsibility to use this power ethically throughout the speechmaking process. (p. 14)

preparation outline   Also known as the working outline, this document presents a speaker's thoughts in one place; it lets the speaker plan the order of the ideas while ensuring that those ideas relate to one another logically, are well balanced, and are adequately supported. (p. 217)

primacy   The principle that audiences are more likely to remember the points the speaker makes first. (p. 367)

primary research   Research that is collected directly from experiments, case studies, surveys, observation, and interviews. (p. 146)

problem-cause-solution pattern   A pattern of organization in which the first point defines a problem, the second argues the causes for this problem, and the third proposes a solution that lessens or eliminates the cause. (p. 206)

problem-solution pattern   A pattern of organization that defines a problem and offers a feasible solution for it. (p. 206)

problem-solving group   A type of group in which people address some sort of issue or challenge. (p. 407)

process speech   A speech that describes a series of actions or events that result in a specific outcome or end product. (p. 351)

pronunciation   The way a speaker forms the sound of a word—where the stress is and how many syllables there are. (p. 326)

proxemics   A category of nonverbal communication defined by interpersonal distance; how close or how far a speaker stands from the audience. (p. 332)

pseudo-listening Pretending to listen without actually being engaged; fake listening. (p. 38)

psychological context The moods and frames of mind of the people engaged in the public speaking transaction. (p. 111)

public listener A person actively working to access, understand, and interact with a public message. (p. 6)

public memory theory A contemporary persuasive theory that points to the power of TV, music, radio, film, and memorials to persuade people about the past and the way they remember it. (p. 371)

Q

Q&A "Question-and-answer" session, wherein audience members query the speaker or make comments on the speaker's content at the end of the speech. (p. 254)

R

racist language Words and phrases that tell a listener that a speaker organizes the world according to race, most often in reference to ability, occupation, behavior, and preferences. (p. 320)

reasoning The process of supporting a claim using sufficient, true (or probable), and relevant evidence, which is logically arranged and linked to the claim by a warrant. (p. 378)

reasoning backward Arguing from effect to cause during causal reasoning. (p. 386)

reasoning forward Arguing from cause to effect during causal reasoning. (p. 386)

receiver The person who receives the sender's message; an audience member; a listener. (p. 17)

recency The principle that audiences are more likely to remember the points the speaker makes last. (p. 367)

red herring fallacy An occurrence of unsound reasoning that raises an irrelevant topic in order to divert attention from the original issue. (p. 393)

References A list, in alphabetical order by last name of author, editor, and so on, of full citations to any work cited, referenced, or paraphrased in a speech. It's typically used when using APA (American Psychological Association) style. (p. 227)

referent power A type of power that comes from possessing qualities that others find attractive. (p. 413)

reflective-thinking process A well-defined five-step process for making a meaningful group decision. (p. 415)

relational dialectics Leslie Baxter and Barbara Montgomery's theory noting that communication—interacting with others—is used to construct relationships and understanding within those relationships. (p. 12)

relationship-oriented role A type of group role that helps group members work well together. (p. 412)

relevance A criterion for ensuring that supporting material has some sensible or logical connection to the idea being communicated. (p. 172)

repetition A figure of speech that uses a recurring word or phrase. (p. 400)

resolution The part of a narrative, after the climax, where the conflict is resolved. (p. 176)

rhetorical participation The result of a speaker inviting listeners to contemplate an issue, consider a scenario, reflect on a value, or mull over a proposal without making a verbal response. (p. 114)

rhetorical question A question that inspires thought without requiring an answer. (p. 242)

S

scene The part of a narrative that explains where and when the action is taking place. (p. 176)

search engine A software program that lets users access information about a given topic; Google, Yahoo! and Bing are among the most popular search engines. (p. 147)

secondary research Existing research that is gathered, collected, or organized from other sources. (p. 146)

self-serving role A type of group role that serves the individual at the expense of the group. (p. 412)

sender A person motivated to send a message; the speaker. (p. 17)

setup The part of a narrative where the character(s) and scene are introduced and the action starts. (p. 176)

sexist language Words and phrases that tell a listener that a speaker organizes the world according to sex or gender, most often in reference to occupation, ability, or behavior. (p. 320)

signpost A word or brief phrase that indicates to listeners where the speaker is in the speech, or indicates the relationship of one idea to the next; a signpost comes in the form of a number, a common transition word, a short phrase, or a question. (p. 260)

simile A figure of speech that compares two things by using the word *like* or *as*. (p. 400)

slander   False statements that defame another's character, potentially harming that person's standing in the community or at work. (p. 72)

slang   Words used and immediately understood within a specific group, be it a small collection of friends, a city, a region, a co-culture, or a country. (p. 321)

slideware   Presentation software, such as PowerPoint, Prezi, or Keynote. (p. 271)

slippery slope fallacy   An occurrence of unsound reasoning that argues an inevitable connection from one event to another, bypassing possible or probable links that may or may not exist. (p. 391)

small group   A small number of individuals who work together toward an identified goal while influencing each other during the process. (p. 406)

spatial pattern   A pattern of organization that discusses the topic according to the way things fit together in a physical space of any size. The supporting points relate to one another according to a geographical pattern or a relative physical relationship, such as top to bottom, east to west, inside to outside. (p. 205)

speaker credibility   A perceived quality a speaker earns through displaying knowledge, preparation, confidence, and a commitment to ethics and civility; it assures listeners that the speaker is the right person for the specific speech. (p. 82)

speaker's energy   The preferred label (rather than nervousness or anxiety) for the rush of adrenaline many speakers feel prior to a public speech. (p. 53)

speaking logistics   The details of the speaking event, including the date, time, and schedule of events and speakers. (p. 297)

speaking notes   The set of notes prepared from a preparation outline a few days in advance of the presentation; they consist of the words, phrases, and symbols the speaker needs to remember what to say while speaking. (p. 228)

speech of acceptance   A special-occasion speech given by someone receiving an award or honor. (p. 404)

speech of commemoration   A special-occasion speech that recognizes an event, a place, or an idea. (p. 404)

speech of definition   An informative speech that gives a fuller understanding of a term, typically one that refers to an object or a concept. (p. 347)

speech of description   An informative speech wherein the speaker provides a collection of details, uses vivid words, and shows pictures that allow the audience to "see" something in a new way. (p. 349)

speech of explanation   An informative speech that begins with something that is or was—an event, an object, a theory, a process, a situation, a fact—and provides reasons or causes for its existence or looks at potential consequences of its existence. (p. 348)

speech of introduction   A special-occasion speech that prepares an audience for an upcoming speaker or event. (p. 402)

speech of tribute   A special-occasion speech that pays honor or respect to another person. (p. 403)

speech to inform   A general type of speech that helps listeners understand new or useful ideas from the world around them. (p. 125)

speech to inspire   A special-occasion speech that encourages, moves or rouses listeners to create positive change. (p. 405)

speech to instruct   An informative speech that teaches the audience about a procedure or task, providing tips, pointers, and directions on how listeners can achieve better results in the future. (p. 348)

speech to mark a special occasion   A general type of speech that celebrates important people or places, honors memorable events, or shares humorous ideas. (p. 125)

speech to persuade   A general type of speech that aims to create, change, or reinforce the thinking or actions of others. (p. 125)

speech to report   An informative speech wherein the speaker collects information from various sources and combines it in an easily understood package to allow listeners to better understand situations. (p. 349)

statistics   Numerical data that describe some sort of relationship. (p. 181)

storyboarding   A visual thinking process that involves sequencing a series of images to tell a story. (p. 282)

subjective support   Forms of support that are based on thoughts, opinions, experience, or feelings; includes emotional proof and personal experience. (p. 186)

subordinate idea   An idea within the speech that supports another idea; it is less important than a superior idea. (p. 217)

subpoints   A point within the speech outline that supports a main point. (p. 217)

substantive warrant   A warrant that uses the reliability and sometimes the quantity of the evidence to support the claim. (p. 381)

sub-subpoints   Points within the speech outline that support a subpoint. (p. 217)

superior idea   An idea within the speech that needs other ideas to support it; it is more important than a subordinate idea. (p. 217)

SWOT analysis   A tool that businesses and organizations use to distinguish themselves from their competitors and successfully compete in their market according to their strengths, weaknesses, opportunities, and threats. Public speakers can use a version of this tool to help identify talents and opportunities in public speaking. (p. 59)

syllogism   A form of deductive reasoning that claims absolute relationships between the major premise and the minor premise. (p. 385)

T

take-away   An idea, instruction, or suggestion for further action, typically given in the conclusion of a speech. (p. 252)

task role   A type of group role that helps the group achieve its mission. (p. 412)

teleprompter   A device displaying a prepared text on a screen at the speaker's eye level, giving listeners the impression of eye contact; speakers read their speech from a teleprompter. (p. 312)

temporal context   The point at which a speech is given, relative to the time of day, to the time in history, or to other presentations on the same topic. (p. 110)

testimony   Words from other people that support an idea a speaker is trying to make. (p. 188)

thesis   Also known as the central idea, it's the one or two sentences typically offered in the introduction of a speech that state exactly what the listeners should know, do, or believe by the end of the speech; the point the speaker is trying to make and how he or she intends to make it. (p. 133)

time limit   The allotted window of time a speaker has to present. (p. 297)

time management   Making effective use of time when faced with conflicting priorities or limited time in which to act. (p. 300)

timeline   A kind of chart that shows key events arranged chronologically. (p. 286)

toast   A special-occasion speech that briefly honors a person or an event. (p. 401)

topic   The subject matter of the speech. (p. 122)

topical pattern   A pattern of organization that divides the topic into subclasses or subtopics based on their similarity; also known as classification or division pattern. (p. 199)

transactional communication   A communication situation in which messages flow in two directions simultaneously, with the speaker and the audience both acting as senders and receivers. (p. 18)

transitions   Overt verbal clues that help listeners follow the progression and relationship of ideas within the speech. (p. 257)

triggers   The key words and phrases on speaking notes that prompt the speaker; used in extemporaneous and impromptu speaking. (p. 307)

true thesis   A thesis that contains one central idea and is backed up by main points that are inevitable and not easily substitutable. (p. 133)

truthiness   A devotion to information one wishes were true even if it's not. (p. 179)

U

uptalk   A pattern of producing statements with an upward inflection, as if asking a question. (p. 338)

urban legend   Stories that many or most people believe to be true, but are not. (p. 178)

V

verbal junk   Sounds such as *uh, like, um.* (p. 336)

virtual library   A general, international, discipline-specific, or topic-specific digital library, containing much of what is found in print collections, but is accessed in digital format. (p. 148)

visual literacy   Effectively understanding and conveying ideas through visual means. (p. 268)

visual support   Material like images, animations, charts, and models that enhance speaking ideas. (p. 268)

volume   How loud or how soft a speaker's voice is. (p. 335)

W

warrant   The link between the evidence and the claim, used while reasoning. (p. 381)

Works Cited   A list, in alphabetical order by last name of author, editor, and so on, of full citations to any work cited, referenced, or paraphrased in a speech. It's typically used when using MLA (Modern Languages Association) style. (p. 227)

Chapter Notes

Chapter 1

1. Special thanks to Andrew D. Wolvin, Roy M. Berko, and Darlyn R. Wolvin, *The Public Speaker/ The Public Listener*, 2nd ed. (Los Angeles: Roxbury, 1999), 74–76; Donald L. Rubin, "Listenability = Oral-Based Language + Considerateness," in *Perspectives on Listening*, ed. Andrew D. Wolvin and Carolyn G. Coakley (Norwood, NJ: Ablex, 1993), 261–281; and Francis A. Cartier, "The Social Context of Listenability Research," *Journal of Communication* 2, no. 1 (May 1952): 44–47.
2. Lyman K. Steil, Larry L. Barker, and Kittie W. Watson, *Effective Listening: Key to Your Success* (New York: McGraw-Hill, 1993), 51.
3. Mikhail Bahktin, *The Dialogic Imagination*, ed. Michael Holquist, trans. Caryl Emerson and Holquist (Austin: University of Texas, 1981).
4. Leslie A. Baxter and Barbara M. Montgomery, *Relating: Dialogues and Dialectics* (New York: Guilford Press, 1996). See also Leslie A. Baxter, "A Tale of Two Voices: Relational Dialectics Theory," *Journal of Family Communication* 4, nos. 3 and 4 (2004): 181–192.
5. Em Griffin, *A First Look at Communication Theory*, 7th ed. (Boston: McGraw-Hill, 2009), 166.
6. *Julia Ward Howe and the Woman Suffrage Movement: A Selection from Her Speeches and Essays* (Dana Estes & Co., 1913), p. 192.
7. Community College Survey of Student Engagement, 2010 Annual Report, http://www.ccsse.org (accessed May 24, 2011).
8. National Survey of Student Engagement, 2010 Annual Report, http://nsse.iub.edu (accessed May 24, 2011).
9. National Association of Colleges and Employers, "Job Outlook 2011 Spring Update," April 2011, p. 8.
10. Randall S. Hansen and Katherine Hansen,"What Do Employers Really Want? Top Skills and Values Employers Seek from Job-Seekers," http:// quintcareers.com/job_skills_values.html (accessed July 24, 2005); and "Skills and Tasks for Jobs. A SCANS Report for America, 2000" (Washington, DC: Department of Labor).
11. John Poulakos, "Terms for Sophistical Rhetoric," in *Rethinking the History of Rhetoric: Multidisciplinary Essays on the History of Rhetoric*, ed. Takis Poulakos (Boulder, CO: Westview, 1993), 56.
12. H. D. F. Kitto, *The Greeks* (1951; Baltimore, MD: Penguin Books, 1968), 120.
13. James Herrick, *The History and Theory of Rhetoric*, 2nd ed. (Boston: Allyn & Bacon, 2001), 32.
14. Andrew Ford, "The Price of Art in Isocrates: Formalism and the Escape from Politics," in *Rethinking the History of Rhetoric*, ed. Takis Poulakos (Boulder, CO: Westview, 1992), 37.
15. All ideas on nineteenth-century oratory come from "Public Speaking in an Outspoken Age: Oratory in 19th Century America," *E Pluribus Unum Project: Archiving 1850s America*, http://www.assumption .edu/ahc/rhetoric/oratory.html (accessed May 23, 2011).
16. Ibid.

Chapter 2

1. Andrew D. Wolvin and Carolyn G. Coakley, *Listening*, 5th ed. (Boston: McGraw-Hill, 1996), 21–25.
2. Author interview with Tom Riggs, vice president of the American Sign Language Teachers Association, November 9, 2005.
3. University of California–Los Angeles, "Multi-tasking Adversely Affects Brain's Learning, UCLA Psychologists Report," *ScienceDaily*, July 26, 2006, http://www.sciencedaily.com (accessed May 29, 2011).
4. "Facts about Stuttering," Stuttering Foundation, http://www.stutteringhelp.org (accessed May 29, 2011).
5. Andrew D. Wolvin and Carolyn G. Coakley, *Listening*, 5th ed. (Boston: McGraw-Hill, 1996), 151–361.

Chapter 3

1. Michael T. Motley, *Overcoming Your Fear of Public Speaking: A Proven Method* (Boston: Houghton Mifflin, 1997), 6–7.

2. Peter D. MacIntyre, Kimly A. Thivierge, and J. Renée MacDonald, "The Effects of Audience Interest, Responsiveness, and Evaluation on Public Speaking Anxiety and Related Variables," *Communication Research Reports* 14 (1997): 157–168.

3. Including Joe Ayers, Tim Hopf, and Elizabeth Peterson, "A Test of Communication-Orientation Motivation (COM) Therapy," *Communication Reports* 13 (2000): 35–44.

4. MacIntyre et al., 158.

5. Richard Doetkott and Michael Motley, "Performing vs. Conversing Public Speakers: Audience Preference and Recollection in a College Population," Top Paper, Basic Course Division, National Communication Association Annual Conference, November 2009.

6. Desiree C. Duff, Timothy R. Levine, Michael J. Beatty, Jessica Woolbright, and Hee Sun Park, "Testing Public Speaking Anxiety Treatments Against a Credible Placebo Control," *Communication Education* 56 (2007): 72–88; and Amber N. Finn, Chris R. Sawyer, and Paul Schrodt, "Examining the Effect of Exposure Therapy on Public Speaking State Anxiety," *Communication Education* 58 (2009): 92–109.

7. First developed by Edmund P. Learned, C. Roland Christiansen, Kenneth Andrews, and William D. Guth, *Business Policy, Text and Cases* (Homewood, IL: Irwin, 1969).

Chapter 4

1. Immanuel Kant, *Groundwork of the Metaphysics of Morals,* trans. H. J. Paton (New York: Harper Torchbooks, 1964), 88.

2. *Chaplinsky v. New Hampshire,* U.S. Supreme Court decision, 1942, cited on the American Civil Liberties Union website, http://www.aclu.org (accessed June 14, 2011).

3. *New York Times Co. v. Sullivan,* U.S. Supreme Court decision, 1964, cited on the American Civil Liberties Union website, http://www.aclu.org (accessed June 14, 2011).

4. Examples from the list compiled by the Center for Media and Democracy, http://www.sourcewatch .org/index.php?title=Doublespeak (accessed June 14, 2011).

5. Plagiarism.org, *Types of Plagiarism,* http://www .plagiarism.org/plag_article_types_of_plagiarism .html (accessed June 14, 2011).

6. Jurgen Habermas, adapted from Richard L. Johannesen, *Ethics in Human Communication,* 5th ed. (Prospect Heights, IL: Waveland Press, 2002), 45.

7. "Northern Parula," Boreal Songbird Initiative, http://www.borealbirds.org (accessed June 14, 2011).

8. Thanks to the University of Texas, Office of the General Counsel, for their student-friendly interpretation of fair use, http://copyright.lib .utexas.edu/copypol2.html (accessed June 15, 2011).

9. This and other ideas about civility come from P. M. Forni, *Choosing Civility: The 25 Rules of Considerate Conduct* (New York: St. Martin's Griffin, 2002).

10. Guy Burgess and Heidi Burgess, "The Meaning of Civility," Conflict Research Consortium, University of Colorado, http://www.colorado.edu/ conflict/civility.htm (accessed June 15, 2011).

11. Civil Dialogue is a trademark of Black Mountain Communications, Inc.

12. Interview with author, June 16, 2011.

13. Civil Dialogue, "Sample Opening Host Statement," http:www.civil-dialogue.com/howto.html (accessed January 1, 2012).

14. Forni, 6.

15. Lea Winerman, "'Thin Slices' of Life," *Monitor on Psychology* 36, no. 3 (March 2005): 54–57.

16. V. P. Richmond and J. C. McCroskey, *Nonverbal Behavior in Interpersonal Relations* (Needham Heights, MA: A Pearson Education Company, 2000).

Chapter 5

1. "Stages of Intellectual Development in Children and Teenagers," Child Development Institute, http://www.childdevelopmentinfo.com (accessed June 17, 2011).

2. Gulf Citrus Growers Association, www.gulfcitrus .org (accessed June 17, 2011).

3. Adapted from "Presentation Tips and Information: Presenting to People with Disabilities," American Educational Research Association, http:// www.aera.net/meetings/Default.aspx?menu_ id=22&id=490 (accessed June 17, 2011).

4. Carson, Clayborne, ed., "The Autobiography of Martin Luther King, Jr." (New York: IPM/Warner Books, 2001), as cited on The Martin Luther King, Jr., Research and Education Institute website, http:// mlk-kpp01.stanford.edu (accessed July 15, 2011).

Chapter 7

1. Alison J. Head and Michael B. Eisenberg, "Finding Context: What Today's College Students Say about Conducting Research in the Digital Age," *Project Information Literacy Progress Report,* February 4, 2009, 5.
2. Michael Liedtke and Joelle Tessler, "FTC Probing Google's Search-Engine Tactics," Associated Press, as printed in the *Arizona Republic,* June 24, 2011, A15.
3. Ann Roselle, Phoenix College Library faculty, interview with author, June 27, 2011.
4. Ibid.
5. OCLC (Online Computer Library Center), *Perceptions of Libraries, 2010: Context and Community* (report): 60.
6. Debbie Abilock (ed.), "Information Literacy from Prehistory to K–20: A New Definition," *Knowledge Quest* 32, no. 4 (March/April 2004): 9.
7. Michael B. Eisenberg, "Information Literacy: Essential Skills for the Information Age," *Journal of Library & Information Technology* 28, no. 2 (March 2008): 39–47.
8. CRAAP test—Meriam Library at California State University, Chico.
9. Head and Eisenberg, 2.
10. OCLC, 54.
11. Eszter Hargittai, Lindsay Fullerton, Ericka Menchen-Trevino, and Kristin Yates-Thomas, "Trust Online: Young Adults' Evaluation of Web Content," *International Journal of Communication* 4 (2010): 468–494.
12. Liedtke and Tessler, A1.
13. OCLC, 54.
14. Ibid., 61.
15. Head and Eisenberg, 12.
16. Jaron Lanier, *You Are Not a Gadget* (New York: Alfred A. Knopf, 2010), 142.
17. Peter Suber, "A Very Brief Introduction to Open Access," http://www.earlham.edu/~peters/fos/brief.htm (accessed July 1, 2011).
18. Amy Dockser Markus, "ALS Study Shows Social Media's Value as Research Tool," *Wall Street Journal,* April 25, 2011, http://online.wsj.com (accessed July 1, 2011).
19. As of August 2011.
20. University Libraries, University of North Carolina, "Evaluating Books: Credibility," http://www.lib.unc.edu/instruct/evaluate/books/credibility.html (accessed June 29, 2011).
21. Free Press, "Ownership Chart: The Big Six," http://www.freepress.net/ownership/chart/main (accessed July 1, 2011).
22. Society of Professional Journalists, Code of Ethics, http://www.spj.org/ethicscode.asp (accessed June 28, 2011).
23. Michael Finkel, "Bedlam in the Blood: Malaria," *National Geographic,* July 2007, 58.

Chapter 8

1. Walter R. Fisher, *Human Communication as Narration: Toward a Philosophy of Reason, Value, and Action* (Columbia: University of South Carolina, 1987), 24.
2. Walter R. Fisher, "Narration as a Human Communication Paradigm: The Case of Public Moral Argument," *Communication Monographs* 52 (1984): 347–367.
3. Author interview with Chiedza Mutsaka, Zimbabwe native, October 16, 2007.
4. International Shark Attack File, "ISAF Statistics for the World Locations with the Highest Shark Attack Activity (2000–2010)," Florida Museum of Natural History, University of Florida, http://www.flmnh.ufl.edu/fish/sharks/statistics/statsw.htm (accessed July 3, 2011).
5. "Bottle Royale," Snopes.com, http://www.snopes.com (accessed July 3, 2011).
6. Paul Rogat Loeb, *Soul of a Citizen* (New York: St. Martin's Griffin, 1999), 34–35.
7. Nell Greenfieldboyce, "Study: 634 Million People at Risk from Rising Seas," *National Public Radio,* March 28, 2007.
8. John R. Pleis, Brian W. Ward, and Jacqueline W. Lucas, "Summary Health Statistics for U.S. Adults: National Health Interview Survey, 2009," Division of Health Interview Statistics, 18.
9. John McPhee, *Oranges* (New York: Noonday Press, 1966), 42.
10. Interview with Dr. Leonard Corte, founding president of the Southwest Center for Psychoanalytic Studies and a member of the American and International Psychoanalytic Association, Tucson, AZ, November 16, 2006.
11. E. O. Wilson, as quoted in Michael Capuzzo, *Close to Shore: A True Story of Terror in an Age of Innocence* (New York: Broadway Books, 2001), epigraph.
12. Scott Bowles, "Leo Eases into Howard Hughes' Shoes," *USA Today,* October 5, 2004, http://www.usatoday.com (accessed January 4, 2012).

Chapter 9

1. Unless otherwise noted, all elephant information comes from S. K. Eltringham, ed., *The Illustrated Encyclopedia of Elephants: From Their Origins and Evolution to Their Ceremonial and Working Relationship with Man* (New York: Crescent, 1991).
2. David Montgomery, "PETA, Ringling Bros. at Odds over the Treatment of Baby Circus Elephants," *Washington Post,* December 16, 2009, http:www .washingtonpost.com (accessed July 6, 2011).
3. "Elephant Conservation," Elephant Care International, http://www.elephantcare.org/ conserve.htm (accessed July 7, 2011).
4. A. H. Monroe, *Principles and Types of Speeches* (Chicago, IL: Scott, Foresman, 1935).
5. Douglas Fox, "Wildlife Contraception," *Conservation Magazine* 8 (October/December 2007), http://www .conservationmagazine.org (accessed July 18, 2011).

Chapter 11

1. Melinda S. Womack, *Speak to Me!* (Dubuque, IA: Kendall/Hunt, 1991), 67–69.

Chapter 12

1. Dale Cyphert, "Presentation Technology in the Age of Electronic Eloquence: From Visual Aid to Visual Rhetoric," *Communication Education* 56, no. 2 (April 2007): 174.
2. Cliff Atkinson and Richard E. Mayer, "Five Ways to Reduce Presentation Software Overload," April 23, 2004, http://www.sociablemedia.com/PDF/ atkinson_mayer_presentation software_4_23_04 .pdf (accessed August 4, 2011).
3. Kathleen H. Jamieson, *Eloquence in an Electronic Age: The Transformation of Political Speechmaking* (New York: Oxford University Press, 1998).
4. Cyphert, 170.
5. Garr Reynolds official website, www.garrreynolds .com. Quote edited by permission of Garr Reynolds.
6. Examples include Garr Reynolds, Nancy Duarte, Seth Godin, Dale Cyphert, Cliff Atkinson, Richard E. Mayer, and Edward Tufte.
7. Edward R. Tufte, *The Cognitive Style of PowerPoint* (Cheshire, CT: Graphics Press, 2003), 3.
8. Anna Patty, "Research Points the Finger at PowerPoint," *Sydney Morning Herald,* April 4, 2007, www.smh.com/au (accessed August 21, 2011).
9. David G. Levasseur and J. Kanan Sawyer, "Pedagogy Meets PowerPoint: A Research Review

of the Effects of Computer-Generated Slides in the Classroom," *The Review of Communication* 6, nos. 1 and 2 (January 2006): 116.
10. Tufte, 5.
11. William Langewiesche, "Columbia's Last Flight," *Atlantic Monthly,* November 2003, http://www .theatlantic.com/doc/200311/langewiesche (accessed August 21, 2011).
12. Tufte, 19.
13. Dave Paredi, http:www.thinkoutsidetheslide.com/ survey2007.htm, as retrieved from Isa Engleberg, "How Do Trade Books Advise Us to Use Power-Point?" (paper presented at the National Communication Association annual convention, November 12–15, 2009, Chicago, IL).
14. Ibid.
15. Thanks to Garr Reynolds, *Presentation Zen* (Berkeley, CA: New Riders, 2008); and Nancy Duarte, *Slide:ology* (Sebastapol, CA: O'Reilly Media, 2008).
16. Reynolds, 163.
17. Walter Fisher, *Human Communication as Narration: Toward a Philosophy of Reason, Value and Action* (Columbia: University of South Carolina Press, 1987), as interpreted by Cyphert, 178.
18. Cyphert, 180.
19. Cyphert, 184.

Chapter 13

1. Kent E. Menzel and Lori J. Carrell, "The Relationship between Preparation and Performance in Public Speaking," *Communication Education* 43, no. 1 (1994): 17–26.
2. E. T. Hall and M. R. Hall, *Understanding Cultural Differences: Germans, French, and Americans* (Boston: Intercultural, 1990).
3. Frances Yates, *The Art of Memory* (Chicago: University of Chicago, 1966), 1–2.

Chapter 14

1. For more on slang, see Michael Adams, *Slang: The People's Poetry* (New York: Oxford University Press, 2009).
2. Robert Delaney, "Dialect Map of American English," http://robertspage.com/dialects.html (accessed October 31, 2011).
3. "Do You Speak Presidential?" from *Do You Speak American?* http://www.pbs.org/speak/seatosea/

standardamerican/presidential (accessed March 2, 2012).

4. For more on nonverbal communication, see Judee K. Burgoon, Laura K. Guerrero, and Kory Floyd, *Nonverbal Communication* (Boston: Allyn & Bacon, 2009); and Mark L. Knapp and Judith A. Hall, *Nonverbal Communication in Human Interaction,* 7th ed. (Boston: Wadsworth, 2009).

5. Albert Mehrabian, *Nonverbal Communication* (Chicago: Aldine-Atherton, 1972), and Ray L. Birdwhistell, *Kinesics and Context* (Philadelphia: University of Pennsylvania Press, 1970). See also Judee K. Burgoon, "Nonverbal Signals," in *Handbook of Interpersonal Communication,* ed. Mark L. Knapp and G. R. Miller (Beverly Hills, CA: Sage, 1985), 344–390.

6. Thanks to Garr Reynolds, *Presentation Zen: Simple Ideas on Presentation Design and Delivery* (Berkeley: New Riders, 2008), 185.

7. Valerie Manusov, "Perceiving Nonverbal Messages: Effects of Immediacy and Encoded Intent on Receiver Judgments," *Western Journal of Speech Communication,* 55 (1991): 107.

Chapter 16

1. Kathleen Hall Jamieson, *Eloquence in an Electronic Age: The Transformation of Political Speechmaking* (New York: Oxford University Press, 1998).

2. Abraham Maslow, *Motivation and Personality* (New York: Harper & Row, 1954).

3. Icek Ajzen and Martin Fishbein, *Understanding Attitudes and Predicting Social Behavior* (Englewood Cliffs, NJ: Prentice-Hall, 1980).

4. Thanks to Marouf Hasian Jr. and Robert E. Frank, "Rhetoric, History, and Collective Memory: Decoding the Goldhagen Debates," *Western Journal of Communication* 63 (1999): 95–104; Cheryl Jorgensen-Earp and Lori Lanzilotti, "Public Memory and Private Grief: The Construction of Shrines at the Sites of Public Tragedy," *Quarterly Journal of Speech* 84 (1998): 150–170; and Marouf Hasian, "Authenticity, Public Memories, and the Problematics of Post-Holocaust Remembrances," *Quarterly Journal of Speech* 91 (2005): 231–263.

5. Jone Johnson Lewis. "Bra-Burning Feminists: NOT Another Myth about Women's History," About.com: Women's History, http://womenshistory .about.com/od/mythsofwomenshistory/a/bra_ burning.htm (accessed October 2, 2011).

6. Judee K. Burgoon and Jerold Hale, "Nonverbal Expectancy Violations: Model Elaboration and Application to Immediacy Behaviors," *Communication Monographs* 55 (1988): 58–79.

7. Cindy Griffin, *Invitation to Public Speaking Handbook* (Boston: Wadsworth, 2011), 381. Adapted for public speaking from Sonya K. Foss and Cindy L. Griffin, "Beyond Persuasion: A Proposal for an Invitational Rhetoric," *Communication Monographs* 62 (1995): 1–18.

8. Griffin, 400–402.

9. Example comes from George Lakoff, *Don't Think of an Elephant!* (Boulder, CO: Chelsea Green Publishing Company, 2004).

Chapter 17

1. Stephen Toulmin, *The Uses of Argument* (London: Cambridge University Press, 1969).

Chapter 18

1. http://www.chrisgardnermedia.com/about/bio (accessed March 31, 2012).

2. Peter D. Hart Research Associates, Inc., conducted on behalf of the Association of American Colleges and Universities, "How Should Colleges Prepare Students to Succeed in Today's Global Economy?" December 28, 2006, 2.

3. Gloria J. Galanes and Katherine Adams, *Effective Group Discussion,* 13th ed. (New York: McGraw-Hill, 2010), 193.

4. Susan Sorensen, "Grouphate" (paper presented at the International Communication Association, Minneapolis, May 1981).

5. Some of these are adapted from the Teamwork VALUE Rubric, American Association of Colleges and Universities, 2010.

6. Randy Y. Hirokawa, Daniel De Gooyer, and Kathleen Valde, "Using Narrative to Study Task Group Effectiveness," *Small Group Research* 31 (October 2000): 573–591.

7. Carol A. Roach and Nancy J. Wyatt, "Successful Listening," in *Small Group Communication: A Reader,* 6th ed., ed. Robert S. Cathcart and Larry A. Samovar (Dubuque, IA: Wm. C. Brown, 1992), 301–325, as discussed in Galanes and Adams, 32.

8. Irving L. Janis, *Groupthink: Psychological Studies of Policy Decisions and Fiascoes,* 2nd ed. rev. (Boston: Houghton Mifflin, 1983).

9. Kenneth D. Benne and Paul Sheats, "Functional Roles of Group Members," *Journal of Social Issues* 4 (1948): 41–49.

10. Gay Lumsden, Donald Lumsden, and Carolyn Wiethoff, *Comunicating in Groups and Teams: Sharing Leadership* (Boston: Wadsworth, 2010), 313–314.

11. E. P. Hollander, *Leadership Dynamics* (New York: Free Press, 1978), 13–16.

12. Anthony T. Pescosolido, "Informal Leaders and the Development of Group Efficacy," *Small Group Research* 32 (February 2001): 74–94.

13. John Dewey, *How We Think* (Boston: D. C. Heath, 1950).

14. Galanes and Adams, 235.

15. Adapted from A. F. Osborn, *Applied Imagination: Principles and Procedures of Creative Problem Solving* (New York: Scribner, 1963).

16. Special thanks for these brainstormed ideas to my Honors public speaking class, Phoenix College, Fall 2011.

17. Lumsden, Lumsden, and Weithoff, 302–310.

Credits

Text

Page 158: © Celia L. Kutcher, CHHC, AADP, BFRAP/FoodHealer; **p. 159:** © Celia L. Kutcher, CHHC, AADP, BFRAP/FoodHealer; **p. 163:** © Jessica Abel and Matt Maddenl; Reprinted by arrangement with Henry Holt and Company, LLC; **p. 276 (top):** Columbia Accident Investigation Board/NASA; **p. 276 (bottom):** Office of the U.S. Joint Chiefs of Staff; **p. 285:** © Leah Buley and Brandon Schauer/Adaptive Path; **p. 286 (bottom):** U.S. Census Bureau, Census of Population and Housing; **p. 287:** U.S. Census Bureau/U.S. Department of Commerce. Economics and Statistics Administration; **p. 371:** © Photodisc/Veer.

Photos

Contents

Page vi: © Colin Anderson; **p. vii (top):** © Ocean/Corbis; **p. vii (bottom):** © Fuse; **p. viii (top):** © The McGraw-Hill Companies, Inc./Mark A. Dierker, photographer; **p. viii (bottom):** © Punchstock/Digital Vision; **p. ix:** © Ocean/Corbis; **p. x (top):** © PhotoStock-Isreal; **p. x (bottom):** © Ryan D. Budhu; **p. xi:** © Fuse; **p. xii (top):** © Elisabeth Coelfen/Alamy; **p. xii (bottom):** © BlueMoon Stock; **p. xiii (top):** © Bloomberg via Getty Images; **p. xiii (bottom):** © The McGraw-Hill Companies, Inc./Mark A. Dierker, Photographer; **p. xiv:** © Hill Street Studios/Blend Images/Corbis; **p. xv (top):** © Pixtal/AGE Fotostock; **p. xv (bottom):** © uniquely india; **p. xvi (top):** © Radius Images; **p. xvi (bottom):** © Lauren Burke; **p. xx:** photo by Steve Emrick, author provided; **p. xxv:** © iTVk.com staff photographer.

Tab 1

Page 1 (top): © Colin Anderson; **p. 1 (top middle):** © Ocean/Corbis; **p. 1 (bottom middle):** © Fuse; **p. 1 (bottom):** © The McGraw-Hill Companies, Inc./Mark A. Dierker, photographer.

Chapter 1

Page 3: © Colin Anderson; **p. 5:** © Catharine Yuelet; **p. 9 (top right):** © Asia Images Group/age footstock; **p. 9 (top left):** © Bronwyn8; **p. 9 (bottom):** © Photodisc Collection/Getty Images; **p. 10:** © Image Source/Getty Images; **p. 13:** © Library of Congress Prints and Photographs Division; **p. 18:** © The McGraw-Hill Companies, Inc./Jill Braaten, photographer; **p. 26:** © iTVk.com staff photographer.

Chapter 2

Page 29: © Ocean/Corbis.

Chapter 3

Page 47: © Fuse; **48:** © CJMGrafx; **p. 50:** © Stockphoto4u; **p. 51:** © John Cooke; **p. 62:** © Photodisc/Getty Images; **p. 63:** © Asia Images/Getty Images.

Chapter 4

Page 68: © The McGraw-Hill Companies, Inc./Mark A. Dierker, photographer; **p. 72:** © Jennifer Mackenzie; **p. 74:** © t_kimura; **p. 77 (top):** © Barış Muratoğlu; **p. 77 (bottom):** © Barış Muratoğlu.

Tab 2

Page 93 (top): © Punchstock/Digital Vision; **p. 93 (top middle):** © Ocean/Corbis; **p. 93 (bottom middle):** © PhotoStock-Isreal; **p. 93 (bottom):** © Ryan D. Budhu.

Chapter 5

Page 95: © Punchstock/Digital Vision; **p. 97:** © Ingram Publishing; **p. 106:** © Photodisc/Getty Images; **p. 115:** © Alloy Photography/Veer; **p. 117:** © Blend Images/Getty Images.

Chapter 6

Page 121: © Ocean/Corbis; **p. 123:** © Dave and Les Jacobs/Blend Images LLC; **p. 124 (top):** © CDC/Cade Martin; **p. 124 (bottom):** © Taylor Hinton; **p. 125 (top right):** © Photographer's Choice/Getty Images; **p. 125 (top left):** © Hill Street Studios/Blend Images LLC; **p. 125 (middle right):** © C Squared Studios/Getty Images; **p. 125 (middle left):** © Nick Koudis/Getty Images; **p. 125 (bottom left):** © Oleg Prikhodko; **p. 125 (bottom right):** © Kriss Russell; **p. 126:** © Tolga Sipahi; **p. 129:** © Izabela Habur; **p. 136:** © Digital Vision/Getty Images.

Chapter 7

Page 140: © PhotoStock-Isreal; **p. 142:** © The McGraw-Hill Companies, Inc./Christopher Kerrigan, photographer; **p. 148:** © Ingram Publishing; **p. 154:** © Rawdon Wyatt/Alamy.

Chapter 8

Page 171: © Ryan D. Budhu; **p. 179 (top):** © Ingram Publishing/Alamy; **p. 179 (bottom):** © AP Photo/Adam Rountree.

Tab 3

Page 195 (top): © Fuse; **p. 195 (middle):** © Elisabeth Coelfen/Alamy; **p. 195 (bottom):** © BlueMoon Stock.

Chapter 9

Page 197: © Fuse; **p. 198 (top):** © WireImage; **p. 198 (bottom):** © Foodcollection; **p. 199:** © Photodisc.

Chapter 10

Page 216: © Elisabeth Coelfen/Alamy; **p. 218:** © NASA/JPL/Space Science Institute; **p. 228:** © Tolga Sipahi; **p. 229:** © wdstock.

Chapter 11

Page 239: © BlueMoon Stock; **p. 242 (top):** © Image Source/Getty Images; **p. 242 (bottom):** © Fancy Photography/Veer; **p. 243:** © Peter Booth.

Tab 4

Page 265 (top): © Bloomberg via Getty Images; **p. 265 (middle):** © The McGraw-Hill Companies, Inc./Mark A. Dierker, Photographer; **p. 265 (bottom):** © Hill Street Studios/Blend Images/Corbis.

Chapter 12

Page 267: © Bloomberg via Getty Images; **p. 270 (right):** © Kent Knudson/PhotoLink/Getty Images; **p. 270 (left):** © Jess Carroll; **p. 272:** © David Cooper/Toronto Star/ZUMA/Corbis; **p. 273 (top right):** © Scala / Art Resource, NY; **p. 273 (top left):** © Erich Lessing / Art Resource, NY; **p. 273 (bottom left):** © Courtesy NASA/JPL-Caltech; **p. 273 (bottom right):** © Digital Vision/Getty Images; **p. 277:** © Brand X Pictures/PunchStock; **p. 280 (top):** © Liz O'Brien; **p. 280 (middle):** © McGraw-Hill Companies, Inc./Ken Karp, photographer; **p. 280 (bottom right):** © McGraw-Hill Companies, Inc./Jill Braaten, photographer; **p. 280 (bottom middle):** © Liz O'Brien; **p. 280 (bottom left):** © McGraw-Hill Companies, Inc./Jill Braaten, photographer; **p. 288:** © Jeremy Kern, JFHQNCRMDW Public Affairs; **pp. 292, 293:** © Erich Lessing/Art Resource, NY.

Chapter 13

Page 295: © The McGraw-Hill Companies, Inc./Mark A. Dierker, Photographer; **p. 302:** © Fancy Photography/Veer; **p. 308:** © Image Source/Corbis; **p. 309 (top):** © Image Source/Getty Images; **p. 309 (middle):** © Image Source/Getty Images; **p. 309 (bottom):** © Purestock/PunchStock; **p. 316:** © Ingram Publishing.

Chapter 14

Page 318: © Hill Street Studios/Blend Images/Corbis; p. 328: © Jen Grantham; **p. 331 right side in descending order:** © Image Source/Getty Images; © Rubberball/Getty Images; © PhotoAlto/Getty Images; © Jaimie Duplass; © Rubberball/Getty Images; **p. 331 (left):** © drbimages; **p. 333:** © Ingram Publishing; **p. 335:** © 4FR; **p. 339:** © Purestock/SuperStock.

Tab 5

Page 341 (top): © Pixtal/AGE Fotostock; **p. 341 (top middle):** © uniquely india; **p. 341 (bottom middle):** © Radius Images; **p. 341 (bottom):** © Lauren Burke.

Chapter 15

Page 343: © Pixtal/AGE Fotostock; **p. 346 (top):** Banksy, Boston, 2012; **p. 346 (middle):** © The McGraw-Hill Companies, Inc./Andrew Resek, photographer; **p. 346 (bottom):** © The McGraw-Hill Companies, Inc./Barry Barker, photographer; **p. 348 (top):** © Taphouse Studios; **p. 348 (middle):** © Stockbyte/Getty Images; **p. 348 (bottom):** © Alan and Sandy Carey/Getty Images; **p. 349 top feature, (top):** © DreamPictures/Blend Images LLC; **(middle):** © Purestock/SuperStock; **(bottom):** © Digital Vision/Getty Images; **p. 349 bottom feature, (top):** © Steve Allen/Brand X Pictures; **(middle):** © Getty Images/Brand X; **(bottom):** © Photodisc/Getty Images; **p. 350 (top):** © franckreporter; **p. 350 (bottom):** © Ingram Publishing; **p. 351 (top):** © Anna Williams/Getty Images; **p. 351 (bottom):** © Pete Souza/The White House; **p. 352:** © The McGraw-Hill Companies Inc./Ken Cavanagh, photographer.

Chapter 16

Page 358: © uniquely india; **p. 363 (top left):** © The McGraw-Hill Companies, Inc./ Mark Dierker, photographer; **p. 363 (top right):** © C. Zachariasen / PhotoAlto; **p. 363 (middle left):** © ERproductions LTD/Blend Images LLC; **p. 363 (middle right):** © Blend Images; **p. 363 (bottom left):** © Brand X Pictures / Jupiterimages; **p. 363 (bottom right):** © Stocktrek Images/Getty Images; **p. 370 (top):** © Susan H. Smith; **p. 370 (middle):** © Jason Swarr; **p. 370 (bottom):** © Photodisc/Superstock.

Chapter 17

Page 377: © Radius Images; **p. 378:** © Anna Williams/Getty Images.

Chapter 18

Page 396: © Lauren Burke; **p. 402:** © Pixtal/SuperStock; **p. 404:** © david franklin; **p. 407:** © René Mansi; **p. 408 (right):** © Image Source/Getty Images; **p. 408 (left):** © Klaus Tiedge/Blend Images/Getty Images; **p. 413:** © t_kimura.

Index

Page numbers in boldface refer to glossary terms.